Freedom from Want

PUBLISHING FOR THE WORLD
125 Years
THE JOHNS HOPKINS UNIVERSITY PRESS

New Studies in American Intellectual and Cultural History
Howard Brick, Series Editor

Freedom from Want

American Liberalism and the Idea
of the Consumer

Kathleen G. Donohue

The Johns Hopkins University Press
Baltimore and London

The Johns Hopkins University Press
2715 North Charles Street
Baltimore, Maryland 21218-4363
www.press.jhu.edu

Library of Congress Cataloging-in-Publication Data

Donohue, Kathleen G., 1958–
   Freedom from want : American liberalism and the idea of the
consumer / Kathleen G. Donohue.
      p.   cm.—(New studies in American intellectual and cultural
history)
Includes bibliographical references and index.
   ISBN 0-8018-7426-2 (hardcover : alk. paper)
   1. Liberalism—United States—History. 2. Consumption (Economics)—United States—History. 3. United States—Intellectual
life. I. Title. II. Series.
JC574.2.U6D66 2003
320.51′3′097309041— dc21
                              2002156767

A catalog record for this book is available from the British Library.

To my children and my mother

"And what do you mean to be?"
  The kind old Bishop said
As he took the boy on his ample knee
  And patted his curly head.
"We should all of us choose a calling
  To help society's plan;
Then what do you mean to be, my boy,
  When you grow to be a man?"

"I want to be a consumer,"
  The bright-haired lad replied
As he gazed up into the Bishop's face
  In innocence open-eyed.
"I've never had aims of a selfish sort,
  For that, as I know is wrong,
I want to be a Consumer, Sir,
  And help the world along.

"I want to be a Consumer
  And live in a useful way;
For that is the thing that's needed most,
  I've heard Economists say.
There are too many people working
  And too many things are made.
I want to be a Consumer, Sir,
  And help to further trade.

"I want to be a Consumer
  And work both night and day,
For that is the thing that's needed most,
  I've heard Economists say.
I won't just be a Producer
  Like Bobby and James and John;
I want to be a Consumer, Sir,
  And help the nation on."

—adapted from Patrick Barrington, "I Want to Be a Consumer," and reproduced with permission of Punch Ltd.

Contents

Acknowledgments

As many historians before me have observed, scholarship is a collaborative process. I have benefited from that process more than I can ever adequately acknowledge here. I am deeply grateful to F. J. Schlink. Had he not been willing to spend many an afternoon relating his experiences to me, this book would never have come to be. Early on I received invaluable insights from Edward Ayers, Joseph Kett, Ann Lane, Julia McDonough, Walter Opdyke, and Dorothy Ross. At a critical stage Thomas Bender urged me to take this project in the direction of intellectual history and, even more important, suggested how to do so. As the project began to take shape, Leon Fink and Kathryn Kish Sklar read and commented on early chapters. In addition, I benefited along the way from the comments and insights of generous colleagues such as Donna Gabaccia, Cindy Kierner, Rob Schneider, and Peter Thorsheim as well as those of good friends such as Laird Hart, Sue Hemberger, and Rosie Zagarri.

I owe special thanks to Alan Brinkley, Daniel Horowitz, Michael Kazin, and Daniel Rodgers, all of whom took time out of their busy schedules to read part or all of the penultimate manuscript and give me numerous suggestions. My debt to Lizabeth Cohen and Robert Westbrook is even greater. Both gave the manuscript an extremely thorough and insightful reading not once but twice. The book also benefited considerably from the invaluable feedback of Lawrence Glickman.

I have long heard horror stories about the production process. My experience, however, was thoroughly enjoyable. Robert Brugger was supportive, patient, and extremely accommodating. His many substantive suggestions have made this a better book. Melody Herr was always helpful. And Elizabeth Gratch, with her ear for language and her eye for detail, caught many an awkward phrase and, even more important, quite a few errors. Finally, I want to thank Thomas Rockwell for his kind generosity.

I also want to thank the several agencies that provided financial support for this project, specifically Wayne State University for a Kaiser Travel Grant and

Wilkes University for a Research Fellowship. This work was also supported in part by funds provided by the University of North Carolina at Charlotte.

My greatest debt, however, I owe to my family. Without my mother's, Edith Donohue's, support—intellectual as well as emotional—this project would never have been completed. And, without Bronwyn, Aidan, Blair, and Laird, it would not have been worth doing. They have brought balance into my life. I'm not sure I can say I have brought the same into theirs. Laird's, Aidan's, and Blair's earliest phrases included "mommy's working" and "no touch the 'puter." And Bronwyn, who grew up with this book, recently decided to write a book of her own. It took her a half-hour, and she wondered what had taken me so long. To them I dedicate this book and so much more.

Freedom from Want

Introduction

In 1941 Franklin Roosevelt identified "four essential human freedoms." Three of them—freedom from fear, freedom of speech, and freedom of religion—had long been fundamental to liberalism. As early as the seventeenth century, no less a liberal theorist than John Locke had suggested that the reason individuals formed a civil society was to enable them to live free from fear. And by the late eighteenth century political thinkers on both sides of the Atlantic had established freedom of speech and freedom of religion as defining principles of liberalism. So fundamental were these three political freedoms to a liberal order that they remained defining principles even as classical liberalism gave way to its modern American counterpart.

Roosevelt's fourth freedom, freedom from want, had not been a defining principle of classical liberalism. Indeed, classical liberals had been able to imagine few systems less liberal than one that would guarantee freedom from want. The problem with such a freedom, William Graham Sumner charged, was that it would allow "those who eat and produce not . . . [to] live at the expense of those who labor and produce."[1] In so doing, it violated what was a defining economic freedom of classical liberalism, the freedom to enjoy the full product of one's labor.

This book is the story of how freedom from want, an economic freedom denied by classical liberalism, became one of the "essential human freedoms" of modern American liberalism. Much of that story focuses on a half-century debate over the place of the consumer in the political economy. For it is, I believe, the changing ideas about the consumer and producer, about consumption and production, which provide the key to understanding why classical liberals found it impossible to recognize a freedom from want while modern American liberals had no such difficulty.[2]

At the center of classical liberal theory was the idea of laissez-faire. To the vast majority of American classical liberals, however, laissez-faire did not mean no government intervention at all. On the contrary, they were more than willing to see government provide tariffs, railroad subsidies, and internal improvements, all of which benefited producers. What they condemned was intervention on behalf of consumers.

American classical liberals were far more tolerant of government intervention on behalf of producers than consumers because they did not value those identities in the same way. In their view producer was the most noble of identities and production the most valuable of activities. Consumer and consumption, however, were far more problematic categories. While classical liberals were willing to concede that humans had to consume, they nevertheless remained convinced throughout the nineteenth century that only the most moderate consumption should be designated what economist Amasa Walker called "right consumption." Anything beyond that they quickly denounced as "luxury."[3]

In part American classical liberals owed their attitudes toward consumption to the European liberal tradition. By the early nineteenth century that tradition had become profoundly producerist, treating production not as a means but an end and consumption not as the ultimate purpose of production but, instead, a threat to it. Classical liberals on both sides of the Atlantic took as a self-evident truth English economist David Ricardo's assertion that the entrepreneur who "avoided an increased expenditure on objects of luxury, enjoyment, and liberality . . . would get rich faster" than the one who did not.[4] Throughout much of the nineteenth century they remained convinced that consumption was little more than the destruction of wealth that could have been used to increase productive capital.

It was not only European economic theory, however, which shaped American classical liberal attitudes toward consumption. Those attitudes were also influenced by an American intellectual tradition that had long imbued both *consumption* and *consumer* with pejorative connotations. As early as the seventeenth century, Puritan thinkers had associated excessive consumption with religious failure, convinced that those who could not control their consumption had failed to find favor with God. By the late eighteenth century republican theorists were equating excessive consumption with political failure, warning that only the abstemious could provide the civic virtue on which a republic depended. Given this intellectual heritage, it was hardly surprising that American classical liberals were unwilling to advocate a freedom that would benefit the consumer at the expense of the producer.[5]

American liberal theorists would have denied that they had a problem with consumption itself. Their only concern, they would have insisted, was with excessive consumption, what they labeled luxury. But, although they were quick to denounce luxury as a threat to the economic well-being of the nation, they found it far more difficult to identify exactly what luxury was. Most, for example, could agree that it was the consumption of more goods than one produced. But that did not mean that American classical liberals believed producing much gave individuals or their dependents the license to consume much. And most could agree that luxury involved the consumption of goods beyond the basic necessities or even a few comforts. But they found it impossible to achieve a consensus on what constituted a basic necessity or a comfort, in large part because most of them were convinced that comforts and necessities for one class were often luxuries for another.

The classical liberal inability to define what constituted luxury went a long way toward calling all consumption into question. Once classical liberals had labeled limited consumption a virtue, they found it almost impossible to avoid the assumption that the more limited an individual's consumption, the more virtuous that individual. That assumption extended the negative connotations associated with luxury to even the most moderate consumption.

While misgivings concerning the consumer had long been an important strain in the American intellectual tradition, the apotheosis of the producer was a more recent phenomenon.[6] It was not that earlier thinkers had neglected production and the producer. On the contrary, Puritans had listed industriousness as one of the identifying characteristics of their "visible saints." And republican theorists had placed the hardworking yeoman farmer at the center of their political order. But, even as they had touted producerist virtues, both had valued other virtues even more. Puritans had emphasized godliness above all else; republicans had stressed independence. Neither group had regarded productivity as the supreme virtue. Neither had placed the producer at the center of their worldview.

Classical liberals, however, did just that. Throughout the nineteenth century they glorified society's producers, especially the capitalists, whose efforts, they insisted, were primarily responsible for the phenomenal productivity of the nineteenth-century economy. And they insisted that the best political system was one that encouraged prosperity by making it easy for producers to produce. Even when classical liberals turned their attention to the eradication of poverty, they continued to emphasize production rather than consumption. If one was entitled to consume only what one had produced, then, classical liberals reasoned, the only way that government could eliminate poverty was by increasing productivity.

Classical liberals were not the only nineteenth-century theorists to advocate a producerist approach to the political economy. American thinkers across the political spectrum defined civic identity in terms of the producer. They might not have included the same individuals within the producer category. But all assumed that only those who were members of that category were entitled to exercise the full rights and responsibilities of citizenship. All agreed that that category and the rights that went with it should be reserved for free adult males. And all insisted that the political economy should function on behalf of the producer, however they might define that identity. In the nineteenth century the producerist worldview reigned supreme.

That producerist worldview was largely a response to industrialization. In the phenomenally productive nineteenth-century economy the producer seemed to be the most logical identity around which to organize the political economy. Yet, ironically, the very forces that made the producer such a positive identity were also eroding the foundation on which a producerist mindset rested. As machines played an ever greater role in production, American thinkers, whatever their political sympathies, found it increasingly difficult to answer basic economic questions. Who, for example, should benefit from the manifold increase in productivity which machines made possible? The workers who built and operated the machines? The capitalists who owned the machines? All of society, whose accumulated technological know-how made the machines possible? And who should determine how the machines were used? The capitalist, whose primary concern was profit? The worker, whose primary interest was wages? All of society, whose needs would be met by those machines? Socialists offered one set of answers, classical liberals another, agrarian populists yet another. For a growing number of American thinkers in the late nineteenth and early twentieth centuries, however, none of these answers was particularly satisfactory.

The thinkers who would challenge the prevailing producerist wisdom were a disparate lot. They did not belong to a single political party or subscribe to one worldview. They came from a variety of professions. Some, like Simon Patten, Thorstein Veblen, and Richard T. Ely, were academics; others, such as Edward Bellamy and Florence Kelley, were reformers. Some supported capitalism; others opposed it. Most were sympathetic to socialism. A few were even sympathetic to a producer-oriented political economy. All, however, were troubled by the paradox of poverty amid plenty. All were convinced that the existing answers to the economic questions would do nothing to resolve that paradox. And all, even the most producerist of them, assumed that any solution to that paradox would require rethinking the consumer's place within the political economy. They spent the last several decades of the nineteenth century and the first several of the twentieth doing just that.

At first glance it is surprising that the process of rethinking the consumer's place in political and economic theory took so long. At least by the eighteenth century, if not earlier, Americans were already participating in what historians have dubbed a "consumer revolution."[7] By the late nineteenth century industrialization and urbanization had radically increased both the scope of what would come to be called a consumer society and the number of individuals who could participate in it. Yet, despite the rapid emergence of a consumer society, the vast majority of American political and economic theorists were, in some cases, unwilling and, in others, unable either to rethink the traditional meanings associated with producer and consumer or to substitute the consumer for the producer as the pivotal identity around which the political economy should revolve. Not until the early twentieth century did they construct a version of the consumer which lacked many of the pejorative connotations so long associated with that identity.

In the 1910s and 1920s a second generation of public thinkers, among them Walter Weyl, Stuart Chase, Rexford Tugwell, and Robert Lynd, drew on the new thinking about the consumer as they attempted to bring liberalism into line with current economic conditions. They retained the liberal faith in material abundance as the key to general well-being. But, because they had come to believe that classical liberal means had ceased to be conducive to liberal ends, they insisted that the only way to realize the promise of liberalism was to construct a political economy that functioned on behalf of consumer-citizens.

Initially the purview of a small group of left liberals, these ideas began to have an impact on public policy after the collapse of the economy in 1929. Throughout the New Deal administration of Franklin Roosevelt, government officials found it far more necessary than had earlier administrations to focus on the consumer's role in the economy and to think of civic identity in increasingly consumerist terms. By 1941 few liberals questioned Roosevelt's identification of freedom from want as one of the "essential human freedoms." That freedom may still have violated the most basic of producerist principles. By the 1940s, however, those principles had long since lost their monopoly on political economic thought.

The liberalism that emerged in the 1940s was not exactly what most of those who had been advocating a consumer-oriented political economy since the 1880s had envisioned. Sympathetic to socialism and skeptical about capitalism, they had assumed that the interests of consuming citizens and those of business were fundamentally opposed. In the pursuit of profit, they had insisted, businesses adulterated and misrepresented products and, perhaps worst of all, manipulated consumers into buying what they neither wanted nor needed. It was this manipulation of the consumer which had prompted most consumerist thinkers in the half-century before Franklin Roosevelt took office to distinguish between a consumer-oriented economy, in which business produced exactly what consumers needed—no less and, just as important, no more—and a consumption-oriented economy, in which business enjoyed high profits because consumers purchased abundantly.

The liberalism that would dominate American politics in the post–World War II period did not distinguish between a consumer-oriented and a consumption-oriented economy. On the contrary, by the end of the war most liberals had become convinced that a disciplined capitalism could provide consumers with an abundance of high-quality goods while simultaneously providing capitalists with ample profits.[8] In short, much like Adam Smith almost two centuries earlier, they believed that a consumption-oriented and a consumer-oriented economy were one and the same. Unlike Smith, however, they were firmly convinced that laissez-faire policies were incapable of realizing the consumerist potential of a capitalist economy. Instead, they relied on Keynesian policies, strong regulatory measures, and a broad welfare program to realize that potential. By the 1940s even consumerist left liberals who had long been profoundly skeptical about capitalism were no exception. After living through a decade during which much of the nation had lacked even the most basic of necessities, they, too had come to believe that a regulated capitalism was the system most likely to solve the paradox of poverty amid plenty.

Why did consumerist thinkers ultimately pin their hopes on liberalism rather than socialism? The privation of the Depression and the phenomenal productivity of the post–World War II economy played an important role. So, too, did the increasing tensions between the Soviet Union and the United States—tensions that encouraged many American intellectuals to rethink their position on both capitalism and democracy. Nevertheless, well before the 1940s consumerist liberals, even those on the left-most edges, had been unable either to embrace socialism fully or to reject capitalism completely. Despite the promises of socialism, they could never quite forget that Karl Marx had called for a worker state while Adam Smith had insisted that "the interest of the consumer" should take precedence over "that of the producer."[9] And, despite the abuses of capitalism, they could never quite abandon the idea that the consuming population would be better served by increasing wealth rather than by redistributing it. Once they replaced the producer with the consumer as the pivotal identity in the political economy, the logic of their ideas not only made socialism unavailable. It also pushed them, much to their chagrin, almost inevitably toward capitalism.

Between the end of the Civil War and the end of World War II, the United States experienced phenomenal social and economic changes. Not surprisingly, these changes called into question many of the prevailing assumptions concerning the role of government. Thinkers across the political spectrum responded to this crisis in political economic thought by constructing alternatives to the laissez-faire liberalism that dominated late-nineteenth-century American politics. Most of these alternatives remained rooted in a producerist worldview. One of the few exceptions was the challenge to the producerist paradigm mounted by the late-nineteenth- and early-twentieth-century economists and reformers who rethought the place of the consumer and the producer in the political economy. This is the story of their ideas and the role these ideas played in transforming classical liberalism into its modern American counterpart.

CHAPTER ONE

The Producerist Worldview, 1870–1900

Americans achieved a remarkable consensus in the nineteenth century. In the midst of major class, sectional, religious, ethnic, race, and gender conflicts, they were all but unanimous in their conviction that the producer was the proper identity around which to organize a political economy. They agreed that individuals were entitled to the products of their labor. They took for granted that industriousness was a virtue and sloth a vice. They assumed that producing wealth was more admirable than consuming it. And they shared the belief that government's main task was to protect and further the interests of producers.

This consensus was all the more remarkable because it transcended major political differences. Much separated the political programs of the nineteenth century, but proponents of those various programs shared a common producerist language and relied on the same producerist principles both to justify their own program and to denounce those of their opponents. Classical liberals, for example, defended the private ownership of capital by insisting that capital embodied past labor. Marxists found that the best way to discredit capitalism was to argue that capital had been created not by the labor of capitalists but by that of the working class. In good producerist fashion they insisted that only by nationalizing the means of production would producers once again be able to enjoy, albeit collectively, the full product of their labor. Working-class republicans were as eager as Marxists to guarantee workers the products of their labor, although their solution was a cooperative commonwealth in which everyone could enjoy the status of independent producer. As for agrarian populists, they built a powerful political movement on the assumption that Wall Street and the railroads were denying farmers the fruits of their labor.

The centrality of the producer was not only evident in nineteenth-century political thought. It was also apparent in the economic theories of the period. The classical economists who formulated these theories approached the economy as a system of production. Their focus was on maximizing the production of wealth. Their virtues were the producerist virtues of thrift and hard work. Their heroes were those who produced wealth.

While the classical economists were quick to assign the producer a central role in their economic theory, they were not quite so sure how they should cast the consumer. On one side, they believed that consumption and consumers were critically important. After all, it was consumers who regulated the economy in the classical economic model, rewarding producers who best served the needs of consumers, punishing those who did not. And it was consumption, as Adam Smith put it, which was "the sole end and purpose of all production." Indeed, it was the classical economists' belief in the importance of consumption and the consumer which had, in large part, prompted them to reject the mercantilist ideas that had dominated economic thought in the seventeenth and eighteenth centuries. As Adam Smith explained it, the fundamental weakness of mercantilism was that "the interest of the consumer is almost constantly sacrificed to that of the producer; and it seems to consider production, and not consumption, as the ultimate end and object of all industry and commerce."[1]

The mercantilist sacrifice of consumers' interests to those of producers was the natural result of certain mercantilist assumptions. According to mercantilism, the amount of wealth in existence was relatively static. The only way for one nation to increase its wealth was to do so at the expense of another nation, something that it could accomplish by establishing a favorable balance of trade and exporting more than it imported. Domestic consumption threatened national well-being in two ways. It reduced the amount of goods available for export, and it increased the amount of goods which had to be imported. In the mercantilist scheme of things domestic consumption was little more than a drain on the national treasury, its only impact to diminish the potential wealth of a nation.[2]

Classical economists disagreed. The economy, as they saw it, was not static but dynamic, something the mercantilists had failed to recognize because of their faulty understanding of wealth. The best way to measure a nation's wealth, according to the classical economists, was in terms not of the bullion that it possessed but of the goods and services that it produced and consumed. Thus, it would seem that for the classical theorists consumption was not so much the antithesis of production as its complement.

Or was it? Classical economists might chastise mercantilists for sacrificing the interest of the consumer to that of the producer, but the logic of their theories could lead them to demand a similar sacrifice. Although classical economists made room for consumption, they nevertheless remained convinced that production drove the economy and that consumption only followed production. But, if production drove the economy, then the best way to further general well-being was to increase production. And the best way to increase production was to increase capital—that is, to develop more machines and build more factories.

It was at this point that consumption began to seem as problematic an activity for classical economists as it had been for mercantilists. The only way to accumulate capital was to save—in short, to forgo consumption. In the classical economic view, then, not only were those who produced of far greater value to society than those who consumed but also those who limited their consumption were of far greater value than those who indulged in it. Consumption might be related to production in classical economic theory but only dialectically. Consumers, it would seem, remained the antithesis of producers.

Although the almost exclusive focus on the producer was a logical outgrowth of certain classical economic assumptions, it was the work of Jean-Baptiste Say which provided the major theoretical justification for that focus. While most of his contemporaries followed Smith's lead and concentrated on "the nature and causes of the wealth of nations," Say gave more than passing attention to consumption. Indeed, in *Treatise on Political Economy* (1803) he devoted an entire section to the topic. But Say's extended treatment of consumption was the exception that proved the rule.[3] He was well within the classical fold, as convinced as any of his contemporaries that production was a far more worthwhile activity than consumption. Indeed, the only reason that Say gave more than passing attention to consumption was to establish that passing attention was more than enough.

What came out of Say's examination of consumption was Say's law, the idea that production created its own demand. That law freed classical economists to focus almost exclusively on production, confident that consumption would take care of itself. But, in doing so, Say's law only reinforced in classical economic theory the very tendency that Smith had denounced in mercantilism. Classical economists might agree with Smith that the chief weakness of mercantilism was that it treated production rather than consumption "as the ultimate end and object of all industry and commerce," but they were well on their way to constructing a theory of their own which did just that.[4]

Say's treatment of consumption not only went a long way toward reinforcing the producerist focus of the classical system of economic thought. It also revealed the deep ambivalence about the consumer at the heart of that system. Like his contemporaries, Say assumed that production was a far more admirable activity than consumption, an assumption that was evident in his definition of *production* as the "creation of new value" and *consumption* as the "destruction of value." It was also apparent in his distinction between productive and unproductive consumption, the latter which Say defined as consumption "with no other end or object in view, than the mere satisfaction of a want." Given such a limited end, unproductive consumption was not to be valued as highly as "productive consumption," which "does not immediately satisfy any human want" but instead results in the creation of new value. Finally, his reservations concerning consumption (as well as his producerist sympathies) were reflected in his conviction that avarice was less of a vice than prodigality. As Say explained it, the miser, "in the dread of losing his money, . . . hesitates to turn it to account" and thus does "nothing to promote the progress of industry." "But, at least," Say stressed, "he can not be said to reduce the means of production." The same, however, could not be said of the spendthrift who, according to Say, "squanders and makes away with the capital that should be the support of industry."[5] Convinced of the centrality of production, Say logically concluded that extravagantly consuming spendthrifts were far more problematic than nonconsuming misers because spendthrifts had a negative impact on production.

Say's attitudes toward the relative merits of production and consumption ultimately prevented him from following up the logic of his own law. Once he had demonstrated that supply created its own demand, he could then have easily concluded that consumption rather than production drove the economy and, therefore, consumption had a positive impact on the economy. Say, however, was quick to reject both conclusions. He warned his readers not to make the same "great" mistake as those who "have confounded the cause with the effect." Just because production always equals consumption, he insisted, it did not follow that "consumption originates production" or that "frugality is directly adverse to public prosperity" or "that the most useful citizen is the one who spends the most." On the contrary, he insisted, "the road to affluence . . . results from activity of production, seconded by the spirit of frugality."[6]

The all but exclusive focus on production and the producer remained a central feature of classical economic thought throughout the nineteenth century. As for the deep misgivings toward consumption and the consumer, they only intensified. Indeed, few nineteenth-century classical economists seemed even to remember that Smith had once identified consumption as "the ultimate end and object of all industry and commerce."[7] Their ideas about the impact of consumption on the economy were shaped instead by the most dismal of the dismal scientists, Thomas Malthus and David Ricardo.

Thomas Malthus's contribution to ideas about consumption was to adapt old assumptions to new conditions. In preindustrial agricultural economies, in which the amount of wealth produced did not seem to vary much from year to year, the prevailing assumptions were that wealth was finite and, perhaps more important, that any person who increased his or her wealth did so at the expense of someone else.[8] Surprisingly, the rapid economic expansion brought on by industrialization did not bring an end to such assumptions. That it did not was largely because of the intellectual efforts of Malthus. In 1798 he suggested that economic expansion was irrelevant because population tended to increase at such a rate that it would ultimately threaten to outstrip the food supply. In a Malthusian world wealth was not so much finite as shrinking. In an economy in which an exponentially increasing population competed for an agricultural output that was at most increasing geometrically, each individual's share of the wealth was becoming ever smaller.

Two decades later David Ricardo only intensified the anti-consumption bias in classical economic thought by establishing the relevance of Malthus's ideas to an industrial workforce. According to Ricardo, wages represented the workers' food supply. It followed, therefore, that any increase in wages would only encourage workers to reproduce, thereby increasing the supply of workers. As soon as workers started reproducing, their increasing numbers would once again force wages down to the subsistence level. What Ricardo had done was to persuade the majority of classical economists that any attempt to increase the material well-being of a nation's workers would have, at best, temporary results.

But Ricardo did not stop there. He insisted that such attempts were not only futile; they actually left society worse off. According to Ricardo, capitalist well-being depended upon an ability to attract workers through adequate wages. The problem was that what constituted adequate wages was continually increasing. Why? Because every increase in wages led to an increase in the number of workers, which in turn required the production of more food. But the only way that farmers could grow more food was to bring ever more marginal land under cultivation. Not surprisingly, it cost more to produce food on such marginal land. The result was higher food prices. Higher food prices meant higher wages, since it took an ever increasing amount of money to keep workers at the subsistence level. Thus, Ricardo predicted, any profits that capitalists might expect to earn because of an expanding economy would be literally eaten up in wages.

By the late nineteenth century such classical economic thinking had resulted in a worldview that was not only profoundly producerist but also one in which both *consumption* and *consumer* were replete with pejorative connotations. And with good reason. For much of the century classical economic theories seemed consistent with economic reality. Between the mid-1840s and the early 1870s American economic growth was fueled by the growth of capital goods. In such an economy any wealth that was used for personal consumption *was* wealth that had been diverted from the production of wealth. And, equally significantly, for much of the nineteenth century the amount of labor required to produce goods remained constant. The only way to increase the amount produced was to hire more workers. In such an economy it was not surprising that producers would be seen as far more economically beneficial than consumers.[9]

The economic conditions that gave a producer-oriented liberalism its explanatory power had already begun to disappear in the very years in which classical liberal ideas were reaching their peak. By the 1880s the capital goods sector had entered a period of stagnation at the same time that the consumer goods sector was rapidly expanding. Indeed, in the 1880s American spending on consumer goods increased more rapidly than in any other decade between 1869 and 1914. The consumer goods industries not only benefited from such spending. They also went to great lengths to encourage it. Manufacturers of consumers goods such as Quaker Oats, Pillsbury Flour, and Campbell Soup developed national markets and employed mass marketing techniques such as standardized products and packaging, brand names, and advertising to increase their sales. And by the 1890s retailers such as John Wannamaker, A. T. Stewart, Roland H. Macy, and Marshall Field had effected a revolution in retailing with the creation of the department store, an institution that had been all but nonexistent before 1876.[10]

Such changes could not help but have an impact on economic and social thought. It proved far easier, however, to bring economic thinking into line with such changes than either social or political thinking. While orthodox economists attributed the depression of the 1870s to such traditional causes as "over-spending, over-consuming, destroying more wealth than is reproduced," a minority began to suggest that the problem was not too much consumption but too little. In 1877 the free trader David A. Wells suggested that "the country . . . is suffering to-day, strange as the proposition may at first thought seem, not because we have not, but because we have; not from scarcity, but from abundance." And by the mid-1880s director of the U.S. Bureau of Labor Statistics Carroll D. Wright was warning that "the United States has gone on perfecting machinery, duplicating plant, crowding the market with products, until to-day, this country is in the exact position of England, with productive capacity far in excess of the demand upon it, and her industries . . . stagnated, the wages of labor reduced, prices lowered, and the manufacturers and merchants trying to secure an outlet for surplus goods."[11]

Theorists who were primarily concerned with the economic implications of the changing relationship between production and consumption, between producer and consumer, may have found it easy to come to terms with these changes. Those who were primarily interested in the political and social implications of those changes did not. The majority of social and political thinkers in the late nineteenth century remained convinced that the only good society was one that focused on the needs and guaranteed the rights of producers. And, if they ever thought about a consumer-oriented good society, it was only to dismiss it as an oxymoron. Their late-nineteenth-century writings revealed both the durability of producerist assumptions and the enduring potency of the pejorative connotations associated with consumption.

While most late-nineteenth-century thinkers continued to subscribe to a producerist worldview, few did so with the uncompromising zeal of the influential Yale sociologist William Graham Sumner. Unlike many of his contemporaries, who believed that it was necessary to adjust a producerist worldview slightly to account for the conditions of an industrial economy, Sumner remained convinced that the same producerist principles that had been relevant at the beginning of the nineteenth century remained so at the end of the century. Indeed, as far as he was concerned, many of society's problems could be traced to a growing tendency to depart from fundamental producerist principles.

In 1883 Sumner laid out his version of the producerist worldview in an article entitled "The Forgotten Man," a version that changed little in subsequent essays. As far as he was concerned, society was divided into producers and nonproducers. The poor were poor because they did not produce. Any attempt to alleviate their condition, therefore, would have to come at the expense of producers. "Whatever capital you divert to the support of a shiftless and good-for-nothing person," he warned, "is so much diverted from some other employment and that means from somebody else. If you give a loaf to a pauper you cannot give the same loaf to a laborer." It was therefore necessary to decide who would get that "loaf." According to Sumner, the loaf should not go to the nonproducing "worthless member of society" but, rather, to the productive member. Any other decision would merely reward those who were lazy and improvident at the expense of those who, through "struggles and self denial," had produced wealth.[12]

One of the worst offenders in Sumner's view was the government, because it functioned as a misguided Robin Hood, robbing from the productive and giving to the nonproductive. It did this through pensions, internal improvements, and the maintenance of museums, libraries, and parks, none of which, Sumner insisted, was actually necessary for public well-being. And it established protective tariffs that enriched certain individuals at the expense of the producing masses. "Wealth comes only from production," Sumner insisted, "and all that the wrangling grabbers, loafers, and jobbers get to deal with comes from somebody's toil and sacrifice." That somebody was the

"Forgotten Man," the individual who had to foot the bill for every govern-ment proposal to help the nation's nonproducers.[13]

Having divided the world into producers and nonproducers, Sumner had to figure out where to place consumers. One possible approach would have been to argue that everyone, producer and nonproducer alike, was a con-sumer. Sumner, however, was reluctant to make such an argument because, like many of his contemporaries, he considered *consumer* a pejorative term. Rather than saddle the producer with the consumer's negative connotations, he chose instead to divide society into workers and savers, on the one hand, and idlers and spenders, on the other. In Sumner's world not only were con-sumer and producer mutually exclusive categories; *consumer* was synonymous with *nonproducer*.

Making *consumer* synonymous with *nonproducer* effectively denied con-sumers any claim to political representation in Sumner's good society. Because he defined such a society as one that revolved around the producer-citizen, he assumed that any "man who is present as a consumer" but who "drops out of the ranks of workers and producers" should automatically be denied any claim to a civic identity. "On no sound political theory," he insisted, "ought such a person to share in the political power of the State."[14] For Sum-ner consumer-citizen was not a legitimate political identity.

The reformer and journalist Henry George was as convinced as Sumner that the world was divided into producers and nonproducers. But he did not place the same individuals in each group. Sumner's nonproducers were pri-marily the unemployed poor. George, on the other hand, reserved the desig-nation for the idle rich. The "luxurious idler, who does no productive work either with head or hand, but lives, we say, upon wealth which his father left him securely invested in government bonds" does not live on "wealth accu-mulated in the past." On the contrary, his subsistence comes "from the pro-ductive labor that is going on around him." As far as George was concerned, "what this man inherited from his father, and on which we say he lives, is not actually wealth at all, but only the power of commanding wealth as others produce it."[15]

George not only dismissed the notion that the idle rich lived off their past labors. He also rejected Sumner's idea that the unemployed poor were para-sites, idle by choice. On the contrary, George insisted, throughout the nation "men who wish to labor, in order to satisfy their wants, cannot find opportu-nity. . . . The real trouble must be that supply is somehow prevented from satisfying demand, that somewhere there is an obstacle which prevents labor from producing the things that laborers want."[16]

In his phenomenally successful *Progress and Poverty* (1879) George traced both the ability of the idle rich to command society's produce and the inability of the poor to secure work to the system of landownership. The poor were poor, George insisted, not because they refused to work, as Sumner suggested, but because they were denied access to the land. "If one man can command the land upon which others must labor, he can appropriate the produce of their labor as the price of his permission to labor." The result was that "one receives without producing, the others produce without receiving." According to George, the right to charge rent, a right that was implicit in the private ownership of land, was an egregious violation of producerist principles, because it stripped "the many of the wealth they justly earn, to pile it up in the hands of the few, who do nothing to earn it."[17]

George's solution was a "single tax" on land. Such a tax would make the monopolization of land unprofitable, thereby eliminating the "rent" that the poor had to pay for the privilege of working. With the introduction of this one tax, he insisted, "the great cause which concentrates wealth in the hands of those who do not produce, and takes it from the hands of those who do, would be gone."[18]

Like Sumner, George had been strongly influenced by the ideas of David Ricardo. It was not Ricardo's theory of wages, however, but his theory of rent which captured George's imagination.[19] According to that theory, rent was the difference between the cost of producing food on the least fertile land and the cost of producing food on more fertile land. For example, if Farmer Jones, who tilled a marginal piece of land, could produce ten dollars worth of food per acre, and Farmer Smith, who tilled more fertile land, could produce fifteen dollars per acre, then the rent on Farmer Smith's land would be five dollars. If Farmer Smith tilled his own land, he could pocket the five dollars. If he leased out his property he could charge the five dollars as rent. In either case the five dollars went to Farmer Smith.

What George took from all this was that rent represented an "unearned increment." Farmer Smith did no more work than Farmer Jones, and yet he received five dollars more per acre. Why? Because he had managed to monopolize more fertile land than Farmer Jones. But, according to George, it was not only agricultural land that produced an unearned increment. Urban land did as well. The city landlord could charge more per square foot for the use of his land than could a landowner in the wilderness. In the case of urban land it was not fertility but location that created the unearned increment. Nevertheless, George pointed out, the principle was the same. Like the affluent Farmer Smith, the city landlord did no extra work to earn that increment. He had merely managed to monopolize land that was high in value.

To the producerist-minded George the problem with an unearned increment was that it denied producers the full product of their labor. Wage workers, in his view, should certainly pay farmers a fair price for the labor involved in growing crops. And they should certainly pay landlords a fair price for the labor involved in constructing and maintaining apartment buildings. But wage workers ended up paying far more than a fair price for the landlord's or farmer's labor because included in the cost of food and lodging was the unearned increment that went to those who had managed to monopolize valuable land.

Sumner found George's analysis flawed. As far as he was concerned, the landholder well deserved any so-called unearned increment. Land, he insisted, "is only a *chance* to prosecute the struggle for existence, and the man who tries to earn a living by the subjugation of raw land makes that attempt under the most unfavorable conditions, for land can be brought into use only by great hardship and exertion." It was to be expected that the pioneer who cleared the land should find "a profit in the increasing value of land as the new State grows up" and rightly so. That pioneer had worked hard, enduring hardships that the rest of society had been unwilling to endure. "It would be unjust," Sumner insisted, "to take that profit away from him, or from any successor to whom he has sold it."[20]

At first glance the worldviews of George and Sumner seemed diametrically opposed. But the two agreed on one important issue. Central to both was the idea that the political economy should revolve around the producer. Sumner and George might not have defined the producer in the same way, but both were firmly convinced that a system that condemned "producers to a life of toil while non-producers loll in luxury" was unacceptable.[21]

Why did two social thinkers who were equally committed to a producerist worldview disagree so fundamentally on what constituted an equitable economy? Much of the explanation can be found in their understanding of how industrialization had altered the economy. As far as Sumner was concerned, it had not. He assumed that the conditions that had existed in a traditional economy dominated by small, independent producers continued to be relevant. He believed that each individual retained some control over his economic fortunes and that the relationship between work and prosperity remained a direct one.[22] Those who possessed "industry, energy, skill, frugality, prudence, temperance, and other industrial virtues" emerged victorious in the economic struggle. Those who lacked these virtues were doomed to fail.[23]

George, by contrast, believed that industrialization had profoundly altered a traditional economy. The small independent producer of old had given way to widespread wage labor and extensive capital accumulation. In such an economy it became increasingly difficult to attribute failure to individual shortcomings. More than industrial virtue separated the poor from the wealthy. In the modern economy, George maintained, the industrially virtuous worker quickly discovered that "the very power of exerting his labor for the satisfaction of his wants passes from his own control, and may be taken away or restored by the actions of others, or by general causes over which he has no more influence than he has over the motions of the solar system."[24] In an economy in which forces beyond one's control determined one's standard of living, the industrially virtuous were no better off than those lacking industrial virtue.

It was not only their different views on the impact of industrialization which accounted for George's and Sumner's fundamentally different understanding of economic equity. Their views on the ultimate source of wealth also influenced that understanding. According to George all wealth came from the land. "Man creates nothing. The whole human race, were they to labor forever, could not create the tiniest mote that floats in a sunbeam—could not make this rolling sphere one atom heavier or one atom lighter." Only when humans mixed their labor with "pre-existing matter" did they create wealth. Therefore, George concluded, the creation of wealth required access to the land.[25]

Because George pointed to land, something not produced by human labor, as the source of wealth, he never considered the single tax a violation of a producer's rights, as Sumner did. To Sumner taxation expropriated a portion of the producer's labor and bestowed it on the nonproducer. George, however, could maintain that the single tax would not divert funds from producers to nonproducers because "the value of land . . . is not created by individual effort." On the contrary, land value depended on its location, specifically its proximity to population. But, if the value of land was a function of population, then this value was ultimately created by society. Thus, George reasoned, according to good producerist logic, it was only fair that the value "be taken by society for social needs." Those social needs included the support of museums, parks, and libraries, the very public institutions that Sumner had opposed on the grounds that they were maintained for the enjoyment of the nonproducer at the expense of the producer. According to George, however, the revenue that would support these institutions had been created by the community and should thus "be applied to the common benefit."[26]

Sumner did not share George's ideas about the source of wealth. Land itself, he insisted, was worthless. "It is covered with trees, or stones, or swamps; or hostile animals of various kinds occupy it; or malaria stands guard over it." Before it could be of any use, there was "a series of obstacles to be overcome; dangerous and toilsome work to be done." But through "labor and self-denial" producers had transformed worthless land into capital.[27] Not land but capital was for Sumner the key to wealth.

The way that George and Sumner each identified the source of wealth had important implications. By identifying land, something not created by human labor, as the source of wealth, George weakened the link between one's role as a producer and one's right to consume wealth. Sumner, by contrast, identified capital, something produced through human exertion, as the source of wealth, a choice that only emphasized the relationship between one's labor and one's claim to material well-being.[28]

George's and Sumner's theories suggest how much of a threat industrialization posed to a producerist worldview. Sumner responded to the threat by refusing to acknowledge that there was any incompatibility between older producerist principles and newer economic conditions. The result was a view of the economy that was perhaps not the most compassionate but one that left the producerist edifice intact. The same could not be said of George's approach. Unlike Sumner, George believed that the emerging industrial economy did not function according to basic producerist notions of equity and justice. But, although his goal was an economy in which producerist principles would reign supreme, the very arguments he used to critique the existing system were ones that could be used to question producerist principles themselves.

George's analysis of unemployment was only one example of how his producerist ideas had consumerist implications. George denounced the existing system because it denied workers the opportunity to work and then told them that because they did not work they could not eat. He did so because he wanted to establish a right to work. What is striking about his critique, however, was that it could just as easily serve as a starting point for establishing a right to eat.

The consumerist implications of George's producerist analysis were even more evident in his discussions of value. In the nineteenth century most economists believed that value was something that was determined in the productive sphere. George was no exception. Indeed, it was his reliance on a cost theory of value which prompted George to develop his single tax in the first place. According to this theory, value was determined by the costs that went into a product, specifically interest, wages, and rent. For George only two of the three costs represented a reward for labor, specifically the reward to the capitalist producer through interest and the reward to the wage-working producer through wages. The same, however, could not be said of rent. "The value of land," he insisted, "is not created by individual effort, but arises from the existence and growth of society."[29] The task, decided the producerist-minded George, was to eliminate the one cost of production which was not related to labor.

George's goal was a producerist one. Yet his means had distinct consumerist implications. He may have argued that "the value of land . . . arises from the existence and growth of society" only because he wanted to demonstrate that a single tax would redirect wealth from nonproducers to producers. But it was an argument that could also be used to call into question producerist theories of value. And, perhaps even more significantly, it was one that could lead quite logically to a definition of *value* which credited consumers with its creation.[30] It did not require much of an intellectual leap to ask why land was more valuable in a densely populated city than in an uninhabited area, to reason that consumer demand for that land was greater than the demand for similar land in an uninhabited area, and then to conclude that it must, therefore, be consumers rather than producers who were responsible for its value. It was a conclusion that the producerist-minded George had no intention of reaching, but he nevertheless provided a few guideposts for those who wanted to travel in just such a direction.

The consumerist implications of George's producerist arguments were also evident in his assertion that any recognition of political rights was meaningless without a recognition of economic rights. "It is not enough that men should vote," he stressed; "it is not enough that they should be theoretically equal before the law."[31] At first glance such an assertion would seem compatible with a consumer-oriented outlook. But the economic rights that George was advocating were not the same ones that consumerist thinkers would demand. The latter wanted recognition of every citizen's right to live free from want, irrespective of his or her role in production. The economic right that George called for, however, was the right of every individual "to the free use of his powers in making a living for himself and his family." In short, rather than demanding a right to consume, George demanded a right to work. And he demanded the right of all who worked "to retain for their own uses the full fruits of their labour."[32] Beyond that, the producer-minded George was unwilling to go.

Nevertheless, George's attempts to understand how the existing economy had failed the producer led him to a number of ideas that would be central to a consumer-oriented worldview. Among them was the notion that work was not an end but a means. According to George, the prevailing focus on work instead of goods, on the means instead of the ends, led to certain fantastic assumptions. The government passed tariffs because it assumed "that the more work we do for foreign nations and the less we allow them to do for us, the better off we shall be." And, according to George, much of the public assumed that those who created jobs made an important contribution to the nation while those who developed labor-saving machinery threatened general well-being because they lessened "the amount of work to be done."[33]

Inherent in all these assumptions, George maintained, was the idea that the fundamental problem confronting society was how to create work rather than how to create goods. "To listen to much that is talked and much that is written," he lamented, "one would think that the cause of poverty is that there is not work enough for so many people, and that if the Creator had made the rock harder, the soil less fertile, iron as scarce as gold, and gold as diamonds; or if ships would sink and cities burn down oftener, there would be less poverty, because there would be more work to do."[34]

Nowhere was the extent to which economic thinkers had confused means with ends more evident to George than in their constant warnings about the dangers of overproduction. "What can be more preposterous," he asked, "than to speak in any general sense of over-production? Over-production of wealth . . . when so many must stint and strain and contrive, to get a living; when there is poverty and actual want among large classes!" "There can be no real scarcity of work," he declared, "which is but the means of satisfying material wants until human wants are all satisfied."[35]

In George's view the problem with such misguided ideas was that they encouraged misguided economic policies. This "constant fear . . . not that too little, but that too much, will be produced" prompted governments to levy tariffs "for fear the people of other countries will overwhelm us with their goods." It kept machines and men idle. And it encouraged businesses to combine in an effort to limit production. "In whatever direction we look we see the most stupendous waste of productive forces." The result was a widespread poverty that was completely unnecessary.[36]

George's understanding of *overproduction* had profoundly consumerist implications. Sensing that the term was being applied only when a certain volume of goods could not all be sold at a particular price, George suggested that business could respond to overproduction in one of two ways. It could reduce production, or it could lower price. If it chose the former, the result would be a contraction in the economy, because reducing production would throw laborers out of work, thereby curtailing their power to consume. This would further reduce demand, resulting in a greater contraction of the economy. Business, however, had another option. It could lower its prices rather than the volume of goods, which would lead to an expansion of the economy. Lowering prices would increase demand. To meet that demand businesses would have to hire additional laborers, who, with their new paychecks, would join other consumers in demanding more goods.[37]

What was significant about George's analysis of overproduction was that it called into question the prevailing assumption that increasing consumption led inevitably to poverty. In so doing, it helped to remove some of the negative connotations that had long surrounded consumption. Throughout the late nineteenth century prevailing economic orthodoxy held that "labor, exercised conjointly with skill and frugality, was the only path for the permanent attainment of material abundance."[38] George suggested, however, that not frugality but increasing consumption was the key to the nation's economic health. It was an understanding of consumption which had distinctly positive connotations.

By 1883 a thinker who insisted that the political economy should revolve around the producer had laid much of the groundwork for a consumer-oriented worldview. He had called into question the preoccupation with work, insisting instead that the proper focus should be on goods. He had argued that the waste inherent in the profit-oriented industrial system prevented the emergence of abundance. He had suggested that the real driving force in the economy was not production but consumption. And he had argued that a guarantee of political rights was meaningless if economic rights were ignored.

That ideas such as George's posed a real threat to the producerist worldview did not go unnoticed. Indeed, one of the most fervent supporters of this worldview, William Graham Sumner, took great pains to discredit such ideas. "Projects to abolish poverty," he warned, "are worthy of an age which has undertaken to discuss the abolition of disease. Why not abolish death and be as gods once for all?" There was only one way, he repeatedly insisted, to improve the material well-being of society, and that was through the "enhancement of the industrial virtues. . . . industry, self-denial, and temperance." It was the lack of such virtues which brought poverty. "There is a plain question," he insisted: "Is there any other man in the world who is to blame for the fact that I am poor?"[39] George would have answered in the affirmative. Sumner insisted that the only valid response was no.

At the same time that Sumner rejected the notion that poverty could be abolished, he also dismissed the idea of a right to live free from want. Just as George had tapped into the pejorative connotations surrounding *luxury* when he denounced the lifestyle of the "idle rich," Sumner drew on those connotations to disparage the demands of the "idle poor." "The popular doctrines of the last hundred years," he declared, "have spread the notion that everybody ought to enjoy comfort and luxury—that luxury is a sort of right. Therefore if anybody has luxury while others have it not, this is held to prove that . . . the state in which such a condition of things exists has failed to perform its function."[40]

Sumner's word choice was deliberate. By suggesting that the poor wanted luxury rather than an end to poverty, he was able to portray their demands as unjustified. But the very fact that Sumner could equate an end to poverty with luxury suggests the extent to which there were no firm boundaries between acceptable and unacceptable consumption. Without such boundaries it would be impossible to define acceptable consumption. Until such a definition could be established, even seemingly moderate consumption would carry with it some of the pejorative connotations surrounding *luxury*.

Sumner tried to discredit the right to live free from want not only by tapping into pejorative associations but also by dismissing the very notion of rights. Any claim to a natural right to material well-being, he insisted, was "destitute of sense," ignoring the "facts of our existence on earth." It assumed that "just because [a man] has been born, he ought to have and enjoy all the acquisitions of civilization without labor, self-denial, or study, and that he is a victim of injustice if he does not possess all those good things." The biggest problem with recognizing a right of the needy and the impoverished to live free from want, Sumner argued, was that it would require those who possessed material goods to fulfill that right. The thrifty and the hardworking would be forced to support the lazy and improvident. Giving the state that responsibility was no different from giving it to the producing individual because all the state would do would be to take wealth "from those who have earned and saved it, and give it to him who needs it and who, by the hypothesis, has not earned and saved it."[41]

Despite all the differences, what is ultimately most striking about Sumner's and George's thought are the similarities. Both found it impossible to step outside the dominant producerist paradigm of the day. Thus, they both demanded an order in which "a man shall not be interfered with while using his own powers for his own welfare." And both called for a system that would guarantee the producer the "fruits of his labor."[42] Although they did not agree on how this would be done, both assumed that the only valid way to organize the political economy was around the producer.

In *The Labor Movement in America* (1886) Richard T. Ely, an economics professor at the Johns Hopkins University, found it as difficult as George and Sumner to step outside the producerist paradigm. Like them, he assumed that the only equitable way to organize the political economy was around the producer. And, like them, he looked to a system in which individuals controlled their own labor. He did not, however, share Sumner's and George's conviction that the most compelling problem confronting society was the tendency of the existing system to deny producers the full fruits of their labor.

In Ely's view increasing class conflict was society's most pressing issue. Industrialization, he warned, was creating two distinct and hostile classes. "Already they scarcely understand each other even when they speak the same language." As far as Ely was concerned, "nothing of graver import has ever befallen this people of the United States. Unless powerful forces calculated to keep alive the unity of civilization among us can be brought into action, our future downfall will be inevitable."[43] As a Christian socialist, Ely believed that the best way to unify civilization and bring about "a peaceful organization of society" was through the application of Christian principles. In a social order organized around "the doctrine of human brotherhood" and the command-ment "love thy neighbor as thyself," oppression would disappear. And with the end of oppression would come social harmony, as "warfare of all kinds shall cease."[44]

Because Ely's harmonious social order was also a producer-oriented one, he looked to the labor movement, by which he meant the Knights of Labor, as the group most capable of ending class conflict. In his view the labor move-ment had three qualifications that made it the most promising group for in-dustrial peace. First, it was "the strongest force outside the Christian Church making for the practical recognition of human brotherhood." Even more important, it was the only group seeking "the union of capital and labor in the same hands." According to Ely, such a union was important because it would eliminate class struggle by placing everyone in the category of inde-pendent producer, thereby eliminating classes. Finally, the labor movement, as represented by the Knights, proposed to unify capital and labor not through violence but through the creation of "grand, wide-reaching, co-operative enterprises, which shall embrace the masses." Such cooperative en-terprises could mitigate increasing class hostility because, according to Ely, they offered "a practical application of Christianity to business."[45]

In turning to cooperation, Ely joined an ongoing debate over the relative merits and liabilities of an economic order based on the cooperative ideal.[46] Increasingly, that debate would focus on whether a cooperative economy should function on behalf of the consumer or the producer. Cooperative theorists were forced to address the issue earlier than most social thinkers because cooperation came in two forms. One version focused on producer cooperatives, worker-owned-and-operated workshops. The goal of this ap-proach was to eliminate the employer and return control of the production process to the workers themselves. Thus, those who favored producer cooper-ation inevitably advocated a political economy organized around the pro-ducer.

The other approach to cooperation called for the creation of consumer co-operatives, stores that were owned and operated by those who patronized them. At first glance such stores would seem to be more compatible with a consumer-oriented view. And, indeed, a number of twentieth-century, con-sumerist thinkers would advocate the creation of consumer cooperatives as the best way to guarantee all members of society a high standard of living. With consumers in control of the distribution and even the manufacture of goods, they would argue, the needs of the consuming population rather than the profit motive would govern economic decisions. Organizing the economy around consumers would usher in an economy of abundance and thus a higher standard of living for all.

Throughout the nineteenth century, however, consumer cooperation remained a producerist ideology. The twenty-eight weavers from Rochdale, near Manchester, England, who developed the Rochdale model of consumer cooperation, established a consumer cooperative because they were convinced that the savings they could realize by eliminating the middleman would enable them to amass the capital necessary to begin a producer cooperative. Most of those who organized consumer cooperatives on this side of the Atlantic also saw them as a means to an economy organized around producer cooperatives. That had been true of the New England Workingmen's Association, and it was true of the Knights of Labor. Even groups that focused exclusively on consumer cooperatives, such as the Sovereigns of Industry and the Patrons of Husbandry, did so because they were convinced that the industrial system denied producers a portion of their labor not only in the workplace through low wages and low agricultural prices but also in the marketplace through high prices. Consumer cooperatives could prevent such expropriation in the marketplace.[47] Thus, for a number of reasons consumer cooperatives were compatible with a producer-oriented world view.

It was therefore not surprising that consumer cooperation was initially a working-class movement. It did, however, attract supporters from the ranks of the middle class, including such high-profile middle-class reformers as E. L. Godkin, editor of the *Nation,* and Horace Greeley, editor of the *New York Tribune.* These reformers were not drawn to cooperation in spite of its producer orientation but because of it. What they saw in producer cooperatives was a way to eliminate the growing tensions between laborers and industrialists by replacing the wage labor system with one organized around independent producers.[48]

In many ways Ely was typical of the middle-class thinkers who turned to cooperation. Like them, he favored producer over consumer cooperatives. If the goal was to unite labor and capital in the same hands, then producer cooperation offered the quickest means of doing so. Consumer cooperation was of more limited value, in his view, because it failed to address the primary problem, namely "the relations between capital and labor." At best it was a beginning, offering an education in the principles of cooperation. It taught the worker "thrift and frugality" and provided "an opportunity to invest his savings." But it aided each member "as a consumer . . . not as a workingman." The best that Ely could say for consumer cooperation was that it would "lead to better things," by which he meant it was a step on the road to "a co-operative system which embraces the industrial life of the people" by controlling both production and distribution.[49]

Ely's producerist assumptions made it impossible for him to grant the consumer a pivotal role in any reorganization of the political economy. Seeking the best means to achieve social harmony in a producer-oriented world, he was drawn to producer cooperation because it offered a way of ending class conflict. Producer cooperation would replace the two hostile categories of employers and employees with one category, independent producers. Once society consisted exclusively of independent producers, class conflict would cease to exist because classes would cease to exist. From his producerist perspective consumer cooperation did not have the same transformative power. It might assist workers, it might train them in cooperative principles, but it was not capable of eliminating class conflict by creating a universal category of independent producer.

Equally indicative of Ely's producerist leanings were his views about what constituted acceptable labor tactics. Although he had no problem with strikes, convinced that they were legitimate weapons in the arsenal of organized labor, he could not countenance "that terrible weapon of labor, the 'boycott.'" The problem with boycotts, he insisted, was that they denied a producer his customers.[50] What distinguished strikes from boycotts, however, was that the former was a strike by producers, whereas the latter was a strike by consumers. For Ely there was only one identity around which workers should organize, and that was their identity as producers.

Ely was unable to see the consumer identity as a legitimate political identity in large part because of the pejorative connotations he associated with consumption. Unlike Sumner, he was willing to grant that not all consumption was motivated by a desire for luxury. But he worried that any attempt to fulfill legitimate needs could quickly degenerate into the pursuit of less than legitimate desires. Not surprisingly, his inability to separate consumption from luxury made it difficult for him to advocate a political economy that revolved around the consumer.

Ely's biggest problem with luxury was that in his view it exacerbated the division between the classes, "injuring those who indulge in it, and exciting envy and bitterness in the minds of those who are excluded." Thus, it was partially responsible for the very weakness in the social order which Ely was most determined to eradicate. But he was also concerned about the close connections between luxury and poverty. "Many who live in worry and discomfort," Ely maintained, "have a sufficient income to satisfy all rational wants, were it well expended." Most people, however, were not content with satisfying their rational wants. Instead, they tried to outdo one another in their consumption. "Men spend more than they can afford. . . . Wasted fortunes, blighted careers, broken hearts, boundless opportunities forever lost,—these are the end of which the beginning is self-indulgence."[51] Like Sumner, Ely assumed that the pursuit of luxury pushed many an individual into the ranks of the impoverished.

The assumption that luxury was responsible for poverty was an old one. But it had not gone uncontested. As early as the eighteenth century, Bernard Mandeville had argued that the private vices of the consumer resulted in public benefits. Consumers, he granted, might be guilty of envy, vanity, selfishness, and pride, but their desires "nursed Ingenuity," which resulted in economic progress and stimulated the economy, which, in turn, increased the standard of living for the poor as well as the rich.[52]

Ely, however, had little patience with Mandevelian arguments. As a consumer, he acknowledged, you "are bound to employ labor when you spend money but God gives you a choice. You may employ the labor to work for yourself, or you may give labor such a direction that others will receive benefit therefrom." Spending money on a fancy dress, he maintained, had little socially redeeming value. "It is said it gives employment to labor—as if every expenditure of money did not do that! . . . That same money spent for cheaper dresses for old ladies in a home would give quite as much employment." As far as Ely was concerned, true Christians limited their consumption to necessities and diverted any remaining funds into charitable works. Only then did they avoid the corrupting effects inherent in consumption.[53]

There is a certain irony in Ely's inability to remove the pejorative connotations surrounding consumption. That inability made it extremely difficult for him to shift his focus from the producer to the consumer and, in so doing, denied him an organizing principle that was more suited to his purposes than the producer identity was. In the 1910s and 1920s cooperative theorists would suggest that only a cooperative economy organized around the consumer—one in which consumers owned and worked in not only their own stores but also their own factories—could usher in a classless society. More significantly, in an industrial economy characterized by wage labor and capital, the consumer identity was readily available, whereas the independent producer seemed to be rapidly disappearing. Ely hoped that producer cooperatives would be able to bring the independent producer back. By the end of the century, however, most cooperative theorists had given up such a hope, convinced that wage labor would be a permanent feature of an industrial economy.

The Labor Movement in the United States proved to be one of the last gasps of a producer cooperative ideal. By the late nineteenth century producer cooperation had come under siege. At the forefront of this assault were European thinkers who suggested that, although producer cooperatives might be attractive ideologically, they were not successful.[54] An economy dominated by small, independent producers had given way to an industrialized order in which huge corporations wielded increasing power. The time had come, they argued, to place cooperation within that order. While this intellectual shift occurred in cooperative circles across Europe, it was the English experience that exerted the greatest influence on American cooperative thought.[55] It was, therefore, not surprising that a British theoretical work, Beatrice Potter's *The Co-Operative Movement in Great Britain* (1891), should first suggest to American cooperative theorists the radical potential of consumer cooperatives. Potter's book had a profound, though somewhat delayed, impact on American cooperative thought.[56]

Like earlier British cooperative thinkers—and American thinkers, for that matter—Potter saw cooperation as a way to improve the existence of society's producers. But she departed from traditional cooperative thought by rejecting producer cooperation. In the modern industrial world, she argued, such cooperatives had little hope of success. At best they were anachronistic, attempting to return society to an earlier stage in which production was organized around small workshops. At worst producer cooperatives were little better than their capitalist competitors, exploiting worker and consumer alike. "It is self-evident," Potter wrote, "that all Associations of Producers whether they be capitalists buying labour, or labourers buying capital, or a co-partnership between the two, are directly opposed in their interest to the interest of the community. . . . They are, and must always remain,

profit-seekers—intent on securing a large margin between the cost of production and the price given." In either case producer cooperatives had proven
thoroughly unsuccessful in correcting the evils of a competitive, capitalist
system.[57]

In discrediting producer cooperatives, Potter had effectively brought one of
the major tenets of American cooperative thought into question: the notion
that consumer cooperatives were only a means to producer cooperatives. If
producer cooperatives ceased to be a goal, could consumer cooperatives—
only a means to that goal—be of any value? Even more specifically, if consumer cooperatives *could* exist in their own right, could they be integrated as
effectively into a working-class ideology as producer cooperatives had been?
Earlier nineteenth-century cooperative thinkers such as Ely had believed that
the answer to those questions must be no. Potter answered both questions in
the affirmative. Potter did not reject producer cooperatives because she considered the producer interest unimportant. On the contrary, she insisted that
the most effective way for the working class to protect its interests was to
organize as consumers as well as workers. Only when the consumer cooperative and the trade union movements joined forces, she argued, with "the
citizens organized as consumers, and the workers organized as producers,"
could labor hope to correct the economic imbalances brought on by industrialization.[58]

Nor was the radical potential of cooperatives limited to the marketplace.
Potter insisted that consumer cooperatives could play a critical role in transforming the production process. Cooperative consumers could maintain adequate working conditions in their own factories. And, even more important,
they could force the introduction of such conditions throughout England
both by refusing to carry "sweated products" in the cooperative stores and by
boycotting any manufacturer whose factory did not maintain an acceptable
labor standard.[59] Consumer, rather than producer, cooperatives were the key
to producer well-being.

Potter's approach to cooperation turned Ely's version on its head. Ely had
stressed the radical potential of producer cooperation while minimizing that
of consumer cooperation. According to Potter, however, producer cooperatives, dependent upon competition and profit, were firmly entrenched in the
capitalist system. It was consumer cooperation that offered the real hope of a
democratic order because it relied on "democratic control" rather than competition to lower prices and raise quality. And it replaced a system dependent

upon individual profit with one in which "each man and woman would work, not for personal subsistence or personal gain, but for the whole community." In short, not producer but consumer cooperatives would be instrumental in forming "out of the present state of industrial war a great Republic of Industry firmly based on the Co-operative principle of 'all for each and each for all.'"[60]

Ultimately, Potter and Ely differed in their attitudes toward cooperation because they did not agree on the social and political order that should and could evolve. Both saw labor as the primary victim of industrial capitalism, and both looked to cooperation to introduce a more equitable order. For Ely an equitable order could best be achieved by eliminating class conflict. Producer cooperatives, by bringing all members of society together in a single class, could do just that. Potter believed, however, that the best way to end class conflict was for the working class to win the conflict. Cooperation offered a way to achieve victory. Although Potter had invested in the consumer an agency that Ely had denied, her equitable economic order remained one that revolved around producers.

The pejorative connotations surrounding *consumer,* which had prevented Ely from entertaining anything but producer-oriented solutions to society's problems, survived well beyond the 1880s.[61] Although those connotations did not go unchallenged, the publication of Charlotte Perkins Gilman's *Women and Economics* (1898) and Thorstein Veblen's *Theory of the Leisure Class* (1899) suggest that they continued to hold their own into the new century. As both Gilman and Veblen constructed their critiques of the existing order, they relied heavily on the negative associations surrounding *consumer* and *producer.*

For Charlotte Perkins Gilman the associations provided an effective means of highlighting the second-class status of women. In *Women and Economics* she criticized an economic system in which men were allowed to be producers while women were forced into the ranks of consumers, "denied free productive expression." The problem with such a situation, according to Gilman, was that humans were first and foremost producers. True, they were also consumers. But, according to Gilman, "consumption is not the main end, the governing force." Humans did not produce to consume. They produced because it was in their nature to do so. Even children exhibited this need to produce, a need that was independent of their need to consume. "'I want to mark!' cries the child, demanding the pencil. He does not want to eat. He wants to mark.

He is not seeking to get something into himself, but to put something out of himself." In Gilman's view "human labor is an exercise of faculty, without which we would cease to be human."[62] Therefore, to deny women their producer identity was tantamount to denying them their humanity.

Excluding women from the ranks of producers not only denied them their humanity. It also denied them their economic independence. "Individual economic independence among human beings," Gilman explained, "means that the individual . . . works for what he gets." She was quick to point out, however, that there was no relationship between how hard women worked and how much they received. "Their labor is the property of another . . . and what they receive depends not on their labor, but on the power and will of another."[63]

The disjuncture between how hard women worked and what they "got" was evident when one looked at the class status of women. "The women who do the most work get the least money," Gilman maintained, "and the women who have the most money do the least work." This was because "their labor is neither given nor taken as a factor in economic exchange. It is held to be their duty as women to do this work." The result, Gilman concluded, was that the economic status of women bore "no relation to their domestic labors." Instead, it was determined by their relationship with a male. "The comfort, the luxury, the necessities of life itself, which the woman receives, are obtained by the husband, and given her by him."[64]

"Debarr[ing] women from any free production" and driving them into the ranks of consumers had certain social consequences as well, Gilman maintained. Compelling half the population to assume an identity as corrupting as that of the consumer, she warned, would result in the corruption of society. "As the priestess of the temple of consumption, as the limitless demander of things to use up," the female created "a market for sensuous decoration and personal ornament, for all that is luxurious and enervating." "To consume food, to consume clothes, to consume houses and furniture and decorations and ornaments and amusements, to take and take and take forever . . . this is the enforced condition of the mothers of the race." What was ultimately most significant about this "enforced condition," however, was its impact not on women but on all those whom they influenced. "What wonder that their sons go into business 'for what there is in it'! What wonder that the world is full of the desire to get as much as possible and to give as little as possible!" The result was a society dominated by "inordinate consumption," "primitive individualism," "brutal ferocity . . . in the market-place," "unnatural greed," and "personal selfishness."[65] Only by granting women entry into the male category of producer could the dehumanizing and corrupting influence of the consumer identity be eliminated.

Gilman harnessed on behalf of women's rights the long-standing concern over the corrupting influence of luxury. Any society that permitted the creation of "an enormous class of non-productive consumers,—a class which is half the world, and mother of the other half," would have to accept the consequences. And the consequences were already apparent. Being responsible for the acculturation of the human race, these maternal nonproductive consumers were creating a species that increasingly divorced "taking . . . from its natural precursor and concomitant of making."[66] As had been the case with Sumner and even George, the power of Gilman's critique lay in her ability to show that the relationship between production and consumption was breaking down.

Gilman's method of challenging women's second-class status suggests how dominant the producerist worldview remained. Like Sumner and George, she knew that she could discredit the existing system by showing that it denied individuals the fruits of their labor. And, like them, she was aware that an even more damning critique of the system would show how some individuals consumed without producing. What was unique about her approach was that she managed to portray those who were forced to consume without producing as the exploited, not the exploiters. That she was able to do so suggests how deeply rooted the pejorative connotations surrounding *consumer* remained at the close of the nineteenth century.

Like Charlotte Perkins Gilman, Thorstein Veblen also relied heavily on the connotations associated with *producer* and *consumer*. In *The Theory of the Leisure Class,* his satirical stab at society's elite, he managed to discredit that group by arguing that they were not producers but consumers—and conspicuous ones at that. By stripping them of any positive connotations associated with *production* and saddling them with negative ones implicit in *consumption,* Veblen was able to cast doubt not only on the economic elite but also on an economic system that allowed such individuals to prosper.

Although Veblen depended upon the negative connotations surrounding consumption, he was actually more tolerant of consumption than were many of his contemporaries. Gilman and Sumner, for example, were poles apart in the way each defined the good society. Yet both could agree that only work gave human existence any meaning. Veblen, however, considered consumption a more central human activity. "Goods," he insisted, "are produced and consumed as a means to the fuller unfolding of human life."[67] The problem was not consumption itself, as Sumner and Gilman seemed to believe, but the cultural meanings that had become associated with consumption.

Veblen traced the origin of those cultural meanings to the fact that goods, like leisure, provided an effective means of making "invidious comparisons" among individuals. In so doing, they transformed the struggle for goods from a struggle for subsistence into one for status. In the process moderate consumption had lost any appeal it may once have had, since "no merit would accrue from the consumption of the bare necessaries of life." In order for consumption to be an effective means of signaling status, Veblen explained, "it must be an expenditure of superfluities. In order to be reputable it must be wasteful." Thus, expensive goods, particularly those whose costs far exceed their utility, were preferable to cheap ones because they provided "evidence of relative ability to pay."[68]

Like Sumner and George, Veblen's ultimate concern was a system that tended to reward nonproducers rather than producers. He parted company with his two predecessors, however, in that he placed capitalists in the nonproducer category. Sumner had defined capitalists as the quintessential producers. Even George had initially included capitalists in the producer category alongside labor, relegating only landowners and the idle rich to the ranks of nonproducers. Only in the early 1880s did he take the first tentative steps toward excluding capitalists from the producer category when he suggested that there was a distinction between the "production of wealth" and the "grabbing of wealth."[69] Veblen developed that distinction.

According to Veblen, there were two types of economic institutions, pecuniary institutions, which focused on acquisition, and industrial institutions, which focused on production. "The former category," he explained, "have [sic] to do with 'business,' the latter with industry, taking the latter word in the mechanical sense." As he saw it, the leisure class was more interested in business, its relation to the economic process "a relation of acquisition, not of production; of exploitation, not of serviceability." Members of this "parasitic class" were intent on diverting "what substance they may to their own use, and [retaining] whatever is under their hand."[70]

In Veblen's view only the "working classes" had any real claim to the producer identity because they were the only ones whose primary interest lay "chiefly in the industrial [employments]." Yet the existing system was weakening even their commitment to industrial virtues. Members of the working classes realized that "entrance to the leisure class lies through the pecuniary employments." And, even more significantly, they found that, in the day-to-day struggle to survive, pecuniary virtues were more relevant than industrial ones. As Veblen explained it, "the pecuniary struggle produces an underfed class, of large proportions." As the members of this underfed class "struggle for the means with which to meet the daily needs," they take on the pecuniary focus of those higher up the social hierarchy. Each member of the underfed class concentrates increasingly on "his own invidious ends alone, and becomes continually more narrowly self-seeking." Thus did the industrial virtues become obsolete. As Gilman, Sumner, George, and Ely had done before him, Veblen warned that the existence of a large class of nonproducers threatened to corrupt the entire society.[71]

It was not only in placing capitalists in the nonproducing class that Veblen parted company with Sumner and George. He also did so over the merits of capitalism. Sumner championed capitalism because he believed it was a producer-oriented system that rewarded those who displayed such producer characteristics as frugality and industriousness. Even George insisted that his target was not the capitalist system. Like Sumner, he believed that capitalism was basically a producer-oriented system. It had, however, developed a few weaknesses that prevented it from functioning completely on behalf of the producer. George's goal was to eliminate those weaknesses and reestablish the producer orientation of capitalism. Because his target was not capitalism but its shortcomings, he, like Sumner, emphasized the sanctity of private property and the importance of guaranteeing that any wealth produced by the individual belonged to that individual. "For my part," George told his readers in *Social Problems* (1884), "I would put no limit on acquisition. No matter how many millions any man can get by methods which do not involve the robbery of others—they are his: let him have them. . . . If he gets without taking from others, and uses without hurting others, what he does with his wealth is his own business and his own responsibility."[72]

Veblen, however, *was* taking aim at capitalism. He did not believe that it was, or indeed ever could be, a producer-oriented system because its focus was not on production so much as ownership, not on industry so much as acquisition. And he disagreed with Sumner that the capitalist system fostered frugality, industriousness, or productivity.[73] A quick look at the existing order revealed that the most productive members of the economy occupied the lowest rungs of the social order while those who were the least productive and practiced the most wasteful consumption occupied the highest. A system that placed so little value on producer values could not be defined as one that functioned on behalf of the producer.

Like Gilman's critique of existing gender relations, Veblen's attack on the capitalist system highlighted the extent to which the traditional connotations surrounding consumption and production remained strong. Only in a society in which producers were held in high esteem and consumers were seen as parasites could Veblen's assertion that the captains of industry were consumers cast doubt on the existing system. As had been the case with Gilman, the power of Veblen's critique depended upon an audience of readers who considered work an honorable activity and excessive consumption a problematic one. In the late nineteenth century Veblen, like Gilman, could assume such an audience.

Veblen had one problem. Readers would not only assume that the producer was a positive identity and the consumer a negative one but also that the producer was male and the consumer female.[74] Veblen, however, had no interest in establishing women as society's economic exploiters. He was reserving that dubious honor for the captains of industry. In order to make his satire effective he would have to establish the consumer as a male identity.

Veblen solved the problem by suggesting that women were not so much consumers in their own right as vicarious consumers. Upper-class males, he suggested, not only engaged in conspicuous leisure themselves but also supported an entire retinue of servants as well as a wife whose sole duty was the "non-productive consumption of time."[75] High status reached ludicrous proportions with the development of a social system in which "one group produces goods for [the master], [while] another group, usually headed by the wife, or chief wife, consumes for him in conspicuous leisure, thereby putting in evidence his ability to sustain large pecuniary damage without impairing his superior opulence."[76]

Fashion, Veblen suggested, provided the most graphic illustration of a conspicuous display of exemption from work. The primary purpose of elegant fashion, he declared, was to suggest "that the wearer cannot when so attired bear a hand in any employment that is directly and immediately of any human use." Such attire implied that the wearer could afford high levels of consumption, but, even more to the point, "it argues at the same time that he consumes without producing."[77]

What was evident for men's fashion was even more apparent in women's. The corset, according to Veblen, was "in economic theory" nothing less than "a mutilation, undergone for the purpose of lowering the subject's vitality and rendering her permanently and obviously unfit for work." It was no accident, he insisted, that women rather than men wore corsets, long skirts, and high-heeled shoes. If "conspicuous waste and conspicuous leisure are reputable because they are evidence of pecuniary strength," then it would defeat the purpose if the evidence of waste and leisure was taken to such an extent as to indicate "obvious discomfort or voluntarily induced physical disability." Instead, such wasteful expenditure and disability was performed by women "in behalf of some one else to whom she stands in a relation of economic dependence." In short, women "are servants to whom, in the differentiation of economic functions, has been delegated the office of putting in evidence their master's ability to pay."[78] Having once been the "drudge and chattel of the man," responsible for producing the goods he consumed, woman had "become the ceremonial consumer of goods which he produces. But she still quite unmistakably remains his chattel in theory; for the habitual rendering of vicarious leisure and consumption is the abiding mark of the unfree servant."[79]

Like Gilman, Veblen managed to absolve women of any blame associated with consumption by showing that they were not independent agents. He, too, assumed that women occupied the ranks of the exploited rather than the exploiters. For Gilman that assumption meant that the consumer identity itself must be an exploited one. For Veblen it meant that women could not be included within the ranks of consumers because that identity was reserved for exploiters, specifically, the male captains of industry.

Veblen tapped into the connotations of exploitation surrounding *female* not only to exclude women from the consumer category but also to establish the exploited status of the producer category. Obliged to explain why productive work was held in low regard by the elite, Veblen maintained that this work lacked high value because in an earlier "barbarian" age "industrial" employments had been women's work. At that time men had been exempt from such employments and had engaged, instead, in hunting, fishing, and other "predatory" activities. Although these activities provided much of the food supply for the community and were obviously productive, the barbarian male had insisted that "he is not a laborer, and he is not to be classed with the women in this respect; nor is his effort to be classed with the women's drudgery, as labor or industry." So intent was the barbarian male upon distinguishing his "exploit" from women's work that he made sure that he acquired goods only in ways that bore no resemblance to productive labor. It was not long before "the obtaining of goods by other methods than seizure [came] to be accounted unworthy of man in his best estate."[80]

Although the barbarian male went the way of history, Veblen maintained that his attitudes toward work survived. In the modern period class, rather than gender, separated those who engaged in industrial employments from those who were exempt. But the barbarian distinction between drudgery and exploit continued in the contemporary distinction between the "unworthy" industrial or productive occupations and the "worthy" nonindustrial, exploitative ones.[81]

Both Veblen's and Gilman's pairing of *female* with *producer* suggests to what extent combining identities could either reinforce or weaken traditional connotations. Both realized that *consumer* and *female* occupied much lower rungs on the social value hierarchy than *producer* and *male*. Gilman believed that one way to push *female* several rungs higher was to disassociate that identity from *consumer* and associate it with *producer*. Veblen knew that the best way to move the producer several rungs lower was to establish it as a female identity.[82]

By the end of the nineteenth century the producerist worldview was at its peak. That worldview had been so completely internalized by much of the population that the most powerful indictment of capitalism which Veblen could make was to suggest that it elevated the consumer over the producer. And the most powerful example of the exploitation of women which Gilman could provide was to argue that they had been denied their producer identity and forced, instead, to define themselves strictly as consumers. Perhaps the most striking indication of the pervasiveness of that worldview, however, was the extent to which thinkers across the political spectrum, who had little else in common, all took producerist assumptions for granted. There was much that separated the thought of a classical liberal such as Sumner, a Christian socialist such as Ely, and a Socialist feminist such as Gilman, but all agreed that the only equitable political economy was one that revolved around the producer.

Yet, even as the producerist consensus seemed to be ascendant, it had already begun to break down. Even some of the most devoted adherents of a producer-oriented worldview had found that it could not always account for the conditions in an industrial economy. As early as the 1880s, George had begun adapting his producerist ideas. Although he continued to insist that the only equitable political economy was a producer-oriented one, his analysis of the existing economic order nevertheless challenged the foundation of that economy. By the early 1890s Ely would begin rethinking the producerist principles, to which he had clung so tightly, and questioning the traditional connotations surrounding consumers and producers, which he had taken for granted. And in a series of books written during the first two and a half decades of the twentieth century Veblen would show how the existing order exploited the consuming masses by preventing the emergence of an economy of abundance.

CHAPTER TWO

Legitimizing the Consumer, 1880–1900

The producerist worldview that dominated nineteenth-century thought depended largely on the widespread acceptance of two related sets of ideas. The first consisted of ideas that characterized the producer and production as far superior to the consumer and consumption. The second consisted of a handful of assumptions that led directly to producerist answers but, even more important, made it difficult to ask anything but producerist questions—what one might call a producerist paradigm. In the late nineteenth century a number of political economic thinkers began to challenge both sets of ideas. Not surprisingly, having come of intellectual age in a producerist world, none managed a wholesale rejection of the producerist worldview. For most of them the easier target was the traditional definitions of *producer* and *consumer,* which could be rethought from within the confines of the producerist paradigm. But, in rethinking such definitions, these thinkers took an important first step toward rejecting the paradigm because they called into question one of the main assumptions on which it rested, namely the supremacy of the producer.

As would so frequently be the case, Simon Patten was an exception. A professor at the Wharton School of Business from 1887 until 1917 and, along with Richard T. Ely, one of the founding members of American Economics Association, Patten found it far easier to challenge the producerist paradigm than to reject the pejorative connotations surrounding the consumer. Indeed, what is most striking about the early writings of an economist who is generally credited with providing much of the theoretical foundation for a consumer-oriented political economy is the extent to which he found consumption a problematic activity.[1]

Patten's early ideas about consumption were laid out in *The Premises of Political Economy* (1885). In that book Patten argued that poverty could be alleviated. Like most nineteenth-century thinkers who made that argument, he found it necessary to take into account the ideas of David Ricardo. Specifically, he had to address Ricardo's assertion that any economic progress would not alleviate poverty but, instead, would only enrich landholders. Ricardo had argued that any rise in wages would only encourage workers to propagate. The growing population would increase the demand for food, which would, in turn, cause more marginal land to come under cultivation. The cultivation of more marginal land would increase rent, thereby pushing up food prices.

Like Henry George and William Graham Sumner, Patten found such logic compelling. But, while Sumner took from Ricardo the idea that poverty was inevitable, Patten learned a different lesson. Like George, he concluded that poverty could be eliminated. The trick was to abolish rent. According to George, the best way to do so would be to tax rent at 100 percent. The single tax, George maintained, would take the fruits of increasing productivity from those who had appropriated them through their monopolization of land and return them to producers. By doing so, the single tax would guarantee producers the full product of their labor.

Patten disagreed. The problem with George's single tax, he insisted, was that it addressed the symptoms rather than the disease. It focused on redistributing existing wealth when workers would have been far better served by an increase in the amount of wealth in existence. Because the single tax did nothing to increase productivity, it could not "compensate for the reduction in the average return for labor" which occurred as marginal land was brought under cultivation. "Neither the nationalization of land nor even the appropriation of all the means of production," Patten concluded, "can increase the average income to such a degree as to make the possessor comfortable and happy."[2]

How, then, to increase the "average return for labor"? According to Patten, the only way to do so was by altering society's consumption choices. "Nature," he maintained, "is not equally productive of all kinds of wealth and men cannot expect to choose those forms of wealth of which nature is least productive and receive the same reward as if they chose for consumption those articles supplied most abundantly by nature." If, however, humans could alter their consumption, bringing it into line with nature's productive capabilities, then it would be possible "to preserve a low price of food and increase the average return for labor." For Patten changes in consumption rather than changes in production or the system of taxation were the best way to ensure that each individual "obtain all that reward which nature offers for labor and abstinence."[3]

Redirecting society's consumption to goods produced abundantly by nature would increase the average return for labor not only because it would harness nature's productivity but also because it would eliminate rent. Patten illustrated how consumption could affect rent by examining the economic impact of a shift in demand from whiskey and beer to coffee. Whiskey and beer, he explained, placed pressure on land "on which high rent is paid . . . since these drinks are made from the common cereals used for food." Coffee, by contrast, was grown on a type of land "of which but small portion is in use." Thus, he concluded, "a change of demand for whiskey and beer to coffee would much reduce the rent of lands on which the common cereals are grown, while much more coffee could be produced without a material increase in price."[4]

For Patten, then, the best way to get rid of rent was to make all land prime land. George's single tax could redistribute rent, but it could do nothing to eliminate it. Only by doing away with marginal land would it be possible to eliminate rent. And the only way to do away with marginal land was to use all land to produce goods for which it was ideally suited. Furthermore, the advantages of bringing land use into line with nature's productivity extended beyond the elimination of rent. Efficient land use would also greatly increase available wealth by increasing productivity. The only real solution to poverty, Patten concluded, depended upon changes in consumption.

By showing that changes in consumption could eliminate rent, Patten had found his answer not only to George but also to Ricardo. Patten was willing to grant that poverty might be inevitable under certain conditions. "The Ricardian theory of rent," he conceded, was "true of a civilization where the mass of the people prefer those commodities which can be produced by nature only in relatively small quantities." In such a civilization poverty increased with every increase in productive power because, "as soon as the productive power of men is increased, it is not used to augment their supply of commodities, but to enable them to obtain articles produced by nature less abundantly than those formerly consumed." But the Ricardian theory of rent did not hold in a civilization that used land to grow products that nature could produce abundantly. Poverty, Patten insisted, was not caused by the "niggardliness of nature," as the Ricardian theory implied, but by "the universal disposition on the part of men to prefer those forms of wealth of which nature is least productive, instead of other commodities of which nature offers a generous supply."[5] And a universal disposition could be changed.

Patten's refutation of Ricardo had important implications. As long as Ricardo's theories about poverty and consumption held sway, constructing a consumer-oriented political economy to eliminate poverty would be worse than pointless. Not only had Ricardo argued that it was impossible to end poverty; he had also insisted that the ultimate cause of poverty was increasing consumer demand. But, if consumer demand were indeed the culprit Ricardo thought it was, then a consumer-oriented political economy, far from providing a way to eliminate poverty—as consumerist thinkers would argue—would merely guarantee its perpetuation. Patten, however, offered an analysis of the economy which suggested that it was indeed possible to alleviate poverty and, even more to the point, that the *only* way to do so was through consumption. In so doing, he not only provided an alternative to a Ricardian economic view but also helped to remove some of the pejorative connotations surrounding consumption.

The notion that inappropriate consumption caused poverty was not a new one. Numerous American thinkers, from Puritan divines to classical liberal economists, had warned of the deleterious effects of such consumption. These thinkers, however, had not defined *inappropriate* in the same way that Patten did. Inappropriate consumption, as they had defined it, was primarily a quantitative rather than a qualitative concept. Excessive consumption was the problem; limited consumption the solution.

Patten, however, was not troubled by the amount consumed so much as by what was consumed. As he defined it, inappropriate consumption was the consumption of goods that nature could produce only with difficulty.[6] Although his examples frequently focused on such morally charged goods as whiskey and beer, his definition nevertheless implied that poverty was not caused by immoral consumption so much as by the inefficient and wasteful use of nature. And, equally important, it implied that the key to prosperity was not moderation, as the critics of consumption assumed, but efficiency.

Shifting the focus from morality to efficiency weakened the luxurious connotations associated with consumption. As long as consumption was judged primarily in terms of morality and immorality, it would be all but impossible to champion an economic order dedicated to increasing consumption. But, once the criteria for judging consumption became efficiency and inefficiency, then increasing consumption ceased to be antithetical to a moral order and became, instead, the goal of an efficient economy.

By focusing on efficiency rather than morality, Patten not only made it possible to see consumption as something other than luxury; he also made it possible to see the consumer as something other than a parasite. And, what is more, he did so in a way that was completely consistent with producerist notions of equity. According to Patten, "the gross produce of any nation is mainly determined by the economy and the consumption of food, and not by the greater productivity in manufacturing." But, if the consumer played a critical role in determining the amount of wealth society had at its disposal, then, according to the dictates of even the most orthodox producerist principles, consumers should have the right to a share of that wealth, even though they played no role in the actual production process.[7]

Patten's theories helped both to legitimize the consumer identity and to weaken the producer's exclusive claim to wealth. In so doing, his theories prepared the ground for a consumer-oriented political economy. As long as the consumer was considered as nothing more than a parasite, advocating a system that revolved around the consumer rather than the producer was worse than ridiculous. It was offensive. Establishing the consumer as a contributing member of the political economy, however, helped to move the notion of a consumer-oriented political economy out of the realm of the perverse and toward that of the possible.

Patten's knack for turning prevailing attitudes on their head was evident when he transformed consumption from an activity associated with waste into one associated with efficiency. And it was evident when he suggested that consumers were more important than producers in helping a society to maximize its wealth. Therefore, it should have been no surprise to his contemporaries when he insisted that Sumner's frugal and abstemious producer was far more of a threat to society than were workers who demanded the comforts of life. Why? Because, according to Patten, workers who insisted on a higher standard of living were unwilling to pay as large a portion of their income in rent as were those whose "wants are small." A society made up of high-consumption workers would therefore have low rents. And, by the same token, a society consisting of low-consumption workers would have high rents, because those workers were both willing and "able to give a greater surplus as rent than the higher classes can do."[8]

High-consumption workers pushed down rents not only by refusing to devote as large a proportion of their income to rent but also by demanding a far greater variety of consumer goods than low-consumption workers. According to Patten, the problem with the "ignorant and inefficient" workers' willingness to subsist at the poverty level, consuming the bare minimum of products, was that they were unable to modify their consumption. Although it was true that they might have fewer desires than the "skilled and efficient workers," these desires were inflexible and could only be met by a limited number of specific goods. Such workers were, therefore, unable to bring their consumption into line with nature's productive capabilities. The "skilled and intelligent" workers, by contrast, had more eclectic wants. Because they could satisfy these wants with any number of different goods, high-consumption workers were able to choose goods that nature supplied abundantly and forgo goods that nature could supply only with difficulty. Thus, unlike the ignorant and inefficient workers, they were able to harness nature's productive capabilities.[9]

In a number of ways, then, Patten helped lay the groundwork for a consumerist worldview. He called into question Ricardo's assertion that poverty was inevitable. He suggested that consumption could be a positive activity and frugality a negative one. He insisted that the consumer played an important role in determining how much wealth society had at its disposal. He hinted at the feasibility of an economy of abundance. And he weakened the producer's exclusive claim to society's wealth.

It is, therefore, all the more significant that a thinker who could make such contributions to a consumerist worldview ultimately found consumption a problematic activity. That Patten did was evident in his inability to follow many of his ideas to their logical consumerist conclusions. Again and again, he proved willing to challenge the prevailing producerist orthodoxy but stopped short of advocating a consumer-oriented political economy.

Patten's deep ambivalence was evident in his tendency to adopt positions that seemed closer to those of an uncompromising producerist thinker such as William Graham Sumner than to those of thinkers who were more sympathetic to a consumerist worldview. His conviction that inappropriate consumption caused poverty was only one example. It was true that Patten and Sumner did not define *inappropriate* in the same way. As far as Sumner was concerned, all but the most necessary consumption was inappropriate. Patten, by contrast, reserved the term for the consumption of a particular class of goods, namely those that nature produced with difficulty. Nevertheless, he was as quick as Sumner to blame the consumer for the existence of poverty. Not surprisingly, Patten's depiction of consumers as responsible agents who willingly engaged in irresponsible consumption did not make the consumer an appealing candidate for the pivotal identity around which to organize the political economy.

Patten's economic theories not only cast doubt on the consumer's suitability as the organizing principle for a political economy. They also transformed consumption into a far more dangerous activity than it was for a more committed critic of consumption such as Sumner. While Sumner was as convinced as Patten that individuals were in complete control of their consumption choices, Sumner assumed that individuals who consumed unwisely consigned only themselves and perhaps their families to poverty. The drunkard paid the price for his folly. But Sumner was confident that, as long as "society" did not interfere with "nature's remedies against vice" and pick the drunkard up out of the gutter, the impact of the drunkard's unwise consumption would not extend beyond his immediate circle.[10]

Patten, by contrast, believed that those who consumed inappropriately dragged the rest of society right down with them. "A demand for whiskey or beer," he insisted, "is a demand for a class of lands already in use and on which high rent is paid." The problem with "the use of liquor, and the other means by which the food-supply is wasted, is not merely a destruction of capital, which only interests the consumers, their families and friends." The real problem was that the consumption of alcohol pushed up rent. Increasing rent meant that "all persons, even those who do not drink," paid the price for the drunkard's unwise consumption because all persons were "forced to pay that much more for their food than they would otherwise have to do."[11]

It was not only drunkards in the lower echelons of society who threatened the survival of society with their unwise consumption. In Patten's view deleterious consumption practices were also evident among the more well-to-do.

Anticipating Veblen, he maintained that "rich persons, as a class, do not desire commodities so much for the pleasure which can be derived from them as for the display of their wealth." The problem with such consumption, he warned, was that it placed a premium on products produced by nature with difficulty, thereby increasing rent. What was worse, the mode of consumption adopted by the wealthy became the model of consumer behavior for the rest of society. This meant that all classes, not just the rich, desired "articles rarer and more costly than those lower in life can afford to purchase," resulting in "a great waste of labor and material" as consumers, driven by the dictates of fashion, replaced goods long before they wore out.[12]

While Patten's focus on efficiency rather than morality would ultimately help to reduce the pejorative connotations surrounding consumption, initially it merely served to reestablish inappropriate consumption as the social threat it had once been. By the late nineteenth century political economic thinkers tended to see immorality as a personal affair rather than the more general threat to society which Puritan and republican thinkers had assumed it was. Inefficiency, by contrast, was no longer considered a failing that just penalized the individual. Instead, late-nineteenth-century economic thinkers began to identify it as something that had repercussions for all of society. By insisting that efficiency and inefficiency were the criteria by which consumption should be judged, Patten reestablished consumption as an activity that could threaten society's very survival.

Nowhere was Patten's unwillingness to follow his ideas to consumerist conclusions more evident than in his discussions concerning the producer's consumer identity. The idea of workers' organizing around their consumer identity was not a new one.[13] It had, for example, been central to all working-class ventures in consumer cooperation. And it would be a basic premise of consumerist thought. The proponents of both worldviews assumed that producers were as exploited in the marketplace as they were in the workplace and that only by organizing as consumers would producers be able to prevent any increase in their wages from being siphoned off through higher prices and shoddier goods. Organizing as consumers could mean boycotts and protests or the creation of consumer cooperatives or even intensive lobbying efforts. But for both labor and consumerist theorists it meant consumer activism.

At first glance Patten seemed to share such sentiments. Indeed, he went so far as to suggest that the consumer identity offered a better organizing principle than did the producer identity. "If the laborers ever advance far enough to investigate the causes which determine the prices of the articles which they consume," he announced, "they will see how much more powerful a lever for increasing real wages they have in combining to influence the price of food than in combining to increase money wages." Such a conviction suggested that Patten was sympathetic to the idea of a consumer-oriented political economy.[14]

Patten, however, was not calling for consumer activism when he advocated "combining to influence price" over "combining to influence money wages." Instead, he was calling for efficient consumption. Such consumption would serve the worker far better than would any agitation for higher wages, he insisted, because an increase in wages "reduces the profit of capital." The problem with reducing profit, according to Patten, was that profit created jobs. Reduce it, and workers would find themselves unemployed. Changes in consumption choices, by contrast, gave the worker more disposable income by reducing rent rather than profit.[15]

What stands out in Patten's call to working-class producers to organize around their consumer identity is his defense of profits. Neither consumerist thinkers nor working-class theorists were particularly tolerant of profits. The latter usually argued that profits came from the capitalist expropriation of the producer's labor. The former insisted that profits were derived either from overcharging consumers or from selling them shoddy or adulterated goods. Consumerist and labor theorists might not agree on whose exploitation created profits, but both insisted that profits were something to be minimized, if not eliminated.

Patten, however, rejected any solution that was rooted in consumer or working-class activism. Such activism was inappropriate because it implied a struggle against the business interests and had as its goal the redistribution of wealth. "The losses to the laboring classes occasioned by an unequal distribution of wealth," he maintained, "are very small when compared with what is lost through a disregard, on their part, of the conditions by which the food supply is increased."[16] The only way to have a real impact on the living standards of the working class was to increase the amount of wealth at society's disposal. And the only way to do that was to consume efficiently.

Patten was not alone in seeking ways to reduce the class tensions of the late nineteenth century. Numerous theorists expressed concern over the animosity between the classes, particularly since these animosities often led to violent clashes between labor and capital. The method most theorists favored for eliminating class tensions, however, involved bringing all members of society into the same class. Richard Ely, for example, had advocated measures that would make everyone an independent producer. Edward Bellamy's solution would be to bring everyone into the middle class. But, whether the goal was a working-class or a middle-class society, the result would be the same: a society without class conflict.

Patten adopted a different approach. Rather than seeking to eliminate classes and with them class struggle, he sought to make class struggle unnecessary. The more that efficient consumption increased society's wealth, the less reason there would be for capitalists and laborers to struggle over scarce resources. With plenty for everyone, the working class could improve its standard of living without bringing down the well-to-do. All classes could coexist peacefully.

Patten's solution to class struggle reveals yet again his initial unwillingness to follow his ideas to consumerist conclusions. In suggesting that efficient consumption could solve the problems caused by scarce resources, he began to hint at an economy of abundance. But, because he found it impossible to ignore the pejorative connotations surrounding consumer, he stopped well short of suggesting that abundance might be the foundation for a consumer-oriented political economy. The most he was willing to argue was that abundance could prevent workers from seeking the redistribution of wealth. But advocating an economy of abundance because it could prevent working-class challenges to capitalist profits was an ideological position far removed from a consumerist worldview.

In a number of ways, then, Patten's attitudes seemed to bear more resemblance to those of William Graham Sumner than to those of consumerist thinkers. Like Sumner, Patten rejected solutions rooted in class conflict, convinced that the key to prosperity was prosperous capitalists. Like Sumner, he blamed the lower classes for their own poverty. Like Sumner, he considered inappropriate consumption the culprit. Yet, despite such similarities, Patten was not a producerist thinker. The common ground that he and Sumner shared was not so much the idea that the economy should function on behalf of the producer as it was the conviction that consumption could be a harmful activity.

That Patten did not subscribe to a producerist worldview was evident in his disregard for traditional producerist concerns. Even producerist thinkers from opposite ends of the political spectrum such as George and Sumner tended to focus on the same sorts of topics. Both devoted most of their energy to the exploration of such producerist issues as how best to define *producer* or how best to guarantee producers the full product of their labor. They might not arrive at the same answers, but they nevertheless asked the same questions.

Patten, by contrast, showed little interest in such topics. And, because he was not bound by producerist concerns, he was able to look at the economy from a completely new perspective. Yet, although he was willing to challenge the reigning producerist paradigm, his sensitivity to the pejorative connotations surrounding consumption prevented him from advocating a consumer-oriented approach to the economy. Consumption remained for Patten a problematic activity. Not until the twentieth century would he begin to develop the consumerist logic of his early ideas. And, even then, he would leave it to others to realize the full consumerist potential of these ideas.

Ultimately, if Patten pushed social thought in a consumerist direction, it was not because of his answers so much as his questions. In the 1880s he was not prepared to argue that citizens had a fundamental right to consume. Nor was he willing to suggest that the consumer should replace the producer as the pivotal identity within the political economy. But he did challenge most of the reasons for limiting consumption. And he reexamined many of the traditional assumptions concerning the producer's claim to society's wealth. In so doing, he played a critical role in laying the groundwork for a consumer-oriented political economy.

If Patten questioned the existing producerist logic, Bellamy responded to it with a consumerist logic of his own. Much less sensitive to producerist criteria for "good" and "bad" than most late-nineteenth-century intellectuals, Bellamy was able to go beyond the measured challenges to the producerist worldview that his contemporaries mounted. Yet, even he, who found it so easy to dismiss the traditional connotations associated with *consumer* and *producer,* never quite managed to function completely outside the producerist paradigm.

Bellamy developed his version of a consumerist good society in two utopian novels, *Looking Backward* (1888) and *Equality* (1897). In both books Bellamy compared the logic behind a producer-oriented political economy with that of a consumer-oriented economy. He did so by transporting a nineteenth-century Bostonian, Julian West, to Boston in the year 2000. In numerous discussions with his twentieth-first-century host, Dr. Leete, West was forced to examine his producerist assumptions, and, even more to the point, he was forced to do so in an intellectual environment in which producerist ideas had lost their monopoly. Not surprisingly, given Bellamy's consumerist intent, West's producerist notions could not survive once they were forced to compete in a free marketplace of ideas.

Although Bellamy told a similar story in both books, he did so from two distinct perspectives. The decade separating the two books accounts for much of the difference. In *Looking Backward,* he found it necessary to spend most of his time justifying a consumer-oriented order, never an easy task in the producerist intellectual environment of the late nineteenth century. By the time he wrote *Equality,* however, the pejorative connotations surrounding consumption were weaker than they had been a decade earlier. Bellamy, therefore, no longer felt compelled to focus on defending a consumer-oriented system and could, instead, turn his energies to attacking the existing producer-oriented one.

While it was the changing attitudes toward consumption and the consumer which enabled Bellamy to take the offensive in *Equality,* Bellamy himself played a critical role in shaping these attitudes. In *Looking Backward,* a novel that enjoyed wide circulation and even launched a political reform movement, he managed to justify a version of the good society which violated most of the principles on which the producerist version of a good society rested. His version challenged the prevailing assumption that work was a noble activity that gave meaning to life while consumption was merely an unfortunate necessity. It dismissed the notion that one's right to consume was contingent upon one's role in the production process. And, finally, his version rejected the idea that rights of citizenship were rooted in the producer identity. At a number of points, then, Bellamy sought to defend what amounted to the antithesis of a producer-oriented political economy.

In the twentieth century producerist ideas would lose their monopoly on political economic thought, making it easy to reject a producer-oriented political economy, as the philosopher Horace Kallen would do, on the grounds that it forced people "to live to work instead of living to live." In Bellamy's day, however, it was not quite so easy to challenge the producerist definition of a meaningful existence. So dominant was that definition in the late nineteenth century that Charlotte Perkins Gilman could identify labor as "an exercise of faculty without which we would cease to be human." So strong were the connotations surrounding *producer* and *consumer* that Gilman could suggest that barring women from the ranks of producers and relegating them to the ranks of consumers constituted a subjugation of the worst kind. And, indeed, denying women their producer identity was a form of subjugation in a political economy that revolved around that identity.[17]

To justify his version of the good society, Bellamy had to weaken the producerist hold on political economic thought. His first task was to alter the connotations surrounding work and consumption. Depicting work as "a necessary duty," rather than the opportunity for creative expression which Gilman considered it, was a step in that direction. In Bellamy's utopia workers were not independent producers controlling their own labor. Instead, they were members of a highly regimented industrial army, required to serve a two-decade tour of duty.[18]

Once he had transformed work from creative expression into regimented service, Bellamy then found it easy to suggest that labor was not "the main business of existence." When his spokesman for the nineteenth-century producerist worldview, Julian West, expressed concern that "to be superannuated at [forty-five] and laid on the shelf must be regarded rather as a hardship than a favor by men of energetic dispositions," Dr. Leete chided West on the "rare quaintness" of his nineteenth-century notions. "The labor we have to render as our part in securing for the nation the means of a comfortable physical existence," he explained to West, "is by no means regarded as the most important, the most interesting, or the most dignified employment of our power." Work was merely something the citizens of Boston in the year 2000 had to do before they could devote themselves exclusively to "the intellectual and spiritual enjoyments and pursuits which alone mean life."[19]

It would take more than weakening the positive connotations surrounding production to challenge the producerist definitions of *good* and *bad*. Bellamy would also have to reduce the negative connotations surrounding consumption. Few nineteenth-century thinkers tapped into these connotations as effectively as William Graham Sumner. In Sumner's view consumption was the antithesis of production, destroying the fruits of labor and preventing the accumulation of capital so necessary for production. Sumner's hostility toward consumption was apparent in his assertion that the important virtues were not only those that furthered production, such as industriousness, but also those that limited consumption, such as thrift and temperance. And it was even more evident in his dismissal of the demand for comfort as nothing more than a desire for luxury.[20]

If Bellamy hoped to justify a consumer-oriented political economy, therefore, he would have to establish not only that limited consumption was no virtue but also that comfort was no vice. Much in the same way that Sumner had denigrated a desire for comfort by labeling it luxury, Bellamy tried to discredit limited consumption by equating it with parsimony. Even more to the point, he blamed such behavior on the instability of the existing economic system. "In your day," Dr. Leete told Julian West, "men were bound to lay up goods and money against coming failure. . . . This necessity made parsimony a virtue." But in Boston in the year 2000 "the nation guarantees the nurture, education, and comfortable maintenance of every citizen from the cradle to the grave." Parsimony was no longer necessary to survival, and, "having lost its utility, it has ceased to be regarded as a virtue."[21]

Having called into question the virtue of limited consumption, Bellamy had next to establish that a demand for comfort was not the same as a desire for luxury—a task to which he devoted a considerable amount of effort. Indeed, his numerous safeguards to ensure the moderate consumption of his utopia's inhabitants suggest yet again how firmly connotations of luxury still clung to consumption, even in the late nineteenth century. These safeguards included setting the yearly income at a level that discouraged conspicuous consumption and the hoarding of goods. And they included giving the state the power to control the income of any individual who could not keep his or her consumption within the limits set by the nation.

Bellamy was not satisfied with merely removing the opportunity for luxury in his consumer-oriented utopia. At some level he realized that only when consumers could be trusted to consume moderately in the face of abundance would a consumer-oriented political economy be justifiable. He, therefore, found it necessary to prove that even the desire for luxury would no longer exist in his consumer-oriented order. He did so by blaming luxury on the capitalist system. That system, he maintained, fostered luxury in two ways. First, it created extremes of income, which encouraged individuals all along the economic spectrum to acquire goods they could ill afford, merely "to make people think them richer than they were." In Bellamy's utopia, however, there would be no extremes of income because everyone would receive the same portion of the nation's wealth. But, once everyone knew exactly how rich everyone else was, the incentive to acquire goods for ostentation would disappear. And, once goods lost their ostentatious value, consumers would select goods only "for their actual use or the enjoyment of their beauty."[22] Focusing exclusively on use value, consumers would have no reason to take any more than they actually needed, and luxury would cease to exist.

Bellamy placed only part of the blame for luxury on the capitalist system's tendency to encourage conspicuous consumption. The more fundamental problem with that system, in his view, was that it was based on the profit motive. Because of the insatiable quest for profit, businessmen did whatever they could to induce "customers to buy, buy, buy, for money if they had it, for credit if they had it not, to buy what they wanted not, more than they wanted, what they could not afford. . . . The more wasteful the people were, the more articles they did not want which they could be induced to buy, the better for these sellers. To encourage prodigality was the express aim of the ten thousand stores of Boston."[23] To Bellamy it was not consumers but businessmen who were responsible for the existence of luxury.

Blaming luxury on the profit motive was one of Bellamy's most significant contributions to consumerist thought because it transformed the consumer from a villain into a victim. If luxurious behavior was not something that consumers engaged in willingly but was, instead, forced on them by businessmen in their insatiable quest for profit, then consumers were absolved of any wrongdoing. Once consumers joined the ranks of the exploited, the notion of a political economy that functioned in the consumer's interests began to have some appeal.

Attributing luxury to the profit motive not only transformed the consumer from a villain into a victim; it also helped to remove the connotations with luxury which had been associated with consumption. In the late nineteenth century *luxury* still tended to be synonymous with *excessive consumption*. The problem with such a definition was that "excessive" was a relative concept—so much so that William Graham Sumner was able to label even a desire for comfort as a pursuit of luxury. Bellamy's definition, by contrast, established a clear distinction between the desire for comfort and the pursuit of luxury. If luxury was consumption that was forced on the consumer by the business interests' drive for profit, then consumption that originated with the consumer was not luxury.

Like Patten, Bellamy had redefined inappropriate consumption from a quantitative to a qualitative concept and, in so doing, had helped to remove some of the connotations of luxury surrounding consumption. Patten's definition, however, continued to hold the consumer responsible for any inappropriate consumption. His definition might have redeemed increasing consumption, but it did nothing to reduce the risk associated with giving consumers control of the political economy. Bellamy's definition, by contrast, not only absolved the consumer. It did so in such a way as to shift the blame for luxury to the very individuals who were supposed to personify thrift and self-denial, Sumner's capitalist producers.

It was a brilliant approach. In one stroke Bellamy managed not only to call into question the ability of a producer-oriented political economy to minimize luxury but also to suggest that, far from encouraging inappropriate consumption, a consumer-oriented political economy was the only system that could eliminate not only "poverty with the fear of it" but, even more important, "inordinate luxury with the hope of it."[24]

In challenging both the positive connotations surrounding production and the negative connotations surrounding consumption, Bellamy did more to erode the foundation of a producer-oriented worldview than did any of his contemporaries. But he did not stop there. He went on to challenge even the producerist definition of citizenship. And, as he did so, he found himself confronting what would prove to be the most difficult obstacle to a consumer-oriented worldview, the close connection between one's right to consume and one's identity as a producer.

Challenging the producerist definition of citizenship went against two centuries of American political thought. According to Lockean liberal theory, government was established in large part to protect property, which Locke defined as the result of mixing one's labor with nature. A Lockean civil government was thus, in essence, little more than a contract among producers for the mutual protection of their interests. According to Smithian liberal economic theory, government's job was to guarantee an economic environment in which individuals were free to pursue their own self-interest. In theory this meant complete laissez-faire. In practice it meant that government could and did interfere in the economy to help producers by levying tariffs, enforcing contracts, and even providing direct economic aid in the form of land grants. But government refrained from regulating business on behalf of the consuming population. As for republican theory, it held that the key to a republican government's survival was civic virtue, and such virtue depended upon a citizenry consisting of independent producers. Thus, the systems of thought on which American political economic theory rested tended to root civic identity in the producer and to define the primary function of government as the advancement of the interests of its producer-citizens.

As long as the right to consume was based on one's role in the production process, the producerist definition of government's function made perfect sense. If the only way to increase one's consumption was to produce more, then the best way for government to improve the standard of living of its citizens was to help them increase their productivity. For consumerist thinkers, then, the real challenge was not to dissociate *producer* and *citizen* so much as *production* and *consumption*. Once they could establish a right to consume which did not depend upon any role in the production process, then separating *producer* and *citizen* would be easy.

Bellamy ultimately failed to separate production from consumption, revealing the extent to which even he never managed to function entirely outside of a producerist paradigm. He continued to assume that producers played at least some role in the production of goods and that those who contributed to the production of goods had a right to them. Because of these two assumptions, the only right to consume which he was able to establish was an individual's right to consume the fruits of someone else's labor. It was not a right that was easy to defend.

There was, however, some precedent for such a right. Family members, for example, had a claim to the product of other family members' labor. Ideally, this meant that able-bodied males supported their wives and children. But in difficult economic times able-bodied males might find themselves supported by the labor of their wives or children. Indeed, one of the few claims that able-bodied men had to consume without producing was based upon their identity as a family member. Their claim to the labor of other family members, however, was limited, not to be utilized except in the most extreme circumstances. Only women and children had a general right to familial support.

The other precedent for claiming a share of the nation's wealth distinct from the producer identity was the claim of the weak and the helpless to communal support. Like the familial claim, it had long existed, but it too stressed that those who could work should do so. An 1821 Massachusetts report on pauperism, for example, recognized the right of those "incapable of work, through old age, infancy, sickness or corporeal debility" to support by the community but was quick to insist that the able-bodied poor had to support themselves. The almshouses of the mid–nineteenth century were equally willing to provide shelter to the weak and the helpless and were equally intent on discouraging the able-bodied from seeking help. And in the late-nineteenth-century debates concerning outdoor relief the issue was never whether individuals incapable of self-support had a right to communal support but, instead, how to keep the able-bodied poor off the relief roles.[25]

Bellamy's task, therefore, was not so much to establish a right to consume without producing, which already existed for a number of groups, but to establish that right for able-bodied males. He was well aware that such a right violated nineteenth-century notions of equity at the most basic level. That was why he provided several different justifications for this right. And it was why he had his spokesman for the nineteenth century, Julian West, have more difficulty accepting the idea that able-bodied males should have this right than any other of the ideas West encountered in late-twentieth-century Boston. Finally, it was why Bellamy chose to expand the existing categories of nonproducing consumers to include men, rather than attempting to defend any fundamental right on the part of independent, able-bodied males to consume without producing.

The most promising of the existing nonproducing consumer categories was the familial one. Bellamy attempted to tap into it by arguing that all men were brothers in one great family. This was no rhetorical flourish on his part. If he could establish such a brotherhood, then he could extend the familial claim to the product of another's labor from family members to all members of society. Thus, when West suggested that Leete did not mean to compare a general sort of brotherhood "except for rhetorical purposes, to the brotherhood of blood, either as to its sentiment or its obligations," Leete was quick to assure his nineteenth-century guest that he meant just that. Twentieth-century Bostonians, unlike their nineteenth-century counterparts, defined the brotherhood of all men to include, first and foremost, the familial right to support.[26]

While the familial right to support represented the stronger claim to consume distinct from the producer identity, Bellamy also attempted to tap into the dependent claim to communal support. He did so by suggesting that in an advanced economy all men were mutually dependent upon one another. "There is no such thing in a civilized society as self-support," Leete told West. "As men grow more civilized, and the subdivision of occupations and services is carried out, a complex mutual dependence becomes the universal rule." Once Bellamy established able-bodied males as members of the dependent class, he could then claim for them the right to consume without producing on the basis that "the necessity of mutual dependence should imply the duty and guarantee of mutual support."[27]

The one major drawback with using dependency to establish a right to consume distinct from one's identity as a producer was that, unlike familial support, public support carried with it connotations of charity. A man's wife and children had a right to a portion of his labor. His support of them could not be defined as an act of charity. The same, however, could not be said of his support of the local widow and her offspring. Neither she nor her children had any right to his labor. The most that could be said was that he had a moral obligation to contribute to their support, but that did not change the fact that his contributions were charity.

In order to establish a right to consume without producing by drawing on the precedent of public support of dependents, Bellamy had to transform such support from a form of charity into a right. One way to do this was to make public support a right of citizenship. When West suggested that giving "the lame, the blind, the sick and the impotent . . . the same income" as those who worked was "charity on such a scale [that] would have made our most enthusiastic philanthropists gasp," Dr. Leete was quick to correct him. Just as in the nineteenth century all citizens had a right to be protected even if they were incapable of serving in the military, in the late twentieth century citizens had a right to consume a share of the nation's wealth regardless of their ability to serve in the industrial army. To deny citizens that right because they were incapable of working was to deprive them of their citizenship in the same way that denying protection to anyone unable to perform military service was to deprive them of theirs.[28]

What is significant about Bellamy's attempt to establish public support as a civic right is that it was an implicit rejection of the producerist definition of *citizen*. According to that definition, producers were the only members of society entitled to full civic rights. Bellamy, however, had outlined a civic identity that was not rooted in one's identity as a producer. As Dr. Leete told Julian West, "the worker is not a citizen because he works, but works because he is a citizen."[29]

Perhaps even more significantly, however, Bellamy's attempts to remove the connotations of charity called into question the producer's exclusive claim to the products of his labor. When West found it difficult to understand how "they who produced nothing [could] claim a share of the product as a right," Leete asked him "how happened it . . . that your workers were able to produce more than so many savages would have done?" Was it not because West and his contemporaries had inherited "the past knowledge and achievements of the race, the machinery of society. . . . which represent nine parts to one contributed by yourself in the value of your product?" For Leete producers and those incapable of producing were "joint inheritors" and "co-heirs" to the knowledge necessary to create society's wealth. As such, both were entitled to a share of that wealth. By taking exclusive title, producers had robbed their "unfortunate and crippled brothers" of their share and then added "insult to robbery when [they] called the crusts charity?"[30]

Bellamy's argument that the creation of wealth depended as much upon inherited knowledge as it did upon individual labor held the key to removing a major obstacle to a consumer-oriented system. That obstacle was the inequity inherent in granting the nonproducing consumer a right to the products of another's labor. As William Graham Sumner pointed out, if "a man has a natural right to whatever he needs," then the obvious question was: "who is bound to satisfy it for him?" For Sumner "it must be the one who possesses what will satisfy that need." "The consequence would be that the industrious and prudent would labor and save . . . to support the idle and improvident."[31]

There was, however, a way to counter such arguments. If producers were not exclusively responsible for the creation of wealth, then they were not entitled to any exclusive claim to that wealth. Bellamy's assertion that all production depended upon the inheritance of past knowledge offered a way to challenge the producer's exclusive claim. If one accepted that assertion, then granting consumers the right to a share of society's wealth did not violate any producerist notion of equity. On the contrary, the real inequity lay in giving producers an exclusive claim to goods that had been created with intellectual capital that belonged as much to consumers as to producers.

In *Looking Backward* Bellamy was not prepared to follow the logic of his argument to its logical conclusion. Although he did question the producer's exclusive right to goods, he was not yet prepared to use these arguments to establish a general right to society's wealth. Instead, he preferred to rely on the rights and customs associated with nonproducing dependency, extending them to all of society. Such an approach, however, failed to address the inequity of granting consumers a right to the products of another's labor and thus proved to be less than successful.

That Bellamy's initial attempts to sever the links between production and consumption were not particularly successful does not diminish their significance. Bellamy was one of the first thinkers to realize the extent to which a producerist worldview rested upon these links. And he was one of the first to understand that the key to justifying a consumer-oriented economy lay in severing them. Eventually, other thinkers would discover more effective ways to divorce consumption from production. But it was Bellamy who demonstrated how critical such a separation was for the development of a consumer-oriented political economy.

Although Bellamy realized that the best way to justify a consumer-oriented political economy was to replace a producerist system of logic with a consumerist one, his initial challenges to a producerist paradigm—and Patten's too, for that matter—occurred from well within that paradigm. Bellamy called into question an exclusively producerist approach to wealth distribution by suggesting that consuming citizens were the owners of intellectual capital. As such, they should have the same rights to a share of the nation's wealth as any other owner of capital. As for Patten, when he set out to discredit the exclusive focus in economic thought on the producer and production, he did so by suggesting that consumers played a central role in determining the amount of wealth in a society. In short, both thinkers attempted to legitimate the consumer by demonstrating the degree to which consumers resembled producers.

If Bellamy had only written *Looking Backward,* he would still have been one of the primary architects of a consumerist worldview. He went on, however, to write *Equality,* a book that was perhaps even more significant in the development of this view. John Dewey certainly thought so. "What *Uncle Tom's Cabin* was to the anti-slavery movement," he wrote, "Bellamy's book may well be to the shaping of popular opinion for a new social order."[32] It was no surprise that Dewey preferred *Equality* to *Looking Backward.* Although both books touched on the same topics, they did not give them equal emphasis. *Looking Backward* focused on the individual's political and economic rights. *Equality,* by contrast, concentrated on the larger political and economic processes, examining in considerable detail such topics as the shortcomings of profit-oriented capitalism, the ways in which it exploited consumers, and the impossibility of introducing abundance under such a system, all topics that Dewey explored in his own writings.

Bellamy's rejection of profit-oriented capitalism as a system antithetical to the interests of the consuming population may not have surprised Dewey. But it would have puzzled Adam Smith. Smith had advocated a laissez-faire approach to the economy precisely because he believed that profit-oriented capitalism would automatically function in the best interests of the consuming population. Consumers, he had reasoned, would patronize businesses that best met their needs, bringing prosperity to those that could supply high-quality, low-priced goods and financial ruin to those that could not. In a Smithian world, with business' well-being dependent upon meeting the needs of the consuming population, consumers and capitalist producers existed in perfect symbiosis. As for government, the best service it could render to the public would be to assist capitalist producers in pursuing their own self-interests. Indeed, according to Smithian logic, the most effective way to guarantee that the political economy would revolve around the consumer was to construct a political economy that revolved around the capitalist producer.

Bellamy found this logic seriously flawed. He saw no reason to believe that allowing capitalists to pursue their self-interest would further the well-being of the consuming population. On the contrary, he insisted, the capitalists' "only object was to secure the greatest possible gain for themselves without any regard whatever to the welfare of the public."[33] And more frequently than not, Bellamy warned, they secured this gain by exploiting the consuming population rather than by serving it.

Smith had been well aware that capitalists, if confronted with a choice, would pursue their own interests at the expense of the consuming public. He had been confident, however, that such a choice would rarely, if ever, occur. The key was competition. In a competitive market any business that violated the consuming public's interest would lose its customers to its competitors. Competition guaranteed that businesses would take great care not to violate the consuming public's interest, because any violation of that interest would inevitably be a violation of their own as well.

Bellamy, however, had much less faith in the ability of competition to maintain an equitable system. For him competition, far from being "a palliative of the profit system. . . . was a grievous aggravation of it." He granted that in a competitive market capitalists might find it in their best interest to keep prices low. But he was quick to point out that, according to the same logic of self-interest, "the capitalist would prefer to reduce the prices of his goods in such a way, if possible, as not to reduce his profits." This meant that "most of the reductions of price effected by competition were reductions at the expense of the original producers or of the final consumers, and not reductions in profits." According to Bellamy, capitalists adulterated goods, cut wages, and introduced labor saving machinery, all in an attempt to lower prices without affecting profits.[34]

How could Smith and Bellamy hold such diametrically opposed views concerning the operation of profit-oriented capitalism? One explanation can be found in the economic changes that occurred in the century between the appearance of Smith's book and Bellamy's works. Because the market had been more local and business enterprises had been smaller in the late eighteenth century than in the late nineteenth, consumers had been better able to judge the quality of their purchases and to hold the seller accountable for them. By the late nineteenth century, however, the increasing reliance on processed and ready-made goods and the growth of the advertising industry made it difficult for consumers to make informed decisions about the safety, quality, or even price of the products they purchased. At the same time, industry's ability to limit competition through the creation of giant corporations, not to mention pools and trusts, the increasingly impersonal nature of market relationships as national manufacturing and distribution systems replaced local ones, and the growing complexity of the market all meant that that market was much less responsive to consumer dissatisfaction than it had been in the days of Adam Smith. Given such changes, it was not surprising that Bellamy had much less faith in the ability of the consumer to police industrialists and regulate the marketplace than Adam Smith had had.

Equally important in accounting for the difference between Smith and Bellamy was the increasingly rigid application of Smith's laissez-faire doctrines at the very time when changes in the economy were undercutting the consumer's influence. Smith had advocated a laissez-faire approach to the economy because he believed that giving capitalist producers a free rein would guarantee economic progress and with it a healthy and prosperous population. He had not championed the producer's interests at the expense of the consuming population. Indeed, it had been mercantilism's tendency to do just that which had been, in his view, one of its most serious weaknesses.[35] When Smith sought to further the producer's interests, he had done so because he believed that it offered the best way to further the interests of the consuming population. In short, his producer-oriented economy *was* a consumer-oriented economy.

By the late nineteenth century, however, it was not so clear that advancing the producer's interests was an effective way to secure the welfare of the consuming population. In light of the economic changes of the previous century, this welfare depended, at the very least, on reestablishing the consumer's influence in the marketplace. A more sweeping alternative would have been to abandon a producer-oriented political system altogether in favor of one that functioned directly on behalf of the consuming population. Late-nineteenth-century public policy makers, however, continued to champion the interests of capitalist producers, ignoring the fact that these interests frequently ran counter to those of the consuming population. The producer-oriented policies that Smith had championed as a means to an end had, by the late nineteenth century, become the very end that he had decried in mercantilism.

While Bellamy's socialist leanings made it easy for him to reject a Smithian capitalist order, his consumerist leanings made him reluctant to replace it with a Marxist one. Marx and Smith might not have envisioned the same good society. But both believed that such a society should revolve around the producer, however that identity might be defined. And both assumed that the good society would function according to producerist notions of equity and justice. Bellamy, by contrast, wanted to place the consumer at the center of his economic order. He therefore attempted to construct consumerist alternatives to the prevailing producerist principles on which the vast majority of economists, including Marx and Smith, relied.

His redefinition of *profit* was a case in point. As a late-nineteenth-century critic of capitalism, Bellamy could have easily adopted a Marxist definition, one that defined *profit* as that portion of the worker's labor which the capitalist expropriated. As a consumerist thinker, however, he was unwilling to rely on a definition that treated profit as something that came exclusively from the exploitation of workers. Capitalists, he insisted, could just as easily make their profit by overcharging consumers as they could by underpaying workers. When they "turn[ed] out goods expressly made with a view to wearing as short a time as possible, so as to need the speedier renewal," forcing consumers to make repeated purchases of a product they should only have needed to purchase once, capitalists engaged in a form of exploitation that had nothing to do with the worker. The same could be said for advertising expenses that were "added to the price of the goods and paid by the consumer, who therefore could buy just so much less than if he had been left in peace and the price of the goods had been reduced by the saving in advertising."[36] Passing on the costs of advertising to the consumer was a form of exploitation that had nothing to do with denying the worker the fruits of his labor.

What was striking about Bellamy's critique of capitalism was how rooted in the producerist paradigm it was. Even staunch defenders of capitalism such as David Ricardo had acknowledged that competition and capitalist self-interest did not operate to the benefit of workers. Bellamy merely suggested that these market forces were of no benefit to consumers either. Similarly, critics of capitalism had long argued that profit included what Henry George had called an "unearned increment." Bellamy merely pointed out that this unearned increment could come from consumers as well as producers. Much as he had done nine years earlier, Bellamy preferred to tap the consumerist potential of existing categories rather than create new ones. And, in so doing, he challenged the producerist paradigm on its own terms.

The same could not be said of the handful of economists who launched what would come to be known as the "marginalist revolution." As early as the 1870s, economists such as Stanley Jevons in England, Léon Walras in France, and Karl Menger in Austria had begun suggesting that consumption rather than production was the driving force of the economy. They were able to arrive at this conclusion because they rejected the classical economic definition of *value*. In their view the most meaningful way to measure value was not in terms of labor or production costs but, rather, in terms of the amount of satisfaction which a product gave to the consumer.[37]

It was this redefinition of *value* which constituted not merely a rebellious but a revolutionary act. Once the marginalists identified the consumer as the individual responsible for value, they found it necessary to shift the focus in economics from cost to utility, from supply to demand, and from production to consumption. And, in so doing, they forced economists to rethink many of the basic assumptions of a producerist worldview. What had once seemed self-evident principles were suddenly no longer so.

The widespread acceptance of marginalist ideas by American economists occurred in the 1890s, when economic conditions in the United States seemed to demand a shift in economic thinking. As American economists witnessed both a stagnation in the producer goods sector of the economy and a boom in the consumer goods sector in the 1880s, they began to suspect that consumption rather than production was driving the economy. And, as they lived through the Depression of the 1890s, they began to worry that the problem to be solved was not an economy that produced too little but one that produced too much. For a couple of reasons, then, marginalist theory seemed far more relevant to existing conditions in the late nineteenth century than did the classical economic theories on which economists had long relied.[38]

Marginalist ideas had both conservative and radical implications. On the one hand, they provided supporters of capitalism with a rebuttal to the socialist critique of capitalism. If consumers rather than producers were responsible for value, then the argument that workers were entitled to the entire product of their labor was not particularly meaningful. By replacing the labor theory of value with a utility theory of value, marginalist theories called into question the primary justification for a worker state.

Marginalist theories also provided supporters of capitalism with a justification for what socialists labeled the "inequitable distribution of wealth." According to the American marginalist economist John Bates Clark, the utility theory of value applied not only to consumer products but also to such "commodities" as the physical labor of the working class and the mental labor of capitalists. Just as the price that consumer goods could command was determined by the utility of these goods, so too was the price that both physical and mental labor could command. Applying the marginalist theory of utility to the productive realm, Clark insisted that "the distribution of the income of society is controlled by a natural law, and that this law, if it worked without friction, would give to every agent of production the amount of wealth which that agent creates." In Clark's view capitalists received so much not because they expropriated the labor of the working class but because their contribution to the production process was worth so much.[39]

Marginalist theories may have provided powerful arguments in support of capitalism. But they also had more subversive implications. Not only did those theories shift the focus from production to consumption, a shift that could benefit capitalists at the expense of the working class. They also moved the focus from the producer to the consumer. Implicit in this shift was a consumerist challenge to the profit system and capitalist control of the economy.

At the most mundane level marginalism helped to provide a new vocabulary with which to discuss consumption. As economic discussions about consumption came to revolve around highly mathematical and complex marginalist models, the moralistic rhetoric on which these discussions had long relied ceased to be appropriate. Beginning in the 1890s, American economists quickly abandoned that language in favor of the more neutral and objective language of science. And, in so doing, they eliminated some of the pejorative connotations that had long been associated with consumption and the consumer.[40]

Marginalist ideas made not only the moralistic language of consumption obsolete but also the producerist definitions of *consumer* and *producer*. If consumers were responsible for the value of goods, as the marginalists argued, then it became difficult to define them as parasites. But it was also not possible to move them to the producer category. Indeed, neither of the categories made much sense. With a marginalist definition of *value*, the producerist division of society into producer and parasite began to break down.

So, too, did a producerist definition of *exploitation*. According to this definition, individuals were exploited when they were denied the fruits of their labor. If one accepted a marginalist theory of value, however, then it became possible to identify a form of exploitation which had nothing to do with the producer. When manufacturers produced few goods and sold them at high prices, for example, they did not exploit producers so long as they paid high wages. But they did exploit consumers. By creating an artificial scarcity, they increased the value—now defined in terms of utility to the consumer—of their products. As for manufacturers who adulterated goods, they too were guilty of exploiting consumers, in this case by tricking consumers into paying a price for their goods which far exceeded their actual utility.

Ultimately, what was striking about marginalist ideas was that they could push thinkers in a variety of directions. By portraying the capitalist economy as a finely tuned instrument dedicated to providing consumers with exactly what they wanted, marginalists helped to recapture the consumerist implications that had originally been inherent in a liberal economy. Like Adam Smith, the marginalists made consumers the regulator of the economy and consumption the purpose of production. But, implicit in these ideas was also a critique of capitalism. If consumers created value and if consumers were exploited by capitalists, then, at the very least, capitalism ought to be regulated so that it functioned on behalf of the consuming public. And it might even be necessary to replace a capitalist order with a socialized economy that truly functioned on behalf of the consuming masses.

The extent to which marginalism forced American economists to rethink their assumptions about the consumer is evident when one compares Richard T. Ely's popular economic textbook, *An Introduction to Political Economy*, published in 1889, with his major revision of this text, renamed *Outlines of Economics* and published four years later. Even the most cursory examination of his 1893 volume reveals an influence of marginalism which had been absent from his earlier work. In his 1889 volume he only briefly mentioned value and then only in an attempt to show how contested a concept it was.

In 1893, by contrast, he provided his readers with an extended discussion of utility and value along marginalist lines. He informed them that value was not "something inherent in the good itself, but something attributed to it by human desire."[41] And he referred them to numerous marginalist works—something he had not done in the earlier version of his text—identifying a marginalist work, Eugen v. Böhm-Bawerk's *Positive Theory of Capital,* as the "best existing statement of the theory of value."[42]

Marginalist ideas forced Ely to rethink not only his ideas about value but also his attitudes toward the consumer and consumption. His treatment of consumption in 1889 relied on the approach developed by the classical economists. A standard part of the classical treatment of consumption was the classification of consumption as either productive or unproductive. Adam Smith had hinted at such a division, but it was Jean-Baptiste Say who developed explicit definitions for each. *Productive consumption,* the French economist had insisted, was the consumption of goods for the purpose of production, and *unproductive consumption* was consumption that merely satisfied a want. At midcentury John Stuart Mill revised Say's definitions but only in such a way as to reinforce the producerist criteria on which Say had depended. Say had labeled all consumption intended to satisfy wants, including the wants of the laborer, as unproductive. Mill, by contrast, was willing to recognize the laborer's consumption as productive consumption so long as it was not the "consumption on [sic] pleasures or luxuries" which "must be reckoned Unproductive," "since production is neither its object nor is in any way advanced by it."[43]

In 1889 Ely relied on Mill's definitions. Productive consumption, he told his readers, was the "consumption of a useful member of society." Unproductive consumption was "the use of mere luxuries even by a useful member of society . . . and every consumption of whatever sort by a useless member of society. Such a person," he concluded, "is a mere cumberer of the ground. His consumption is mere waste, and he does not deserve to live."[44]

Four years later, however, the marginalist challenge to classical economic thought forced Ely to rethink his categories. He began by jettisoning unproductive consumption and, in so doing, removed from *consumption* what was perhaps the most pejorative of adjectives in the producerist lexicon. He then redefined *productive consumption* far more narrowly than he once had. No longer did he use it to refer to individual consumption. Instead, he reserved the term for the consumption of goods used in the production process, such as machines and raw materials.

What is significant about Ely's redefinitions is that they constituted a rejection of the producerist measures of good and bad on which nineteenth-century classical economists had so long relied. That Ely was able to reject these measures highlights the influence of marginalist ideas on his thinking. Following the marginalists' lead, Ely ceased to evaluate consumption in terms of its impact on production, preferring instead to approach it as an activity in its own right. Not surprisingly, once he quit filtering his analysis of consumption through a producerist lens, consumption all but ceased to be the immoral activity it had once been. It was, however, the marginalist influence that enabled Ely to discard this lens in the first place.[45]

That Ely had abandoned much of the moralism of classical economics by 1893 was evident not only in his redefinition of productive and unproductive consumption but also in numerous other modifications to his 1889 text. In it he had discussed questionable consumption under headings such as "Avarice and Prodigality," "Wasteful Consumption," "Luxury," and "Desirable and Undesirable Wants." He had defined luxuries as those "things which minister to such undesirable wants as love of display, vanity, or selfish desire to exalt one's self above one's fellows." He had regretted that "manifestly we are not even making an effort to love our neighbors as ourselves when we indulge in luxuries so long as they want the necessaries, comforts, or even conveniences of life." In the section entitled "Luxury" he had warned that "among the most pernicious things which satisfy undesirable wants may be mentioned tobacco, opium, intoxicating beverages." But, he had maintained, "there are other objects of foolish and harmful consumption." "How often," he asked, "is the usefulness of women destroyed or lessened by extravagant display of jewelry and precious stones which minister only to vanity and envy!"[46]

In his 1893 text Ely softened many of the moralistic overtones. Gone was his denunciation of women and extravagant display. Gone, too, were the moralistic headings under which he had discussed questionable consumption. Now this discussion took place under two headings, "Luxury" and "Harmful Consumption." And *luxury* had been redefined simply as "excessive consumption." Even more striking was Ely's assertion that "a luxury may be a positive good in itself, a satisfaction which society may well hope to make general, but it is a good which society cannot yet afford because other and greater wants are yet unsatisfied"—a major departure from his denunciation of luxury in the earlier work. Finally, in 1893 he moved his discussion of liquor and other intoxicants from a section dealing with luxury to one entitled "Harmful Consumption." He assured his readers that he had "no intention of assuming the function of the physiologist or the moralist in enumerating the evils which come from the consumption of certain goods." And he explicitly rejected his earlier position that "luxury consists in the use of pernicious goods." "It would be a violation of all language to call the use of intoxicating liquors a luxury in general," he told his readers, "but it is certainly on the whole harmful."[47]

One of the more striking differences between the two works was Ely's recognition in 1893 of a right to consume distinct from one's identity as a producer. "The many who have wants," he insisted, "must have those wants satisfied, and that satisfaction means the right of consumption, a right proportioned to those wants." This was quite a change for a thinker who less than a decade earlier had dismissed luxury as a violation of Christian principles. Although he still found luxury problematic in 1893, he now did so because it violated the consummatory rights of all other members of society.[48]

Ironically, Ely's recognition of a consummatory right had what might seem, at first glance, producerist roots. It was Ely's socialism that had given him an appreciation for "distributive justice." And he praised an approach to the economy in which "production would be carried on for the satisfaction of wants." But the producerist roots were more apparent than real. He explicitly rejected Marxist socialism—which he labeled "a pseudo-scientific presentation . . . full of revolting crudities"—in large part because it was a working-class, and thus producerist, ideology. "It is not by any means necessary to make socialism a purely working-class movement," he insisted in 1894. "The question of socialism is one which concerns all classes of society." He advocated what he called "all-classes socialism" because it did not suffer from "the narrowness as well as the bitterness which accompanies [socialism] if it becomes a working-class movement."[49]

While Ely's concern with class conflict was a long-standing one, his approach to it had changed significantly since the publication of *The Labor Movement in America*. There he had suggested that the way to eliminate class conflict was to bring all members of society into the ranks of independent producers. By the 1890s, however, he took the first tentative steps toward an alternative approach. Because class relationships were based on producer identities, shifting the focus from producer to consumer offered one way to minimize the class struggle implications of a socialist order. And, perhaps even more important, it did so in a way that reinforced the socialist emphasis on distributive justice.

It is worth noting that Ely—and Bellamy, for that matter—could shift the focus from the producer to the consumer without compromising his socialism, something that twentieth-century thinkers would find far more difficult to do. The reason lay in the changing nature of socialism. In the nineteenth century numerous versions of socialism vied for ascendancy, including Ely's Christian socialism and Bellamy's nationalism. In the early twentieth century, however, the forms of socialism that Marx had labeled "utopian" yielded once and for all to Marxism. The ascendancy of Marxism meant the ascendancy of a quintessentially producerist form of socialism and the purging from socialist theory of the consumer-oriented potential that had characterized much nineteenth-century utopian socialism. Thus, although a number of twentieth-century American intellectuals would embrace socialism on their way to a consumer-oriented worldview, unlike their nineteenth-century counterparts, most would find it all but impossible to reconcile the two.

Ely's increasingly tolerant treatment of both consumption and the consumer suggests the extent to which American social thinkers had already begun to rethink consumption even before the turn of the century. But Ely also played a role in that process. Over the next half-century his best-selling textbook, *Outlines in Economics,* would introduce countless college students to basic economic theory. By including in that introduction a sympathetic treatment of consumption, Ely helped to create an intellectual atmosphere in which it was possible to approach consumerist ideas without the same misgivings that had characterized the thinking of many late-nineteenth-century thinkers, including Ely himself.

The late nineteenth century witnessed a number of assaults on the producerist paradigm. While these assaults helped to weaken the producerist edifice, their initial impact was primarily on the connotations surrounding *consumer* and *producer.* Patten's theories concerning the role of consumption in determining wealth, Bellamy's arguments on behalf of consummatory civic rights, the marginalists' redefinition of *value*—all helped to construct a version of the consumer with far more legitimacy than those that had dominated political and economic thought throughout most of the nineteenth century.

The acceptance of that more legitimate consumer was quite rapid. The extent to which Bellamy found it necessary to justify consumption in 1888 and the moralistic treatment Ely gave to consumption in 1889 suggest that the traditional definition remained the dominant one throughout the 1880s. Yet the enthusiastic reception of *Looking Backward,* the far more positive treatment that Ely gave consumption in 1893, and the extent to which Bellamy assumed a legitimate consumer in 1898 suggest that this definition was no longer uncontested.

Why did such a shift occur so suddenly? At one level the answer is that it did not. It was merely the culmination of a rethinking of *consumption* and *consumer* which had been going on for decades as observers had attempted to reconcile traditional ideas about the economy with the new economic conditions brought on by industrialization and the emergence of a mass market. But at another level the timing of the shift was no accident. In 1893 Americans found themselves in the midst of a major depression. With one out of every five workers unemployed, much of the population found it difficult to raise enough funds to purchase food, clothing, and shelter, never mind luxuries. In the midst of such widespread misery the negative connotations surrounding consumers and consumption made far less sense than they once had.

While the Depression of the 1890s might have prompted a number of Americans to rethink the traditional definition of consumer, it did not prompt many to rethink the basic producerist principles that they used to order their political and economic worlds. Those who joined Jacob Coxey in 1894 and descended on Washington, D.C., seeking relief did not call for the recognition of any consummatory rights. They demanded a job. And those who joined William Jennings Bryan in 1896 and called for the coinage of silver did so because they believed an expanded currency would translate into increased opportunities for individual producers. Intellectuals might have already begun to question the connection between the right to consume and one's identity as a producer, but for most of the American public this connection remained intact into the twentieth century.

CHAPTER THREE

At the Crossroads, 1899–1912

In the Progressive Era ideas about the consumer and the producer reached a crossroads. While the largely negative version of the consumer that had long dominated political economic discourse ceased to do so, a predominantly positive version of the consumer could not yet claim to be the preferred version. And, while the producerist paradigm that had long been used to organize political and economic thought had come under siege, it did not seem to be in any danger of disappearing. The result was an intellectual environment awash in possible ways of thinking about the consumer and the producer.

Some thinkers, such as Thorstein Veblen and Florence Kelley, thrived in such a fertile intellectual environment, developing highly innovative strategies to reconcile the irreconcilable. Others, however, found it exceedingly difficult to balance traditional misgivings and profoundly new ways of thinking about the consumer and consumption, few more so than Simon Patten. Even as he bade a not-so-fond farewell to the "age of deficit," with its "disease, oppression, irregular work, premature old age, and race hatreds," and welcomed the "age of surplus," characterized by "plenty of food, shelter, capital, [and] security," Patten remained highly ambivalent about consumption. "Goods," he told his readers in *The Theory of Prosperity* (1902), "do not create happiness." Indeed, in excess they could threaten one's very survival. "Dissipation and over-indulgence," he warned, "are as potent in cutting off the more

productive class as under-nutrition is effective in cutting off the less efficient."[1] The goal, he concluded, was moderate consumption.

But how was one to practice such consumption in the phenomenally productive economy of plenty which Patten described? Patten suggested that the
solution lay in vicarious consumption. "If a man gets pleasure in the welfare
of others and seeks in this direction an outlet for his surplus energy, he avoids
both over-nutrition and under-nutrition." Indeed, in Patten's view the highly
productive individual was literally "saved by his greater altruism" because it
alone enabled him to escape the dangers of overconsumption which continually threatened the survival of those living in an economy of plenty. Not
increased consumption, he concluded, but altruism was the proper "complement to increased productivity."[2]

Thorstein Veblen also had misgivings. His, however, were not about the
consumer or consumption so much as the emerging economic system.
Whereas Patten saw a shift from deficit to plenty, the transition that Veblen
observed was from an "old régime of handicraft and petty trade," with its emphasis on "workmanship," to a "new régime" dominated by "business principles" and "pecuniary motives." While Patten celebrated the end of a "world
where a man's death was his neighbor's gain," Veblen regretted the departure
of an economic order whose guiding principle was "honesty was the best policy" and the arrival of one whose maxim of choice was "charging what the
traffic will bear." And, whereas Patten assumed that the goal of the new civilization was to "utilize the surplus for common good . . . [and] to distribute
the surplus in ways that will promote general welfare," Veblen insisted that
in a system in which "the production of goods and services is carried on for
gain and the output of goods is controlled by business men with a view to
gain. . . . the vital point . . . is the vendibility of the output . . . not its serviceability for the needs of mankind."[3]

It was this distinction between vendibility and serviceability, Veblen insisted in *The Theory of Business Enterprise* (1904), which explained why the
economy could not possibly function in the way that Patten—and, even more
to the point, the classical economists—suggested it would. Underlying both
Patten's economic theories and those of the classical economists was the
assumption that businessmen were interested in the efficient and abundant
production of goods. Veblen disagreed. Businessmen, he pointed out, were
interested in pecuniary gain, not production. And they did not necessarily

maximize that gain through the "unbroken maintenance of the industrial balance" on which the efficient and abundant production of goods depended. Indeed, more often than not, pecuniary gain came "from a given disturbance of the system."[4]

Veblen's was a novel approach. Critics of profit-oriented capitalism had long suggested that it was a harsh and brutal system. And many had argued that it did not work. But even the most ardent critics had assumed that the capitalists knew what they were doing. Not so Veblen. In his portrait capitalists were not savvy exploiters manipulating a system for their own benefit but, rather, benighted warriors blundering through a highly sensitive and technologically sophisticated landscape. In a world that required Connecticut Yankees, they were Arthurian knights.

Like Mark Twain's knights, Veblen's businessmen engaged in battle. And, like those knights, his businessmen were oblivious to the impact of their activities on the community at large. Transactions that "aim to bring a coalition of industrial plants or processes under the control of a given business man" were only one example. According to Veblen, the businessman who wanted to increase his control entered into a struggle against his rivals. "And more often than not the outcome of the struggle depends on which side can inflict or endure the greater pecuniary damage." As might be expected, "pecuniary damage in such a case not uncommonly involves a set-back to the industrial plants concerned and a derangement, more or less extensive, of the industrial system at large." The businessman, however, was unconcerned. That his activities might "act temporarily to lower the aggregate serviceability of the comprehensive industrial process" was as irrelevant to him as the incidental damage and hardship that chivalric duels caused the community would have been to one of Twain's medieval warriors.[5]

This disjuncture between the interests of the business community and those of the community at large were, Veblen suggested, even more apparent in the case of industrial depression. From the perspective of the community at large "a period of depression is a period of underproduction; mills run on half time or none, and the supply of goods that finds its way into the hands of consumers is sensibly scant for the demands of comfort." But from the perspective of the business community the problem was not so much under- as overproduction. "The difficulty is that not enough of a product can be disposed of at fair prices to warrant the running of the mills at their full capacity." As far as businessmen were concerned, "there is too large a productive capacity; there are too many competitive producers and too much industrial apparatus to supply the market at reasonable prices."[6]

The issue, according to Veblen, was not whether one version of reality was more valid than the other. Indeed, validity was ultimately irrelevant, since the business community's control of the industrial system meant that its version would determine industrial policy, valid or not. The real question, as Veblen saw it, was: why did the business community perceive reality in the way that it did? Once again, he suggested, the answer could be found in the fundamental difference between a system organized around vendibility and one organized around serviceability and efficiency. A depression might be a period of underproduction when looking at the economy from the perspective of serviceability and efficiency. But, from the perspective of vendibility, overproduction was the only meaningful way to characterize depression. During a depression there was, indeed, "an excess of goods . . . above what is expedient on pecuniary grounds."[7]

Although Veblen was primarily interested in "the habits of thought which give cogency and effect to the dogma of 'overproduction,'" he did suggest that those habits of thought had some basis in economic facts. The key factor in understanding depressions, according to Veblen, was that the "machine processes, ever increasing in efficiency, turn out the mechanical appliances and materials with which the processes are carried on, at an ever decreasing cost." That meant that those who used those "mechanical appliances and materials" to manufacture goods could produce goods with decreasing costs and increasing efficiency. But it also meant that the later entrants into a field of enterprise had a distinct advantage. Because they could acquire more efficient machines at lower prices than had been available to their predecessors, these later entrants were able to produce more goods at a much lower cost. The downward pressure on prices which resulted from the increasing efficiency of production methods meant that, if the early entrants wanted to remain competitive, they, too, would have to reduce the price of their goods. But, because their machines were both less efficient and more expensive, they found that at the new prices their "older establishments and processes will no longer yield returns commensurate with the old accepted capitalization."[8]

Here, according to Veblen, was the fatal flaw of profit-oriented capitalism. Because "the efficiency of the machine process in the 'instrumental industries' sets up a discrepancy between cost and capitalization. . . . the earning-capacity of any industrial enterprise enters on a decline from the outset, and . . . its capitalization, based on its initial putative earning-capacity, grows progressively antiquated from the start."[9] In other words, it was efficiency and technological progress that threatened to destroy capitalism.

Businessmen could, however, "offset the disastrous cheapening of products through mechanical improvements" and thereby save their economic system. One way was to increase "the unproductive consumption of goods. . . . If the waste is sufficiently large, the current investment in additional industrial equipment will not be sufficient to lower prices appreciably through competition." Unfortunately for the capitalists, however, "wasteful expenditure on a scale adequate to offset the surplus productivity of modern industry is nearly out of the question." "So long as industry remains at its present level of efficiency," Veblen warned, even the most extraordinarily wasteful consumption "is apparently altogether inadequate to offset the surplus productivity of the machine industry."[10]

If wasteful consumption could not offset the "disastrous" effects of efficiency, business had an alternative. It could eliminate "'cutthroat' competition" "by curtailing and regulating the output of goods." The formation of trusts might rescue capitalism because trusts could "adjust the output of goods and services" in such a way as to maintain the price levels necessary to prevent the "received capitalization" from becoming "obsolete even in the face of very radical improvements in the processes of industry."[11]

Limitation and cessation of production were, Veblen admitted, extreme examples of the extent to which the interests of the business community and those of the community at large did not coincide. But, he insisted, even in the "ordinary routine of business," vendibility and serviceability were at odds. Even when "gains come from [the] output of goods and services. . . . it does not follow that the highest serviceability gives the largest gains to the business man." Advertising was a case in point. While it might not interfere with production, it also "does not add to the serviceability of the output. . . . What it aims at is the sale of the output." Nevertheless, "in the modern system, where the process of production is under the control of business men and is carried on for business ends," it was, according to Veblen, "an unavoidable item in the aggregate costs of industry." Why? Because "it gives vendibility, which is useful to the seller, but has no utility to the last buyer. And, even worse, it was the buyer who bore the costs of advertising, which, according to Veblen, were significant. Along with the other costs of competitive selling, he estimated, it "may amount to more than ninety per cent. of the total cost of the goods when they reach the consumer."[12]

Veblen's examination in *The Theory of Business Enterprise* of the ways in which "business methods and business principles . . . influence the modern cultural situation" represented a shift in focus from his earlier work on the consummatory habits of the elite. Nevertheless, his heroes and villains remained the same. He continued to target those who had embraced the pecuniary values of the "new régime."[13] And he continued to sympathize with those who retained the industrial values of the handicraft economy. But, as he turned from the personal to the business habits of the pecuniary minded, his consumers underwent a startling metamorphosis. They ceased to be the idle spendthrifts given to conspicuous displays of dissipation and luxury who had haunted the pages of *Theory of the Leisure Class* and became, instead, the primary victim of the existing system, exploited by a business community willing to sacrifice the interests of the consuming population in a relentless pursuit of profit.

It was precisely because his heroes and villains remained the same that Veblen found it so easy to substitute one definition of the consumer for another. Despite his frequent examinations of consumption, his main interest in the economy throughout his career was as a system of production. It was categories of production such as "handicraft system" and "age of machine industry"—and not consumption categories such as Patten's "deficit" and "plenty"—which Veblen used to distinguish the old economy from the new. It was an impulse connected with production, the "instinct of workmanship," rather than one associated with consumption such as Patten's "altruism" which Veblen believed essential for the proper functioning of the economy. Therefore, it was not surprising, given his approach to the economy, that he should identify his heroes and villains according to their impact on the system of production. But, precisely because his interest in the economy was as a system of production, Veblen did not find it necessary to treat the consumer with the sort of intellectual consistency which he reserved for the producer. "Consumer" might be an economic category for Patten. For Veblen it was merely a rhetorical tool and as such could be adapted to the task at hand.

Veblen's larger project—the one he tackled in his first two books and several later books—was to topple the classical liberal edifice by showing that it rested on a foundation of false premises. His preferred method was to disprove these premises by proving their antithesis. Given the producerist sympathies of the period, it was a doubly effective approach. Disproving foundational premises would certainly call into question the structure that rested on them. And, because these premises revolved around production and the producer, it would do so in such a way as to strip classical liberalism of the producerist credentials that were so essential for any approach to political economy in the nineteenth century.

It was in his search for an antithesis that Veblen first turned to the consumer. In *The Theory of the Leisure Class* the task he set himself was to disprove the classical liberal assumption that the economic elite represented the most industrious members of society—producers par excellence. The antithesis he chose was "consumer par excellence." If *consumer* was to be an effective rhetorical device, however, it would have to be defined in such a way as to be not only antithetical to producer but also replete with negative connotations. Such a definition existed. In fact, it was one of the more common ones. Both William Graham Sumner and Charlotte Perkins Gilman had used *consumer* in just this sense.

In his second book Veblen's overall goal and method remained the same as those of his first. Once again he wanted to call into question the premises on which classical liberalism rested. And again he sought to do so by proving the antithesis. This time the targeted premise was the assumption that the interests of business coincided with those of the community at large and that both would be best served if the enterprises were "so managed as to give the best and largest possible output of goods or services." In order to show that just the opposite was true, that far from being in harmony, the interests of the business community and those of the community at large were, more often than not, directly at odds, he developed his distinction between an economy that functioned according to the dictates of vendibility and one that was committed to serviceability and efficiency.[14]

One consequence of suggesting that the dictates of vendibility violated the interests of the community at large was that such an approach defined those interests in terms of consumption. Veblen's sympathies might lie with workers who retained an instinct of workmanship, but it was as consumers that the community was denied the "best and largest possible output of goods or services." It was as consumers that they saw the trusts "neutralize the cheapening goods and services effected by current industrial progress." It was as consumers that they bore the brunt of "parasitic industries, such as most advertising and much of the other efforts that go into competitive selling." And it was as consumers that they suffered when business attempted to "offset the surplus productivity of modern industry" by "turning out goods for conspicuously wasteful consumption."[15]

If Veblen hoped to indict the classical economic system because it violated the dictates of serviceability and efficiency, he could not have those most disadvantaged by such a system defined as individuals given to self-indulgence, decadence, waste, luxury, and indolence. But, if the traditional definition of the consumer on which Sumner and Gilman had relied was of no use to him, another definition was available, namely that of Edward Bellamy. Bellamy equated consumers with the community at large, the people. And, even more to the point, he identified them as the primary victims of profit-oriented capitalism, forced by capitalists to consume beyond their means, denied the benefits of labor-saving machinery, manipulated by advertising, and prevented from enjoying a comfortable standard of living because of the excessive waste inherent in the system. It was a definition that suited Veblen's needs perfectly.[16]

The ease with which Veblen substituted one definition for another suggests the extent to which the meaning of *consumer* was in flux by the turn of the century. Only because his readers were familiar and comfortable with both definitions was it possible for Veblen to employ such radically different versions of the consumer within a five-year span. Nor were the two definitions on which he relied the only ones available in the early 1900s. The marginalist definition of consumer as the creator of value had been around for several years. And so, too, had Patten's definition of consumer as the regulator of the economy.

Patten's emphasis on the consumer's power and agency was, in part, a response to a growing skepticism about the compatibility of capitalism and the consumer. When Adam Smith first set forth his economic theories, he had assumed that capitalists and consumers enjoyed a close and mutually beneficial relationship. Consumers provided capitalists with profits, and capitalists provided consumers with abundant, high-quality goods at the lowest possible prices. By the late nineteenth century, however, a number of political-economic theorists were much less convinced that capitalists and consumers enjoyed such a symbiotic relationship. That critics of capitalism might have their doubts about capitalism's ability to meet the needs of the consuming population was, perhaps, not surprising. But even a staunch defender such as William Graham Sumner found it difficult to reconcile consumers and capitalism, although, as far as he was concerned, it was consumers who were responsible for any gap between what capitalism promised and what it actually delivered.

Patten, however, believed that the two were compatible, that consumers were good for capitalism and that capitalism was good for consumers. In the 1880s any attempt to reconcile them had required addressing the anticapitalist arguments of socialists as well as the anticonsumer arguments of classical liberals. To advocates of wealth redistribution Patten had suggested that the real task was not so much redistributing as increasing wealth. Modifying consumption choices, he insisted, would do just that. And, to those who asserted that the only way to increase wealth was to produce more and consume less, Patten had once again touted the benefits of modifying consumption choices, in this case because such modifications would have a far more significant impact on the "gross produce of any nation" than would the "greater productivity in manufacturing."[17]

The economic changes that occurred in the last half of the nineteenth century, however, undercut much of Patten's argument. Poverty continued to exist in the United States despite the eightfold increase in the nation's gross national product which occurred in the half-century after the Civil War. And producers rather than consumers seemed to be largely responsible for that increase. American industrial output, which had trailed that of Great Britain, the German states, and France in 1860, had by the turn of the century surpassed that of all other nations.

The same economic changes that undercut Patten's arguments also delivered a mortal blow to the idea that the consumer was bad for capitalism. By the end of the century the nation's phenomenal productive capabilities had convinced all but the most recalcitrant that the real threat to a capitalist economy was not too much consumption but too little.[18] The same productive capabilities, however, only served to strengthen the position of those who argued that such a system was bad for the consumer. Despite the phenomenal productivity of American industry—or, so the argument went, because of it—American consumers found themselves manipulated by advertising, poisoned by adulterated foods and drugs, and overcharged by the trusts.

For many a turn-of-the-century observer the rapid rise of the trusts went a long way toward explaining why the only effect of the phenomenal increase in productivity seemed to be an increase in the vulnerability of the consuming population. The problem with an economy dominated by trusts, these critics maintained, was that it lacked the all-important competitive market forces that kept producers in line. Without these forces trusts could produce shoddy, adulterated goods and charge inflated prices, and consumers—be they midwestern farmers who needed to ship their grain to market or urban housewives who wanted to buy meat for Sunday dinner—had little choice but to lay down their money and take what was offered to them.

Although most Progressive Era social critics agreed that the trusts were responsible for many of the nation's ills, they found it more difficult to achieve a consensus when it came to prescribing a cure for these ills. Some favored trust busting. Only by restoring competition, they insisted, would it be possible to force those who controlled industry to offer high-quality goods at the lowest possible prices. Others, however, were reluctant to exchange the benefits of economic concentration for those of competition. Nor did they believe that it was necessary to do so. The problem, they insisted, was not size but accountability. Government regulation could guarantee the same sort of accountability in an economy dominated by trusts as competition did in one dominated by small enterprises.

Patten rejected both cures. But that was hardly surprising, since he also rejected the diagnosis. Competition had not disappeared, he insisted. It had merely been transformed. Acknowledging that competition among producers supplying the same article might be much weaker in an economy dominated by trusts, he was quick to stress that competition among the producers "of different articles capable of supplying the same want" still thrived. What made this sort of competition an effective regulator of the economy was the "consumer's power of substitution." Any time that a "producer seeks to take an advantage" of a consumer, Patten argued, the consumer could substitute "other goods supplying the same want." If, for example, "the price of beef rises, the consumer may eat more mutton and pork, or he may forego [*sic*] meat entirely and eat more bread and vegetables."[19] In either case the producer of beef would have to reduce his prices if he hoped to regain his share of the food market.

The consumer's power of substitution not only kept prices in line. It also maximized productive efficiency. When consumers began to push prices down through their power of substitution, the more efficient producers responded by increasing their output. Doing so was the only way that they could "get the same total profit with a smaller return on each unit of commodity." Producers who were unable to improve their efficiency enough to survive on the "smaller return" per unit found themselves "permanently displaced." The result was a market "supplied by better producers."[20]

Patten's consumers, who regulated the trusts and maximized productive efficiency, did have a weakness. They were continually developing new wants, and those new wants put an upward pressure on prices. The problem with new wants, according to Patten, was that they were much less susceptible to the consumer's power of substitution. "Old wants may be supplied in many ways," he explained. New wants, however, "demand particular goods only to be had from [a] monopoly." "Every more intense want that the monopolist arouses gives him a greater hold over his public by limiting their power of substitution."[21]

Even when Patten's consumers were able to resist their "new wants," they could still be responsible for higher prices. In the old competitive economy, Patten suggested, it was the action of producers which brought down prices. "All the benefits of improved production" came to consumers "through no effort of their own." But in the new trust-dominated economy "there is no force operating entirely in one group of producers to bring this result to a passive consumer." The consumer had to be active, employing the power of substitution to keep producers in line. "Unless he is active, high prices are forced upon him by those upon whom he has become accustomed to depend."[22]

Ultimately, Patten was not particularly concerned that consumer passivity or the desire for new wants might mean higher prices for consumers. Such prices were the consequence of self-indulgent or lazy behavior. And they were a fair recompense for the monopolist's innovations. Furthermore, such prices were only temporary. Once a new want became an old want, consumers could use their power of substitution to force the price down.[23] The real problem with consumer self-indulgence and passivity was that it threatened to bring government regulation down on the trusts.

Patten worried about government regulation of the trusts because he was convinced that monopolists were largely responsible for prosperity. They were intent on maximizing efficiency because anything below maximum efficiency represented "a loss that could have been avoided" and reduced their "profit below the attainable." And they were the driving force behind economic progress because their profits depended upon developing new wants. Finally, they eliminated the "confusion of ignorance" which characterized the competitive economy of old. Under their direction, Patten maintained, "the regularity of life and the power of predicting events and results are . . .

increased, and all parts of society become more progressive." For numerous reasons, then, Patten considered an economy directed by the visible hand of monopolists far superior to an economy directed by "the conflicting motives of the less efficient but more numerous classes."[24]

So, when consumers allowed themselves to be exploited by the trusts, making it far more likely that government would attempt to limit or even eradicate monopoly power, they were, once again, directly responsible for frustrating abundance. Price controls, Patten warned, would decrease the "rate of progress" and create economic stagnation. The only way to reduce monopoly without destroying its benefits, Patten maintained, was through "the increased power of substitution which improvements bring." If government really wanted to reduce monopoly, it should develop public policies designed to "increase the rate of progress."[25] An increased rate of progress would increase the rate at which new wants became old wants. And once wants became "old" their prices would be regulated not by government but by the consumer's power of substitution.

Patten's definition of the consumer remained quite consistent throughout his career. It was a definition that stressed the phenomenal power of consumers. In the 1880s this had meant that consumers were capable of increasing society's wealth. In the early 1900s it meant that consumers could bring the mighty trusts to heel. But it was also a definition that emphasized the weakness of consumers when it came to resisting their own desires. Because of that weakness, Patten's consumers, though capable of solving most of the economy's problems, often chose instead to engage in self-indulgent consumption. And such consumption had far-reaching effects for all of society. It was the consumer's preference for goods supplied with difficulty by nature, Patten suggested in the 1880s, which prevented a general improvement in the living standard. And it was their inability to resist new wants, he maintained in the early twentieth century, which ultimately threatened "to check progress" and to stagnate the economy by encouraging government regulation of the trusts.[26]

Although Patten's overall definition of the consumer as powerful but self-indulgent remained quite consistent over the years, the connotations associated with that definition did not. In the 1880s Patten's examples of inefficient consumption frequently involved such morally charged products as whiskey and beer. By the twentieth century his consumers were being seduced by new wants. The shift made self-indulgence a far less problematic activity. Instead

of evoking images of moral deficiency, Patten's twentieth-century version of
self-indulgence was associated with progress, as the consumer relentlessly
pursued the new.

Equally important, Patten's twentieth-century version of self-indulgence
no longer implied that irresponsible consumers merely needed to exercise a
bit more self-control. Reflecting the influence of marginalism on his thought,
he had come to see self-indulgence as the result of economic law rather than
weakness of character. The consumer, he now argued, "must seek the greatest
satisfaction, which is obtained . . . by the gratification of the newer and in-
tenser wants."[27] By making self-indulgence inevitable, Patten absolved the
consumer of much of the blame for misguided consumption. By rooting self-
indulgence in economic law, he replaced many of the moral connotations
that he had once associated with consumption with scientific ones.

Ultimately, however, Patten was not willing to absolve the consumer of all
the blame nor to replace all the moral connotations. Although he limited the
instances in which self-control might be applied, he did not eliminate them
altogether. Self-control might be useless when it came to irresistible new
wants, but it still played an important role when it came to old ones that
could be resisted. Therefore, Patten argued, the best way to restrain consumption was to speed up the process by which new wants became old ones. Then
consumers would once again be in control of their consumption, and self-
control would once again be not only possible but also necessary.

What was most striking about Patten's analysis was how ambivalent he remained about the consumer. Indeed, the tension between Patten's profound
reservations regarding the consumer and his conviction that abundance was
the key to social well-being goes a long way toward explaining the apparent
contradictions in his writings. The same individual who argued that "the new
morality does not consist in saving, but in expanding consumption," that "we
encourage self-denial when we should encourage self-expression," and that
"the non-saver is now a higher type of a man than the saver" also suggested
that "abstinence, fortitude, chastity, and thrift" were "the ultimate moral
virtues," that "self-repression . . . is the essence of character building," and
that "primitive men" engaged in extravagance while the new order would be
characterized by "restraint and morality, puritan in essence but various in
form." Patten resolved such apparent contradictions by suggesting that the
inhabitants of a "pleasure economy," far more than those living in a "pain
economy," would need to possess the "ultimate moral virtues" of "abstinence,

fortitude, chastity, and thrift." Without such virtues those who encountered "an abundance of economic goods" would inevitably succumb "to many forms of temptation, disease and vice" and "would be carried off." The "apostle of plenty," it would seem, remained a reluctant one at best.[28]

In the 1880s Patten's ambivalence toward the consumer had prevented him from following the logic of his ideas. Even as he denounced "age-of-deficit" thinking, he had been reluctant to challenge the producerist paradigm. Nor had this been particularly surprising. Throughout the nineteenth century producerist ways of thinking were so hegemonic that as dedicated a champion of the consumer as Bellamy had found it impossible to function completely outside that paradigm. Thus, even as Patten identified efficient consumption as the key to prosperity, he refused to challenge the producer's claim to society's wealth or to argue that citizens had a fundamental right to live free from want or to replace the producer with the consumer as the pivotal identity in the political economy.

By the early twentieth century, however, the producerist paradigm was significantly weaker than it had been even two decades earlier. And the consumer had all but ceased to be a luxury-seeking parasite responsible for poverty. In such an intellectual environment Patten found it possible to mount an attack on the producerist paradigm. His target remained deficit age thinking. His goal remained a system of thought appropriate for an "age of surplus." But he had come to see the extent to which the producerist paradigm stood between him and his goal. And his increasing tolerance of the consumer made him far less reluctant to follow the logic of ideas, even if that logic led directly to a consumer-oriented political economy.

Patten began his attack on the producerist paradigm by challenging what was the cornerstone of that paradigm, the producer's claim to society's wealth. The key to his challenge was the utility theory of value. In the hands of the marginalists such a theory represented a fundamental break from earlier theories of value. It defined value not in terms of the producer's contribution—as did both a labor and cost theory of value—but in terms of the consumer's satisfaction. And it assumed that the producer and consumer perspectives were so fundamentally different that there was little point in attempting to reconcile them within one theory of value.

Patten relied on a marginalist definition of *value*. But he was unwilling to treat the producer and consumer perspectives as antithetical approaches to the measurement of value. And he was unwilling to dismiss the producer's contribution as irrelevant. Ironically, however, his attempt to reconcile the two perspectives and to recognize the producer's contribution to society's wealth ultimately represented a far greater challenge to producerist ideas than the marginalist redefinition of value ever had.

The first step toward reconciling the two perspectives was to account for the gap between the value of goods to the consumer and the cost of producing these goods. Patten was certainly not the first to identify such a gap nor the first to attempt to explain it. Marx, for example, had relied on just such a gap when he had developed his theory of surplus value. Capitalists, he argued, made their profit by underpaying their workers and pocketing the difference. In his view the value of goods was determined by the labor that went into them, and any difference between what the consumer was willing to pay and what the worker received belonged to the worker.

Bellamy also relied on such a gap in his critique of capitalism. Not surprisingly, however, he wanted the consuming population to be the primary beneficiaries of any difference between what the consumer paid for a product and what it cost to produce it. He did so, in part, by suggesting that in their pursuit of profit capitalists exploited consumers as much as they did workers, overcharging them and selling them shoddy and adulterated goods.

Although identifying consumers as covictims of capitalist exploitation denied workers their exclusive claim to what Marx had called "surplus value," it did not eliminate the claim altogether. Nor did it weaken the connection between one's role as a producer and one's right to consume. The consumer's contribution to the value of the product, as Bellamy defined it, was strictly a function of capitalist exploitation. Eliminate that system and the exploitation that went with it, and workers would once again be exclusively responsible for the value of a good.

Bellamy, however, did not rely solely on consumer exploitation to justify a right to consume distinct from one's role as a producer. He also emphasized the extent to which a society's wealth depended upon the "social inheritance of intellect and discovery." As Dr. Leete told Julian West in *Looking Backward,* "the past knowledge and achievements of the race. . . . represent nine parts to one contributed by yourself in the value of your product [and] you inherited it, did you not?"[29] Ten years later, in *Equality,* Bellamy reduced the individual's contribution from one-tenth to one–two hundredth and shifted the focus from the social inheritance of intellect and discovery to the "social organism." It was, he insisted, the "social organism, this vast machinery of human association, which enhances some two hundredfold the product of every one's labor." A worker "toiling in isolation . . . would be fortunate if he could at the utmost produce enough to keep himself alive." But, Bellamy maintained, "working in concert with his fellows by aid of the social organism," that same worker and his fellows "produce enough to support all in the highest luxury and refinement." This wealth that was a product of the social organism Bellamy called the social or general fund.[30]

Although Bellamy had joined Marx in arguing that in a capitalist economy a substantial portion of society's wealth did not belong to those who held title to it, an important difference separated their two analyses. Marx's theory of surplus value identified the workers as the ones responsible for and therefore entitled to society's wealth. Bellamy's general fund, by contrast, was the product of social inheritance and the vast machinery of human association and, therefore, belonged to all members of society. As Julian West concluded, "society collectively can be the only heir to the social inheritance of intellect and discovery, and it is society collectively which furnishes the continuous daily concourse by which alone that inheritance is made effective."[31]

By defining the vast machinery of human association rather than human labor as the most important factor in creating society's wealth, Bellamy was able, theoretically at least, to limit the producer's contribution. But he never managed to eliminate it entirely. Initially, one-tenth and later one–two hundredth of the value of a product remained, according to Bellamy, the result of the individual's labor. Unable to eliminate the contribution, he did the next best thing. He eliminated the claim by making labor a civic responsibility. In his Boston of the year 2000 it was "the duty of every citizen to contribute his quota of industrial or intellectual services to the maintenance of the nation."[32]

Bellamy's inability to sever completely the connection between one's role as a producer and one's right to consume stemmed largely from his inability to step outside the dominant producerist paradigm of the day. His discussion of exploitation, for example, established a consumer's right to surplus value by suggesting that consumers played a role in its creation. And his suggestion that "society collectively" was entitled to the wealth produced by the "vast machinery of human association" was based not only on the general producerist assumption that a product belonged to those who created it but, even more specifically, on a capitalist version of that assumption, namely that a product belonged to those who owned the means of production.

Even his conceptualization of the problem revealed his reliance on a producerist perspective. As he set out to explain the gap between the value of goods to consumers and the costs of production, he asked who or what was responsible for the value of those goods. It was a producer's question. It equated value with production and assumed that those who contributed to the production of value were entitled to the portion that they had contributed.

Like Marx and Bellamy, Patten also wanted to explain the gap between the value of goods to consumers and the costs of production. And, like them, he gave the gap a name. He called it the "social surplus."[33] Unlike them, however, Patten was both willing and able to function outside the producerist paradigm. Rather than approaching the gap by asking who was responsible for value, he wanted to know what had reduced costs. It was a consumer's question. And it made all the difference.

Like Bellamy, Patten began with the assumption that "the goods enjoyed by men are not wholly the results of their labors." And, like Bellamy, he pointed to the "great improvements" that had "been made through inventions, discoveries, and other additions to the general stock of knowledge." But there the similarity ended. Because Bellamy wanted to establish a claim for the consuming population, he suggested that "additions to the general stock of knowledge" were an inheritance and thus belonged to "society collectively." Patten, however, was interested in costs. These additions were important to him not because they established a basis for a claim of ownership but because they "aid[ed] in the reduction of costs."[34]

They did so in two ways. First, all "additions to the general stock of knowledge" were the product of a previous generation's labor. Therefore, members of the current generation could enjoy those additions without having to expend any labor to discover or invent them. In short, the current generation could use them free of charge because a previous generation had picked up the tab. But some of them—specifically, "improvements in the productive processes and machinery"—also reduced costs by performing the labor that humans had once performed, thereby "reduc[ing] work to a minimum." Thus, the efforts of a previous generation absolved the current generation not only from the labor required to invent machines but also from the labor that the machines performed. And reducing labor meant reducing costs. Thus, Patten could conclude that both the portion of a good which depended upon the work of a previous generation and that which had been produced by mechanical labor had no cost.[35]

Nor were additions to the general stock of knowledge the only factors reducing costs. Previous generations had also improved "the original qualities of the land," created "much fixed capital," and "permanently removed" "many obstacles to production," all of which represented work that did not need to be repeated by the current generation, thereby reducing their costs of production even further. Nature also helped to reduce these costs by providing a number of services free of charge. "The natural power of the land, wind, water, and sun," Patten maintained, "help men in production and are employed by men without any costs."[36] Thus, in numerous ways the value of society's wealth far exceeded its costs.

What was so significant about Patten's focus on costs was that it went a long way toward removing one of the most formidable obstacles to a consumer-oriented political economy: the producer's claim to society's wealth. As long as the focus was on value, the producer's right to wealth would remain paramount. No matter how much Bellamy argued to the contrary, according to producerist logic, the consumer's contribution—if it could even be considered a contribution—could never compare with that of the producer because ultimately the consumer did not create anything.

But, once the focus shifted to cost and, even more important, once it was possible to show that costs were far less than value, then a portion of society's wealth ceased to have any costs. And this was the key. Why? Because the producer had no more right to wealth that had no cost than did any other member of society. The shift in focus from value to cost denied producers their preferred status.

Shifting the focus from value to cost also paved the way for a rethinking of the role of machines in the political economy. From a producerist perspective the two significant facts about a machine were that it was the product of human labor and that it was a tool that increased the amount of goods which a human could produce. From these two facts producerist thinkers across the political spectrum could conclude that producers who were responsible for the existence of machines—be they Sumner's capitalist producers or Marx's working-class producers—were entitled to the wealth that those machines produced.

Bellamy altered the equation only slightly. Like producerist thinkers, he assumed that a machine was a tool that magnified human labor. He merely suggested that it owed its existence to the technical knowledge that belonged to society collectively and, therefore, so too did the products created by that tool.[37] But, because Bellamy continued to define a machine as a tool that magnified human labor power, he could not eliminate the producer from the equation.

Patten could—precisely because he did not define a machine as a tool that magnified the producer's labor power. For him a machine was an alternative to human labor power. From there it was but a short step to the sort of argument that his student Rexford Tugwell would make in the late 1920s. Tugwell would argue that the time was not that far off when humans would be replaced by machines and would thus cease to be producers. Instead, they would become consumers, using what machines produced. Such an argument made it possible to establish a right to consume which did not depend upon one's role in the production process, and, even more important, it did so without denying human producers the fruits of their labor. The starting point for such an argument was Patten's nonproducerist definition of a machine as an alternative to human labor power.

Even Patten, however, could not ignore the fact that humans labored, a fact that had been largely responsible for Bellamy's inability to eliminate the producer's claim to society's wealth. But, once again, Patten's focus on cost rather than value allowed him to succeed where Bellamy had failed. Because Bellamy assumed that a claim to wealth was based on one's contributions to the value of goods, the only way that he could eliminate the producer's claim was to show that the producer made no contribution. Not surprisingly, he found that impossible to do. Patten's approach, by contrast, required only that he show that the producer's labor did not constitute a cost, a much easier task than Bellamy's.

Patten began by suggesting that "the theory that costs determine value rests upon the notion that labor is disagreeable." As far as he was concerned, the theory rested upon a false premise. Work, he insisted, "is normally agreeable," although, "in a decreasing degree with each repetition of a given act." If it was carried on too long, work did become painful. But only then, according to Patten, could it be defined as cost. Any work before that point did not constitute a cost because producers had already received compensation for it through the pleasure they derived from their labors.[38]

Central to Patten's argument was the concept of cultural lag—the theory that ideas lag behind technological progress. "Mental habits," he maintained, "continue long after the economic conditions which fashioned them have disappeared." This was certainly the case with work. "Labor is irksome not because regular bodily movements cause pain, but because of the disagreeable associations connected with it." According to Patten, these associations were the product of an earlier time when "a servile class worked" and "the free man showed his superiority by abstaining from production." Under such conditions work came to be "associated with servility" and, not surprisingly, was "socially despised."[39]

If cultural lag identified the problem, it also suggested the cure. Work would cease to be irksome as soon as different associations were formed, "making industrial occupations honorable, and thus making them pleasurable." Once that was accomplished, then it would be possible to envision an economy in which there would be no pain whatsoever. If the individual stopped working before work ceased to be enjoyable, the result, Patten suggested, would be "a perpetual round of production, consumption, rest, revival of energy, and renewed production in which no pain enters." Until that time, he insisted, "social penalties" should not be considered production costs because they did not interfere with the individual's production, only "with his social status."[40]

The theory of cultural lag allowed Patten to eliminate the final and most obstinate cost, that of human labor. That he had to resort to cultural lag was ultimately not surprising. The idea that individuals are entitled to the fruits of their labor was the foundation of the entire producerist system of thought. It therefore would require nothing less than a rejection of the entire system to eliminate the worker's claim. By comparison, removing the negative connotations from consumption had been quite easy. It was no wonder, then, that Bellamy, who had been so successful at legitimizing consumption, ultimately failed when it came to devising an equitable way to deny workers the products of their labor. As long as he functioned within the producerist paradigm, there was no equitable way.

Although cultural lag proved to be an even more powerful analytical tool in the hands of later consumerist thinkers, it was Patten who suggested its potential, showing how it could be used to explain why poverty, which "ought to be disappearing from a rich and lavish world," continued to flourish. According to Patten, the obstacles that prevented an economy of "pleasure or surplus" from replacing "a pain or deficit economy" were social rather than economic. Economic obstacles—those "maladjustments between men and nature, which forced men in the past to submit to a poverty they did not know how to escape"—were slowly being eradicated, "weakened by the application of knowledge, science, and skill." Social obstacles, by contrast, continued to thrive. These obstacles, the social institutions, mental habits, and popular beliefs that had been established "during pervasive and all-powerful poverty," reflected "the passing age of nature's deficit" and were therefore totally unsuited to the new economic conditions. "It is essential to recognize," Patten insisted, "that we have passed from one epoch to another and that our principles and facts must be correspondingly modified." "The economic revolution is here but the intellectual revolution that will rouse men to its stupendous meaning has not done its work."[41]

Both the persuasiveness and the appeal of cultural lag were due largely to its linking of new ideas with economic progress, no small advantage in a nation as committed to economic progress as the turn-of-the-century United States. With the theory of cultural lag the weight of tradition ceased to be an asset and became, instead, a liability, the onus of proof shifting from new to old ideas. Suddenly older ideas were placed on the defensive, forced to show that, despite rather than because of their longevity, they remained functional. As for newer ideas, they had the benefit of the doubt merely because of their newness. Such a theory had obvious consumerist potential.

Patten left the development of that potential to later consumerist thinkers. They were only able to develop that potential, however, because Patten had cleared the ground of several producerist impediments. By focusing on cost rather than value, he had identified one way to sever the connections between one's role as a producer and one's right to consume. By defining social surplus as that portion of society's wealth which had no cost—rather than the unreimbursed or overlooked contribution of a particular group, as Marx and Bellamy had done—he found a way to give consumers the same right to society's wealth which producers had. By suggesting that a deficit economy had given way to one characterized by surplus, he helped to shift the focus from problems of production to those of distribution and consumption. And, perhaps most important, by using cultural lag to discredit the existing system of ideas and institutions, he cleared the ground for the construction of a consumerist edifice.

Although Patten's assault on the producerist paradigm had important implications for a consumerist worldview, his goal had never been a consumerist one. Instead, like many of his contemporaries, he wanted to find a way to reduce the conflict that seemed to be threatening the very survival of the existing order.[42] Defining the social surplus as wealth that had no cost might have real consumerist potential, but what drew Patten to it was its potential to discredit the age-of-deficit thinking that encouraged class struggle and replace it with "age-of-surplus" thinking, which could foster cooperation. If the social surplus was wealth that had no cost, then, he reasoned, it was possible to use that wealth on behalf of all of society without denying either capitalists or workers the products of their labor.

Similarly, what Patten found appealing in the idea of a surplus economy was not that it could be the foundation of a consumer-oriented system but that it could change the conditions under which a welfare state could emerge. In a deficit economy such a state would be the outcome of a protracted struggle, because only by taking from the rich could it secure the funds necessary to help the poor. In an economy characterized by surplus, however, it became possible to envision a very different welfare state, one that did not advance any particular group at the expense of another and therefore one that was not born of conflict.[43]

Finally, Patten was drawn to the theory of cultural lag not because it provided a justification for a consumerist order but because it could be used to defend his version of the welfare state. Those who opposed a welfare state did so because they assumed that the economy was characterized by scarcity and that wealth was limited. Such conditions meant, as Sumner put it, that "if you give a loaf to a pauper you cannot give the same loaf to a laborer." Patten was convinced, however, that "in modern nations the productive power is more than sufficient to produce the minimum of existence." No longer was it necessary to choose between the two. The new economic conditions made it possible to give loaves to both the pauper and the laborer. Indeed, if a deficit economy had given way to one characterized by surplus, then not to do so had become the real violation of justice.[44]

According to Patten, it was not only the opponents of a welfare state who were guilty of an outmoded, deficit-economy thinking rooted in conflict. Those who advocated a welfare state relied on the same obsolete mental habits. Like Sumner, they divided society into groups with conflicting interests, assumed that goods were scarce, and believed that the only way to elevate the "toilers" was through "a sacrifice of those having economic advantages." Indeed, the only real difference was that they advocated such a sacrifice. Patten argued, however, that in an economy characterized by surplus it was neither necessary nor advisable to eliminate poverty and misery by demanding sacrifice or requiring the well-to-do to give "up positions of advantage." On the contrary, it was far better to create "similar positions for other people." "The extension of opportunity, the growth of efficiency, the spread of knowledge and the increase of health"—these methods, Patten insisted, were far more effective ways to eliminate misery and poverty than the simple redistribution of society's wealth.[45]

Patten was far more interested in constructing a blueprint for an economy without conflict rather than one for a consumer-oriented welfare state. Nevertheless, his rejection of producerist notions of equity and his surplus economy thinking inevitably pushed him in a consumerist direction. The welfare state that he envisioned—he called it "voluntary socialism"—turned out to be far more consumer oriented than the versions that other turn-of-the-century welfare state proponents advocated. Nor was that particularly surprising. Patten had long argued that the most salient interest a worker had was as a consumer. Most welfare state proponents focused on certain producerist rights, such as the right to a safe workplace and the right to the full product of one's labor. By contrast, the rights that Patten's welfare state would guarantee were, for the most part, those that focused on the consummatory interests of the nation's citizens—the right to leisure, to comfort, to relief, to cleanliness, to a home, to develop, and to recreation.[46]

Similarly, advocates of a producer-oriented welfare state assumed that the best way to further the interests of the nation's workers was through measures such as unemployment insurance, workmen's compensation, a minimum wage, maximum hours, retirement insurance, and even industrial democracy. Patten, by contrast, believed that the welfare state should concern itself with "good housing, elaborate sanitation, shorter hours of work, [and] protection from disease," measures that focused primarily on the workers' interests as consumers.[47] And even the one measure that did focus on the workers' producer interests, shorter hours, would advance these interests by reducing the amount of time that workers had to spend as producers.

Arguing that the key to the welfare state was not re-slicing the economic pie but, instead, making it bigger presented Patten with a significant intellectual problem. If economic progress, rather than victory in the class struggle, was the key to ending poverty, then, Patten concluded, the capitalists were indispensable. They had the ability to enlarge the economic pie. And they were most capable of sustaining the economic progress on which a surplus economy depended. Patten was well aware, however, that unchecked capitalists had been largely responsible for much of the misery of the past several decades. How, then, would it be possible to grant capitalists the freedom they required to maximize efficiency and at the same time avoid the disastrous side effects that had accompanied unregulated capitalism in the late nineteenth century?

Patten solved this dilemma by turning yet again to cultural lag. The key, he suggested, was to bring capitalist thinking into line with new economic conditions. And he was confident that this transformation was already occurring. "The growth of large scale capitalism has resulted in the elimination of the unsocial capitalist." As survival in the business world came to depend less on eliminating rivals and more on increasing efficiency, businessmen found it in their best interests to bring "their action into line with public interest." Thus, "trusts, large corporations, and stable industries" were finding "it advantageous to raise wages" because high wages attracted "a high class of laborers" and such laborers were more productive than the "lowest classes." Similarly, any "disposition to take advantage of the public by short-sighted practices" was fast disappearing as businesses discovered that the best way to maximize profits over the long run was to maximize public welfare. Any "delay in the recognition of this principle" was, according to Patten, due "to the holding over of ideas that originated in earlier epochs."[48]

Patten was quick to stress that it was not just capitalists who needed to learn that "progress is due to coöperation and not to conflict." It was equally important for those who were committed to far-reaching social and political change to realize that "general well-being . . . must be secured through social coöperation." "The road to prosperity," he reminded them, "is not through class conflict, with its mulcting of the minority—but is, rather, in social improvements that take men from the margin of production and place them in contact with better resources and in more favorable situations." Attempts to "reduce the evils of poverty" by eliminating the capitalists would merely result in "the destruction of the advantages upon which . . . welfare and the progress of society depend."[49]

Patten's insistence that the state should not regulate production but should provide extensive social services highlights once again the extent to which his shift in focus from production to consumption placed him outside the existing political economic debate. In the Progressive Era this debate was largely one between right-of-center corporate liberals such as Jeremiah Jenks and Arthur Hadley and left-of-center democratic statists such as Richard Ely and H. C. Adams over how much the state should regulate production and how it could best serve producers. Democratic statists were on the left not only be-cause they called for an activist state but also because they tended to favor the interests of wage-earning producers over those of capitalist producers. Corpo-rate liberals occupied the right side of that spectrum in part because they wanted minimal state intervention but also because they tended to emphasize the interests of capitalist producers over those of wage-earning producers.[50]

Patten, however, looked at the economy as both a system of consumption and a system of production. When he approached it from the perspective of production, he focused on maximizing capitalist production and developing a disciplined labor force, a focus that had much in common with that of cor-porate liberals. When he looked at the economy as a system of consumption, however, he moved toward a democratic statist position, advocating exten-sive government intervention on behalf of the needy and redistribution, al-beit voluntary, of income as a developing altruism among capitalists made them willing "to be taxed for public and far-reaching ends."[51] That he could shift from one side of the political spectrum to the other with such ease and that, in the case of voluntary income redistribution, he defied categorization says as much about the spectrum as it does about Patten. What was left and right on a producerist spectrum was not necessarily left and right on a con-sumerist one.

The extent to which producerist notions of left and right made little sense on a consumerist spectrum would plague consumerist left liberals far more than it did Patten. Proud of their leftist credentials, left-leaning consumerist thinkers would again and again try to defend as radical positions that were anything but radical in the producerist scheme of things. Nowhere was this more evident than in their attempts to come to terms with capitalism. Be-cause they began with the assumption that social well-being rested on mate-rial abundance, left-leaning consumerist thinkers would find it far more difficult to reject capitalism than their left-leaning producerist contempo-raries would. At some level left-leaning consumerist thinkers were never quite able to forget that Marx's goal had been a worker state while Adam Smith's had been a political-economic order in which "consumption is the sole end and purpose of all production."[52]

Patten, by contrast, never had any doubts about capitalism. Throughout his career he remained convinced that it was the economic system most con-ducive to an economy of plenty. Not surprisingly, given such a conviction, his ideal political economy bore a far greater resemblance to the political economy that emerged in the post–World War II era than it did to the more statist system that consumerist left liberals would advocate in the early 1930s. Patten envisioned an economic order in which workers would be willing "to accept the discipline of the new industrial régime" in exchange for a comfortable standard of living—much like the unionized workers of the 1950s and 1960s. And he envisioned one in which those who were better off financially were, theoretically at least, willing "to be taxed for public and far-reaching ends"—like Dwight D. Eisenhower's highways or Lyndon Johnson's Great Society programs.[53]

But the greatest similarity between Patten and the post–World War II public policy makers was their common conviction that government could best serve the people not so much by controlling business or even by redistributing income but by promoting prosperity. Patten might not have anticipated Keynesian economics, but he would have been as comfortable with its methods and goals as John F. Kennedy and Lyndon Johnson were and, certainly, more so than Eisenhower ever was. Like the American disciples of Keynes, Patten believed that capitalists were quite capable of creating prosperity. And, like them, he favored measures that required only limited government involvement in the economy. He would have found Keynesian fiscal measures infinitely preferable to the government regulation and government direction of business favored by many of the 1920s and 1930s consumerist left liberals—including his own student Rexford Tugwell.[54]

Why did Patten find it so much easier to embrace capitalism than the consumerist left liberals ever did? Why, unlike the left liberals, was he willing to entrust prosperity to the capitalists? One explanation might be that his academic position was at the Wharton School of Business. But many of his contemporaries who did not teach at business schools were equally convinced that the new corporations had a largely positive impact on the economy. And during the Progressive Era there were reasons for such a conviction. To many an observer the corporations seemed to have brought "order" to the economic chaos of the late nineteenth century. And they seemed to have brought scientific efficiency, thereby greatly expanding the amount of consumer goods produced. The result, many a progressive concluded, was a higher standard of living for much of the American population. Indeed, so successful did corporate methods appear, that even reformers enthusiastically adopted them—the reorganization of numerous municipal governments being only the most obvious example.

Nor was it only the corporate business methods that made it easy for reformers to assume that corporations had a progressive influence on the economy. Industrialists engaged in numerous philanthropic enterprises. And corporations were often instrumental in securing the passage of regulatory legislation. The Meat Inspection Act, Workmen's Compensation, railroad regulation, all might have furthered the interests of business, but that did not change the fact that such legislation left workers and consumers better off than they had been before its passage. For a number of reasons, then, it was easy for not only Patten but also numerous social critics to find room for the corporations in their particular versions of the good society.

By the 1920s this was far more difficult to do. The post–World War I suppression of labor, the rapid growth of advertising, the uneven prosperity that favored business and the well-to-do but failed to reach many workers and most farmers, the extent to which a federal government that refused to use the power of the state on behalf of the needy was more than willing to use it on behalf of business, all contributed to a growing conviction that a business-oriented political economy would not, perhaps even could not, operate on behalf of workers and consumers.

It was this growing skepticism about capitalism which ultimately explains why Patten had a limited influence on consumerist thinkers. How limited was made painfully clear in the late 1930s when the *New Republic* asked its readers to identify the books that "changed our minds." Respondents mentioned Thorstein Veblen more than any other author. No one mentioned Patten.[55] The obvious question is why. Patten's iconoclastic and idiosyncratic ideas and his opaque writing style might help explain why he was overlooked, but it is difficult to absolve Veblen of any of these charges. The answer probably has more to do with timing. To left liberals confronting the corporate-dominated economy of the 1920s and the collapsed economy of the 1930s, Veblen's critique of capitalism seemed to make far more sense than Patten's celebration of it. And Veblen's version of the consumer as a victim of capitalism seemed to mirror reality far more than Patten's version of the consumer as a powerful regulator of the market place. By the 1950s, when capitalism's performance might have been used to vindicate Patten's theories, few remembered him.[56]

Not surprisingly, their different attitudes toward business allowed Patten and the consumerist left liberals to reach different conclusions about how society should be organized. Although Patten insisted that the economic focus should be on consumption rather than production and although he demanded the recognition of a number of consummatory rights, he nevertheless continued to assume that humans were producers. His good society was one that would reduce conflict by focusing on a common interest in expanded consumption which both wage earners and capitalists shared. For wage earners such consumption meant a higher standard of living; for capitalists it meant higher profits. An economy dedicated to expanding consumption would thus be one that advanced the interests of all producers.

What Patten did by shifting the focus from production to consumption was to show how it might be possible to reestablish the harmony of interests which had been so central to Smithian economic theory. A political economy dedicated to furthering consumption rather than production would be one, he believed, in which one group's gain could once again be that of another.[57] But these groups remained groups of producers. It was workers and capitalists who found common ground in expanded consumption. Patten's good society was not so much a consumer-oriented as a consumption-oriented one.

Consumerist left liberals in the 1920s and 1930s would adopt a very different approach. Rather than emphasizing that all producers shared a common interest in expanded consumption, they would insist that all humans shared a common identity as consumers. It was an important distinction and one that led to fundamentally different versions of the good society. If humans were first and foremost consumers, then the good society was one in which consumers, not capitalists or workers, were in control. That control might mean extensive government regulation of the economy on behalf of consumer-citizens. Or it might mean consumer-owned and -operated businesses. But in either case it meant that producers did not have rights as producers, only as consumers. Unlike Patten's good society, theirs *was* consumer oriented.

Despite their differences, Patten and the consumerist thinkers agreed on certain characteristics that any version of the good society had to have. It had to function on everyone's behalf. And it had to be free of conflict. It was only when they sought to devise the best way to create a conflict-free system that functioned on everyone's behalf that they parted company. Patten believed that such a system could best be established by focusing on an interest common to all members of society. Consumerist thinkers insisted that the key was to focus on a common identity.

Patten and the consumerist thinkers were not the first to suggest that any good society would have to be free of conflict and function on everyone's behalf. Nor were they the first to struggle with how best to bring such an order into being. Implicit in most nineteenth-century producerist systems of thought was both a similar understanding of the good society and the assumption that the way to guarantee a conflict-free order that functioned on everyone's behalf was to focus on either a common interest or a common identity. Classical liberals, for example, envisioned an order in which various sorts of producers, be they wage workers, independent artisans, or capitalists, would exist in harmony. And they assumed that the key was a common interest that all producers shared in prosperity. Socialists disagreed, insisting that certain groups of producers benefited far more from prosperity than did others. The solution, they decided, was not a common producer interest but a common producer identity. If everyone shared the same identity, then harmony would be inevitable.

In the highly industrialized economy of the late nineteenth century, however, producers seemed to share neither a common interest nor a common identity. Numerous producing groups with competing interests could and did claim the producer label. But a system that functioned on behalf of industrialists would be quite different from one that functioned on behalf of independent artisans. And a system organized according to the needs of industrial workers would have little in common with one organized according to the needs of farmers. The producer identity, it would seem, had lost its ability to function as a universal identity. And a common producer interest, if it had once existed, had long since disappeared. The result was widespread conflict.

Late-nineteenth-century producerist thinkers tried to solve this problem in one of two ways. One approach was to define *producer* narrowly and then force everyone into that narrow producer category. It was the approach implicit in the Marxist worker state. If everyone became a member of the working class, then a society that functioned on behalf of working-class producers would be a society that functioned on behalf of everyone. Although this approach might ultimately result in a harmonious order, it was one that, in the short run, could produce considerable conflict. It was to be expected that certain groups of producers, most notably capitalists, would strenuously resist any attempt to force them to adopt a Marxist version of the producer identity.

The alternative to the Marxist approach was to ignore the differences that existed among the various claimants to the producer identity. It was this approach that both the Knights of Labor and the Populists adopted. Both movements defined producers broadly. The Knights made room for capitalists as well as industrial workers and independent artisans within the producer category. The Populists' "toiling masses" included urban and rural laborers who worked for wages as well as farmers who owned their own farms and worked for profit. Inevitably, however, when it came to devising a specific program, neither group managed to come up with one that would serve all members of their broadly defined producer category equally. Each found it necessary to narrow that definition, the Knights ultimately choosing to champion the interests of wage workers, the Populists pushing for measures that were primarily of interest to the nation's farm owners. Ultimately, both movements failed because they attempted to build a political movement around a universal producer identity that had long since ceased to exist.[58]

During the Progressive Era the search for a universal identity, broadly defined, reached a crossroads with the development of the tripartite commissions. First established by the National Civic Federation and soon adopted by several government commissions, the tripartite approach brought together representatives of labor, industry, and the public.[59] It was the task of the representatives of each interest to find compromise positions, the assumption being that, in a complex industrial economy, the best way to avoid conflict and further everyone's interest was to find a balance among the interests of various groups.

The tripartite approach represented a critical juncture in the transition from a producer-oriented to a consumer-oriented liberalism. By reserving one-third of the votes for the "public," progressives began to move away from the nineteenth-century producerist assumption that *the public* and *producers* were one and the same. Producers retained majority control within the tripartite system. But they could no longer claim to be either a universal interest or a universal identity. One-third of the votes now belonged to an interest that, whatever it was, was not a producer interest.

It was not only in their rejection of a producerist definition of the public that progressives played a critical role in the shift from a producer-oriented to a consumer-oriented liberalism. Equally important were their various attempts to arrive at a new definition. These attempts were anything but successful. But they were, nevertheless, significant, because included among the various contradictory definitions of *public interest* was one that equated it with a consuming interest. In so doing, progressives took a critical step toward developing a new understanding of civic identity, one that was rooted in the consumer rather than the producer identity.

Given the fragmentation of the producer identity, it is not surprising that those who organized the tripartite commissions should have such trouble agreeing on the representatives for each of the producing interests. Who, for example, was best qualified to represent the nation's workers? Was it the Industrial Workers of the World? the Socialist Party of America? the American Federation of Labor? And who could best represent the business interests? Small manufacturers? Corporate leaders? These questions produced a considerable amount of debate.

By contrast, no real debate occurred over who could best represent the public interest. Lawyers, academics, philanthropists, and social reformers were the usual choice.[60] The absence of debate, however, could not be traced to a universal preference for one definition of the public interest from among many. Instead, it resulted from a general failure to define the public interest at all.

Those who organized tripartite commissions would have denied that they lacked a definition. The public interest, they would have insisted, was that which all citizens had in common. And, indeed, such a definition was the one on which they relied as they chose their representatives. Lawyers, academics, philanthropists, and social reformers, they assumed, were the sorts of disinterested individuals whose strongly developed sense of social responsibility made them ideally suited to public service.

But defining the public interest as that which all citizens shared was only one of the definitions on which those who organized tripartite commissions relied. When it came to deciding which three interests would be represented on the commissions, they employed a second definition, one that treated the public as one interest among many. It was this definition that resulted in the creation of boards on which representatives of the public were given one-third of the votes, the remaining two-thirds going to labor and industry. And it was this definition that ultimately revealed the confusion over what actually constituted the public interest. If the public interest was that which all members of society had in common then it made little sense to give representatives of the public only one-third of the votes. Indeed, since the tripartite approach was based on the assumption that balancing the interests of various groups would result in policies that were in everyone's interest, it would have been more logical to deny the public any representation at all.

The third definition—and the one on which the actual representatives of the public interest most frequently relied—equated the public interest with that of consumers.[61] There were at least two reasons for making this equation. First, representatives of the public interest sat on boards that were primarily concerned with the economic interests of capital and labor. It was, therefore, easy for them to assume that their job was to champion the economic interests of the public, which they defined in terms of consumption. But it was also easy for them to treat the public interest and the consumer interest as one and the same because both were interests that all members of society shared.

The contradictions inherent in the various definitions of the public interest did not become apparent during the Progressive Era in large part because no one had anything to gain by separating the consumer and public interests. Those who wanted policies on behalf of consumers, such as the advocates of pure food and drug legislation or municipal control of utilities, found the equation of a consumer interest with a public interest advantageous. The consumer identity might have lost many of its negative connotations, but it had not lost all of them. The legitimacy of the public interest, by contrast, was beyond question. Presenting their programs as ones that were in the public rather than the consumer interest or demanding seats on government commissions for representatives of the public rather than the consumer interest was one way for consumer advocates to increase their chances of success.

Those who opposed giving the consumer any voice in government had even less to gain by separating the public interest from the consumer interest. For one, equating the two made it possible to reject any demand for representation of a distinct consumer interest by arguing that that interest was already adequately represented under the rubric of the public interest. For another, it meant that those who represented the consumer interest did not do so with the same single-mindedness with which the delegates of labor and industry championed their constituencies. Nor should they have. As representatives of the public interest, they were supposed to be above the sorts of interest group politics in which the agents of labor and industry engaged. Any exclusive focus on the consumer interest would have been a violation of their duties.

In the 1930s those who wanted to limit the political influence of the consumer would continue to treat the consumer interest and the public interest as one and the same. But those who wanted to increase that influence would begin to question the strategic value of equating the two. They were only able to do so, however, because the consumer identity had attained a legitimacy that it had lacked in the Progressive Era and, therefore, no longer needed the legitimation that association with the public interest brought. But that new-found legitimacy was in large part due to the earlier association. The equation of *consumer* with *public interest* had played a critical role in removing many of the parasitic connotations that still clung to *consumer* in the early decades of the twentieth century. And, perhaps even more important, it went a long way toward rooting civic identity in the consumer. Once the public interest had been defined in terms of a consumer interest, it did not require much of an intellectual stretch to define *the people* in terms of their consumer identity. For all its disadvantages the Progressive Era equation of *consumer* with *public interest* was an important step in the development of a consumerist worldview.

But, just as the 1930s separation of consumer and public interest depended upon a level of consumer legitimacy which had not existed in the Progressive Era, so too did the Progressive Era equation of the two interests depend upon a more positive version of the consumer. The Progressive Era version of the consumer was in large part a result of the attempt by late-nineteenth-century thinkers to make sense of their rapidly changing social and economic landscape. As these thinkers sought to reconcile their theories with what they observed around them, many found it necessary to rethink the traditional meaning of *consumer*. The result was that by the turn of the century *consumer* could just as easily refer to a victim of the capitalist system or an all-powerful regulator of the economy as it could to a self-indulgent parasite or a corrupter of the body politic. By developing a number of alternatives, late-nineteenth-century political-economic thinkers literally marginalized the traditional definitions, forcing them to inhabit one side of the spectrum of ideas concerning the consumer.

Traditional definitions might have been relegated to one side of the spectrum. But they were still very much in existence. The result was that those who turned their attention to the consumer during the Progressive Era found themselves confronting what amounted to two distinct sets of ideas—an older set, which emphasized production over consumption and treated the consumer as a negative identity, and a newer one, which shifted the economic focus to consumption and defined the consumer in more positive terms. Rather than choosing one set of ideas over another, Progressive Era academics, reformers, and public policy makers usually drew from both the old and the new. The result was a veritable explosion in ways of thinking about the consumer.

While the range of ideas about the consumer in the early twentieth century was remarkable, perhaps even more striking were the various strategies that Progressive Era thinkers developed as they sought to reconcile what were ultimately two irreconcilable intellectual traditions. Nowhere were the difficulties inherent in such attempts more evident than in Simon Patten's efforts to develop a theory of consumption. On the one hand, Patten was more than willing to embrace new ideas about the consumer. Indeed, his theories about expanded consumption as the key to social welfare placed him at the forefront of the new thinking. But, even as he was breaking new intellectual ground, he was not able to free himself from a far older intellectual tradition. The consumer remained for him a problematic identity and consumption a problematic activity. The result was an approach to the consumer and consumption which was frequently ambiguous, sometimes inconsistent, and almost always full of ambivalence.

Patten was certainly not the only turn-of-the-century thinker to have difficulty blending older and newer ideas of the consumer. Indeed, his experience was probably typical. But there were Progressive Era thinkers who did manage to avoid the sorts of problems that Patten encountered. Thorstein Veblen, for example, developed a strategy that proved quite successful, even if it was one that few progressives were prepared to adopt. Veblen had no problem with either the older or the newer definitions of the consumer, but he was very careful to keep the two separate. In his first book he relied exclusively on a traditional version of the consumer. But, when that version proved unsuitable for his second book, he did not hesitate to discard it in favor of a radically different consumer. While Veblen's was perhaps not the most intellectually honest of approaches, it was nevertheless one that allowed him to avoid the sorts of inconsistencies that plagued much Progressive Era thinking on the consumer.

Academics were not the only ones caught in the crossfire of two intellectual traditions battling for ascendancy. Progressive Era reformers and public policy makers also found themselves drawn into the fray. Confronting a wide variety of conflicting ideas about the consumer and consumption, they too had to find ways to reconcile the irreconcilable. Few managed to do so as successfully as did the members of the foremost consumer organization of the period.

The very fact that the National Consumers' League (NCL) was the foremost consumer organization is itself revealing. Its primary aim was not to further the interests of consumers but to harness consumer power on behalf of wage-earning producers. That Progressive Era reformers found it easiest to recognize and organize around their consumer identity if they were doing so on behalf of producers suggests once again that consumer legitimacy had proceeded only so far by the turn of the century. *Consumer* had lost enough of its negative connotations to make it easy for middle-class women to define themselves in terms of that identity. But it retained enough of those connotations to make these women far more comfortable with such an identity if they were using it to improve the lives of disadvantaged producers.

At first glance the NCL approach to consumer organization seemed to be merely a resurrection of an older approach, one that had been in existence for at least a couple hundred years. In the early eighteenth century, for example, British citizens had been more than willing to organize around their consumer identity as they sought to preserve a "moral economy." They had boycotted and even destroyed the shops of individuals whose rising prices, they believed, indicated a selfish desire for private gain at the expense of public well-being. Less than a century later, American colonists had proved just as willing to organize around their consumer identity, this time to resist what they perceived as the tyranny of the mother country. By rejecting the "baubles of Britain" in favor of American-made goods, they hoped to force a change in British colonial policy.[62]

What the eighteenth-century consumer protest movements shared with the NCL effort was a common belief that organized consumers could wield their power on behalf of a moral order and a common conviction that the private act of consumption had important public dimensions. But there were also differences—one of the more important being the extent to which the eighteenth-century movements had equated morality with limited consumption. American opponents of British taxation had worried about the "amazing growth of Luxury" and promised to "discourage and discountenance to the utmost of our power the excessive use of . . . all British and foreign superfluities and manufactures."[63] British advocates of a moral economy—and American opponents of British taxation, for that matter—had engaged in the public destruction of goods, a symbolic act that highlighted their ability to resist their consumer desires.

The NCL, by contrast, expressed little concern over luxury. And its members would probably have had some difficulty decoding the symbolism inherent in the public destruction of goods. Indeed, from an NCL point of view limited consumption, far from being a virtue, could be highly problematic in that it might cost the working poor their jobs. Instead, the NCL's moral consumer was one who purchased only those goods—be they luxuries or necessities—which had been manufactured under acceptable working conditions. As for immoral consumers, they were those whose purchasing decisions involved them, as NCL general-secretary Florence Kelley put it, "in the meanest forms of cruelty, the sacrifice of the weak and the defenseless to the search for cheapness."[64] The NCL might continue to rely on a language of morality. But its definitions of *moral* and *immoral* had little in common with any eighteenth-century understanding of the terms.

The NCL definitions had even less in common with a nineteenth-century understanding of *moral* and *immoral consumption*. While nineteenth-century critics of consumption continued to measure morality in terms of quantity, they added a new criterion. Consumption, they insisted, also had to conform to producerist notions of equity and justice. Thus, committed producerist thinkers such as Sumner and Gilman would assume that immoral consumption was not merely excessive consumption but the excessive consumption of nonproducers. And they would agree that moral consumption was not only limited consumption but the limited consumption of producers.[65]

NCL definitions of *moral* and *immoral consumption,* by contrast, included no such producerist criteria. Indeed, its definitions constituted an implicit rejection of such criteria. If one followed the logic of the NCL definitions, then abundant consumption by nonproducers—as long as it consisted of unadulterated products manufactured under acceptable labor conditions—was moral. And, perhaps even more significantly, limited consumption of adulterated and sweated goods by producers was not.

The NCL redefinitions of *moral* and *immoral* highlighted the ways in which Progressive Era thinkers tended to blend both older and newer ideas about the consumer. The language of morality on which the NCL relied had been in existence for hundreds of years. But it was a language that was no longer appropriate for discussions of the actual consumption of goods—if the writings of the NCL general-secretary were any indication. Kelley could be fierce in her condemnation of irresponsible purchasing. When it came to consumption itself, however, she preferred a far more neutral language, a preference that she shared with a growing number of political economists.[66]

Kelley's preference for a neutral language of consumption was not the only indication of her reliance on new political-economic thinking about consumption and the consumer. Her conviction that "the power of the

purchaser . . . is potentially unlimited" and that "all of us, all the time are deciding by our expenditures what industries shall survive" was one that had far
more in common with the new economic thinking than the old. Her assumption that the best way to define the "whole people" was as consumers
departed radically from earlier producerist definitions of *the people*. Finally,
her recognition of certain consummatory rights, among them the right to
have "goods as they are represented, and to have food pure and garments free
from poison and infection" and her assumption that the government had to
play a role in guaranteeing these rights were assumptions that were all in line
with the new thinking on the consumer.[67]

Kelley might have been more than willing to embrace new thinking about
the consumer and consumption. But, like most of her Progressive Era contemporaries, she blended newer ideas with older ones. Her consumers, for
example, were as flaw-ridden as those of Sumner and Gilman, capable of "ex-
traordinary incompetence," "willing ignorance," "cupidity," and "credulity."
And they were as capable of threatening social well-being as Gilman's and
Sumner's consumers had ever been. "Unintelligent," "unenlightened and un-
organized" consumers, Kelley insisted, were responsible "for some of the
worst evils from which wage-earners suffer" because they "persist in buying in
the cheapest market, regardless of how cheapness is brought about." And they
were responsible for the existence of numerous adulterated and even dangerous goods on the market. "Because the purchasing public, on the whole,
prefers at present not to know the facts, we are all in danger of eating aniline
dyes in tomatoes . . . salicylic acid in our canned peas and other vegetables"
and wearing "germs of tuberculosis and of countless other diseases in our
outer garments." As far as Kelley was concerned, "willingly ignorant" consumers had to carry "a heavy share of the guilt of the exploiting manufacturer
and the adulterating distributor."[68]

Kelley's portrait of the consumer was no more flattering than those of
nineteenth-century producerist thinkers such as Sumner and Gilman. But one
critical difference separated Kelley's negative portrayal from theirs. While
Sumner's consumer was extravagant and Gilman's was greedy, Kelley's was
merely ignorant. What was so significant about such a fault was that it was an
eminently correctable one. Kelley's consumers only needed to be educated—
a task that the National Consumers' League was more than willing to under-
take. Once educated, they would cease to exert their baleful influence on
society.[69] Neither Gilman nor Sumner, by contrast, ever treated their highly

problematic consumer as one who was capable of rehabilitation. The goal, as they both saw it, was not a society in which well-behaved consumers coexisted with well-behaved producers but one in which all inhabitants were first and foremost producers.

Sumner and Gilman found it impossible to make room for consumers in their ideal society primarily because both assumed that the consumer was the antithesis of the producer. Sumner, for example, contrasted "idle and improvident" consumers with the "industrious and prudent" producers. The contrast between Gilman's consumers and producers was even more pronounced. Her producer was an individual characterized by "creative energy," while her consumer was one who "lightly destroys." Her producer was "not seeking to get something into himself, but to put something out of himself." Just the opposite was true of her consumers. Given to "inordinate" "unnatural greed" and "personal selfishness"—"horse-leech daughters," Gilman called them—they were determined "to get as much as possible and to give as little as possible!"[70] As long as Sumner and Gilman defined the consumer as the antithesis of the producer, they could not possibly make room for consumers in their ideal order.

By contrast, the antithesis that Kelley constructed was one that allowed her to include consumers along with producers in her ideal order. In her view the opposite of *bad consumer* was not *good producer* but *good consumer*. What was so significant about Kelley's antithesis was that it presupposed the possibility of good consumers, something that neither Sumner nor Gilman had been willing, or indeed able, to do.

Like the NCL definition of *moral consumption*, Kelley's juxtaposition of "bad" and "good" consumers highlighted the extent to which Progressive Era thinkers relied on both older and newer ideas about the consumer. And it also showed one way to reconcile the irreconcilable. Kelley's redefinition of older concepts in radically new ways allowed her to avoid the inconsistencies and ambiguities that had plagued Patten's attempt to blend older and newer ideas. And it enabled her to rethink the consumer without ever seeming to step outside the mainstream. The result was an approach to the consumer that was as radical as Patten's but one that was far less alien to turn-of-the-century Americans.

The consumerist implications of Kelley's language were evident in her definition not only of the consumer but also of the producer. In her lexicon *producer* meant manufacturer and distributor. Rarely did she use the term to refer to the working class, preferring instead such terms as *wage earners, workers,* and *employés.*[71] The obvious question is why would a left-leaning progressive who championed the working class adopt a definition of *producer* which had far more in common with the definition of a classical liberal such as William Graham Sumner than that of a more left-leaning thinker such as Henry George. The answer lies in the changing meaning of *producer.* And it is an answer that highlights the growing influence of a consumerist way of thinking.

In the early nineteenth century, when the vast majority of individuals had been either artisans or farmers, it had been relatively easy to distinguish between those who "eat and produce not" and those who "labor and produce," as Sumner would later put it.[72] The mechanization of industry, however, changed all that. As more and more labor was performed by machines, it became increasingly difficult to define exactly what a producer was—never mind who was and who was not entitled to claim the label.

Despite the growing gap between those who owned machines and those who tended them, *producer* remained as important a badge of honor as ever. Not surprisingly, therefore, producerist thinkers across the political spectrum fought fiercely for their particular definition of the producer. Those on the left such as Henry George insisted that the quintessential producer was a wage worker. Those on the right such as William Graham Sumner assumed that individuals who had transformed their labor into capital had the best claim to the producer label.

Veblen was one of the first producerist thinkers of the late nineteenth century to avoid the entire issue. He did so by treating *producer* as a historical term, using it to refer primarily to those who had worked in the "system of handicraft and neighborhood industry" that had existed "before the machine's régime and before modern business enterprise." When it came to those responsible for production in an industrialized economy, however, he almost never used the term *producer.* Instead, he preferred to distinguish between *businessmen* and *workmen.*[73]

Ironically, it was Veblen's producerist leanings that prevented him from using *producer.* For Veblen the term remained a badge of honor. But "in conventional speech," he regretfully acknowledged, "'producer' means the owner of industrial plant, not the workmen employed nor the mechanical apparatus about which they are employed."[74] Unwilling to use *producer* to refer to the business interests and, because of the prevailing conventions, unable to use it to refer to those who retained an "instinct of workmanship," he decided to avoid the term altogether.

Veblen's refusal to identify members of the existing economy as producers had certain consumerist implications. Because he did not participate in the usual producerist debate over who was and was not entitled to be classified as a producer, he avoided the usual producerist definition of *consumer* as the antithesis of the producer. But, once *consumer* ceased to be synonymous with *nonproducer,* it became possible to conceive of an alternative to the traditional producerist division of the economy into producing workers and capitalists, on one side, and nonproducing consumers, on the other. In Veblen's economy it was exploited wage workers and consumers who shared one category, while exploiting businessmen occupied another.

Unlike Veblen, both Ely and Bellamy were willing to use the term *producer.* What is striking about their use of the term, however, is that it was more frequent in their later, more socialist writings. One might easily conclude from such an observation that Bellamy's and Ely's increasing use of the term was motivated by an increasingly producerist outlook. A closer examination of the ways in which they used it, however, suggests that the motivation was not so much an increasing producerism as it was an increasingly consumerist socialism.

Bellamy used *producer* infrequently—far preferring terms such as *worker, workingman,* and *working people* or *capitalist.* But, when he did employ the term, he did not do so, as earlier producerist thinkers had done, to identify his "good guys." In Bellamy's lexicon *producer* could just as easily refer to capitalists as it could to workers.[75] His willingness to apply the term to both his heroes and his villains suggests the extent to which, for Bellamy at least, *producer* had become a neutral term, one that no longer possessed the powerful positive connotations that it had once carried.

Ely's use of the term represented an even more fundamental break with producerist notions of good and bad. In both *The Labor Movement in America* (1886) and *The Strength and Weakness of Socialism* (1894) Ely used the term *producer* infrequently. What is significant about his use of the term in the two books, however, is that he relied on two fundamentally different definitions. In his book on labor he treated *producer,* in good producerist fashion, as a badge of honor. It was the heroes of his story, the independent artisans, for whom he reserved the label. Eight years later, however, he had ceased to reserve the term for his heroes. Instead, it was the villains of his piece, the businessmen, whom he labeled producers.[76]

What Bellamy, Ely, Veblen, and Kelly's definitions had in common was that none of them presumed the positive connotations so long associated with *producer*. The ease with which all four thinkers disregarded these connotations highlights the extent to which the legitimizing power of the producer was already in decline by the late nineteenth century. It was a decline that had important implications for a consumerist worldview. Only if the producer ceased to be the touchstone of all social value would it be possible to recognize the nonproducing consumer as a legitimate political identity.

In at least three ways the Progressive Era represented a critical juncture in the development of a consumerist perspective. First, it was during this period that the producerist way of thinking was finally forced to share the political-economic stage with a way of thinking which only a short time earlier had been the purview of utopian writers and eccentric iconoclasts. Only in the Progressive Era did intellectuals figure out how to challenge the producerist paradigm. And only then did academics and reformers make positive definitions of the consumer part of the mainstream political-economic discourse, even though these definitions had been in existence for some time.[77]

But it was not only the breakup of the producerist monopoly on political-economic thought which made the period a turning point. By the end of the Progressive Era the generation of thinkers which had pioneered new ways of thinking about the consumer was giving way to a new generation of thinkers. Veblen, Bellamy, Ely, Patten, and Kelley were all members of a generation of thinkers which shaped American thought from the 1880s until the 1910s. Those who would shape the political-economic discourse concerning the consumer in the 1920s and 1930s were, for the most part, members of a new generation.

Finally, the period was a turning point because it saw a shift in focus from economics to politics. The Progressive Era generation of thinkers had been primarily interested in the economic implications of placing the consumer at the center of the political economy. The consumer legitimacy that they had established was an economic legitimacy. And the producerist principles that they had called into question were economic principles. The next generation of thinkers, by contrast, was far more interested in the political implications of placing the consumer at the center of the political economy. It was they who called for a political system that revolved around the consumer-citizen. And it was they who constructed a consumerist alternative to the producerist paradigm that their predecessors had so effectively challenged. In so doing, they played a critical role in the transformation of classical liberalism into its modern American counterpart.

CHAPTER FOUR

Politicizing the Consumer, 1909–1923

By the second decade of the twentieth century the consumer had become a legitimate economic identity. Economists were giving the same attention to consumption that they had once reserved for production. Social reformers were harnessing the consumer's purchasing power on behalf of society's dispossessed. And policy makers were coming to believe that the economic interests of the nation's citizens included a consuming as well as a producing interest.

It soon became clear, however, that economic legitimacy had political implications. If, for example, consumption was as important an economic activity as production, then was the government's all but exclusive focus on production justified? If consumers had responsibilities, then did they not also have rights? And, if the consumer interest was not only one of the interests of the nation's citizens but the one interest that they all had in common, then did it not make more sense to organize the political system around the consumer rather than the producer? These were the sorts of political questions to which a handful of thinkers began turning their attention in the 1910s.

The thinkers who addressed such questions in the 1910s were part of a larger intellectual movement, one committed to the reconstruction of classical liberal theory. According to the new liberals, the problem with classical liberalism was that in the highly complex economy of the twentieth century its means—self-interest, competitive market forces, the profit motive—had ceased to be compatible with its ends, broad-based prosperity. The task, as they saw it, was to revise liberal theory so that it would once again promote a prosperous society.

Most new liberals agreed that one of the reasons for liberalism's shortcomings was that the economy had ceased to be competitive. But, although they could agree on what ailed liberalism, the new liberals found it far more difficult to achieve any consensus about a cure. For some, such as Louis Brandeis and his followers, the solution was to restore competition. But, while they might share their classical liberal predecessor's faith in competition, they parted company in their conviction that an active government offered the best hope of a competitive marketplace. For others, particularly those who were drawn to Herbert Croly's new journal of liberal opinion, the *New Republic,* the problem was that competition itself was flawed. They, too, looked to government, not to restore competition but to replace it as the regulator of the market.[1]

The *New Republic* liberals' willingness to rethink the place of competition in a liberal economy represented a major departure from classical economic theory. In the classical liberal view it was competition that made the economy function equitably. It protected the consumer by rewarding those who met the needs of consumers and punishing those who did not. And it promoted economic efficiency by favoring those who were efficient and penalizing those who were not. Not surprisingly, therefore, classical liberals had been adamantly opposed to government intervention in the economy. As far as they were concerned, any government intervention would interfere with competitive market mechanisms, thereby reducing productivity and efficiency and compromising social well-being.

The *New Republic* liberals rejected the classical liberal faith in competition. Far from maximizing efficiency, they argued, competition frustrated it, resulting in "unnecessary enterprise" and "the chaos, the welter, the strategy of industrial war." Competition encouraged "needless duplications of plants, the useless sending of cross freights, the absurd vagaries of a boundless, competitive advertising." And the result of all this waste was that industry was able to produce only a fraction of what it was technologically capable of producing.[2]

But limited productivity, the *New Republic* liberals insisted, was not the only cost of competition which the community had to bear. It also had to suffer the antisocial behavior that competition encouraged among members of the business community. "There are a hundred ways of competing," Walter Lippmann warned, "to produce the highest quality at the lowest cost proved to be the most troublesome and least rewarding form of competition. To cheapen the quality, subtract value that does not appear on the surface, lower the standards of workmanship, to adulterate, in short, was a more 'natural' method of competition than the noble Platonic method which economists talked about." Far from channeling self-interest in a socially beneficial direction, the *New Republic* liberals concluded, competition encouraged the most corrupt of business practices.[3]

Nevertheless, the *New Republic* liberals were well aware that an economy no longer regulated by competition would have to be regulated by something else. So, they looked to government to do the job that competition had once done, to punish those who pursued self-interest at the expense of the community, to reward those whose self-interest resulted in socially beneficial behavior, to maximize efficiency, and to discourage waste. For Croly this meant taxation of excess profits and the creation of regulatory commissions. For his editorial associates at the *New Republic,* Walter Lippmann and Walter Weyl, it meant government regulation and, in some industries, public ownership. For left liberals in the post–World War I period it meant "economic planning," namely the substitution of the visible hand of government for both the invisible hand of the market and the visible hand of business.[4]

Although the *New Republic* liberals parted company with classical liberals over such seemingly fundamental issues as government regulation and the value of competition, what is striking is the extent to which the two groups shared certain political assumptions. Like their classical predecessors, the *New Republic* liberals defined the good society in terms of economic prosperity. Like their predecessors, they assumed that the key to maximizing productivity was maximizing efficiency. Croly even retained a faith in the socially beneficial results of self-interest. He was confident that "a corporation management which was thoroughly alive to its own interest would endeavor to arrange a scale of prices, which, while affording a sufficient profit, would encourage the increased use of the product." But he was as aware as any classical liberal that unchecked self-interest could lead to antisocial behavior. "Short-sighted management," he admitted, "may prefer to reap large profits for a short time and at the expense of the increased use of its product or service." Classical liberals had relied on competition to discourage such self-interested behavior. Croly, however, was convinced that government could channel self-interest in socially beneficial directions as surely as competition ever had. And, what was more, it could do so without the wasteful side effects of competition.[5]

Croly could call for government regulation and still remain a liberal because regulation for him was a means to an end rather than an end in itself. Indeed, he was quick to stress the dangers of confusing the two. "Rigid and comprehensive official supervision" of the corporations might "eradicate many actual and possible abuses," he admitted. But it would also "be just as likely to damage the efficiency which has been no less characteristic of these corporate operations." "The only reason for recognizing the large corporations as desirable economic institutions," he emphasized, "is just their supposed economic efficiency; and if the means taken to regulate them impair that efficiency, the government is merely adopting in a roundabout way a policy of destruction."[6] Croly's point was clear. Neither government regulation nor competition were ends in themselves. They were merely means. And as such they should be abandoned as soon as they ceased to promote the real liberal end, a prosperous economy and, even more to the point, a prosperous people.

Weyl and Lippmann were as intent as Croly on distinguishing between means and ends. Even more than Croly, the two were convinced that socialistic methods could play an important role in constructing a liberal order. Both, for example, believed that the creation of such an order might require government ownership. But both insisted that the goal, as Weyl put it, "was not government ownership for itself, but merely as much government ownership, regulation, or control as may be necessary to a true socialization of industry." Even Weyl's use of the term *socialization of industry* highlighted the extent to which the new liberals were willing to draft socialist means on behalf of liberal ends. In demanding the "socialization of industry," Weyl was not calling for the nationalization of industry, the confiscation of property, the redistribution of wealth, or the abolition of a capitalist system. All he meant by the term was the "viewing of our manifold business life from the standpoint of society and not solely from that of the present beneficiaries or directors of industry." And he meant "a coördination of business as will permanently give the greatest happiness and the highest development to the largest number of individuals, and to society as a whole."[7] According to such a definition, Adam Smith had also been seeking the socialization of industry.

Indeed, his competitive market mechanisms had been designed to deliver nothing less.

New liberals were intent on distinguishing between means and ends in large part because their late-nineteenth-century predecessors had failed to do so. As industrialization radically altered the economic landscape, classical liberals had responded by clinging ever more tightly to laissez-faire principles. In so doing, they had created a political order that functioned for the well-being of a few while consigning the many to abject poverty, dangerous working conditions, and unsafe, unsanitary living conditions. In an economy in which liberal means ceased to be productive of liberal ends, late-nineteenth-century classical liberals had found it necessary to choose one or the other. They had chosen liberal means, in the process sacrificing liberal ends.

The new liberals, however, were unwilling to make this sacrifice. If liberal means ceased to result in liberal ends, then, the new liberals insisted, it made far more sense to jettison the means. Thus, they rejected laissez-faire principles in favor of extensive government involvement in the economy. Doing so, however, did not make the new liberals socialists. On the contrary, it made them better liberals than their late-nineteenth-century predecessors had been.

Nowhere was this distinction between means and ends more evident than in the emphasis on the consumer by two of the *New Republic* liberals. Walter Lippmann and Walter Weyl were certainly not the first liberals to give priority to the consumer. No less a liberal theorist than Adam Smith had stressed that "consumption is the sole end and purpose of all production." And he had insisted that "the interest of the producer ought to be attended to, only so far as it may be necessary for promoting that of the consumer."[8] Ultimately, however, Smith believed that the two interests were related. In his view the best way to promote the interest of the consumer was to attend to the interest of the producer. Why? Because producers were interested in maximizing profit, and, according to Smith, the best way to maximize profit was to give consumers exactly what they wanted. For Smith, then, a producer focus had been a means to an end, a way to construct a political economy that functioned on behalf of the consumer.

So, too, had been his celebration of laissez-faire principles. Like his producer focus, Smith's advocacy of such principles was motivated by his desire to construct a consumer-oriented political economy. Without government intervention in the economy, he reasoned, it would be consumers who would decide what should and should not be produced. It would be consumers who would punish those who manufactured poor-quality goods or attempted to sell goods at inflated prices. And it would be consumers who would reward productive and efficient entrepreneurs. In advocating a laissez-faire system, Smith might have freed producers from government tyranny but only to deliver them into the hands of a much less forgiving tyrant, the consumer.

The consumer's power, however, was not absolute. It depended upon two preconditions. The market had to be a competitive one, and the consumer had to be informed. Only in a competitive market would consumers be able to punish a producer who did not produce high-quality, low-cost goods by taking their business elsewhere. And only if consumers were informed about the products they purchased would they be able to distinguish high quality from low, good value from bad. As long as those two preconditions were met, however, Smith had been confident that in a laissez-faire economy consumers would be in charge.

Walter Lippmann did not share Smith's confidence. "The consumer," he told his readers in *Drift and Mastery*, "is sometimes represented as the person whose desires govern industry." Lippmann, however, was "sure that few consumers feel any of that sense of power which economists say is theirs." Nor should they. Lippmann's observations of the modern economy convinced him that it was not the consumer who dictated to the producer but the reverse. "The consumer takes what he can get at the price he can afford. He is told what he wants, and then he wants it."[9] If consumers had ever ruled the marketplace—and Lippmann doubted that they had—producers were now in full control.

Why were producers in full control of the economy? Why was it that "in our intricate civilization," as Lippmann put it, "the purchaser can't pit himself against the producer?" The answer, for Lippmann, was quite simple. Consumers lacked both the knowledge and the power "to make the bargain a fair one." Lippmann blamed this lack of power on the classical liberal faith in the ability of competition to channel self-interest into socially beneficial directions. Competition, he insisted, was just as likely to encourage adulteration, misrepresentation of products, shoddy workmanship, and price agreements. It was not long, Lippmann concluded, before "the consumer began to realize that he couldn't trust to the naïve notions of the nineteenth century."[10]

If Lippmann's consumers lacked power because competition was a less than perfect economic mechanism, they lacked knowledge because the modern economy had grown impossibly complex. The consumer, he pointed out, had neither the time nor the expertise to "candle every egg he buys, test the milk, inquire into the origins of the meat, analyze the canned food, distinguish the shoddy, find out whether the newspapers are lying, avoid meretricious plays, and choose only railroads equipped with safety devices." And the one source of information most readily available to consumers, advertisements, only compounded the problem by violating the separation of economic powers on which Smith's liberal economy had depended. As Lippmann saw it, advertising was nothing less than "the effort of business men to take charge of consumption as well as production. They are not content to supply a demand, as the text-books say; they educate the demand as well." In such an economy, Lippmann concluded, consumers became "a fickle and superstitious mob, incapable of any real judgment as to what it wants or how it is to get what it thinks it would like." Little wonder they were incapable of performing the regulatory role that Smith had assigned to them.[11]

Although Lippmann doubted that consumers had the economic power necessary to bring business to heel, he did not believe that they were powerless. By organizing politically, they could force government to "impose upon business a maximum of quality and a minimum of cost." Not market forces but politics, he concluded, would be "the chief method by which the consumer enforces his interests upon the industrial system."[12]

What is striking about Lippmann's call for politically organized consumers is how supremely liberal it was. The entire Smithian economic edifice had rested on the assumption that consumers could and would control the market. Lippmann had shown that, in a highly industrialized corporate economy, economic control was impossible. He had not done so, however, in an effort to topple the liberal edifice. On the contrary, his goal was to repair its faulty foundation. If consumers had lost economic control, then they had to "develop new instruments for controlling the market." And, he insisted, they were well on their way to doing just that. Politically organized consumers, he predicted, "are going to dominate the government." Once they did so, they could use government regulation instead of market forces to keep business in line.[13] Their old "instrument" had been purchasing power. Their new one would be political power.

Lippmann's call for politically organized consumers was not only supremely liberal; it was also consumerist. Despite his brief encounter with socialist politics (Lippmann had been a member of the Socialist Party and had served as assistant to the Socialist mayor of Schenectady)—or perhaps because of it—Lippmann looked to a day when consumers, not labor, would control the government, and government regulation would be on behalf of the consuming rather than the laboring population. But, despite his willingness to grant consumers all but exclusive control of the state, he did not abandon labor. He remained a strong proponent of powerful unions, convinced that "labor is compelled to organize its power in order not to be trodden by gigantic economic forces." He blamed employers rather than workers for much of the so-called labor violence. He even believed that workers should "participate in the control of industry."[14]

Such pro-labor attitudes were not a remnant of Lippmann's brief sojourn into producer-oriented, socialist politics. On the contrary, they were an integral part of his rapidly developing liberal and consumerist worldview. Underlying his ideas about labor was the assumption that workers would best be served not by socialism but by a disciplined capitalism. It was an assumption that he shared with Adam Smith, albeit for different reasons. According to Smith, employers would treat their workers fairly because it was in their best interest to do so. If employers abused their workers, they would soon find themselves without any employees. If they treated their workers fairly, they would be able to count on a large supply of eager, diligent workers. Realizing that profits depended upon good labor relations, employers would take great pains to address the needs and concerns of their labor force.

Smith's theory that capitalism was as good for workers as it was for employers was one of the first of his theories to go by the wayside. Classical economists, from Malthus to Ricardo to Marx, had all insisted that a capitalist economy, far from being benevolent, inevitably relegated a large portion of the population to utter misery. Indeed, it had been their insistence on the inevitability of such misery which had earned for economics the unflattering sobriquet *dismal science.*

Unlike the dismal scientists, Lippmann believed that capitalism could be made to function in such a way that it would benefit workers as well as employers. But he did not place his faith in Smithian self-interest. In an industrial economy, he maintained, self-interest was no more capable of preventing the exploitation of workers than it was of encouraging the production of high-quality, low-priced goods. Why? Because business had grown so powerful that neither consumers nor workers could keep it in line.[15] The task, then, was to figure out how to increase both consumers' and workers' power so that both could once again perform the function that Smith had assigned to them. The key for Lippmann was collective action. Like politically organized consumers, unionized workers would have the power to keep business in line. And, once both groups had that power, liberalism would cease to be an outdated theory with little relevance to an industrial economy. Instead, it would become a theory that could be used to establish an economic order capable of producing abundant industrial wealth and, even more important, distributing that wealth fairly.

At first glance Lippmann's approach to the economy seems remarkably similar to that of the tripartite commissions. Yet there were critical differences that revealed, once again, both how liberal and how consumerist Lippmann's approach was. The organizers of tripartite commissions had taken a tentative step in a consumerist direction when they decided to appoint representatives for the public interest. But their failure to agree on a definition of the public interest—was it the consumer's interest, or was it the interest that all citizens had in common?—largely neutralized whatever consumerist implications their recognition of a public interest might have had. Ultimately, their commissions were producerist bodies. The representatives of business and labor worked out compromises concerning such producer issues as workmen's compensation and regulation of the trusts.[16] As for those representing the public interest, their job was not to bring new issues to the table but to figure out whether the public's interests would best be served by siding with labor or business.

If the tripartite organizers' definition of the public interest meant that they were never quite sure whether society was divided into two groups or three, Lippmann suffered from no such confusion. For him the public was a distinct interest group, namely consumers. It was a definition that had far-reaching consumerist ramifications. At the most obvious level making *public* synonymous with *consumer* radically altered the notion of a "public interest." No longer did that interest evoke images of apolitical, disinterested citizens making decisions on behalf of a greater good. Now the public interest was as narrow and self-serving as the interests of labor and business. And, as such, it could be pursued with the same sort of relentless, self-interested determination that had once been the exclusive prerogative of labor and business. "The public," Lippmann warned, "is capable of oppression." "And," he continued, "when I say that consumers are going to dominate the government I do not state the fact with unmixed joy. There will be a tyranny of the majority for which minorities will have to prepare."[17]

Equating *public* with *consumers* also had certain class implications. When progressives had defined the public interest broadly, as an interest that all members of society shared, they had constructed a category that transcended class. Lippmann rejected that definition in favor of one that treated the public not only as a far narrower category but, even more important, as a category rooted in an economic interest, that of consuming. And he positioned his public with its narrow economic interests between two other groups with narrow economic interests, namely the working and the business classes. Lippmann's consuming public, it would seem, was nothing other than a middle class. And, more significantly, it was a version of the middle class which defined that class as the one whose interests were rooted not in production—as were those of workers and capitalists—but in consumption.

By the mid–twentieth century Lippmann's definition of the middle class as the class whose interests were most closely connected with issues of consumption would be commonplace. In the 1910s it was anything but. Into the early twentieth century the vast majority of Americans remained reluctant to relinquish their Victorian definition of *middle class,* which defined that class in terms of moral rather than economic interests. Most Americans in the 1920s and 1930s would have recognized Lippmann's definition. But progressives remained far more comfortable with the sort of definition on which Florence Kelley had relied when she called on members of the middle class to use their consuming power not in their own interests so much as in the interests of a moral economy.[18]

Equating *public* with *consumer* not only redefined the public interest—and, for that matter, the middle class. It also weakened the producerist hold on political discourse. In the tripartite scheme the focus was inevitably on producer interests. Should workers work eight or ten hours a day? Should business have to pay workers who had been injured on the job? Labor and business might not agree on how to answer such questions, but they nevertheless could agree that these were the questions that had to be answered. Once the consumer entered the political arena as an equal player, however, it became far more likely that consumer-oriented issues would command a hearing. Consumers had merely to join forces with either workers or capitalists to push through their own agenda.

Whereas conservatives were more likely to suggest that consumers were better served by joining with capitalists, Lippmann was convinced that consumers and workers shared a common interest. Both groups, he maintained, "are interested directly in making industry produce the greatest quantity and the best quality of goods at the least possible cost in effort." Why? Because it was they who "pay all the cost of waste, parasitism and inefficiency" in the form of higher prices and lower wages. But once consumers and workers were powerful enough to prevent business from "cover[ing] waste by reducing wages or raising prices," then business would have no alternative but to eliminate wasteful practices. The result would be a more efficient and thus more productive industrial system. And it was just such a system, Lippmann insisted, that was the real goal of both organized consumers and organized labor.[19]

Lippmann was not the first to suggest that consumers and workers shared a common interest. Florence Kelley, for one, had also envisioned a consumer-labor alliance. Hers, however, had been an alliance devoted to producerist goals. She called on consumers to use their purchasing power to improve conditions in the workplace. Lippmann's alliance, by contrast, was not designed to end exploitation in the workplace. In his view that was organized labor's job. Instead, "consumers and workingmen" had a common interest in seeing industry substitute what Veblen had called "industrial values" for "pecuniary" ones.[20] Or, as Patten might have put it, they had a common interest in a disciplined capitalism.

That Lippmann was able to construct a consumerist theory in which the ideas of a strident critic of capitalism such as Veblen seemed to merge with those of an enthusiastic champion of business such as Patten is remarkable. Ultimately, however, the achievement was not so much his as Walter Weyl's. Lippmann's consumerist sympathies turned out to be as short-lived as his socialist ones, acquired while writing *Drift and Mastery* and dispensed with shortly thereafter. Even more to the point, they came largely from Walter Weyl. And, if Lippmann's consumerist worldview ultimately differed from that of Weyl, it was because Lippmann's genius lay in his ability not only to recognize and borrow good ideas but also to adapt these ideas to suit his purpose. It was a talent of which Weyl was wary. "Walter has the faculty for taking what he can without giving any credit whatsoever," Weyl once complained. "I have not the slightest desire to be exploited at his pleasure."[21]

Weyl had taken his first steps toward a consumerist worldview in 1890, the year after Lippmann was born, when he began studying economics at the Wharton School of Business. It was not long before Weyl came under the influence of Simon Patten. Indeed, it was Patten who got Weyl a fellowship to graduate school. And, although Weyl did not write his dissertation under Patten's direction, he nevertheless credited Patten with being responsible for "the very best of my poor stock of political and social philosophy." Patten's influence continued well after Weyl had left Wharton. When *The New Democracy* came out, Weyl wrote Patten that the original idea for the book was to "simplify the first chapter of your *New Basis [of Civilization]* and to give it a statistical foundation."[22]

But Weyl also had more than a passing familiarity with Veblen's ideas. Indeed, if much of his cure for society's ills came from Patten, much of his diagnosis came from Veblen. According to Weyl, the reason why the phenomenal increase in the nation's productive capabilities had not brought an end to poverty was because industry was controlled by a "plutocracy." It was a term that Veblen would have appreciated. Even more to the point, it was a term whose definition came straight from the pages of *The Theory of Business Enterprise*. As Weyl explained it, "the plutocracy stands for 'business,' which is concerned uniquely with profits, and not, like industry, with production. Business means gaining money, not making things. Business destroys, when it pays to destroy, as it upbuilds when it pays to upbuild. Whether profits are secured through monopoly, adulteration, advertised poisoning, or the making of good bread and good shoes at fair prices, the end of business is the same—the maximum of profits."[23]

Ultimately, Weyl relied more on Patten's theories than he did on Veblen's. But his Veblenian leanings proved to be important because they helped him bring Patten's excessively optimistic outlook into line with the harsh realities of industrial capitalism. Indeed, much of the power of Weyl's analysis came from his ability to navigate a middle ground between Patten's panegyric to corporate capitalism and Veblen's excoriation of it.

Finding that middle ground was no easy matter considering the fundamental differences between Patten's and Veblen's worldviews. Indeed, even when the two economists began with the same premise, as on occasion they did, they inevitably arrived at radically different conclusions. Both, for example, adopted an evolutionary approach to the economy. But Patten assumed that evolution was in the direction of progress, as an economy of deficit gave way to a surplus economy. The evolution that Veblen observed was not from deficit to surplus but, rather, from a handicraft to a business economy. And he had his doubts that the latter was an improvement over the former.

Similarly, both might blame misery on "habits of thought" or "mental habits," rather than any deficiency in the nation's productive capabilities.[24] But in Patten's view the problem was that outdated mental habits rooted in self-interest and competition had not yet given way to the sorts of cooperative, altruistic mental habits demanded by a surplus economy. Veblen, by contrast, insisted that the problem was not the failure to develop new habits of thought but the disappearance of old ones. It was the substitution of pecuniary values for an older instinct of workmanship which accounted for the gap between the productive potential of the industrial system and what it actually produced.

Finally, both assumed that efficiency was the key to an economy of abundance. But Patten assumed not only that efficiency was increasing but also that the trusts were largely responsible for that improvement. Veblen, by contrast, was convinced that efficiency was on the decline. And, more to the point, he insisted that trusts, far from maximizing efficiency and productivity, were far more likely to frustrate it.

That Patten and Veblen could begin with similar ideas but end up with radically different conclusions is not merely an interesting intellectual phenomenon. The two were the foremost Progressive Era economists developing theories with significant consumerist implications. Their theories would go a long way toward determining what form a consumer-oriented political agenda would take. If consumerist thinkers adopted Patten's reasoning, they would identify a disciplined corporate capitalism as the most consumer-oriented of systems. If they accepted a Veblenian view of how the economy functioned, they would be much more skeptical about the potential of corporate capitalism to serve the consuming population and be much more likely to demand extensive government control of industry on behalf of that population.

In the 1920s and 1930s consumerist left liberals would be quick to acknowledge their intellectual debt to Veblen.[25] And rightly so. To Veblen they owed much of their critique of capitalism. But the same thinkers remained largely unaware that they also owed an intellectual debt to Patten. It was from Patten that they got two of their basic concepts, their idea of an economy of abundance and their theory of cultural lag.

That they recognized their intellectual debt to Veblen and not to Patten is not particularly surprising. Late in the 1910s Veblen was enjoying a brief renaissance. H. L. Mencken reported that Veblen "was all over *The Nation, The Dial, The New Republic*" and that "everyone of intellectual pretensions read his works." *The Theory of the Leisure Class* was reissued, and in 1921 *The Engineers and the Price System,* the Veblen work most frequently mentioned by consumerist thinkers, appeared. When the latter was reissued in 1932, it became a best-seller.[26]

Whereas consumerist thinkers in the 1920s and 1930s, more often than not, read Veblen in the original, they tended to get their Patten ideas second-hand. Most of Patten's books were out of print by the 1920s. And the writings that were still in print, specifically a collection of economic essays edited by Rexford Tugwell, were hardly likely to appeal to a wide audience.[27] But, if few consumerist thinkers were reading Patten in the original, most of them had already absorbed many of Patten's ideas. That they had already done so was largely due to Walter Weyl.

Anyone with left liberal leanings in the 1920s would have been familiar with Weyl's ideas. Weyl had been one of the foremost progressive intellectuals, his *New Democracy* identified by Theodore Roosevelt as one of the two "true books of the [progressive] movement" (the other being Croly's *Promise of American Life*). He had been a prominent political journalist, whose articles appeared in all the major publications of the day.[28] And he had been one of the founding editors of the *New Republic,* the journal to which consumerist thinkers in the 1920s and 1930s looked for both inspiration and an outlet for their articles. As one of the original editors, Weyl left his stamp not only on the magazine but also on his colleagues. It was from Weyl, for example, that Lippmann took his Patten ideas.[29] And Lippmann incorporated those ideas into yet another one of the major Progressive Era publications written by a *New Republic* editor, *Drift and Mastery.* For a number of reasons, then, Weyl was primarily responsible for making Patten's ideas a part of mainstream left-liberal thought by the 1920s. Yet, because most left liberals got their Patten ideas second- and even thirdhand, they were largely unaware of the origin of those ideas.

Weyl may have been instrumental in transmitting Patten's ideas, but he did not transmit them without significant modifications. And it was Weyl's modifications that gave Patten's ideas their appeal to 1920s left liberals. In their original form Patten's ideas were pro-capitalist and, if not anti-consumer, at least ambivalent about consumers. When Weyl got through with them, however, these ideas had become the foundation of both a thoroughgoing critique of capitalism and a consumer-oriented political theory.

In constructing his consumerist political theory, Weyl began with several assumptions that came directly from Patten. He took for granted that a deficit economy had given way to one characterized by surplus. He agreed with Patten that certain "mental habits" were appropriate for each economic stage. Following Patten's lead, he identified mental habits rooted in struggle and conflict as those most appropriate for a deficit economy, insisting that a surplus economy would demand a more cooperative ethos. Finally, he blamed existing misery on cultural lag. Only when the mental habits appropriate for an economy of scarcity gave way to those more suitable for a surplus economy would the full potential of the nation's phenomenal productivity be realized.

Such ideas were not inherently consumerist. But they did have significant consumerist potential, which Weyl developed. Weyl reasoned that, if a deficit economy was one in which the members of society were forced to struggle over scarce goods, then the most useful mental habits in such an economy would be those that encouraged production. A deficit economy would therefore, by necessity, be a producer-oriented one. More significantly, Weyl concluded that, if the primary concern in a surplus economy was not the production of more wealth but the equitable distribution and consumption of existing wealth, then the only way to enjoy the full benefits of a surplus economy was to replace outmoded producer-oriented mental habits with consumer-oriented ones.

Once Weyl had constructed his producerist/consumerist version of economic evolution, he found it easy to develop the consumerist potential of not only Patten's ideas but those of other thinkers as well. In the early twentieth century, for example, Veblen was no more interested than Patten in a consumer-oriented economy, and his producerist sympathies were far stronger than Patten's. Those sympathies were evident in his conviction that the problem with the emerging economic structure was not that it was too producerist but that it was not producerist enough. It encouraged pecuniary rather than industrial values and, in so doing, all but eliminated the instinct of workmanship which had been so central to a handicraft economy organized around small, independent producers.

Weyl found it easy to incorporate Veblen's distinction between industrial and pecuniary values into his evolutionary framework. But he incorporated neither Veblen's reasoning nor his producerist sympathies. According to Veblen, a pecuniary economy was at odds with producerist principles. Weyl, by contrast, insisted that such an economy was supremely producerist. Its goal was to increase the profits of corporate producers often at the expense of the consuming population. It was, he believed, industrial values that were consumerist, emphasizing as they did production for use rather than production for profit.[30] Therefore, substituting industrial for pecuniary values meant substituting a consumer for a producer orientation.

While developing the consumerist potential of Patten's and Veblen's ideas was an important contribution to consumerist thought, Weyl's primary contribution was to transform what had been ideas with economic implications into a political worldview. Although other thinkers had tried, most notably Edward Bellamy, Weyl was the first major thinker to have both the economic background that made it possible for him to break free of the producerist paradigm and the political leanings that made him want to do so.

Like Bellamy before him, the political idea in which Weyl was most interested was democracy. For him democracy was a political system that could only exist under certain economic conditions. "Without an excess of wealth," he warned, "no democracy on a large scale was possible." Why? Because, "however it may be clothed in legal rights and political immunities, democracy means material goods and the moral goods based thereon." Without the existence of enough wealth "to provide a livable life for all the populations," he insisted, the only viable political system was despotism. But, with the growth of a surplus, "the denial to the people of wealth and rights, which had found its moral justification in the early poverty of society, became ethically untenable," and "democracy became ultimately inevitable."[31]

Weyl was quick to warn that the existence of surplus did "not mean that a democracy is attained, but only that it is attainable." A survey of U.S. history convinced him of that. Americans, he pointed out, had long pursued democracy. But, as he saw it, they had not yet managed to establish a real democracy. Initially, the problem had been an economic one. The nation simply did not have the wealth to support a real democracy. The best that it had been able to do was to construct what Weyl called the "shadow democracy of 1776." Only in the nineteenth century did Americans begin to amass the sort of wealth on which a real democracy might rest. But, unfortunately, even as they tore down the economic obstacles to a democracy, Americans fortified the intellectual ones. The very characteristics that fitted them for amassing wealth, Weyl noted regretfully, "gave to American development a tendency adverse from the evolution of a socialized democracy."[32]

What were these characteristics forged during the "conquest of the continent" which impeded the evolution of a democracy? They were certainly not those that William Graham Sumner had identified. For Weyl the transformation of virgin land into farms and factories had not promoted thrift and industriousness. Nor had it been a process in which competition had brought out the best in each individual. On the contrary, Weyl insisted, it had been a process that had encouraged excessive waste, excessive greed, and, perhaps most of all, excessive individualism, all pursued at the expense of the community. As for competition, far from promoting the best in the producer, it had encouraged "bribery . . . false pretense, the buying off of rivals' agents, the damaging of rivals' wares, ingenious chicanery of all sorts."[33]

What was striking about Weyl's description of the conquest of the continent was his reversal of the connotations associated with *producer* and *consumer*. Producerist thinkers had traditionally assumed that greed, waste, and the valuation of self over society were all characteristics associated with consumption. Indeed, they often pointed to the example of Rome, as Richard Ely had done in 1889, warning that "wanton luxury" was inevitably "accompanied by loose morals, decay of civic virtues, general rottenness, while the magnificence of the few contrasts vividly with the beggarly wretchedness of the depraved masses."[34] Weyl, however, attributed to the producer the very characteristics traditionally associated with the consumer. For him loose morals, eroding civic virtues, general rottenness, and extreme disparities of wealth were all far more characteristic of a society obsessed with the production of wealth than one that was primarily interested in the distribution and consumption of wealth.

Weyl was not the first thinker to alter the traditional connotations associated with *consumer* and *producer*. He was, however, the first to place this redefined consumer at the center of the political economy. It was a major achievement. Although several of his predecessors had been instrumental in legitimizing the consumer identity and had even begun to rethink the consumer's place within the political economy, none had taken the step that Weyl did. Either unwilling or unable to substitute a consumer-oriented political economy for a producer-oriented one, most had ended up advocating a system that made room for both.

Weyl, by contrast, was both able and willing to abandon producerist principles. His ability he owed to Patten, one of the first economists to develop an alternative to the producerist paradigm. Ironically, however, he owed his willingness to his strong labor sympathies. Weyl's labor credentials were more solid than those of most middle-class intellectuals. He had worked with John Mitchell of the United Mine Workers during the anthracite coal strike of 1902. And he had written extensively on behalf of the labor movement.[35] But Weyl came to believe that workers would do far better in the existing industrial order if they defined their interests in terms of their consumer identity.

How central Weyl's labor sympathies were to his consumerist worldview becomes evident when one looks at the fundamental differences between his ideal order and that of his mentor. Patten had moved workers into the consumer category not because of any strong labor sympathies—he did not possess any—but because he wanted to eliminate class conflict.[36] As long as both workers and capitalists focused on their identity as producers, Patten insisted, their interests would be in conflict. Workers would agitate for higher wages and shorter hours, while their employers would attempt to maximize profit by reducing wages and extending the workday. But in an economy of abundance, Patten reasoned, workers had only to embrace their consumer identity, and their interests would cease to be in conflict with those of their employers. In such an economy consumer-workers could enjoy a high standard of living at the same time that their producer-employers enjoyed ample profits.

Ultimately, it was Patten's aversion to labor radicalism which prompted him to call for a consumption-oriented, rather than a consumer-oriented, system. At some level he realized that, once he had transferred workers from the producer to the consumer category, a consumer-oriented political economy would, by definition, function on behalf of the nation's workers. A consumption-oriented economy, by contrast, would not only neutralize labor radicalism, it would also guarantee capitalist well-being.

Not surprisingly, Patten's version of the good society held little appeal for someone with labor sympathies as strong as those of Weyl. Indeed, Weyl's ideal order was the antithesis of Patten's; it would guarantee not capitalists' but workers' well-being and would neutralize not labor but corporate power. Yet, even though Weyl was far more committed to labor than Patten had ever been, his ideal order was far more consumerist. And it was more consumerist precisely because Weyl was as convinced as Patten that, once workers were transferred from the producer to the consumer category, a consumer-oriented political economy would function on behalf of the nation's workers.

If Weyl was so committed to an order that would function on behalf of the nation's workers, why did he reject the producer identity as an organizing principle? The reason, as he explained it, was that that identity had become too "highly differentiated" to be an effective identity around which to organize the people. "The producer (who is only the consumer in another role) is. . . . banker, lawyer, soldier, tailor, farmer, shoeblack, messenger boy. He is capitalist, workman, money lender, money borrower, urban worker, rural worker."[37] Any attempt to establish a democratic order around such a fragmented identity, he warned, would run aground on the question of "which producer." And, however that question might be answered, the result would be that one group of producers would benefit at the expense of another.

The same, however, could not be said about a democratic order based on the universal identity of consumer. Individuals as diverse as "the Polish slag-worker and the Boston salesgirl and the Oshkosh lawyer" might not have much in common as producers, but, Weyl insisted, they all shared "a similar interest (and a common cause of discontent) as consumers of the national wealth." Thus, he concluded, it made little sense to define the people in terms of a producer identity. The most salient interest that the people shared was rooted in their identity as consumers.[38]

Ultimately for Weyl what was significant about the consumer interest was not merely that it was the most salient interest the people *shared*. Even more to the point, it was the most salient interest that the people *had*. Weyl granted that in an earlier time production had been the "sole governing economic fact of a man's life." But, he insisted, "to-day many producers have no direct interest in their product." It was, for example, "a very attenuated interest which the Polish slag-worker has in the [tariff] duty on steel billets." But that same Polish slag worker had a very real interest in seeing "the greatest possible production of articles worth consuming" at "the lowest possible cost in effort . . . and so distributed as to give the greatest possible satisfaction in their consumption."[39] And it was an interest that he shared not only with other slag workers but with all members of society.

In retrospect it seems inevitable that *the people* would eventually cease to be defined exclusively in terms of the producer identity and come to be defined increasingly in terms of the consumer identity. For several decades a number of political economic thinkers had been moving in just that direction. But all had stopped short of calling for a consumer-oriented order to replace the producer-oriented one. Bellamy had done so because he had never

managed to topple the producerist edifice. Kelley and Veblen had been unwilling to topple it. And, although Patten had been both able and willing, he
had refused to replace that edifice with a consumerist one. Weyl, however,
shared the leftist sympathies of Bellamy, Kelley, and Veblen, and he was well
versed in Patten's theories. Possessing both the inclination and the theoretical tools, he alone found it easy to use the building blocks constructed by previous thinkers to erect a consumerist edifice.

That inclination and ability were both critical for the construction of a
consumer-oriented theory becomes evident when one compares Weyl's ideas
with those of his predecessors. Bellamy, for example, had been more than willing to construct a consumer-oriented political system. He had just lacked the
ability to do so. Trapped within a producerist paradigm, he never figured out
how to eliminate completely the producer's claim to society's wealth. As long
as the producer retained even the tiniest claim to wealth, Bellamy could not
argue that a system that functioned exclusively on behalf of the consuming
population was a just one. He had resigned himself, therefore, to an order
that eliminated the "profit takers" but made room for both the "original
producers" and "final consumers."[40] And, when it came to identifying the
source of the people's rights, he had avoided economic categories altogether.
Instead, he had opted for the political identity of citizen. Whatever rights the
inhabitants of Bellamy's utopia possessed, they did not possess because they
were consumers or producers but because they were members of the body
politic.

Unlike Bellamy, Weyl had no trouble defining the people as consumers or
arguing that a political economy that functioned exclusively on behalf of the
consuming masses was an equitable one. He found it easy to do so because,
unlike Bellamy, he never had to figure out how to make the nonproducer's
claim as legitimate as that of the producer. Patten had done that for him.
Armed with Patten's idea of a social surplus, Weyl was able to dismiss the producer's exclusive claim to society's wealth. Once he had done this, the rest was
easy.

If Patten's social surplus allowed Weyl to reach consumerist conclusions
that Bellamy had been unable to reach, it prompted him to pursue a consumerist logic that Kelley had been unwilling to pursue. Although Kelley was
as convinced as any consumerist thinker that "in a civilized community every
person is a consumer," she nevertheless remained a producerist thinker. For
her the challenge facing society was to end exploitation, something, she

maintained, that was done to wage workers by manufacturers and consumers. She granted that manufacturers might try to sell adulterated products to consumers. But such efforts, she insisted, did not constitute exploitation. Consumers could choose not to buy these products. Indeed, according to Kelley, the only reason that these goods existed at all was because of the "willing ignorance of the masses." Workers, by contrast, were not a party to their own exploitation. They had little choice but to accept whatever inhumane treatment was a condition of their employment, and, in Kelley's lexicon, such treatment constituted exploitation.[41]

Kelley's cure for society's ills was as producerist as her diagnosis. Although she had begun with a consumerist proposition, namely that everyone was a consumer, she did not call for a democratic order based on a universal consumer identity. Instead, she insisted that numerically superior consumers had to use their economic influence on behalf of less numerically powerful, working-class producers.[42] In Kelley's view, consumers should commit themselves to a producer-oriented good society.

Like Kelley, Weyl wanted to see an end to the exploitation of the masses. But, unlike her, his definition was a consumerist one. Exploitation, he maintained, involved "excessive claims upon the [social] surplus." Such a definition shifted the focus from the people's interests as producers of the nation's wealth to their interests as consumers of it. More to the point, it made consumers rather than producers the primary victims of business's pursuit of profit. "When the trust raises prices, obtains valuable franchises or public lands, escapes taxation, secures bounties, lowers wages, evades factory laws, or makes other profitable maneuvers," Weyl argued, "it is diverting a part of the social surplus from the general community to itself." It was actions such as these which constituted exploitation for Weyl. But, if the "chief offense of the trust" was not its capacity to injure the producer but, rather, "its capacity to injure the consumer," then it made little sense to call for a producer-oriented political economy.[43] Numerically superior consumers should demand a system that functioned not on behalf of numerically inferior wage-earning producers but on their own behalf. The only way to end exploitation, Weyl concluded, was to construct a consumer-oriented political economy.

That a consumerist Weyl and a producerist Kelley could arrive at fundamentally different versions of the good society is perhaps not particularly surprising. What is surprising is that Weyl and Patten were also able to do so, particularly since Weyl based his economic worldview on Patten's ideas. Weyl owed to Patten not only the idea of a social surplus but also an evolutionary approach to the economy, a theory of cultural lag, a conviction that conflict and struggle were unnecessary for progress, and an appreciation of the social and economic contributions of the trusts.

Such heavy reliance on Patten's ideas might have prompted Weyl to adopt some of Patten's more conservative political attitudes. And indeed, at first glance, this seemed to be the case. It was, for example, one of Patten's ideas which prompted the left-leaning Weyl to reject a Marxist solution to society's problems. Like Patten, he was convinced that a surplus economy made the Marxist program, with its emphasis on increasing misery, class conflict, and confiscation of property, obsolete. Such a program, he acknowledged, may have been appropriate in an economy of scarcity. In an ever-expanding economy, however, not only was the Marxist emphasis on increasing misery misguided, so too was the assumption that any "progress of democracy will involve a wholesale confiscation of the property of the rich." "Where wealth is growing at a rapid rate," Weyl insisted, "the multitude may be fed without breaking into the rich man's granary."[44]

Patten's influence was also evident in Weyl's conviction that trusts were a significant improvement over the small, competitive businesses of the preceding era. Even more than Patten, Weyl emphasized the trusts' role in "reduc[ing] chaos to order." And he was willing to grant that the trusts had a "broader ethical basis and a wider program of social reform" than their predecessors had possessed. "The growing popularity of company-paid pensions to employees, of welfare work, even of reductions in hours—although these have another side—is indicative of a certain rudimentary sense of responsibility on the part of big business."[45]

Despite such pronouncements, Weyl turned out to share few of Patten's political convictions. Far less tolerant of capitalism and far less sympathetic to the business interests than Patten, Weyl frequently found it necessary to modify Patten's economic ideas. Inevitably, his modifications transformed Patten's relatively conservative ideas into the foundation for a radical rethinking of the political economy.[46]

Weyl's understanding of the trusts was only the most obvious example of how he incorporated Patten's theories into a worldview far more radical than that of his mentor. Patten believed that the trusts were adopting socially responsible policies because they were rapidly developing the altruistic values that were appropriate for an age of surplus. It was these values that prompted "upper class men," moved by "sympathy for the laborer," to seek "to improve the conditions of the lower classes." And, according to Patten, it was a process that was already well under way. "The striking fact of recent industrial organization," he announced, was that the new economic conditions had all but weeded out the "unsocial capitalist," leaving the trusts largely in the hands of "socialized" capitalists who emphasized "public welfare" over "temporary gain."[47]

Weyl may have joined his mentor in crediting the trusts with rationalizing the economy and adopting a social view, but, when it came to explaining why they had done so, he opted for a Veblenian explanation. According to Weyl, those who controlled the trusts—the plutocrats, as he called them—did what they did, be it socially responsible or merely exploitative, for one reason and one reason only: "the desire for profits." It was, Weyl insisted, their "standard of pecuniary preeminence," their "pecuniary ambitions," which determined what sorts of policies the plutocrats adopted. And, if they "accept[ed] certain industrial responsibilities," it was only because they had discovered that "with increasing concentration of business control . . . it is becoming wiser to mitigate certain evils of unregulated employment, and make the additional cost a fixed charge to customers, rather than let things go and pay the cost of negligence in taxes."[48] For Weyl profit, not altruism, was the motive behind the trusts' socially responsible policies.

Not that Weyl believed profit was necessarily bad. Indeed, he conceded, profit had played an important role in establishing an economy of abundance. It had been the desire for profit which had prompted the plutocracy "to bring order out of chaos." But, if Weyl joined Patten in crediting the plutocracy's pecuniary motives for the economic progress of the nineteenth century, he nevertheless was as convinced as Veblen that these same motives made the trust an inappropriate form of economic organization for the twentieth century. Like Veblen, he believed that an economy committed to pecuniary goals could not possibly function on behalf of the people in the same way that one dedicated to industrial goals could.[49]

Weyl was able to incorporate the ideas of both Veblen and Patten into a single theory primarily because his focus was on politics rather than economics. Veblen and Patten might have been at opposite ends of the political spectrum, but they, nevertheless, shared some common intellectual ground. Both, for example, were primarily economic thinkers, their main concern the production of wealth. They might not agree on the answer, but both asked the same question: was the trust a form of economic organization which could produce abundance?

Weyl, by contrast, asked political questions. Indeed, he usually dispensed with the economic questions by following Patten's lead. He was, for example, quick to grant that "the plutocracy, with its brand-new tool, the trust," was largely responsible for the existing prosperity. But for him the important question was not whether or not the trust was a form of economic organization which could usher in prosperity but, rather, "who gets the prosperity?" "Why," he asked, "after the wastes of production have been so largely eliminated, do we still suffer from overwork, child labor, sweating, industrial disease, preventable accident, slums, poverty, wretchedness? Why do wages remain low after the plutocracy has established a little order in industry?"[50] These were not economic but political questions.

More often than not, Weyl turned to Veblen for answers to his political questions, which at first glance is surprising. Veblen might have had the requisite left leanings, but he was also convinced that the good society was one that revolved around the producer. If all Weyl had needed was a producerist critique of capitalism, he did not need to rely on Veblen. Any number of socialist thinkers could have provided him with such a critique. Veblen, however, was not merely a left-leaning producerist thinker; he had also been heavily influenced by Edward Bellamy. The result was a powerful critique of capitalism with considerable consumerist potential, albeit one that Veblen had not yet chosen to develop.

This potential was evident in Veblen's conviction that abundant production did not necessarily translate into a better life for all members of society, a conviction that Patten did not share. In both *The Theory of the Leisure Class* and *The Theory of Business Enterprise* Veblen had argued that the traditional indicators of an economy's success, abundant consumption and abundant production, were actually poor measures of social well-being. Far more important than the amount produced or consumed, he believed, were the reasons. Were goods consumed because they satisfied needs or merely because they signaled status? Similarly, were goods produced because they could be used or merely because they could provide profits? These questions were not only central to Veblen's work. They were also at the heart of a consumerist worldview.

Not surprisingly, Weyl preferred Veblen's measures of social well-being to Patten's. The critical test for the good society, he insisted, was not whether it poured forth an abundance of goods but whether it was able to guarantee its citizens a full life. It was a test that the plutocracy had failed. "What the people want," Weyl insisted, "is not wealth, but distributed wealth; not a statistical increase in the national income, but more economic satisfactions, more widely distributed." The plutocracy, however, had made no such distinctions. "It is exactly as though the plutocracy . . . had trebled our production of coal," Weyl suggested, "but had distributed the fuel so badly, overstoking some boilers and understoking others, that the total production of heat was not greater than before." What a "shivering people" needed, however, was "not more coal, not more smoke, not more ashes, but more heat." Believing with Patten that the trusts represented an economic advance, Weyl was adamant that economic advances were meaningless without political advances. "Without a readjustment in the distribution and consumption of wealth," he argued, "improvements in production will be of no permanent advantage."[51] Only by modifying the political structure would it be possible to translate the phenomenal productivity of the trusts into social well-being.

Weyl's conviction that the trusts represented an economic advance but not a political one was also evident in his ideas about economic evolution. Weyl took his basic evolutionary framework from Patten. Like Patten, he believed that the economy was evolving from scarcity to abundance. And, like Patten, he assumed that it was moving in the direction of progress. But, when it came to deciding where to place "large scale capitalism" on the evolutionary scale, he parted company with his mentor. Patten insisted that large-scale capitalism was the most highly advanced stage of economic evolution because it was capable of producing the phenomenal amounts of wealth necessary for an economy of surplus. Weyl, by contrast, placed an economy organized around the trusts much lower down the evolutionary scale. He granted that the plutocracy had put "an end to the waste and brutality of an unregulated business war" and, having done so, was "superior to what had preceded it." But, because the peace it had imposed was merely the "peace of industrial despotism," the plutocracy, with its trusts, "was by no means the last word in industrial development." At best it was "a stage in our development from the anarchic industry of half a century ago to the completely socialized industry of half a century hence."[52]

Weyl's use of the term *despotism* was no rhetorical flourish. In his lexicon it meant the "denial to the people of wealth and rights," and, as he saw it, this was exactly what the plutocracy had done. The plutocracy, as he defined it, was the "system of industry in which a large and increasing portion of the income of society flows into great reservoirs (usually natural or legal monopolies) which are preempted and controlled by private corporations." A form of economic organization which thrived by expropriating the people's wealth, Weyl concluded, could not possibly qualify as the highest stage of evolution.[53] The plutocracy's economic advances might entitle it to a relatively high position on the evolutionary scale. Its political abuses disqualified it from occupying a position anywhere near the pinnacle.

The extent to which Weyl rejected Patten's politics even as he relied on his economics becomes even more apparent when one looks at the system that Weyl chose to place at the pinnacle. Patten had always assumed that the good society would be a capitalist one. Convinced that "altruism is . . . the complement to increased productivity," he believed that the capitalists were rapidly becoming "socialized," a transformation that was evident in their growing "desire to improve the conditions of the lower class." The "lower classes," he insisted, should respond by ceasing to work "for their own betterment," trusting the capitalists to run the economy on their behalf. When the socialization process was complete, Patten predicted, capitalists would produce abundantly but would then willingly divert much of the resulting wealth to the public to be used for "social purposes."[54]

Weyl had little faith in the capitalists and little interest in a political economy dominated by them. For him capitalists in a "plutocratic" economy were not the altruistic benefactors of society whom Patten described but expropriators of the people's wealth, intent on "diverting a part of the social surplus from the general community to itself." Capitalists, he insisted, sought to maximize wealth when the real task was to maximize the "range of economic satisfactions." They thought of profits when they should have been thinking of "recreation, leisure, a wise expenditure, and a healthful toil." They were determined to save wages when the real goal was the "saving in labor."[55]

Ultimately, however, Weyl did not find fault with the capitalists themselves so much as the system within which they operated. That system forced "men in certain positions either to sin or to surrender their places to men who will." Socializing the capitalists was impossible, therefore, as long as they operated within a capitalist economy. Only by changing the system itself would it be possible to end capitalist abuses. The task, Weyl decided, was not the socialization of the capitalists but the "socialization of industry."[56]

Ironically, it was Patten's idea of the social surplus which made it possible for Weyl to call for the socialization of industry. Only because Patten had identified a fund of wealth which did not belong to the producer was Weyl able to reject the producerist definition of *profit* which had long dominated radical thought. As Weyl saw it, it was not the worker's labor but the social surplus that the capitalists expropriated in their relentless pursuit of profit. Once Weyl defined profit as wealth taken from the consuming rather than the producing masses, it became possible to argue that the cure for society's ills was not a worker state but, rather, the socialization of industry on behalf of the consuming masses.

In advocating the socialization of industry, Weyl did not mean the "rigorous nationalization of the means of production." Indeed, he did not mean any "definite industrial program" at all. For him socialization was "a point of view," an "animating ideal of a whole industrial policy," "a standard by which industrial conditions and industrial developments must be adjudged." Specifically, it was "a viewing of our manifold business life from the standpoint of society and not solely from that of the present beneficiaries or directors of industry." That might require "government ownership of some industries." It might require "government regulation of others." But, however socialization might be implemented, it would mean "an enlarged power of the community in industry." And, most important, it would mean "an increased appropriation by the community of the increasing social surplus and of the growing unearned increment."[57]

What was striking about Weyl's socialized democracy was how consumerist it was. Most leftists advocated nationalizing the means of production because they believed doing so was the only way to guarantee producers the full product of their labor. Their socialized system was a worker state. Weyl, however, believed that the plutocracy exploited consumers even more than producers. The task, therefore, was to replace the plutocracy with a system that would function according to "the common interest of the citizen as a consumer of wealth." His socialized democracy would do just that. Through "a conservation of life and health, a democratization of education, a socialization of consumption, a raising of the lowest elements of the population to the level of the mass," Weyl's socialized democracy would further the well-being of the nation's citizens as consumers rather than producers.[58]

Weyl's call for a socialized democracy highlighted both the radical potential of consumerist ideas and their limits. On the one hand, his "new democracy" represented as fundamental a challenge to the existing system as did any leftist version of the ideal order. Like those on the left, Weyl demanded an end to the capitalist economy and the construction of a socialized system. Like them, he wanted to see the people vanquish the plutocracy. Indeed, his very choice of *the people,* a term with a long radical tradition, rather than the more moderate *public,* which Patten had employed, signaled his reliance on a radical diagnosis of society's ills.[59] Patten had used *the public* precisely because it was a term that minimized conflict, suggesting, as it did, that there was a greater interest that all members of society shared. Weyl relied on a term that was rife with contentious meanings.

But, even as Weyl adopted a radical language, he did not rely on radical definitions. In the radial lexicon *the people* was a term with not only conflictual but also producerist connotations. Throughout the nineteenth century that term had been synonymous with the *producing masses.*[60] Weyl, however, was committed to a consumer-oriented system. He therefore chose to redefine the people exclusively as consumers rather than producers.

For at least two reasons Weyl's exclusively consumerist definition of *the people* went hand in hand with what was ultimately a liberal understanding of the economy. Liberalism may have become increasingly producer oriented during the nineteenth century, but it had considerable consumerist potential. When Smith constructed his economic model, he had assumed that consumers would be its primary beneficiaries. Radical worldviews, by contrast, were profoundly producerist. Much might separate a revolutionary socialist, a syndicalist, and a guild socialist. But all of them championed the "workers of the world." All relied on producerist notions of equity to justify the overthrow of capitalism, arguing that workers as the creators of wealth were the only members of society with a legitimate claim to it. And all looked to a worker state to replace the existing order.[61] Weyl, by contrast, was as convinced as Smith that consumers should be the primary beneficiaries of the economy.

It was not only Weyl's preference for a consumer-oriented system which made his ideas more compatible with liberalism than radicalism. So, too, did his reliance on a liberal definition of *consumer* and *producer.* Implicit in Smith's insistence that the consumer interest should take precedence over the producer interest was the notion that consumers and producers were two distinct groups. Smith—and, indeed, classical economists in general—might be confident that a liberal economy could further the interests of both consumers and producers, but they assumed that those interests were distinct—even antithetical. Consumers wanted low prices, producers high prices. Consumers wanted an abundant supply; producers wanted to keep supply limited. It was this distinction between the supply side of the economy and the demand side which made it difficult for classical liberals to conceive of individuals as both consumers and producers.

That consumer and producer were treated as distinct identities in the producerist environment of the nineteenth century was not particularly surprising. But, even as a number of intellectuals in the early twentieth century began to question whether the two identities were as antithetical as late-nineteenth-century thinkers such as Gilman and Sumner had suggested, they did not challenge the assumption that the two identities were distinct. Florence Kelley, Simon Patten, Walter Lippmann, and even Thorstein Veblen may have all envisioned an alliance between consumers and producers. But the very fact that they called for an alliance suggests how much they continued to view them as two different groups.

So deep was the liberal conviction that consumer and producer were distinct identities that thinkers who relied on a liberal definition found it necessary to minimize, even deny, the producer identity of working-class consumers. Sumner, for example, divided society into workers and savers, on the one hand, and spenders and idlers, on the other, the implication being that, if one was a spender, then one was disqualified from membership in the worker category. And Patten envisioned a political economy in which capitalists would be the producers while members of the working class would ignore any interests they had as producers and function instead as wage-earning consumers. Even Walter Weyl, who had far more sympathy for workers than either Sumner or Patten, found it impossible to treat the worker as both a producer and a consumer. Convinced that the producer identity had become obsolete in the highly industrialized economy of the early twentieth century, he opted for an exclusively consumerist definition of *the people*. And he defended his definition by suggesting that it was far more consistent with actual conditions than were producerist definitions. "Men who voted as producers," he insisted, "are now voting as consumers."[62]

What was significant about the liberal distinction was that it forced those who relied on it to choose between a consumer- and a producer-oriented system. And, because liberalism was more consumer oriented than most versions of radicalism, social thinkers who emphasized the consumer over the producer—even those who were highly critical of capitalism—ultimately found themselves being pushed in a liberal direction. How much so becomes evident when one looks at consumer cooperative theory. Since its inception consumer cooperation had been primarily a working-class movement, dedicated to advancing the interests of producers. By the late nineteenth century most cooperative theorists had come to believe that consumer, rather than producer, cooperatives were far more likely to achieve working-class victories. By providing workers with a way to prevent capitalists from recovering in the marketplace any wage gains made by workers in the workplace, consumer cooperatives could give workers the edge they needed to win the class struggle and establish a worker state. It was precisely because consumer cooperatives had the potential to improve the conditions of the working class that consumer cooperation in Europe was so closely linked to socialist politics and the trade union movement. And even in the United States consumer cooperation and labor radicalism enjoyed a close relationship. As one historian has noted, when government repression immediately after World War I resulted in the collapse of socialist politics, cooperation, for many labor radicals, "came to serve not as a complement to a thriving Socialist Party, as it did in Europe, but as a substitute."[63]

The individuals who were most responsible for shaping cooperative theory on this side of the Atlantic were Albert Sonnichsen and James Peter Warbasse. Sonnichsen was a secretary for the Co-operative League of the United States of America (CLUSA), the national umbrella organization for consumer cooperatives, and editor of its official organ, the *Coöperative Consumer*. In 1919 he published *Consumer's Coöperation*, the first major American work to focus on consumer rather than producer cooperation. Warbasse's influence was even greater. As the founder and president of CLUSA, he was often called upon to provide advice and support to various groups seeking to establish consumer cooperatives. In 1919 he spent several days in Seattle, for example, helping strikers to organize their broad network of consumer cooperatives.[64] He was also a prolific writer, publishing numerous articles, pamphlets, and books. His first major work on cooperation, *Cooperative Democracy* (1923), remained the bible of the consumer cooperative movement for decades.

Warbasse and Sonnichsen were as adamant as any European cooperative theorist that consumer cooperation was "an anti-capitalist, revolutionary movement." And they were as convinced that consumer cooperation was a labor movement. The problem with the "present system," Warbasse maintained, was that "the people who do the labour get but a part of what they produce." As convinced as any labor radical that "he who produces more than he consumes, is exploited . . . and he who consumes more than he produces is a parasite," Warbasse insisted that only a cooperative order could bring consumption into line with production. By "harmonizing . . . labour and consumption," consumer cooperation would ensure that "the workers get what they make, and the consumers make what they get." And, in so doing, Warbasse concluded, consumer cooperation would end the parasitism and exploitation that were endemic to the existing order.[65]

It was not merely because it would guarantee workers the full product of their labor that cooperation could claim to be a radical labor movement. According to Sonnichsen and Warbasse, cooperation would also give workers control of the means of production. Warbasse pointed out that, "when more than half of the consumer members are employed in the co-operative industry, it is evident that the voice of the workers becomes the majority voice. What begins as consumers' control," he concluded, "moves slowly on till it becomes workers' control of industry." Sonnichsen agreed. He looked to a time when cooperation would be a "universal institution." When that happened, "the entire membership of all the coöperative societies would consist of workers, organized as consumers." But, if "the workers and the consumers . . . [were] completely identical," then "the workers in the coöperative factories would be their own employees and, through their coöperative societies, would have full power to regulate working conditions to suit themselves."[66]

Sonnichsen and Warbasse found it easy to place the consumer at the center of a radical worldview because they relied on a radical definition of the consumer. American labor activists had long stressed that producers had critical interests as consumers. "We have been led to suppose that the producer and the consumer were totally separate individuals, with separate and distinct interests," complained one contributor to the *Journal of United Labor* as early as 1884, "when in reality all producers are consumers."[67] Sonnichsen and Warbasse were thus able to assume what no liberal could, that the consumer was also a producer.

Having available a version of the consumer who was a member of the working class was a real advantage. By uniting consumer and producer, labor radicals had constructed a consumer who possessed the positive virtues of the producer. The very term *working-class consumer* evoked images of hardworking individuals saving what little they earned and going from store to store in search of meager necessities at a price they could afford. Labor's consumer, it would seem, could lay claim to the producerist virtues of thrift, self-discipline, and diligence.

Warbasse's and Sonnichsen's membership in an intellectual tradition that relied far more on labor radicalism than liberalism meant not only that they had access to a far more positive version of the consumer but also that they did not need to choose between a consumer- and a producer-oriented system. Labor radicals had long envisioned an ideal order that would demand from each "according to his ability" and provide for each "according to his need." They might have insisted that it was "workers of the world" who had to unite, but what they promised was an economic order in which workers would be guaranteed a right to consume. In labor radical circles a call for a producer-oriented system was not implicitly a rejection of a consumer-oriented one.

Given their ties to labor radicalism, Warbasse and Sonnichsen could easily have championed a cooperative system that would simultaneously further the interests of workers as both producers and consumers. They chose not to do so. Although they remained firmly committed to improving the well-being of the working class and continued to emphasize that workers were both producers and consumers, they nevertheless came to believe that the only way to realize the radical potential of consumer cooperation was to emphasize the consumer identity. In so doing, they found themselves on the same slippery slope as other consumerist critics of capitalism. The cooperative order that they envisioned began to sound far more Smithian than Marxist.

According to Warbasse and Sonnichsen, the real problem with the various versions of labor radicalism was that they concentrated on producers rather than consumers. Seeing production as the purpose of all industry and "labor as the chief social end," labor radicals misclassified the "workers as workers." The result was that they tried "to organize society as a society of workers," their goal "to have the workers get control of the industries." But what if "the workers in any industry" were to "get all they are asking for"? Warbasse asked. What if they were to "secure control and ownership of the industry"? What if they "control the marketing of the produce"? What if they were "in a position to have 'the full value of the wealth they produce'"? According to Warbasse, they would merely "become monopolistic and proceed to exploit the rest of society. . . . the history of the self-governing workshop or syndicalized industry confirms this statement." Indeed, because "it does not touch the fundamentals of the motive of production and monopoly in ownership," he concluded, "the so-called 'revolutionary movement' in which so many workers are interested . . . would only superficially change one set of bosses for another." Sonnichsen agreed. "An industrial democracy founded on labor," he declared, "is no democracy at all."[68]

If labor radicalism's focus on the producer prevented it from "effect[ing] radical changes," then the solution, Warbasse and Sonnichsen reasoned, was to focus on the consumer. Consumer cooperation did just that. Its "primary hypothesis," Warbasse explained, ". . . is that the consumers are everybody, and that all of the machinery of industry and the organization of society should be for them." Consumers, he granted, were just as likely as workers to "organize for their mutual interest." But there was a critical difference. Workers were only interested in the well-being of producers. "The consuming masses," he maintained, "are interested in the total good of society, for they are society."[69]

Warbasse and Sonnichsen never dismissed the producer identity as obsolete or irrelevant. But, even as they repeatedly stressed that in a cooperative economy the consumers would be the producers making "the interests of producer and consumer . . . one," both were adamant that the consumer was the paramount identity. Any attempt to correct the economic injustices of the existing system had "to begin with the consumers because the interests of the 4,800,000 working-class consumers is superior to that of the 50,000 working-class producers. It is in this simple fact," Warbasse concluded, "that the fundamental common sense of the Consumers' Co-operative Movement resides."[70]

By giving the consumer identity priority over the producer identity, Warbasse and Sonnichsen began a transformation of American cooperative theory which would culminate a decade later in the work of the preeminent cooperative theorist of the 1930s, New School philosopher Horace Kallen. Kallen did not merely give preference to the consumer identity. He completely dismissed the producer identity. "We are," he insisted, "consumers by nature and producers by necessity. We are born consumers, and remain consumers all our lives. But we are not born producers. We become producers under coercion, contingently, and we stay producers also under coercion, in response to the police-power in the hands of our 'betters'; we are compelled to live to work instead of living to live." Convinced that "the intrinsic or natural end of life is not labor but leisure," Kallen looked to consumer cooperation because, he believed, it alone "is directed toward the fulfillment of the original nature of man." It alone could usher in a "consumer-controlled economy of abundance."[71]

It was no coincidence that, at the same time Kallen was placing the consumer at the center of cooperative thought, he was also moving consumer cooperation in a liberal direction. Any consumer-oriented economy, he argued, would have to rely on the very "institutions basic to the capitalist structure"—namely "private property, the price system, and the profit-motive"—because these were the only ones capable of "maintain[ing] a continuous economy of abundance." Furthermore, the cooperative economy would be far more consistent with the foundational principles of liberalism than was the existing "producer-capitalism." "The American philosophy of life uttered in the Declaration of Independence," he declared, "rests upon the paramountcy of the consumer." "Life, liberty, the pursuit of happiness are . . . consummatory . . . rights." In Kallen's hands consumer cooperation became more Smithian than Smith, more Lockean than Locke.[72]

How much an exclusive emphasis on the consumer identity was responsible for pushing American cooperative theory in a liberal direction becomes evident when one looks at the ways in which European social democrats incorporated consumer cooperatives into their political theories. In the late nineteenth and early twentieth centuries social democrats across Europe were as determined as many an American progressive to construct a socialist alternative to Marxism, one that extended beyond the working class.[73] And, like American thinkers, they were struggling with the tensions between the consumer and the producer identity. Indeed, Beatrice Webb suggested that "the citizens organized as consumers, and the workers organized as producers" were "two opposite but complementary corporations." But Webb never felt compelled to choose one group over the other. Unlike Weyl, Warbasse, and Sonnichsen, she remained convinced that British democracy rested upon associations of consumers "in organic connection with an equally ubiquitous organization of the producers by hand or by brain (in trade unions and professional associations)."[74] For her, and indeed for most social democrats, the goal was not a consumer-oriented system but one that was committed to advancing both the producing and the consuming interests of the masses.

Precisely because European social democrats were determined to further both the producing and the consuming interests of citizens, they found it far more difficult than did American progressives to come to terms with capitalism. Capitalism might have had considerable consumerist potential, but its ability to serve the producing interests of the working class was more questionable. Thus, European social democrats rejected capitalism, convinced that a socialist order would improve the well-being of the people as both consumers and producers. By contrast, American consumerist thinkers—be they advocates of a cooperative order such as Sonnichsen and Warbasse or proponents of a "socialized democracy" such as Weyl—ultimately chose the consumer instead of the producer. And, in so doing, they helped to move American progressivism in a liberal rather than a socialist direction.

By the 1920s Lippmann, Weyl, Sonnichsen, and Warbasse had not only constructed two versions of a consumer-oriented economy. They had also transformed *consumer* from an economic to a political category. And they had called on the American people to use their identity as consumers to take control of the political system. That call went unheeded. Not until the 1930s would consumerist ideas have much of an impact on American politics.

The lack of interest during the 1920s in a consumerist approach to politics had more of an impact on liberal consumerist ideas than it did on cooperative consumerist ones. In cooperative circles the consumer-oriented cooperative theory that Warbasse and Sonnichsen had developed remained largely intact. And it did so because Warbasse dominated consumerist cooperative discourse throughout the decade and, indeed, well into the 1940s.

Liberals, by contrast, enjoyed no such continuity in intellectual leadership. Once war broke out in Europe, both Weyl and Lippmann turned their attention to international events, and neither returned to consumerist issues when the hostilities were over. Weyl died of cancer in 1919, only forty-six years of age at the time. As for Lippmann, he abandoned the liberalism of his youth. Having once been a supporter of strong federal control on behalf of the consuming population, he had become convinced by the 1920s that "decentralization of the federal political power and the reduction of government at Washington is the paramount political issue of our time."[75] It was a position that placed him at odds with the liberal community.

Without a prominent intellectual such as Weyl or Lippmann to advocate a consumer-oriented liberalism, most liberals quickly forgot about the consumer. Like Weyl and Lippmann, they too spent the latter half of the 1910s focusing on the war in Europe and its impact at home. And, when the hostilities were over, they turned their attention to domestic issues. They championed labor and Sacco and Vanzetti. They worried about the impact of the emerging mass society on culture and values. And they decried the "illiberalism" of the 1920s even as they debated whether government should be "by the people" or merely "for the people."

In the early 1920s, however, a small handful of liberals once again began to think about the political economy in consumerist terms. They did not do so because they had been rereading Weyl and Lippmann. Instead, almost all came to the consumer by way of Veblen. Nevertheless, Weyl's and Lippmann's writings were indirectly responsible for the burgeoning consumerist liberalism of the late 1920s. The left liberals who were so quick to identify the consumerist implications in Veblen's work were avid readers of and frequent contributors to the *New Republic*. As such, they had been exposed to Weyl's and Lippmann's consumerist critiques of capitalism. Thus, when they began looking for alternatives to the existing political economy in the late 1920s, they found it easy to advocate what few of their contemporaries had even begun to contemplate: a consumer-oriented system. They may have owed the details of their consumerist system to Veblen. Their willingness even to consider such a system they owed to Weyl and Lippmann.

CHAPTER FIVE

"What's an Economic System For?" 1917–1933

Shortly after the end of World War I, Americans decided to "return to nor-
malcy" by supporting the conservative "Republican ascendancy." Nowhere
was Republican conservatism more conservative than in its exclusive focus on
the producer. Warren G. Harding, Calvin Coolidge, and especially Herbert
Hoover were more than willing to part company with their conservative and
even progressive predecessors when it came to using government power. All
three headed administrations that were deeply involved in the economy. But
all three were well within the conservative fold when it came to deciding who
the beneficiaries of such government involvement should be. In their view
production and producers (by which they meant business) were the proper
focus for government energies.

Such an exclusive focus on the producer was not merely conservative. It
was reactionary. In the Progressive Era the federal government had begun
moving in a more consumer-oriented direction. Progressives had included
among their various definitions of the public interest one that equated it with
a consuming interest. And they had pushed through legislation that was designed to protect the nation's consumers, most notably the Meat Inspection
Act and the Pure Food and Drug Act in 1906. So, when Republican leaders decided that consumption and consumers could and, even more to the point,

should take care of themselves, they were not so much preserving an exclusive focus on the producer as returning to it.

Republicans, however, were not the only "reactionaries" in the 1920s. Throughout the decade most Democrats and Socialists were also convinced that the political system should revolve around the producer. Where they differed from the Republicans and one another was over whom to include within the producer category. For the Republicans the producer was a manufacturer, an entrepreneur, a corporate leader. Democrats were more than willing to identify the capitalist as a producer, but they wanted to define the category a bit more broadly, making room for workers and perhaps even farmers. As for Socialists, they wanted to exclude capitalists altogether. But all agreed that producers, whoever they may be, were the proper beneficiaries of public policy.[1] In the producer-dominated political environment of the 1920s, the consumer was once again relegated to the margins of political economic discourse.

At first glance this marginalization of the consumer may seem surprising. The 1920s, after all, was a decade in which large numbers of Americans joined the consumer society. They bought cars, radios, iceboxes, and numerous other consumer goods—often on credit. They learned about their imperfections from Madison Avenue. They learned about most everything else from Hollywood. In a decade as given to consumption as the 1920s, it made little sense for political economic thinkers to ignore the consumer.

Or did it? Precisely because so many Americans were consuming at record levels did it make sense to focus on the producer. For the Republicans 1920s prosperity was the strongest justification for their producer-oriented (by which they meant business-oriented) policies. This orientation, they repeatedly insisted, was responsible for the flood of consumer goods that had deluged the nation. As they saw it, government's job was to maintain that flood. And the most effective technique for doing so, they maintained, was to stimulate production by stimulating profits. In short, the best way to further the interests of consumers was to further the interests of producers.

Opponents of the Republican ascendancy were even less likely to demand an increased focus on the consumer. According to many a cultural critic, the fundamental problem with the Republican program was that it was doing too much to encourage consumption. Republican policies, they argued, were rapidly transforming the American people into a mindless, self-oriented mass of consumers whose herd mentality left no room for aesthetic or communitarian sensibilities.[2] As for the more politically minded critics, they dismissed the notion that Republican policies were designed to benefit producers. These policies, they granted, might have sent corporate profits skyrocketing, but they had done so at the expense of the nation's real producers, the men and women who worked in the factories and on the farms. In a decade that saw the largest jump in GNP to date, workers' wages rose only slightly, and farmers' incomes actually declined. Thus, whether they denounced Republicans for creating a consumer society or for abandoning producers, critics of Republican policies were unlikely to suggest that the cure for the nation's ills was a more consumer-oriented political economy.[3]

Consumerist cooperators were an exception. While James Peter Warbasse and his followers were quick to agree that Republicans had abandoned the producer, they were equally quick to insist that Republicans had also abandoned the consumer. Excessive consumption, they argued, was characteristic of a profit-oriented system, not a consumer-oriented one. Only by creating a system that truly functioned on behalf of the consumer, they maintained, would it be possible to end both the mindless consumption and the economic inequities that the Republican administrations were encouraging.

In the 1920s consumerist left liberals found it more difficult than did the cooperative theorists to argue that a consumer-oriented political economy would solve the problems caused by Republican policies. The cooperators were able to champion a consumer who was also a member of the working class. Left liberals, by contrast, belonged to an intellectual tradition that had long treated consumer and producer as mutually distinct identities. And, perhaps even more important, that tradition had increasingly come to associate the consumer with the middle class. In liberal circles, therefore, a call for a consumer-oriented political economy was not merely a rejection of the producer in favor of the consumer. It was also a rejection of the working class in favor of the middle class.

It was not easy for consumerist left liberals to abandon working-class producers in favor of an identity associated with shopping. For one, they were well aware that doing so would call into question whatever radical credentials they might have. But it was not merely their own self-image that gave them pause. In the 1920s producers seemed to be having a far harder time than consumers. Labor faced yellow-dog contracts, open shop campaigns, and unfavorable judicial decisions. And farmers found themselves confronting hard times almost a decade before the rest of the nation. Consumers, by contrast, seemed to be enjoying a frenzy of self-indulgence. The intellectual task facing consumerist left liberals, therefore, was not only to reestablish the consumer as a victim but also, far more challenging, to justify abandoning the working-class producer.

In the 1920s consumerist left liberals did figure out how to reestablish the consumer as victim. And they even managed to justify abandoning the producer. But they stopped short of advocating the sort of consumer-oriented democracy which both Walter Weyl and Walter Lippmann had envisioned a decade earlier. They did so not because of any reservations about the consumer but because of their doubts about democracy. Nor were they alone. In the 1920s thinkers across much of the political spectrum were becoming increasingly convinced that the "people" were incapable of making rational political decisions, a conviction that made any call for democracy, consumerist or otherwise, problematic.

Ironically, one of the first intellectuals to articulate such concerns was Lippmann. Never the unabashed champion of democracy which Weyl had been, Lippmann had nonetheless assumed that, even with their shortcomings, the people were capable of governing themselves. By the end of World War I, however, he had changed his mind. Having witnessed the ease with which wartime propagandists had manipulated public opinion, he insisted in *Public Opinion* (1922) that the basic premise of democratic government—that every citizen could "acquire a competent opinion about public affairs"— was an "intolerable and unworkable fiction." The only way that democratic government could work, he concluded, was if the "common interests" were "managed only by a specialized class." For Lippmann the best way to guarantee that democracy would function *for* the people was to make sure that it was not *by* the people. No wonder John Dewey, writing in the *New Republic,* identified Lippmann's book as "perhaps the most effective indictment of democracy as currently conceived ever penned."[4]

World War I may have destroyed the left liberals' faith in the people, but it strengthened their faith in government. Before the war progressives had believed that government could best serve the public interest by maintaining some sort of balance among the various interest groups. Progressives had applauded government efforts at antitrust, the regulation of interstate commerce, food and drug control, and labor legislation. By the end of the war, however, such regulatory efforts, once deemed a major expansion of governmental authority, had come to seem insignificant in comparison with the sorts of powers government had claimed during the hostilities.

When the United States entered World War I, it was clear that victory would depend on industrial productivity as well as manpower. Not only would the nation's factories have to clothe and feed the domestic population; they would also have to keep the American armed forces supplied with weapons and materials—and all this at a time when access to raw materials was restricted by the hazards of wartime transportation and a large portion of the labor force was overseas, fighting in the trenches.

Initially, it looked as if the nation's economic system would not be up to the challenge. The military had no coordinated system for securing its supplies. The nation's railroad system proved incapable of handling the increase in traffic, causing shortages in many parts of the country. Wartime demand for labor and goods began pushing up wages and prices. And many of the workers who did not share in the pay increases further reduced the nation's productive capabilities by going out on strike.

Well aware that the entire war effort could founder on an inability to harness the nation's productive potential, the federal government began to intervene in the nation's economy. It established a Food Administration and a Fuel Administration, which were responsible for increasing the amount of food and fuel available for the war effort. It created the National War Labor Board to mediate labor disputes and regulate wages. It took temporary control of the railroads, transforming a chaotic transportation system into an extremely efficient one. And it established the War Industries Board (WIB) to oversee industrial production for the war.

Under the direction of Bernard Baruch, the WIB took the first tentative steps toward economic planning. It developed sophisticated techniques for the collection and analysis of data concerning the productive capabilities of the economy. With enforcement of the antitrust laws suspended, it encouraged businesses to cooperate and share information. It decided how raw materials would be allocated. And it eliminated much of the waste and inefficiency in production by promoting standardization of both the production process and the products themselves.[5]

The phenomenal productivity that occurred under wartime planning affected a generation of American political thinkers. These thinkers, however, did not attribute that productivity to the same cause. For members of the business community who served on the WIB, such as Hugh Johnson and Gerard Swope, the lesson to be learned was the value of business cooperation—by which they meant the exchange of information concerning markets, prices, and technology. When the WIB had replaced competition with cooperation, the economy, in the words of Hugh Johnson, had "poured forth such a flood of production for the uses of war as the world had never seen in one country." Johnson and other members of the business community concluded that "if cooperation can do so much maybe there is something wrong with the old competitive system."[6]

Left liberals drew their own lessons from the nation's brief experiment with economic planning. They had little interest in a corporate liberal version of planning on behalf of the business interests. But they were convinced that, under the right sort of control, economic planning might eliminate poverty. Echoing other left liberals, Stuart Chase would later write: "War control lifted the economic system of the country, stupefied by decades of profit seeking, and hammered it and pounded it into an intelligent mechanism for delivering goods and services according to the needs of the army and of the working population."[7] This had been in wartime. How much more, the left liberals wondered, could such planning accomplish in the less destructive environment of a peacetime economy? In 1921, when he published *The Engineers and the Price System*, Thorstein Veblen gave them their answer.

According to Veblen, the problem with the industrial system was that it was managed by businessmen. Businessmen, he emphasized yet again, were not interested in producing goods and services but, rather, in maximizing profits. And they preferred to maximize profits by keeping prices high. In the modern economy, however, businessmen had a problem. "The mechanical industry of the new order is inordinately productive." The only way that businessmen could keep prices high, therefore, was to engage in a "conscientious withdrawal of efficiency," what Veblen called "sabotage." By limiting "the productive use of the available industrial plant and workmen," businessmen could prevent the high levels of production which would result if the industrial system were allowed to operate at capacity.[8]

Not all individuals involved in the production process, however, were motivated by pecuniary principles. According to Veblen, the actual mechanical operations were the responsibility of technicians. And the technicians were far more interested in efficiency than in profits, in maximizing production than in limiting it. Convinced that "the material welfare of the community" depended upon the efficient operation of the industrial system, Veblen concluded that it would be in the best interests of the general population to give control of the industrial system to "the engineers, who alone are competent to manage it."[9]

What Veblen was advocating was economic planning. He wanted to see "the country's productive industry . . . competently organized as a systematic whole." He wanted that "systematic whole" to be "managed by competent technicians with an eye single to maximum production of goods and services" rather than "by ignorant business men with an eye single to maximum profits." And he predicted that, if such changes in the nation's economic organization were to take place, "the resulting output of goods and services would doubtless exceed the current output by several hundred per cent."[10] The left liberals had their answer.

What was significant about *The Engineers and the Price System* for the left liberals, however, was not merely that Veblen advocated a planned economy but that he did so in consumerist terms. Indeed, Veblen's increasingly consumerist outlook—evident not only in *The Engineers and the Price System* but also in his 1923 publication, *Absentee Ownership and Business Enterprise in Recent Times*—was perhaps the strongest testament to the increasing legitimacy of consumerist ideas. By the 1920s the author who had once used the pejorative connotations surrounding *consumer* to discredit the captains of industry had come to believe that consumers were the primary victims of "business as usual."[11]

In retrospect Veblen's growing consumerist sympathies were not totally unexpected. He had always been more tolerant of consumption than had many of his nineteenth-century contemporaries. Even in *The Theory of the Leisure Class,* a work in which he had relied on a pejorative definition of *consumer,* Veblen had not condemned consumption itself, only the meanings associated with the act of consuming. And five years later, in *The Theory of Business Enterprise,* he had abandoned his earlier definition of consumer as parasite in favor of one that defined the consumer as a victim of profit-oriented capitalism.

Nevertheless, despite his willingness to redefine the consumer in 1904, Veblen's producerist sympathies had remained intact. His villains were still those who lacked a producerist instinct of workmanship, namely the leisure class and the captains of industry. His heroes were still those who had managed to retain such an instinct, members of the working class. And what troubled him most was that, in placing a premium on pecuniary rather than industrial values, the existing system rewarded those who lacked producerist sensibilities at the expense of those who possessed them.

Initially, Veblen's producerist convictions prevented him from developing whatever consumerist potential his ideas might have had. In 1904 he was willing to acknowledge that the consumer suffered under profit-oriented capitalism, but for him what the consumer suffered was inconvenience, a far cry from the real anguish that workers had to endure. The wasteful practices of the "modern business system," he insisted, involved no "curtailment of the community's livelihood." The worst that could be said about the impact of a pecuniary economy on the consuming public was that in economic good times it encouraged consumers to engage in the "unproductive consumption of goods" or to pay artificially high prices. And in economic bad times it forced consumers to expend a bit more effort to achieve their usual levels of "comfort."[12]

Veblen had so little sympathy for the plight of the consumer in 1904 because he was convinced that they enjoyed their comforts at the expense of labor. The only reason why the wasteful practices of the modern business system did not involve a "curtailment of the community's livelihood," he insisted, was because that system "makes up for its wastefulness by the added strain which it throws upon those engaged in the productive work." Only by forcing "men [to] work hard and unremittingly" was the existing system able to provide consumers with an abundant array of goods.[13] And, even worse, the same system that minimized the consequences of its wasteful practices by overworking the labor force in good times reduced the impact of economic bad times by discharging much of that labor force. In short, the only reason that consumers suffered so little was that workers suffered so much.

Veblen never lost his deep producerist convictions. But eventually he began to develop the consumerist potential that had always been implicit in his ideas. By 1921, when he published *The Engineers and the Price System,* Veblen had come to believe that it was in fact consumers who bore the brunt of the wasteful practices that he had long identified as an integral part of the pecuniary economy. When businessmen allowed "material resources, equipment and manpower" to stand idle, adulterated products, engaged in "systematic dislocation, sabotage and duplication," and produced "superfluities and spurious goods," Veblen insisted, they limited the output of an "inordinately productive" economic system to a level "below the needs of the community."[14] Denied not merely comforts but even the most basic of necessities, consumers had become by 1921 the main victims of Veblen's pecuniary economy.

Veblen's willingness to substitute consumerist conclusions for his producerist ones was even more apparent two years later in *Absentee Ownership and Business Enterprise in Recent Times*. These conclusions were all the more striking because he managed to reach them without altering the analysis of the economy on which he had relied for years. As in his previous works, Veblen continued to portray the existing system as a "business economy" characterized by pecuniary principles. He continued to suggest that this business economy was the culmination of an economic transformation that had begun with the rise of the "handicraft economy"—although he now gave far more attention to the period immediately preceding "recent times," a period he called the "era of free competition." And, finally, he continued to insist that what distinguished the earlier economic stages from the business economy was that the previous stages had rewarded those who were productive and efficient, whereas the business economy rewarded those who limited productivity. But in a dramatic departure from his earlier work Veblen no longer characterized the preceding economic stages as merely more producerist than the business economy. Now he argued that those stages had also been more consumerist than the economy that grew out of them.[15]

Ironically, what made Veblen's earlier economic stages more consumerist was the very thing that had made them more producerist, an emphasis on workmanship. But it was only after he had abandoned his definitions of the consumer as a luxury-seeking parasite or even an individual in pursuit of comfort that the consumerist implications of this emphasis became clear. Once the consumer became an individual who was denied even the basic necessities of life by an economic system that made its profits by restricting the production of goods, then it followed that any economic system committed to providing these basic necessities was more consumerist than one that frustrated their production.

Although Veblen portrayed earlier economic stages as more consumerist than the business stage, he was under no illusions about the economic motives of individuals who had pursued a livelihood in these earlier times. They had been as eager as any 1920s corporate leader to make a profit, he believed, but they had operated under fundamentally different economic conditions. And, according to Veblen, it had been these economic conditions that encouraged workmanship as surely as the economic conditions in the 1920s encouraged "sabotage." Before the end of the nineteenth century, he maintained, the "industrial system never reached such a pitch of efficiency that it could properly be called inordinately productive." In an economy that was not "continually in danger of outrunning the capacity of the market," the best way to make a profit was "by underselling an increased output of serviceable goods in an open market." Only in the late nineteenth century, when the economic system was becoming "inordinately productive," did business enterprises come to realize that the best way to maximize profits was "by maintaining prices and curtailing the output."[16]

Even though Veblen became far more consumerist over the years, he never abandoned his producerist convictions. He was as convinced in the 1920s as he had been at the turn of the century that the producer was the superior identity. And, linguistic conventions to the contrary, he continued to believe that only those who possessed an instinct of workmanship could legitimately claim the title of producer. Veblen regretted that by the 1920s workers were rapidly losing this instinct and with it any right to the producer label. But there were individuals, he insisted, who continued to approach production from an industrial rather than a pecuniary perspective. The "industrial experts," the "skilled technologists," the "production engineers," were "driven by no commercial bias" but were, instead, "responsible to their own sense of workmanship." Their only interest was in maximizing efficiency.[17] Not surprisingly, it was they and not victimized consumers who had become Veblen's heroes.

Veblen's strong producerist convictions left their mark on his consumerist ideas. Unlike many earlier thinkers, he never assumed that it was necessary to choose between a producer-oriented and a consumer-oriented system. Nor did he believe that in an industrial economy producers had to abandon their producer identity in favor of their identity as consumers. Not surprisingly, Veblen's determination to make room for both consumers and producers resulted in a set of consumerist ideas that diverged in significant ways from those of earlier consumerist thinkers such as Bellamy, Lippmann, and Weyl.

The most surprising divergence was Veblen's attitude toward competition. Bellamy, Lippmann, and Weyl had all believed that competition operated to the consumer's disadvantage. Bellamy had dismissed competition as one of the "great wastes," arguing that, if the workers' energies had been "expended in concerted effort," it would have increased productivity enough to "have enriched all." Lippmann and Weyl had suggested that, far from encouraging the efficient production of high-quality, low-cost goods, competition was more likely to reward cheapened quality and lower standards of workmanship. The trust, by contrast, with all its faults, did more for the consumer. It "at least prevent[ed] some of our earlier reckless wastes" and was the "beginning of a collective organization." Although neither Lippmann nor Weyl saw the trust as "the last word in industrial development," they were nevertheless convinced that "it was superior to what had preceded it."[18]

Veblen did not share their conviction. Not only did he dismiss the notion that the trust was "superior to what had preceded it"; he also rejected the idea that the trust had reduced or eliminated competition. On the contrary, it had only transformed it. For most of the nineteenth century, Veblen maintained, competition had "run mutually between the producing-sellers," in what "might be called a competition in workmanship." Such competition meant that goods "were made profitable by low costs." What was significant for Veblen about a competition in workmanship "between producing-sellers" was that it encouraged the efficient production of high-quality, low-cost goods. And, in so doing, it "inured to the benefit of the consumers."[19]

The same, however, could not be said of competition in a corporate economy. According to Veblen, in such an economy "the competition which . . . used to run mutually between the producing-sellers has . . . increasingly come to run between the business community on the one side and the consumers on the other." The problem with such businesslike competition, Veblen maintained, was that it used "salesmanship and sabotage" to gain an advantage, both of which furthered the interests of business at the consumer's expense. Salesmanship, as Veblen defined it, "means little else than prevarication," its end "to get a margin of something for nothing at the cost of the consumer in a closed market." "And sabotage," he continued, "means a businesslike curtailment of output," its goal to maintain artificially high prices.[20] Neither one was particularly consumer oriented.

What was striking about Veblen's 1920s views on competition was how much they had come to resemble those of Adam Smith. Veblen had spent much of his career exposing the weaknesses in liberal economic theory. Yet, near the end of his career, he found himself embracing the central tenet of Smithian economics, the notion that competition was an effective regulator of the economy. Veblen was able to do so because he had historicized competition, distinguishing between the "competitive selling" of the corporate economy and the "competitive production of goods" which had operated in Smith's time. He was no more convinced than Bellamy, Weyl, or Lippmann that the cure for the economy's ills in the 1920s was a return to a competitive market. But he parted company with them in his unwillingness to dismiss what Lippmann had disparagingly referred to as the "naïve notions of the nineteenth century." For Veblen competition had at one time been an effective market mechanism.[21]

Even more to the point, competition had been an effective market mechanism that had advanced the interests of both consumers and producers. Consumerist thinkers such as Bellamy, Weyl, and Lippmann had all assumed that it was necessary to choose between a producer-oriented and a consumer-oriented economy. Veblen, however, was unwilling to do so. And Smith's economic model suggested that he did not have to. Veblen had no intention of adopting Smith's approach. He was well aware that the rise of a corporate economy had made competition an ineffective way to harmonize the opposing interests of consumers and producers. Nevertheless, Veblen's interest in constructing an economic model that would function on behalf of both consumers and producers made him far more sensitive to the consumerist implications of competition than Bellamy, Weyl, or Lippmann had ever been.[22]

It was no accident that a strident critic of liberal economic theory such as Veblen managed to come to terms with Smithian economic theory in the very years that he was developing consumerist sympathies. Indeed, many left-leaning consumerist thinkers would spend the 1920s and 1930s struggling to reconcile their preference for a socialist alternative to profit-oriented capitalism with the realization that it was not Karl Marx but Adam Smith who had placed the consumer at the center of his political economy. And, as they witnessed the National Recovery Administration's disappointing experiment in economic planning, the failure of the Soviet planned economy to raise the living standard of the Russian people, and the phenomenal productivity of the U.S. economy in the early 1940s, most consumerist left liberals would eventually opt for an economic system that was far more Smithian than Marxian.[23]

If Veblen's nascent consumerist sympathies made him appreciate Smith's ideas more than he once had, the same could not be said for his attitude toward Simon Patten's ideas. At first glance it might seem that by the 1920s Veblen was on the same road Patten had traveled several years earlier. Both suggested that the ideal economy would make room for producers *and* consumers. And both parted company with most of their contemporaries in arguing that a corporate economy remained a competitive one. These similarities, however, proved to be more apparent than real. Patten might have championed the producer, but his producer was the corporate capitalist, the very individual whom Veblen blamed for the anticonsumer direction the economy had taken in the twentieth century. And Patten might have argued that the corporate economy remained a competitive one, but the competition he identified was one that existed among the corporations as consumers practiced their "power of substitution." The competition that Veblen observed, by contrast, did not empower consumers. On the contrary, existing "between the business community on the one side and the consumers on the other," it gave all the advantage to the corporations.

Ultimately, what distinguished Patten's ideal order from Veblen's was that Patten's was consumption oriented, Veblen's consumer oriented. Indeed, Veblen could imagine few things worse than an economic system designed merely to increase consumption. One of his biggest complaints about the 1920s corporate economy was the extent to which it permitted "the fabrication of customers . . . as a routine operation, quite in the spirit of the mechanical industries and with much the same degree of assurance as regards the quality, rate and volume of the output."[24] A consumer-oriented economy, by contrast, might very well discourage consumption, if doing so were in the best interests of the consuming masses.

Veblen was not the first thinker to distinguish between a consumer-oriented political economy and a consumption-oriented one. Indeed, forty years earlier Bellamy had denounced profit-oriented capitalism because it forced consumers to "buy, buy, buy, for money if they had it, for credit if they had it not, to buy what they wanted not, more than they wanted, what they could not afford."[25] But, if Veblen agreed with other consumerist thinkers that the problem with the existing system was that it was consumption oriented, he did not agree with them on how to replace that system with a consumer-oriented one. Bellamy, Lippmann, and Weyl had all been convinced that a consumer-oriented political economy would come into being when consumers seized control of the system from the business interests. According to Bellamy, such a seizure would have required a peaceful revolution. According to Lippmann and Weyl, it would have required the political mobilization of consumer-citizens. Either way, all three had been confident that, having secured control over the government, consumers would use their power to restructure the economy on behalf of the consuming masses.

Veblen rejected such a solution for two reasons. First, he believed that managing an industrial economy was a highly complex and technical task, one that could not be left to consumer-citizens. But, more important, Veblen had serious doubts about the ability of consumers to manage their own consumption. Despite his increasingly consumerist outlook, Veblen had never lost his early misgivings about the consumer. Although he had come to regret that they were victimized by the existing system, he nevertheless blamed consumers for much of their own predicament. They allowed the business interests to use "up their productive forces, with nothing better to show for it than an increased cost of living." They willingly purchased "superfluities and spurious goods." They seemed incapable of resisting advertising, seeing beyond "fancy packages and labels," or identifying adulterated goods. The consuming masses, Veblen concluded, were both "credulous" and docile, hardly the stuff of which revolutions were made, peaceful or otherwise.[26]

Weyl, Lippmann, and Bellamy had not been without their own misgivings concerning the ability of the masses to consume rationally. Lippmann had regretted the "disastrous incompetence of the ultimate consumer." "A bewildered child in a toy shop," he had asserted, "is nothing to the ultimate consumer in the world market of to-day." Bellamy had worried about the consumers' inability to resist either the dictates of fashion or the pressures of sales clerks. And Weyl had denounced both the conformity of the consuming masses ("There are women," he suggested, "who are heterodox in religion, politics, and cooking, who nevertheless dare not wear a small hat when other women wear their hats large") and their lack of any sense of social responsibility.[27] "We are consuming without judgment, without moderation, without regard to our individual interests or to the interests of society." "Much of our expenditure," he asserted, "is a pure competition of display. Fashion, conspicuous waste, absurd extravagance, even among the poor, destroy an astonishing proportion of the national product. The pleasure of Americans consists largely in the breaking of expensive toys."[28]

At first glance it would seem that Bellamy, Lippmann, and Weyl had had as many misgivings concerning the consumer as had Veblen. Why, then, did they believe consumers could manage a consumer-oriented political economy and Veblen did not? The answer lies with how each identified the source of the consumer's failings. Bellamy, Lippmann, and Weyl all blamed consumer misbehavior on the profit system. They were convinced that businesses manipulated consumers into "consuming without judgment, without moderation, without regard to [their] individual interests or to the interests of society."[29] Without such manipulation, they predicted, consumers would either learn to control their consumption or would do so automatically.

Veblen disagreed. Although he was willing to put some of the blame on business, he was convinced that consumers were also culpable. Consumer misbehavior, he insisted, had existed since the earliest stages of human existence. The ideas that goods were effective indicators of one's power and that useless goods were better markers of status than useful ones had their roots in the barbarian stage of history. There was no reason to suppose that consumer misbehavior, which predated profit-oriented capitalism, would not also survive it. But if consumers were indeed incapable of consuming moderately, judiciously, and responsibly, then they were hardly equipped to manage their own affairs. As far as Veblen was concerned, they needed someone to run the system for them.

By the early 1930s most consumerist left liberals had embraced Veblen's notion of a managed economy as the best way to safeguard the interests of the consuming population. In the 1920s, however, the handful of left liberals who had already begun to view society and the economy through a consumerist lens did not rely equally on Veblen's ideas. Popular economist Stuart Chase was the most enthusiastic Veblenian of the group. In a series of books and articles he emphasized the shortcomings of an economy dedicated to producing profits rather than goods. And he insisted that the solution was economic planning, be it under the direction of Veblen's engineers or an "Industrial General Staff, a government body modelled along the lines of the WIB."[30]

Unlike Chase, both economics professor Rexford Tugwell and sociologist Robert Lynd were initially more interested in Veblen's diagnosis of the economy's ills than they were in his cure. Lynd, together with his wife, Helen Merrell Lynd, attributed the stresses and strains of life in Middletown to the dictates of a pecuniary economy. And even Rexford Tugwell, who came to Veblen more slowly than did either Chase or Lynd, eventually incorporated Veblen's distinction between business and industry, insisting that "producing profits does not always mean producing goods."[31] Indeed, by the mid-1930s Tugwell's Veblenian credentials had become so strong that he was chosen to write the essay on Veblen in Malcolm Cowley and Bernard Smith's *Books That Changed Our Minds.*

Tugwell did not travel the same road to a consumerist way of thinking which Chase and Lynd did. For Chase the journey began in the mid-1910s, when, in a series of articles, he chronicled the difficulties confronting one family—his—as it struggled to maintain a middle-class lifestyle in the prewar inflationary economy. When it came to offering a solution to these difficulties, the best that Chase had to offer was to call on individuals to reduce waste and on government to tax luxuries and excess profits.[32]

What was striking about Chase's solution was that, despite a degree in economics from Harvard and long-standing Fabian sympathies, he seemed either unaware of or uninterested in twentieth-century thinking on the consumer. Indeed, his assumption that much of the problem could be traced to a taste for luxury placed him closer to nineteenth-century thinking on the subject. Only in 1919, when he encountered Veblen's articles in *Dial* (which were later published as *The Engineers and the Price System*) did Chase begin to conclude that the difficulties besetting the consuming population were endemic to a profit-oriented system.[33]

Like Chase, Lynd began thinking about the consumer in the mid-1910s, long before he encountered Veblen. Ironically, however, as managing editor of *Publishers' Weekly,* Lynd first approached the consumer from the perspective of the advertiser.[34] And by the late 1910s, when he left *Publishers' Weekly* to pursue a degree in divinity at Union Theological Seminary, Lynd had ceased to think about the consumer from any perspective at all. Only in the mid-1920s, when he began working on *Middletown,* did he return to the consumer. As he observed the residents of Muncie, Indiana, Lynd came to the conclusion that the key to understanding the existing economic system lay in large part in understanding the consumer's place within it. It was a conviction that owed much to Veblen.

By contrast, Tugwell's first exposure to the consumer was as an undergraduate at the Wharton School, when he came under the influence of Simon Patten. It was an influence that Tugwell would long feel. Indeed, Stuart Chase, who dismissed Patten's influence on his own thinking ("I read a bit of Patten in my salad days, but he never made the impression on me that Veblen did or H. G. Wells, or even Scott Nearing") would later remember Tugwell as "a devoted disciple of Simon Patten" who "quoted him at every opportunity." And

Henry Wallace recalled Tugwell trying "to get me interested in Patten. . . . Rex looked on him as a truly great man."[35]

Tugwell may have relied far more heavily on Patten than did other post–World War I consumerist left liberals. But, like another Patten protégé, Walter Weyl, he was quite willing to push Patten's ideas in a far more consumerist direction than Patten had ever intended. And, like Weyl, Tugwell often drew on Veblen to temper Patten's pro-capitalist analysis. Indeed, the task that Tugwell set for himself in his dissertation, *The Economic Basis of Public Interest,* published in 1922, was to justify price controls, the very sort of government regulation which Patten had rejected.

Patten had rejected price controls because he believed they were not only unwise—they would, he warned, lead to economic stagnation—but also unnecessary. Instead, he placed his faith in consumers and capitalists. Consumers, he insisted, could keep capitalists in line through the "power of substitution." Any consumer who found that prices for a product were too high could simply substitute "other goods supplying the same want." Even more important, Patten maintained, because "the growth of large scale capitalism has resulted in the elimination of the unsocial capitalist," capitalists were increasingly willing to keep themselves in line.[36] Not government regulation but altruistic businessmen and vigilant consumers were the key to prosperity as Patten imagined it.

Tugwell, by contrast, was unwilling to trust businessmen with control over the economy. Like Veblen, he was convinced that their motives were not altruistic but, instead, "purely acquisitive," their main concern the "highest possible net profit." Without "perfect and free competition," Tugwell warned, businessmen were far more likely to use their newly acquired "monopoly powers" to limit supply and raise prices than to behave in the socially responsible manner that Patten had predicted. And "when supply is limited in the interest of total net profit," Tugwell concluded, "there is a harm to consumers."[37]

But could not consumers compel businessmen to pursue consumer-oriented policies? Tugwell had his doubts. With "the end of competition in a *laissez-faire* regime," he maintained, ". . . the disadvantage of mere disorganized consumers in dealing with highly organized business has become more and more apparent." And, although he was willing to grant that consumers could exert some influence over business through their power of substitution,

he insisted that relying on this power to regulate the economy placed an unfair burden on consumers. There was, he insisted, "no defensible reason why
consumption habits should be compelled to change so that some one, or even
a group of persons, may gain a profit" through the "artificial manipulations
of prices." Government, not consumers, should be responsible for compelling
business to provide "adequate service at reasonable rates."[38]

Despite his call for government regulation of the economy and his emphasis on acquisitive businessmen, Tugwell's basic view of the economy remained far closer to that of Patten than that of Veblen. Implicit in Veblen's
understanding of the economy was the notion of conflict. No economic system, he believed, could function on behalf of both consumers and business,
because the two had such diametrically opposed interests. Patten, by contrast,
was convinced that it was possible to construct an economic system that
would further the interests of both consumers and business. The key was
abundant production.

Tugwell agreed with Patten that an economy characterized by abundant
production could function on behalf of both consumers and businessmen. He
merely doubted that businessmen were aware of the fact. Business managers,
Tugwell warned, "do not always apprehend that their acquisitive interest may
be served," "by extending sales and accepting low profits per unit in the interest of the large total profits." Indeed, according to Tugwell, one of the
ironies of price controls was that the "rate-fixing bodies" would force business
managers "against their desires into large-scale service and the taking of a
small profit per unit," the very sort of economic behavior which, Tugwell insisted, could maximize profits.[39]

At first glance Tugwell's defense of profits may have seemed inconsistent
with his consumer-oriented left liberalism. Ultimately, however, it was not in
spite of his consumerist leanings but because of them that Tugwell defended
profits. Like Adam Smith, he considered profits a means to an end, that end
being the abundant manufacture of goods. But he was as aware as Veblen that,
in the absence of competition "to protect consumers," profits were far more
likely to encourage restricted production and high prices than abundant production and low prices.

The question, then, was whether profits could be an effective means to
consumerist ends in the corporate economy of the 1920s. Veblen had been
convinced that they could not. Indeed, in his view the only way to guarantee

a consumer-oriented approach to production in a corporate economy was to replace businessmen, who were motivated by profit, with engineers, who were interested in efficiency. Tugwell, however, had far more faith in the consumerist potential of the profit motive. And he looked to price controls to harness that potential. Once government set prices, he predicted, businessmen would quickly realize that it was no longer in their self-interest to make their profits on "high per unit profits on greatly restricted sales." Instead, they would discover that the "cheapest and widest dissemination of goods possible" was the best way to maximize their bottom line.[40]

In calling for abundant production and low prices, Tugwell was advocating a consumption-oriented economy. His version, however, was a far cry from Patten's. Patten had called for expanded consumption because he believed that it could neutralize working-class radicalism and at the same time protect business profits. Tugwell, by contrast, was not particularly concerned about the well-being of either capitalists or workers. His goal was to promote the welfare of the consuming public. If, as he believed, businessmen oppressed consumers by "reduc[ing] the supply of those things which people depend on for their sustenance and happiness," then the way to end such "oppression" was to force businessmen to produce abundant, high-quality, low-cost goods.[41] Tugwell's consumption-oriented economy, unlike Patten's, was also a consumer-oriented one.

It was striking the enthusiasm with which Tugwell made room for capitalists in his consumer-oriented economy, particularly since most of his left liberal contemporaries were far more reluctant to do so. Well into the 1930s consumerist left liberals, with only a few notable exceptions, would remain convinced that corporate capitalists were incapable of directing the economy in a consumer-oriented fashion. Businessmen, they would argue, made their profits either by making goods artificially scarce or by manipulating the consumer into buying harmful or unnecessary products. Only through extensive government intervention in the economy, they would conclude, would it be possible to guarantee that the nation's productive machinery would operate on behalf of the consuming population.

It was not sympathy for businessmen which prompted the left liberal Tugwell to envision a significant role for profit-seeking capitalists within his consumer-oriented system. Indeed, unlike Patten, Tugwell was convinced that given half a chance, capitalists were as likely as not to pursue unsocial policies. Nor was Tugwell motivated by a belief in the sanctity of property. On the contrary, he was as adamant as any consumerist left liberal that the market had to be viewed "as a social mechanism rather than as a private one."[42]

Why, then, did Tugwell make room for capitalists in his consumer-oriented economy? The answer has to do with the extent to which he embraced Patten's version of the "good society." Like Patten, Tugwell assumed that the best way to promote the public interest was to increase the public's access to consumer goods. And, like Patten, he believed that capitalism—albeit with a few modifications—was capable of providing these goods. But, once Tugwell concluded that a consumer-oriented economy also had to be consumption oriented, he found it easy to do what proved far more difficult for the majority of consumerist left liberals, namely rely on profit-oriented businessmen to manufacture the products for a consumer-oriented order.

Not surprisingly, left liberals who took a Veblenian route to a consumerist worldview shared neither Tugwell's belief in the consumerist potential of profits nor his definition of a consumer-oriented economy as one that maximized consumption. Veblen had never had much sympathy with a consumption-oriented economy. Indeed, he had been as critical of business for forcing individuals to consume too much as for limiting their access to consumer goods. In Veblen's view a consumption-oriented economy, far from being one that functioned on behalf of consumers, was dedicated to serving the interests of profit-hungry businessmen at the expense of the consuming public.

Robert Lynd agreed. As he and Helen Merrell Lynd examined the daily activities of Middletowners, they were struck by the "long hours day after day" which their subjects spent working in the "offices, stores, and factories of Middletown." "Why," the Lynds wondered, "do they work so hard?" It was not, the two concluded, because Middletowners enjoyed their labors. On the contrary, as far as the Lynds could tell, "the amount of robust satisfaction they derive from the actual performance of their specific jobs seems, at best, to be slight." Nor was it because "all this expenditure of energy [was] necessary to secure food, clothing, shelter, and other things essential to existence." Instead, the Lynds decided, Middletowners worked so long and hard because they wanted "to buy more."[43]

Although the Lynds were as convinced as any 1920s cultural critic that the emphasis on consumption was destroying the cooperative and communal ethos that had characterized American life only a generation earlier, they parted company with these critics over who was ultimately to blame. According to cultural critics such as Lewis Mumford and Waldo Frank, self-indulgent consumers, enthusiastically engaging in an orgy of materialism, were responsible not only for the demise of communitarian sensibilities but also for their own misery. The Lynds, however, saw consumers not as the perpetrators of excessive consumption so much as its victims. "Whole industries," they warned, "are pooling their strength to ram home a higher standard of living." No longer content to rely on the "relatively mild . . . I-tell-you-this-is-a-good-article copy seen in Middletown a generation ago, advertising is concentrating increasingly upon a type of copy aiming to make the reader emotionally uneasy, to bludgeon him with the fact that decent people don't live the way *he* does: *decent* people ride on balloon tires, have a second bathroom, and so on." In short, the Lynds concluded, it was not self-indulgent consumers but a profit-oriented business system that forced consumers into "running for dear life in this business of making the money they earn keep pace with the even more rapid growth of their subjective wants."[44]

Like the Lynds, Stuart Chase doubted whether a profit-oriented system could ever function in a truly consumer-oriented fashion. His doubts, however, stemmed primarily from his conviction that the system, far from forcing individuals to consume too much, denied them "adequate food, shelter, clothing, education and modest comforts." Chase was quick to stress that it was not any technical inability to produce which failed "to keep the majority of American families above the line of economic insecurity and want." Instead, it was the "waste and leakage of business-as-usual" which was responsible for the "existence of a wide margin of poverty." This waste occurred because workers, who were willing and able to produce, were denied employment because of layoffs, "labor turnover, strikes and the needless agony of industrial accident and disease." It occurred "because individual plants are badly managed." And it occurred "because there is little co-ordination between the requirements of the population to be served by the output of these plants, and their production schedules."[45]

Chase did not limit his analysis to wastes in production and distribution. Yet even as he turned his attention to what he called the "wastes in consumption," he remained focused on the ways in which the existing economic system frustrated the nation's productive potential. By *wastes in consumption* Chase did not mean the sort of consumer behavior which Veblen had decried almost thirty years earlier in *The Theory of the Leisure Class*. Instead, he meant the "wasted man-power" that went into the "production of goods which lie outside the category of human wants." Thus, while he believed it was important to recognize that "the number of people converted into drug fiends or made ill by patent medicines is in its way a waste," what Chase wanted "to know more particularly is how many industrial workers are bottling, packing, advertising and selling the deleterious product."[46]

What was striking about Chase's analysis was the extent to which it absolved consumers of any wrongdoing. Even the Lynds, who denounced advertisers and businessmen for manipulating consumers, nevertheless regretted the zeal with which Middletowners sought to accumulate consumer goods. They recounted story after story of people in Middletown who endured considerable hardship to acquire "an electric washing machine, electric iron," "vacuum sweeper," "icebox," or "$1,200 Studebaker." What the Lynds found particularly discouraging about such struggles was the consumption priorities these struggles revealed. Middletowners, it would seem, were willing to go without even the most basic of necessities before they would deny themselves what the Lynds considered luxuries. And nowhere, the Lynds believed, was that tendency more evident than in the Middletowners' love affair with the automobile. "We'd rather do without clothes than give up the car," one woman with nine children told the investigators. "I'd go without a meal before I'd cut down on using the car," exclaimed another. And, of twenty-six families on whom the Lynds had data concerning both car ownership and bathroom facilities, twenty-one had a car but no bathtub.[47]

Chase was both more critical of business and more tolerant of consumers than were the Lynds. His profit-seeking businessmen were not merely pressuring consumers to buy cars they could ill afford. They were far more nefarious than that, converting consumers into drug fiends and poisoning them with patent medicines. They were profit seekers who deliberately wasted both manpower and natural resources, in the process consigning much of the population to poverty.[48]

As for Chase's consumers, far from being the willing participants in their own manipulation whom the Lynds described, they were the model of restraint—so much so that multimillion-dollar advertising campaigns were necessary to break down their "sales resistance." And so what, Chase conceded, if consumers occasionally engaged in nonutilitarian consumption? "Human nature," he was quick to stress, "is such that it demands to keep up with the Joneses—particularly in democratic countries."[49] Once a threat to the very survival of republican political institutions, conspicuous consumption had become in Chase's hands a fundamental right of democracy.

Despite Chase's defense of consumers' desires, he was as quick as the Lynds to distinguish between a consumer-oriented and a consumption-oriented economy. At best a consumption-oriented economy focused on the "distribution of material goods and services to the ultimate consumer." At worst it emphasized "unlimited purchasing power for unlimited junk." Either way, Chase warned, defining prosperity in terms of the quantity of consumer goods was problematic because it "does not say much about the value of the goods, or their net effect on health, happiness, and habits." "It still escapes me," he concluded, "why a prosperity founded on forcing people to consume what they do not need, and often do not want, is, or can be, a healthy and permanent growth."[50]

Like the Lynds, Chase insisted that a consumer-oriented system was one that emphasized living rather than consuming. And, like them, he saw consumer goods not so much as an end in themselves but as a means to a fuller life. He was as quick as they were to insist that such a life depended upon the ability of all to live "free from the fear of want." It also required, he believed, the application of "technical knowledge to increase . . . physical well-being" and promote health. But both he and the Lynds remained convinced that a full life depended on more than material and physical comfort. To the Lynds the cooperative social relationships that had defined life in Middletown a generation earlier were an essential component of the full life. As for the more sensuous Chase, he wanted "to live in a community where beauty abounded." And, "above all," he wanted "leisure, leisure, a break in the remorseless and meaningless urgencies of the twentieth-century pace."[51] Whatever else Chase's utopia was, it was not producerist!

But was it capitalist? That was the question with which consumerist left liberals would struggle well into the 1930s. Initially, the debate revolved around whether "salesmanship" and "sabotage"—what Veblen had referred to as the "twin pillars of the edifice of business-as-usual in recent times"—were basic to capitalism or merely a perversion of it.[52] In the 1930s the debate expanded to include another issue. Following the collapse of the economy, left liberals would wonder whether the inability to sustain mass purchasing power was a fundamental defect of a capitalist system or merely a correctable flaw.

It was not particularly surprising that in the high consumption economy of the 1920s Tugwell, Chase, and the Lynds should focus more on the impact of salesmanship and sabotage than on the sustainability of mass purchasing power. Nor is it particularly surprising that Chase and the Lynds, all of whom relied more heavily on Veblen's analysis than had Tugwell, were generally far more pessimistic about the consumerist potential of capitalism than he. What is surprising is the extent to which even Chase, the most Veblenian of the bunch, found it difficult to reject capitalism completely. Although he was quick to insist that the only way to construct a consumer-oriented economy was through some sort of economic planning, he was never quite sure whether his planned economy would replace capitalism or merely discipline it.[53]

Tugwell found it far easier than Chase to assume that a consumer-oriented economy was capitalist because he did not diagnose the cause of the economy's ills in the same way that Chase did. Tugwell traced the capitalist "oppression" of consumers to the rapid disappearance of the competitive market forces that were supposed to prevent that oppression.[54] The task, as he saw it, was to find some way to keep capitalists in line now that competition no longer did so. This was where his price and quality controls came in. They were merely a means to an end, just like the competitive market mechanisms they were designed to replace.

The market mechanism that Chase identified, however, was profit. And he was not certain if profit was merely a means to an end or an end in itself. He knew that what he did not like about the existing system—an "acquisitive society," he called it—was that "production to meet necessary requirements" was "a by-product rather than the main end of economic activity." And he knew that what he wanted to see in place of an acquisitive society was a "functional" one, where "industry is devoted primarily to supplying human wants, and where profits are a by-product."[55] What he was not so certain of, however, was whether replacing a profit-driven economy with a planned one constituted a rejection of capitalism or merely a modification of it. Only in the mid-1930s, when he added an inability to provide mass purchasing power to his list of capitalism's defects, did he conclude—and then only temporarily—that a planned economy was not a version of capitalism but, rather, the economic stage that would follow it.[56]

Given his hostility toward profits, it is striking that in one of his most popular works Chase called on consumers to harness the profit motive on their own behalf. The book was *Your Money's Worth*, a best-seller and book-of-themonth-club selection, which he coauthored with F. J. Schlink. Although it represented a major departure for Chase, it was consistent with much of what Schlink would later write. In all likelihood, therefore, this "'Uncle Tom's Cabin' of abuses of the consumer," as Robert Lynd would later call it, owed its economic perspective far more to Schlink than to Chase.[57]

Schlink was an exception among consumerist left liberals in a couple of ways. For one, he was far less interested than they in the political form that a consumer-oriented system would take. Thus, while most of the consumerist left liberals would ultimately remain within the liberal fold, Schlink proved surprisingly adept at changing his political allegiances. A liberal in the mid-1920s, he drifted steadily leftward. By the end of the decade he was well within the ranks of left liberalism and by 1933 was complaining that the platform of Socialist candidate Norman Thomas was too "mild." Shortly thereafter, however, he did an about-turn. By the late 1930s he had become a libertarian and an ardent anti-Communist crusader, funneling information about his former left-leaning allies to the Dies Committee on Un-American Activities.[58]

Schlink was also unique among consumerist left liberals because he alone could lay claim to membership in Veblen's revolutionary cadre of engineers. He had a master's degree in engineering, had spent the 1910s working as a physicist and technical assistant to the director at the Bureau of Standards, and, for much of the 1920s, served as assistant secretary to the newly organized American Engineering Standards Committee. Yet, contrary to Veblen's expectations, Schlink proved to be far more interested in the radical potential of consumer activism than that of Taylorism.

Schlink had discovered the consumer while working at the Bureau of Standards. One of the bureau's primary functions was to test products that the government needed, the results of which were used to design specifications, which the government then used to purchase supplies. In the course of preparing these specifications, the bureau had amassed information on a vast number of brand-name products. Schlink found it regrettable that the bureau refused to share this information with tax-paying consumers. He found it unconscionable that by the 1920s the bureau was using its scientific expertise on behalf of industry.[59]

That Chase and Schlink managed to collaborate is at first glance surprising because the two approached the consumer in such fundamentally different ways. Chase was primarily concerned with the consumer as a user of goods.

The goal, as he saw it, was to prevent the waste that was ultimately responsible for the existence of poverty. He looked to an economic order in which the industrial plant produced enough high-quality, useful goods so that "the last family in the country could be raised above the line of economic insecurity." Schlink, by contrast, saw the consumer primarily as a purchaser of goods. For him the goal was to end the manipulation of consumers by empowering them to make "efficient and economic selection[s]."[60]

Despite their different approaches to the consumer, Chase and Schlink managed to find common ground. Both, for example, denounced salesmanship. Yet, even as they agreed that salesmanship injured the consumer, they did not identify the same injury. For Chase salesmanship was precisely the sort of activity which wasted society's resources. "Under the canons of high-pressure selling and volume turnover," he complained, "we are enjoined directly and indirectly by something in the nature of a billion dollars' worth of advertising and publicity a year, to throw things away before they are worn out, and buy a new model." For Schlink, by contrast, salesmanship was a tool with which business exploited consumers by convincing them to pay inflated prices for what were often substandard and unnecessary products. And what made matters worse, Schlink concluded, was that consumers ultimately had to foot the bill "to be told . . . that Tweedledum and Tweedledee, though both excellent fellows, were each infinitely to be preferred to the other."[61]

Chase and Schlink may not have understood the economic impact of salesmanship in the same way. But the very fact that they were both concerned about its impact meant that they shared certain assumptions. Both distinguished between a consumption- and a consumer-oriented economy. Both assumed that salesmanship would play a dominant role in the former but no role at all in the latter. And both saw the existing economy as hopelessly consumption oriented. "The consumer," they told the readers of *Your Money's Worth*, "is under mounting pressure, directed by ever increasing astuteness, to buy, buy, buy." This pressure meant that consumers "buy not what they freely want but what they are made to want." And it meant that consumers "buy not for the value of the product to meet [their] specific needs but because the story told on every billboard, every newspaper and magazine page, every shop window, every sky sign . . . is a pleasing, stimulating and romantic story." But it was not merely that in a consumption-oriented economy consumers were manipulated into purchasing products that they did not really want or that had little relation to their actual needs. Even more troubling, according to Chase and Schlink, these products were often of poor quality and some-times even dangerous. Why? Because in an economy, in which "turnover is the chief aim," businesses were under "a tremendous temptation . . . to adulterate goods, limit their serviceability, [and] shorten their life." Doing so offered one sure way to "bring the purchaser back the sooner for another sale."[62]

How, then, to liberate this consumer who had been trained "to jump through the hoops of the advertiser—dosing himself with dangerous nos-trums . . . walking Heaven alone knows how many aggregate miles for a cigarette." The answer, Chase and Schlink suggested, was scientific buying. "When goods are bought to specification," the two explained, ". . . the buyer knows exactly what he is getting; the manufacturer knows exactly what he has to produce. Competition must then descend from the cloudy heights of sales appeals and mysticism generally, to just one factor—price."[63]

What was striking about Chase's and Schlink's analysis in *Your Money's Worth* was the extent to which it embraced capitalism. In his other writings Chase, much like Tugwell, had blamed the consumer's problems on the fail-ure of what were fundamental components of capitalism. For Tugwell it was the decline of that most basic of market mechanisms, competition, which was responsible for the "oppression" of the consumer. For Chase it was a central feature of capitalism, the profit motive, which prevented the system from operating on behalf of the consuming population.[64] The two might not have agreed on the specifics, but both assumed that only by abandoning Smithian means would it be possible to achieve the Smithian end of a prosperous, consumer-oriented society.

In *Your Money's Worth*, however, Chase and Schlink embraced Smithian means as enthusiastically as they advocated Smithian ends. They were able to do so because they identified salesmanship as the factor that prevented capi-talism from functioning in a consumer-oriented fashion. What was signifi-cant about salesmanship was that, unlike profit and competition, it was not one of the basic components of Smith's economic model. Thus, while both Chase's call for a planned economy and Tugwell's call for a regulated one rep-resented a departure from a Smithian economy, advocating a system in which consumers were immune to the pressures of salesmanship represented a re-turn to an earlier, more Smithian form of capitalism. This system would con-sist of consumers who would once again be able to perform the function that Smith had long ago assigned to them. Having acquired the knowledge necessary to see past salesmanship, they would be able to reward producers who provided high-quality, low-cost goods and punish those who did not.

Given their strong consumerist leanings, it is perhaps not inconceivable that two left liberals could endorse the consumerist aspects of a Smithian economy. What is far more astonishing is that they were willing to embrace its producerist aspects as well. An impotent consumer, they told their readers, was as bad for business as it was for consumers. "In a reasonable world it would be a kindergarten principle that a thing good for the ultimate consumer is good for industry." But, according to Chase and Schlink, the world was far from reasonable. It was not quality but salesmanship that determined consumer behavior, and this meant that "it is not quality but salesmanship which makes or breaks a business man to-day." "Honest manufacturers," Chase and Schlink concluded, "have gone cascading into eternity because their goods were better than their sales appeal."[65]

How, then, to rescue such "honest manufacturers"? The answer, Chase and Schlink decided, was to reestablish the sort of economy in which "the test of business success is the excellence and serviceability of its product." And this was where the consumer came in. "If and when the consumer arms for his own protection, the vicious circle may perhaps be broken, and the manufacturer of sound goods restored to the place which the higher salesmanship has so often wrung from him." Empowered consumers, Chase and Schlink announced, would protect "an honest manufacturer against the higher salesmanship in the hands of an unscrupulous rival."[66] And, in so doing, they would replace a corrupted capitalist system with one that functioned the way that Smith had envisioned.

What was significant about *Your Money's Worth* was not that it reflected a consensus among consumerist left liberals in the late 1920s nor even that it represented Chase's and Schlink's thinking on capitalism. It did neither. Indeed, over the next several years most consumerist left liberals—Chase and Schlink included—would denounce capitalism far more often than defend it. But *Your Money's Worth* did highlight how difficult it was for left liberal consumerist thinkers, who considered themselves radicals, to reject capitalism. Even as they flirted with ideologies on the left, they could never completely abandon the notion that a system committed to an ever-expanding prosperity might serve the consumer better than one that was dedicated to equity through the redistribution of wealth.

The inability to reject capitalism was only one example of what proved to be a dilemma for consumerist left liberals in the 1920s and early 1930s. Throughout these years left liberals strongly resisted the liberal label. In their view they occupied a position far to the left of liberalism. Chase, for example, insisted that his ideas had more in common with socialism and perhaps even communism than liberalism. And *New Republic* editor George Soule, whose consumerist sympathies would become increasingly evident in the 1930s, suggested that "radical progressivism" was a far better way to describe his political ideas.[67]

But, even as consumerist left liberals rejected the liberal label, they found that their consumerist sympathies pushed them in directions that were anything but left. It had been these sympathies that had prevented them from rejecting capitalism out of hand. And it would be these sympathies that would prompt them to abandon the worker in favor of the middle class. In both cases consumerist left liberals found themselves advocating positions that were far more liberal than radical.

Perhaps even more frustrating, left liberals found that their consumerist sympathies pushed them in directions that called into question their self-image as "political realists." Like many of their contemporaries, left liberals insisted that political theories had to be based on empirical study. Indeed, for them one of the major weaknesses of radical thought was that it lacked an objective, morally neutral foundation. The problem with radicals, George Soule insisted, was that they preferred to denounce "existing institutions . . . on the grounds of abstract principle," whereas he and other left liberals preferred to test these "institutions by the establishment of standards and the record of performance." Stuart Chase was even more direct. "Some years ago," he told the American critic and author Edmund Wilson in 1931, "I came to the conclusion that we are not going to resolve the problems of poverty, waste and human degradation in America by employing [the] standard dogmas. Somebody had to find out what was really going on, not what Karl Marx, seventy years ago, said might go on." Chase was willing to acknowledge that Marx "was a good guesser." But, he insisted, "seventy years is a long time." "I am looking for a synthesis a good way ahead of your orthodox communism, Mr. Wilson, and yet one which can begin to work. Now; here."[68]

According to most political realists in the 1920s, one system that would not work "now; here" was democracy. The problem with democracy, they maintained, was that it depended on informed citizens to make rational and intelligent decisions about how to further their own and the nation's well-being.

But, if Sigmund Freud was right, then humans were anything but rational. And, if the World War I intelligence tests were at all accurate, then the majority of Americans were not particularly intelligent. By the mid-1920s a number of studies by political scientists provided the empirical data that seemed to confirm what the psychological literature had suggested: voters were irrational and ignorant and could not be trusted with governing themselves.[69]

True to their self-image as political realists, consumerist left liberals dismissed democracy as just so much "nonsense." It was not an easy thing for advocates of a consumer-oriented system to do, particularly, since one of the appeals of a consumer-oriented system had long been its democratic potential. Indeed, both Bellamy in *Equality* and Weyl in *The New Democracy* had looked to the consumer identity to reenergize democracy. And cooperative theorists such as James Peter Warbasse and Albert Sonnichsen had insisted that the only "true democracy," as Sonnichsen put it, was a system that functioned on behalf of consumers, because "consumption. . . . is the one interest which we all have in common, and to very nearly the same degree."[70]

Nevertheless, consumerist left liberals managed to downplay the democratic implications in a consumer-oriented system. They did so, in part, by defining the consumer identity in strictly economic terms. By *consumer* they meant a purchaser and user of goods, the demand side of the economic equation, or the regulator of a competitive economy but not a voter or a citizen. They also downplayed these implications by advocating a system that functioned "for the people" rather than "of" or "by" them. For Tugwell this meant price controls. For the Lynds, who were less specific about the exact shape of such a system, it meant "a reëxamination of the institutions themselves." For Chase it meant a "National Planning Board . . . manned by engineers, physical scientists, statisticians, economists, accountants, and lawyers." "If we must have a few figure heads near the top, representing, to preserve the democratic dogma, industry, finance, labor, farmers, or this and that—well, we must have them." But Chase was quite adamant that "the real work, the real thought, the real action, must come from the technicians.[71]

The left liberal rejection of "democratic dogma" had certain implications for consumerist thought. For one, it made much of the recent thinking about the consumer unavailable to consumerist left liberals because that thinking had relied on a definition of the consumer as a citizen in a democracy. Walter Weyl had not only assumed that a consumer-oriented system would be democratic. He had also looked to citizens "voting as consumers" to usher in that "new democracy." Even Walter Lippmann had emphasized the role that politically organized consumers would play in bringing about a "great extension of collectivism."[72] Doubts about the ability of the people to function in a rational and intelligent manner, however, meant that Weyl's and Lippmann's consumerist ideas had little direct impact on consumerist thought throughout the 1920s.

If doubts about human rationality and intelligence had only prevented consumerist left liberals from drawing on Weyl's and Lippmann's theories, they would have been merely inconvenient. But these doubts posed a far more serious challenge to a consumerist worldview because nowhere was human irrationality and ignorance more evident than in the marketplace. To many an observer the phenomenal growth of the advertising industry in the late 1910s and 1920s seemed to bear out the incompetence of American consumers, for it suggested that consumers could be made to want almost anything and, even worse, that the best way to do so was to focus on their subconscious fears and desires, rather than the qualities of the product.[73] But, if consumers were indeed irrational and fickle, lacking both judgment and taste and obsessed with material goods, then they were hardly the sorts of individuals around whom to organize the political economy.

At first glance it would seem that the task confronting left liberal proponents of a consumer-oriented system was to reestablish the legitimacy of the consumer identity. For a number of reasons it did not prove to be a particularly difficult one in the 1920s. By that decade the producerist paradigm, which had made it so difficult for turn-of-the-century thinkers to justify a consumer-oriented system, no longer dominated American economic thought. Nor were Americans as conflicted about their consumer identity as they had been a quarter of a century earlier.[74] Finally, consumerist left liberals had the advantage of being able to draw on fifty years of consumerist thinking as they attempted to relegitimize both the consumer and a consumer-oriented system. For a number of reasons, then, consumerist left liberals found it easy to strip the consumer identity of its newly acquired pejorative connotations.

What they found far more difficult was coming to terms with the democratic implications of their legitimate consumer. If consumers were indeed rational and intelligent, then there was no reason why they should not govern themselves. Once again, left liberals found that the logic of their consumerist ideas pushed them in directions that they did not want to go.

How much their consumerist ideas compromised their antidemocratic convictions became evident with the publication of *Your Money's Worth*. Few left liberals were as dismissive of democracy as Stuart Chase. Indeed, in 1931 he wrote an article for the *Nation* entitled "If I Were Dictator." But, despite such sentiments, he collaborated on one of the few books in the 1920s to recognize, albeit implicitly, the democratic potential of the consumer identity. When he and Schlink called on consumers to organize and put an end to the exploitation of the buying public, the two might have focused on the consumer as an economic identity. But they assumed that consumers could recognize their own economic interests. And they were confident that consumers were capable of organizing to further these interests.[75] Such assumptions had real political potential. And, more to the point, they had democratic potential, one that consumerist thinkers would increasingly develop in the 1930s.

Chase and Schlink began to develop this potential earlier than most. Even before the publication of *Your Money's Worth,* Schlink had begun to put the principles of scientific buying into effect, when he provided his neighbors and fellow church members in White Plains, New York, with lists of products that were good and bad values. The enthusiastic response to *Your Money's Worth,* however, convinced the two authors that their idea might have a national appeal. They organized the Consumer Club. For a two-dollar subscription fee members received the sort of information necessary to buy scientifically.

Chase and Schlink did not test the products themselves. They did not have to. Product testing was not a new idea. Both government and industry had long used product tests to establish purchasing specifications. The insurance industry relied on product test results to set its rates. And the State of North Dakota had been testing products for farmers since the turn of the century. All that the club had to do was to translate what was often highly technical information gleaned from Bureau of Standards specifications and trade and technical journals into a form that could benefit consumers.

Early in 1929 Schlink and Chase moved beyond the translation of technical information. With a grant from the Elmhirst Foundation the two transformed the Consumer Club into the nation's first subscriber-financed, product-testing organization, Consumers' Research (CR). The organization grew rapidly. By October 1932 it had over twenty employees on the staff, almost twenty-five thousand subscribers (forty thousand one year later), and a list of sponsors which read like a who's who of economic and political thinkers. Among those who lent their names to the fledgling product-testing organization were philosopher John Dewey, League for Industrial Democracy chairman Harry Laidler, pacifist and labor movement activist A. J. Muste, Socialist Party leader Norman Thomas, *Nation* editor Oswald Garrison Villard, *New Republic* columnist Paul Blanshard, Veblenian Morris Cooke, law professor Milton Handler, consumer activist Henry Harap, and a number of economists including Rexford Tugwell, Paul Douglas, Wesley C. Mitchell, Isador Lubin, Donald McConnell, Dexter Keezer, Walton Hamilton, Frank Knight, and Robert Brady.[76]

That socialists, pacifists, liberals, consumer activists, and labor activists could all see value in CR suggests that the product-testing organization could mean different things to different people. Indeed, there was considerable debate both inside and outside the organization over exactly what CR's role should be. Kitty Pollock of Brookwood Labor College (where Muste was director) suggested that the greatest value of an organization such as CR was the role it could play in "building up the labor movement" by "winning consumer support in time of labor struggle, showing that advertising etc., is another argument against the system and showing that workers who cannot pay dues . . . may be able to if they buy wisely." The *New Republic,* by contrast, insisted that there was a far "deeper significance to Consumers' Research." "One of the important weaknesses in our industrial system, now creaking along so dismally," a *New Republic* editorial maintained, "is the wretched disorganization of distribution." CR could play a role in reducing this disorganization. By creating a mass of consumers who bought more intelligently, CR would not only eliminate "some of the present wastes which are artificially maintained by the force of high-pressure salesmanship" but would also compel businesses to introduce "more orderly and systematic marketing." In short, the writer concluded, CR could do on this side of the Atlantic what the "the consumers cooperatives which play such a large part in orderly distribution in European countries" were doing on the other side. It could help move the United States "in the direction of a planned economy."[77]

Within CR the debate took a slightly different form. All members of the board of directors were confident that CR would play a role in transforming the existing system. Where they parted company was over exactly what this role should be. On one side were left liberals such as Chase and Soule who were convinced that CR's contribution should be a technical one, namely providing consumers with product test results. Indeed, Soule expressed considerable concern over the increasing number of articles in the CR bulletins which were not reports on product test results but, instead, exposés on the government's treatment of consumers. Such articles, he told Schlink, were "not based upon competent technical advice, but [were] rather a matter of opinion" and, as such, should not be published.[78]

Schlink disagreed. To him CR was more than a technical organization. It also had an important role to play in politicizing consumers and consumer issues. Far from overstepping its bounds, CR was rendering an important service when it analyzed current events in terms of the consumer. "Our subscribers look to us for this kind of information," he told Soule, "and can hardly find . . . an agency better qualified by study or better equipped with relevant reference material, to advise them." Nor was Schlink content with merely making consumers aware of their interests, in the hopes that they would pressure the federal government on their own behalf. CR, he believed, should also bring pressure to bear on behalf of the "eating and wearing and using and buying citizenry at large." He was confident that together CR and organized consumers could push public policy in a more consumer-oriented direction. "Congressmen and Senators," he predicted, "will adjust themselves as readily to articulate demands from ultimate consumers to a share in the economic benefits of the government's operation, as they have in the past to such demands from big business."[79]

Schlink's vision of CR prevailed. Into the mid-1930s the product-testing organization was as active on the political front as it was on the technical. The staff at CR published numerous books and articles denouncing the treatment that the consumer received at the hands of both government and business. They lobbied U.S. representatives and senators for stronger food and drug laws. They demanded the creation of a Federal Department of the Consumer. They talked about organizing a consumers' political party. They harassed public officials who developed public policies that were detrimental to the consumer. They maintained an active speakers bureau. And on occasion they even cooperated with officials in Washington who were attempting to push public policy in a more consumerist direction.[80]

In 1932 Schlink acquired an important ally in his campaign to establish CR as a political force when J. B. Matthews became involved with the organization. An individual drawn to political extremes, Matthews seemed to attract controversy, and his association with CR proved to be no exception. His political "odyssey," as he called it, began harmlessly enough with a stint in Java as a Methodist minister. By the mid-1920s he was teaching at both Scarrit College and Fisk University in Nashville, Tennessee, but managed to lose the Scarrit job because he began hosting interracial get-togethers for his students. He joined La Follette's Progressive Party in 1924 and the Socialist Party shortly after that, although by 1933 he had moved so far beyond mainstream socialism that he was expelled from the latter. Not that he minded. By then he had already become deeply involved in yet another cause, having in 1932 become a CR speaker and then a member of its board of directors.[81]

Initially, Matthews did not find it necessary to jettison his Marxism when he discovered the consumer. But he did modify some of his ideas. No longer did he champion the "workers of the world." Instead, his hero was the "consumer-worker." And, although he might still believe that "all history is the history of class struggle," the "clash of classes" which he currently identified was one that pitted "those whose relationship to goods is primarily a function of use" against "those whose relationship to goods is primarily a function of exploitation." He still looked to a "classless community," but he no longer believed that it would take the form of a worker state or emerge when all members of society had become workers. On the contrary, his "consumer-workers' society of tomorrow" was "an economy oriented to and driven by and for consumers' needs and wants." And it would come into being "only when all men stand primarily in the position of consumers with reference to the available goods and services of a society," because only then would it be "possible to eliminate class differentiations and advantages." Finally, he remained convinced that "the absolutely prerequisite state of mind for any successful opposition to the exploitaters" was the development of a class consciousness, but the class consciousness that he meant was that of consumer-workers.[82]

If Matthews had converted Schlink to such ideas and no more, CR might have remained within the liberal fold. But, as someone who had recently flirted with communism, Matthews had no sympathy for either liberals or the existing government. The problem with the government, he insisted, was that it was in a "predatory alliance" with business, "completely under the control of, and in another sense effectively a partner of, those who work for profits (not wages and salaries) against the interests of consumer-workers." The problem with liberals was that they were determined to close their "eyes . . . to the ugly facts of [that] predatory alliance."[83]

Matthews's strange blend of Marxist economics and consumer activism may not have had much of an impact on mainstream politics. But it did have an impact on Schlink. As he embraced Matthews's political ideas, Schlink began to distance himself and, more important, CR from the liberal community.[84] One of the earliest indications of the increasing distance occurred shortly after Matthews became involved with the product-testing organization, when first Chase and then Soule failed in their reelection bids to the board of directors. By 1935 the split was complete. When CR employees— Matthews's consumer-workers—went out on strike, the liberal community did not hesitate to rally behind the employees, denouncing Schlink's and Matthews's "arbitrary and capricious management" and "autocratic control."[85]

The rupture between Schlink and the liberal community had a significant impact on Consumers' Research. In the 1930s liberals were the primary proponents of a consumer-oriented approach to politics. By alienating liberals, Schlink made it all but inevitable that he and CR would fall into obscurity. Indeed, how important liberal support was to a consumer organization became evident in the late 1930s, when the defeated strikers from CR established Consumers Union, the publisher of *Consumers Reports*. CU would remain well within the liberal fold and, by doing so, would replace CR as the nation's preeminent consumer organization.

If the break between CR and the liberal community had a profound impact on the product-testing organization, its impact on consumerist left liberals was negligible. This was because consumer activism and a consumer-oriented approach to politics had never been one and the same. Consumerist left liberals wanted a consumer-oriented political economy because they believed that only such a system could guarantee freedom from want. They were willing to devote attention to furthering the interests of consumers within the existing system, but their primary goal was to end poverty and raise the general standard of living. Schlink, by contrast, was a consumer activist. When he called for a consumer-oriented political economy, it was not because it would end poverty or raise the general standard of living or even end class conflict. On the contrary, he advocated such a system because it would, by definition, function on behalf of the consumer.

That Schlink and the left liberals were interested in the consumer for fundamentally different reasons is highlighted by the sorts of New Deal public policies on which each focused. Although Schlink put pressure on both the National Recovery Administration (NRA) and the Agricultural Adjustment

Administration (AAA) to adopt consumer-oriented policies, his real interest was food and drug reform. He coauthored a book on the topic. He found funds in the limited CR budget to hire a lobbyist to represent the consumer interest in Washington. He frequently traveled to the capital to fight for stronger legislation. And he even hired a lawyer to draft a food and drug bill, eventually introduced in the House as the Boland bill.[86]

With the one exception of Tugwell—who, as undersecretary of agriculture, was in the very department that was responsible for food and drug control—consumerist left liberals largely ignored food and drug reform. But all, including Tugwell, were profoundly interested in NRA and AAA policy. For them the two agencies were fundamentally changing the role of government in the economy. Consumerist left liberals wanted to make sure that these changes would be on behalf of the consuming population. Reform of the food and drug laws might prevent certain abuses of the consumer, but, as far as left liberals were concerned, the AAA and NRA had the potential to establish freedom from want as a civic right.

Consumerist left liberals, of course, were not alone in their desire to see freedom from want established as a basic human right. For at least a century various types of socialists had been advocating just such a system. But in the twentieth century, as American radicalism became all but synonymous with Marxism, socialists—indeed, American leftists in general—became almost exclusively producer oriented. When American radicals advocated a system that would give "to each according to his need," they assumed that *each* was a producer. Consumerist left liberals, by contrast, argued that the best way to provide for "each according to his need" was to define *each* as a consumer.

This argument did not come easily to consumerist left liberals. All were sympathetic to the cause of labor. Many had, at one time, flirted with socialism. Nevertheless, in the 1920s they became increasingly convinced that an exclusive reliance on either the labor movement or Marxist ideas would not bring about the necessary political changes. In the existing economy, they insisted, capitalists wreaked far more hardship through their control of consumption than they did through their control of production. If the fundamental interest of all members of society was a higher standard of living—and consumerist left liberals believed that it was—then, they reasoned, the only way to achieve this standard was by focusing on consumers and consumption.

The various attempts by consumerist left liberals to establish consumption rather than production as the more significant arena of conflict highlighted the extent to which a consumerist worldview had displaced a producerist one, at least in some political circles. At the turn of the century even political theorists who had already begun to think about exploitation in terms of the consumer nevertheless agreed that the exploitation of the worker was at least as great, if not far greater than that of the consumer. And with good reason. At the turn of the century the abuses that consumers suffered, while at times quite serious, seemed to pale in comparison with the abuses that workers and their dependents had to endure. Consumers might ingest food that was less than healthful or dose themselves with dubious medications. They might find themselves paying "unfair" prices. But it was workers who were paid almost nothing for long hours of work, beaten during strikes, maimed and killed in industrial accidents, discarded when they were no longer capable of working, and forced to send their children into the factories. Little wonder that one of the most noted "consumer" organizers of the period had been Florence Kelley, who had called on consumers to use their purchasing power on behalf of wage workers.

Thirty years later, however, consumerist left liberals found it easy to insist that all members of society—workers included—were far more exploited as consumers than producers. By then the composition of the labor force had changed, and working conditions had improved. Workers were increasingly likely to hold white- or pink-collar rather than blue-collar jobs, hours were shorter, pay was higher, And jobs were safer. Workmen's compensation reduced some of the impact of the industrial accidents that still occurred. And, with the exception of the textile industry, industrial child labor had all but disappeared. To consumerist left liberals it seemed that workers were more vulnerable in the marketplace than they were in the workplace.

Labor activists might not have agreed that workers were more vulnerable in the marketplace than the workplace, but they recognized that workers had interests as consumers. Yet, even as they established consumer cooperatives, organized boycotts, and launched union label campaigns, labor activists remained convinced that the producer interests of the working class were paramount. Indeed, in organizing consumers to boycott or buy the union label, they had not been trying to improve the lot of working-class consumers so much as to harness purchasing power on behalf of producers.[87]

Consumerist left liberals, by contrast, responded to the changes in the economy by dismissing a producer-oriented approach as obsolete. According to Stuart Chase, socialism—and communism, for that matter—were outdated "production-age systems." The Socialists demanded a more just division of what they assumed was a limited volume of goods. "But under 1934 technological conditions," Chase insisted, "the potential volume of goods is all but unlimited." And the Socialists used the "doctrine that labor creates wealth" to justify the "social ownership of the means of production." This doctrine, according to Chase, had been "roughly true in 1850," but "today the mental labor of technicians harnesses inanimate energy to create far more wealth in total tonnage than is created by manual labor." Finally, the Socialists subscribed to what Chase called "rigid conceptions of the class struggle." According to Chase, however, the significant economic conflict in a "surplus economy" was "no longer primarily between producers and owners of the means of production." On the contrary, both workers and capitalists had become far more interested in the technological and ethical implications of consumption than they were in the technological and ethical implications of mass production. "Class struggles we may have, but the lines must be reformed."[88]

Not all consumerist left liberals abandoned the worker when they abandoned the producerist approach. But even those such as Robert Lynd, who retained strong sympathies for the working class, found it necessary to redefine producerist categories in consumerist terms. Lynd did so by rejecting Marxist definitions of class and exploitation in favor of Veblenian ones. Drawing on Veblen's distinction between business and industry, he divided society into a "Working Class," whose members "utiliz[e] material tools in the making of things and the performance of services," and a "Business Class," whose members "address their activities predominantly to . . . the selling or promotion of things, services and ideas."[89] And he shifted the site of class conflict from the workplace to the marketplace. As Lynd described it, the Business Class exploited the Working Class not so much by underpaying workers as by manipulating working-class consumers into purchasing products that they did not want or need.

Although Lynd defined class in Veblenian terms, his equation of the consumer with the working class would have been familiar to most labor activists in the late 1920s.[90] The same, however, could not be said of the role that Soule reserved for organized labor. At first glance Soule seemed to be following in the footsteps of Walter Lippmann. Like Lippmann, he believed that the unions could play an important role in a planned economy. But, whereas

Lippmann assumed that this role would be to safeguard the interests of workers, Soule looked to unions to promote the interests of consumers. Their job, as he saw it, would be to "exert their power in the direction of better management and more productivity in their several industries."[91]

Labor activists would have been equally puzzled by Soule's call on the workers of the world to throw off their chains and usher in a consumer-oriented economy of abundance. Soule was as critical as any Marxist of a system in which "a minority of the population have first claim on what is produced, and can . . . satisfy their own desires while a large number of citizens remain in want." He, too, was confident that producers would play a decisive role in freeing citizens from want. But, when it came to defining this role, Soule relied on Veblen rather than Marx. He looked forward to a time when "the farmers, the workers, the salaried clerks and all the rest of us who live by producing can say 'what we make is ours, and it will be promptly and fairly shared; therefore we can and will make as much as we want.'"[92] For Soule the best way to achieve freedom from want for all was not by guaranteeing workers the full product of their labor, as the Marxists argued, but by unleashing the productive potential of the industrial system.

Not surprisingly, as a Patten protégé, Tugwell did not reform the lines of class struggle in the same way that Veblenian thinkers such as Lynd and Soule did. Rather than relying on a consumerist definition of workers, Tugwell did away with workers altogether. In his view the very category was anachronistic. The only reason why "we are torn between two aims: to protect workers, and to obtain product from machines," he insisted, was because "we still think of physical operations as the tasks of men." According to Tugwell, however, "work, in this physical sense, is no part of man's destiny, but is the sphere of machines." The task, as he saw it, was to replace the existing industrial system with one "which will not only move steadily toward better and cheaper goods, but which will make machines to do the work these men and women and children are now doing."[93] Far from advocating a worker state, Tugwell looked to a system in which there were no human workers at all.

If the left liberals had merely substituted a consumer-oriented system for a worker state or a Veblenian critique of capitalism for a Marxist one, they might have been able to remain comfortably within the ranks of radicalism. It was only when they rejected the working class as the force of change and, even worse, did so in favor of the middle class that they called into question whatever radical credentials they possessed. Nor were they unaware of the consequences of their actions. Indeed, both Soule and Chase tried to defend the radicalism of their approach. "Many of the most earnest exponents of a planned society," Soule asserted, "are certain to be found among those whom an orthodox Marxian would scarcely recognize as true proletarians. And it is a commonplace that our industrial 'proletariat' has been largely assimilated to a 'bourgeois' psychology." It was, therefore, not only unrealistic but also counterproductive for labor radicals to ignore this fact "for the sake of exclusive loyalty to a theoretical class conflict which is now, from an orthodox socialist point of view, disappointingly absent in the realm of action." Stuart Chase was even blunter. "If I appeal now to the middle class, particularly the technician, it is because a decade of working with the labor movement has taught me that for the moment most of American labor is spiritually bankrupt."[94]

Chase and Soule did not dismiss the working class as a force for radical change because they were unsympathetic to the cause of labor. They were merely trying to point out weaknesses in a Marxist approach. Nevertheless, in so doing, they distanced themselves from much of the left. The result was a far closer association of *consumer* with *liberal* than either Soule or Chase wanted. Indeed, by the 1930s many left-of-center political thinkers assumed that the terms *consumer-oriented* and *liberal* were synonymous. How much so became evident during debates over the direction that the League for Independent Action's (LIPA) third-party organizing effort should take.

The LIPA was organized in December 1928—just weeks before Consumers' Research was incorporated—when several dozen progressive intellectuals met to discuss how they might make progressive ideas a force in American politics.[95] By the spring they had formed an executive committee. John Dewey was asked to serve as chairman. Paul Douglas, a professor of economics at the University of Chicago, soon emerged as the most active of the four vice chairmen—the other three were pacifist and novelist Zona Gale, former Socialist vice presidential candidate James Maurer, and black nationalist and *Crisis* editor W. E. B. Du Bois. Additional members of the executive committee included Oswald Garrison Villard as treasurer, farmer-labor activist Howard Y. Williams as executive secretary, as well as radical theologian Reinhold Niebuhr, associate editor of the *Nation* Devere Allen, *New Republic* book review editor Robert Morss Lovett, labor historian Nathan Fine, Stuart Chase, Norman Thomas, Harry Laidler, and A. J. Muste.

Those associated with the LIPA represented a wide range of left-of-center political ideas. All were committed to establishing freedom from want as a basic right. And all agreed that guaranteeing this right would involve some form of economic planning. But beyond that there was less consensus. Some, such as Niebuhr and Thomas, wanted to see the nation take a socialist road to planning. Others were sympathetic to socialist ideas but agreed with Dewey that "the greatest handicap from which special measures favored by the Socialists suffer is that they are advanced by the socialist party as Socialism."[96] Almost all were supporters of the cause of labor; many were labor activists.

If a mild socialism had been all that the LIPA had advocated, it would not have been much different from any of the left-of-center organizations that had appeared on the American political scene in previous decades. The LIPA, however, represented a significant departure from the usual progressive and radical organizations because of the extent to which it incorporated consumerist ideas. Indeed, many of the original members of the executive committee would also be involved with Consumers' Research, most of them as sponsors. Chase, of course, had a more pivotal role. Niebuhr would coauthor the report that blamed Schlink and Matthews for the strike at CR.

The LIPA never became a consumerist organization. Indeed, probably a majority of the membership remained convinced that the primary focus should be on the producer. Nevertheless, most members agreed that no remedy to social problems was possible without giving at least some attention to the perspective of the consumer and consumption. And a significant minority insisted that this perspective should be the primary one.

Both the influence of consumerist ideas and the extent to which they were coming to be seen as liberal were evident in the debate between Paul Douglas and John Dewey over the political role that the LIPA should play. At first glance the two seemed to share a number of ideas. They both believed that the primary function of the organization was to prepare the way for a third party. They both assumed that that party should be dedicated to furthering the interests of wage workers, farmers, and the middle class. And they both maintained that these interests could best be advanced in a planned economy. But, when it came to deciding how economic planning would further these interests, or even what they were, the two parted company.

During the New Deal, Douglas would advocate a consumerist approach to politics. And throughout his subsequent career as a U.S. senator from Illinois he would be interested in consumer issues. Nevertheless, into the early 1930s he remained far less sympathetic to a consumerist approach to politics than did Dewey. While he was as convinced as Dewey that the goal of the LIPA was to further the interests of farmers, workers, and the middle class, he maintained that what these three groups had in common were producer interests. Like wage workers, middle-class workers were "not their own masters but are subject to strict discipline from their employers" and "are miserably paid." Although they might "have sentimentally aligned themselves with the owning rather than with the working classes," Douglas insisted that "their real economic interests are much more closely joined with the latter." The same held true for farmers. Increasingly, according to Douglas, they were being forced into "a permanent wage-earning class, composed of those who are unable to afford the expensive machinery and the large amounts of land needed for successful farming."[97] And, as part of that wage-earning class, farmers shared the same interests as middle-class and industrial wage earners.

Although Douglas remained adamant that the producer interest needed to be the dominant one, he did not discount the consumer interest. Indeed, he devoted a chapter in *The Making of a New Party* to the topic of "How Government Can Further the Interests of Citizens and Consumers." And, although he did try to establish the producer interests of the middle class, he nevertheless ultimately decided that *middle class* was best understood as a synonym for *consumers*. Even more significantly, he equated both terms with *liberal*. As he outlined the three interests that the third party should serve, he used *farmers* to refer to the agricultural interest and either *wage workers* or *labor* to refer to the industrial interest. But, when it came to labeling the third interest, he could not decide among *consumer, middle class,* or *liberal*. Indeed, so closely associated were the three terms for Douglas that he decided they were interchangeable.[98]

The extent to which Douglas considered the middle class / consumer / liberal the least important element in the wage worker coalition is evident in the name that he chose for the new party. Although he considered "People's party," he ultimately rejected it. Such a name, he granted, "would perhaps make a greater appeal to the white-collar and to the professional classes." But he worried that it would not "command the loyalties of the rural and urban workers" to as great a degree.[99] Convinced that these workers had to be the backbone of any successful third-party effort, Douglas ultimately decided on the "Farmer-Labor party" or even just the "Labor party" as the most appropriate way to refer to the new third party.

Neither was a name that John Dewey would have chosen. Although he was as convinced as Douglas that the new party would have to represent the interests of farmers, workers, and the middle class, he insisted that what these three groups shared were consuming interests. And, although he agreed with Douglas that "no movement can ultimately succeed that has not enlisted the hearty support of labor," he nevertheless believed that the middle-class consumer would have to be the mainspring of the new party, precisely because it was the class most closely associated with issues of consumption. Finally, although he did not use *liberal* as a synonym for either the middle class or consumers, he did believe that liberals were the political group most committed to a consumer-oriented planned economy.

Dewey and Douglas envisioned such fundamentally different roles for liberals, consumers, and the middle class in the new party because they diagnosed the current political problems in fundamentally different ways. To the producerist-minded Douglas the goal was an economy that functioned on behalf of the wage-earning population. The problem, as he saw it, was that the "two old parties" were dominated by the "capitalistic class." If industrial, agricultural, and middle-class wage earners wanted to make government responsive to the needs of wage-earning producers, they would have to found their own party.[100]

Dewey, by contrast, did not believe that the struggle was between two different classes of producers so much as between two different ways of understanding the economy. In his view the old parties were "bound up with the interests of production." They promoted policies that were "centered almost wholly upon stimulating production and distribution without any reference to the way they impinge upon consumption." The problem with such a producer-oriented focus, Dewey insisted, was that it was "wholly out of line and out of touch with the realities of American life." "I should like to make the point definite," he told his readers in the *New Republic*. "The needs and the troubles of the people are connected with problems of consumption, with problems of the maintenance of a reasonably decent and secure standard of living."[101]

If, as Dewey believed, "neglect of the consumer and his standard of living at the expense of fostering production is the ultimate cause of much of our present distress," then the solution had to be a consumerist one. For Dewey the only way to "regulate production in the interest of consumption" was through economic planning. Indeed, as he put it, "a planned economy, and industry and finance administered in the interest of consumption, are synonymous terms."[102]

Perhaps the most striking indication of the influence of consumerist ideas on Dewey's political thought was his conviction that the foundation for the third party would have to be the middle rather than the working class. Dewey insisted that the "first appeal of a new party must be to what is called the middle class," in part because he believed that the "middle portion of the community represents most adequately the interests of the consumer." But Dewey's emphasis on the middle class went deeper. For him the aim of a "new political movement" was not only "to protect and render secure the standard of living enjoyed by the middle class." Even more important, it was "to extend the advantages of this standard, in both its cultural and economic aspects, to those who do not enjoy it" while "leveling down the idle, luxurious and predatory group."[103] In short, Dewey wanted to establish a classless society not by making everyone part of the working class but by moving all members of society into the middle class.

Although Dewey joined Soule and Chase in placing the middle class at the center of a new political movement, he managed to do so without alienating those who championed the working class. He stressed that the interests and the participation of industrial workers were of "fundamental importance" to the new party. But he was convinced that the most vital interest of industrial workers was a consuming interest. "Running through" all the concerns of labor—whether yellow-dog contracts, the injunction power of the courts, unemployment, old-age pensions, or a more equitable distribution of national income—was "the fundamental question of obtaining and maintaining a reasonable standard of living."[104]

Nor was it only industrial workers whose interests Dewey redefined in consumerist terms. He was equally convinced that the farmers' interests were more closely related to consumption than production. As he saw it, traditional farm issues such as the tariff, railway rates, and control of credit were also issues in which the "farmers' interest coincides with the general social interest." Once farmers realized that they shared the same consuming interests as most Americans, they would be able to find common cause with large sectors of the American population.[105]

Dewey's version of the new party not only highlighted the influence of consumerist ideas on political ones. It also suggested the extent to which these ideas were coming to be labeled liberal, at least in left-of-center circles. For Dewey it was liberals who were most interested in a consumer-oriented planned economy. Therefore, he maintained, if the LIPA hoped to establish a third party it would have "to discover and to cooperate with liberal groups and individuals throughout the country; to bring them into conscious contact with one another and to promote that sense of solidarity among them which is the condition of further effective political action."[106]

That an intellectual of Dewey's stature should advocate a consumerist approach to the political economy suggests the extent to which these ideas were beginning to have a broader appeal. Dewey, however, also played an important role in extending that appeal. Consumerist ideas may have survived the 1920s largely because of the efforts of consumerist left liberals. But, even as these thinkers had preserved consumerist ideas, they had also transformed them in ways guaranteed to limit their influence. Indeed, the most prolific of the 1920s consumerist left liberals, Stuart Chase, worked hard to cultivate the impression that consumerist ideas were radical ones, pondering in print what he might be able to accomplish were he dictator or questioning why Russians should "have all the fun of remaking a world."[107]

Dewey, by contrast, managed to make radical ideas seem completely reasonable and, even more important, quintessentially American, something the post–World War I generation of intellectuals could not or would not do. Separated by only a few years from the jingoistic and reactionary "one-hundred-percent Americanism" emphasized during World War I, this generation was uncomfortable celebrating anything American. Dewey, however, was a member of the Progressive Era generation and, as such, could remember when *American radicalism* had not been the oxymoron it would become in the 1920s to those on the left as well as the right.

Even more significantly, Dewey could remember when appealing to "the people" had not seemed naive. Democracy may have sounded hollow to the post–World War I generation, but it did not sound hollow to Dewey. Indeed, for him it was one of the few "great issue[s] on which all others converge." To Dewey democracy meant "equal opportunity for everyone to better his condition and that of his children." He was well aware that the "words have lost their magic." But he was confident that "their fundamental meaning remains." "The problem," as he saw it, "is to translate them into terms that signify something vital in the present complex situation."[108] Defining the people as consumers, he believed, went a long way toward solving the problem.

Dewey's definition was not a new one. Fifteen years earlier Walter Weyl had defined the people in consumerist terms and had called for a consumer-oriented political economy. But in the antidemocratic intellectual environment of the 1920s, Weyl's ideas had been all but forgotten. Dewey reestablished the democratic potential of consumerist ideas and, in so doing, greatly expanded their potential political appeal.

Nothing, however, expanded the mainstream political potential of these ideas so much as the economic crisis of the 1930s. As journalists, academics, politicians, and public policy makers all tried to make sense of the catastrophe, they began to take a closer look at consumption and the consumer. And in 1933, when Roosevelt launched his "New Deal," consumers were given a voice within the federal government for the first time in U.S. history. Within the National Recovery Administration, a Consumers' Advisory Board was charged with ensuring that industrial recovery did not come at the expense of industry. Within the Agricultural Adjustment Administration, the Office of the Consumers' Counsel was to perform the same function for agricultural recovery.

It was not inevitable that those within the New Deal—or those outside of it—would devote much attention to the consumer or consumption after 1929. In the depression of the 1890s, for example, the focus had been almost exclusively on production, as capitalists had worried about gold supplies and workers had demanded their right to work. By the 1930s, however, capitalists were far more concerned than they had been in the earlier depression about how to get Americans consuming again. And workers focused more on their right to a minimum standard of living than they did on their right to work.

Neither capitalists nor workers—nor most public policy makers, for that matter—understood *consumer* and *consumption* in quite the same way that the left liberals did. But the very fact that, in the 1930s, Americans were much more aware of the terms than they had been four decades earlier was, in large part, due to the left liberals. It was they who had preserved a consumer-oriented approach to the political economy in the producer-dominated 1920s. So, when New Dealers began casting about for alternatives to the discredited Republican approach to the economy, consumerist left liberals were able to provide a fundamentally different way of understanding both the economy and its collapse.

CHAPTER SIX

The Demise of Economic Planning, 1933–1940

By the spring of 1933 it was already clear that the New Deal administration of Franklin Roosevelt would redefine the role of government in the economy. What was not so clear was what this new role would be. And the two pieces of legislation which went the farthest in altering the economic role of government did surprisingly little to clarify it. Both the National Industrial Recovery Act and the Agricultural Adjustment Act had been written in such a way that they were consistent with a variety of approaches to a government-directed economy. The debate inside and outside the administration was over which of the several approaches the New Deal should embrace. At stake was the definition of *New Deal liberalism.*

Central to much of the debate was the role of consumption and the place of the consumer within the economy. The Roosevelt Administration gave far more attention to both consumption and the consumer than had any of its predecessors. In establishing a Consumers' Advisory Board (CAB) within the National Recovery Administration (NRA) and an Office of the Consumers' Counsel within the Agricultural Adjustment Administration (AAA), the New Deal was the first administration to recognize consumers officially as a major interest group. And, far more than earlier administrations, it treated consumption as a critically important economic activity. Indeed, the most widely accepted explanation within New Deal circles for the economic collapse was that consumption and production had ceased to be in balance.

Although officials throughout the New Deal administration agreed that they had to take both the consumer and consumption into account, they found it more difficult to achieve a consensus about why they should do so. Was it because consumers and consumption were a means to producer well-being? Was consumer well-being an end in itself? Officials within the AAA eventually concluded that the answer to both questions was yes. By contrast, most of those involved with the NRA recovery effort assumed that it was necessary to choose between the producer and the consumer. Both supporters and opponents of NRA policy were convinced that a consumer-oriented and a producer-oriented approach to industrial recovery were, by and large, mutually exclusive. The task, as each side saw it, was to establish their approach at the expense of the other.

That production and consumption were out of balance, few in the new administration could doubt. In the farming regions supply had been outstripping demand since World War I, forcing down the prices of agricultural products. In the industrial region the nation's industries seemed trapped in a downward cycle. With their markets drying up, factories had attempted to limit production and cut costs. As they discharged their workers, however, the number of unemployed grew. More and more people found themselves unable to buy even the most basic necessities. Businesses had responded to the decline in sales by further curtailing production, which meant more unemployment.

The New Deal's initial attempt to bring production and consumption back into balance centered on two pieces of legislation. The Agricultural Adjustment Act was designed to address overproduction in the agricultural sector. The National Industrial Recovery Act (NIRA) was intended to give government the necessary tools to jumpstart a stalled industrial sector. By suspending the antitrust laws, the NIRA would make it possible to organize industries on the basis of "codes of fair competition," which would be used to establish industry-wide minimum wages and maximum hours so that industry could not compete at the expense of labor. The codes would also eliminate certain unfair trade practices such as false advertising, bonuses and bribes paid to customers or their agents, industrial espionage, and cutthroat price cutting. To oversee the organizational process the NIRA created the National Recovery Administration.

Most observers agreed that the NRA represented the "acknowledged and legalized end of laissez-faire." Advocates of a planned economy, however, did not agree on why laissez-faire should be abandoned. According to corporate liberals such as Gerard Swope, Bernard Baruch, and Henry Harriman, all of whom approached the economy from a producer-oriented perspective, the major problem with laissez-faire capitalism was its tendency toward "savage wolfish competition." Such competition, they insisted, had caused the economic collapse. It had forced businesses to cut wages and discharge workers in order to keep costs down. And it had forced businesses to sell goods at prices below cost in order to eliminate rivals, a practice that frequently plunged both combatants into bankruptcy. Producer-oriented corporate liberals looked to the NRA to end destructive competition by replacing laissez-faire with a system in which business and government cooperated to determine price and production schedules. Such a system, they believed, would reestablish the sort of economic environment which would benefit all producers, be they wage workers or capitalists.[1]

Consumerist left liberals were as eager as producerist corporate liberals to see laissez-faire capitalism replaced with economic planning but for fundamentally different reasons. The problem, as they saw it, was not that the economy had been too competitive in the 1920s but that it had not been competitive enough.[2] And the victims of the economic collapse, they insisted, were not businessmen but, instead, consumers and wage workers. Consumerist left liberals looked to the NRA to replace an economy directed by profit-oriented capitalists with one directed by government on behalf of the consuming population.

The person who would decide whether the NRA would adopt a consumerist or a capitalist version of economic planning would be the NRA administrator. To that post Roosevelt appointed General Hugh Johnson. Johnson came to the NRA with a background in both planning and business. During World War I he had served on the War Industries Board under the direction of financial wizard Bernard Baruch. After the war he retired from the army and went into business, serving as general counsel for the Moline Plow Factory. When that company was sold, in 1929, Johnson became increasingly active in politics, primarily under Baruch's patronage. In 1933 he was appointed to head the NRA.[3]

Given his background, it was not particularly surprising that Johnson should rely on a producerist view of the economy. His heroes were businessmen and to a lesser extent workers. And he was a firm believer in the motivating power of the profit motive. "I think the profit motive is the basis of all human incentive," he announced. It encouraged such basic American values as "thrift, hard work, and self-dependence." Destroy these, he warned, and "you destroy everything for which we have fought in this country."[4] To Johnson the profit motive was not the cause of the economic collapse, as some consumerist left liberals suggested, but, rather, the key to recovery.

Having identified profits as the foundation of a prosperous economy, Johnson decided that the only way for the NRA to effect recovery was to reestablish industrial profitability. And the only way to do that, he reasoned, was to make sure that prices were high enough to include a sufficient profit margin. Indeed, according to Johnson, it was low prices that had brought on the economic collapse in the first place: "Destructive price destroys wages which destroy consuming power which again destroys price down to the very depths of the 1933 pit."[5]

But what had been responsible for these "destructive" prices? Johnson thought he knew. Drawing on economic lessons he had learned while in the farm belt, he blamed low prices on the "overwhelming excess of productive capacity" of the industrial sector, a "productive capacity" that constantly threatened to disgorge "a new mountain of undigested and indigestible goods." Indeed, so destructive was this "productive capacity" that it reminded Johnson of nothing so much as "masked batteries of machine-guns waiting to lay down a new barrage of production whenever buying reappears." Anyone wishing to observe the consumerist left liberals' "economy of plenty" in action, he chided, had only to look to the agricultural sector, where it had existed since World War I. If "the sole hope for Agriculture was to starve out all surplus production," Johnson wanted to know, "how could the magnification of surplus be a proper prescription for industry?"[6]

Because Johnson was committed to a producer-oriented recovery, he saw consumption as a means rather than an end. How much so was evident in his call for more profit to go "to farmers and workers and all producers" so that they could "constantly consume more and more." In Johnson's view the real benefit of such expanded consumption was not a higher living standard but, rather, "more employment, more business, more profit." Similarly, Johnson called for "balance among all producing segments" because with it "there would be almost no limit to our consuming capacity." His choice of the word *capacity* was revealing. Once again, increased consumption was, for Johnson, not a goal in itself so much as a foundation on which to build a profitable mass production economy.[7]

Johnson's conviction that prosperity depended upon profits prompted him not only to treat consumption as a means rather than an end but also to assume that consumers had no rights. As far as he was concerned, consumers had one function, to provide the profits on which prosperity depended. As long as they did so, all producers, including wage workers, would benefit. Indeed, he cautioned wage workers not to confuse their real producer interests with their apparent consumer interests. Workers might, for example, think that they have a right to "the lowest prices that any kind of competition can provide." But such prices could threaten the very survival of the economy, undermining either profits or wages. Indeed, he argued that because, more often than not, low prices came at the expense of labor, and most consumers depended upon the paycheck of a wage earner, they were foolish to seek such prices. Just as it was in the best interests of factory-owning producers to pay a fair wage, it was in the best interests of working-class producers to pay a price that included a fair profit.[8]

Much of the disagreement between Johnson and the consumerist left liberals stemmed from their fundamentally different definitions of *abundance*. For Johnson the term was synonymous with *overproduction*. Given this definition, it was not surprising that he wanted to see abundance eradicated. "We can't sell more bread than people eat or make women go back to five and six petticoats to consume our cotton," Johnson announced. In what was undoubtedly a shot at the left liberals, he demanded, "Haven't we had enough of unmanageable surplus?" "The Apostles of Plenty," he warned, "must temper their doctrine."[9]

The "Apostles of Plenty," however, were quick to point out that their call for abundance was not a call for overproduction. The reason why Johnson had equated the two, they maintained, was because he failed to distinguish between the ability to consume and the ability to buy. In a profit-oriented economy, in which consumption was limited by the size of one's pocketbook rather than the size of one's stomach, it was frequently not even possible, they insisted, to sell bread when people were starving. "The ten million unemployed in this country today," Stuart Chase declared, "would gladly take a volume of goods which would make factory wheels hum. The factory wheels are silent because the unemployed have no money." George Soule agreed. "What limited the growth of production was not the lack of profit margins, but the lack of sufficient growth in demand." "There are a few simple principles which it seems impossible for most business men to learn," he concluded, one of which was that "there is a virtually unlimited demand for consumers' goods in general, provided consumers are able to buy them."[10]

What dismayed consumerist thinkers about Johnson's producerist diagnosis of the economy's ills was that it prompted him not only to prescribe cures that had no hope of success but also to ignore those that might be of some benefit. "Our economic existence," Rexford Tugwell maintained, "[depends] upon the purchasing power of the consumer." "If . . . we guarantee profits . . . to all businesses, who is to buy the goods on which the profits are made?" "To put [profits] first is to put the cart before the horse." Columbia University economist Gardiner Means agreed. "If policy is to be determined primarily by persons who seek to produce not things but immediate values, the continuance of . . . the depression . . . seems almost inevitable. Only as policy is determined in the interest of the consumer," he concluded, "will the potentialities of our economy be realized." Stuart Chase was even blunter. "Mass production demands mass consumption." "It cannot function without a vast body of consumers able and eager to receive its mammoth output. . . . always provided the mass production system continues to function at all."[11]

Chase's concerns about the viability of the mass production system were no idle musings. Indeed, the debate over whether the existing system would continue "to function at all" divided consumerist left liberals into two camps. On one side were those such as Tugwell and Means who believed that capitalism could survive but only if a consumer-oriented approach were substituted for the producer-oriented one. On the other side were those such as Soule, Chase, and Robert Lynd who, in the wake of the economic collapse, began to suggest that capitalism was irredeemable. The very structure of capitalism, they maintained, made it impossible for that system to function on behalf of the consuming population. Only in the late 1930s and early 1940s would they begin to rethink their anticapitalist impulses.

One of the factors shaping the ways in which consumerist left liberals viewed capitalism was how each experienced the recovery effort. Tugwell's and Means's primary affiliation was with the AAA, Tugwell serving as the undersecretary of Agriculture and Means as economic advisor to Secretary of Agriculture Henry Wallace. Both found that within the AAA consumerist ideas were guaranteed a hearing, and public policy was designed to benefit consumers as well as producers. Soule, Chase, and Lynd, by contrast, were far more interested in industrial recovery. Industrial recovery, however, was the purview of the NRA, an administration in which producers and consumers were assumed to have antithetical interests and public policy decisions seemed designed to benefit producers at the expense of consumers. It was hardly surprising, therefore, that Soule, Chase, and Lynd considered *consumer-oriented capitalism* an oxymoron.

Ultimately, however, the NRA experience only confirmed whatever doubts the three already had about the consumerist potential of capitalism. Far more reliant on a Veblenian analysis of the economy than either Tugwell or Means, Soule, Chase, and Lynd had long warned that the "price system," with its focus on "vendibility" and profits rather than "serviceability," furthered business interests at the consumer's expense. In the 1920s their critique of capitalism had been a cultural one. Capitalism, they had charged, was a system in which businesses thrived by using salesmanship to get consumers to purchase products that they did not need and could ill afford. What bothered the Veblenian left liberals about such a situation was that, when consumers bought "motor cars, radios and overstuffed davenports on $40 a week," they could not "spend as much for rent, for food, for clothing, or for education." By "forcing in luxuries and alleged comforts at the cost of the prime essentials," capitalism had denied consumers any real quality of life even as it deluged them with unnecessary consumer goods.[12]

The economic collapse of 1929 may have undercut much of the power of a cultural critique of capitalism, but it considerably increased the potency of an economic critique. Veblenian consumerist thinkers such as Chase and Lynd no longer found themselves defending an identity that conjured up images of the self-indulgent, pleasure-seeking flappers who appeared in the nation's magazines, advertising everything from Lucky Strike cigarettes to Fisher automobile bodies. Instead, references to the consuming public were far more likely to evoke images of the gaunt and haunted men and women who stared out from the photos of Dorothea Lange and Walker Evans.

Just as important, Veblenian consumerist thinkers no longer found themselves trying to discredit the existing system by insisting that it forced the public to consume too much. Now they could denounce it for denying the public even the most basic of necessities. Shifting their focus from "salesmanship" to "sabotage," they began to argue that the closing of factories in the wake of the stock market crash was only the most dramatic example of the "conscientious withdrawal of efficiency" which capitalists had long practiced in an attempt to maintain price levels in an "inordinantly productive" economy. "Dire poverty in the midst of plenty," Chase announced, "is a permanent phenomenon in the system known as capitalism; it always has been and probably always will be so long as capitalism in its present form endures." And, while neither Soule nor Lynd possessed Chase's rhetorical gifts, they shared his concerns. Soule warned that "the kind of liberty that goes with security and abundance" could never "really be embodied either in a system of laissez-faire or in a system of regulated capitalism." And Lynd emphasized the "fundamental unsoundness" of assuming that it was possible to meet "the needs of the consumer in our business economy run primarily for profit."[13]

Why was it impossible to meet the consumer's needs within an economy run mainly for profit? Why was "dire poverty in the midst of plenty . . . a permanent phenomenon" of capitalism? Chase, Soule, and Lynd offered numerous explanations. But central to all their explanations was the Veblenian distinction between an economy dedicated to making profits and one dedicated to making and distributing goods. Profits, the three insisted, depended upon "conditions of relative scarcity." "How else," Chase asked, "shall price levels be maintained?" But the scarce conditions so vital to capitalism were fast disappearing. "American agriculture and industry have reached a point where they could provide an ample livelihood for all citizens." Businesses had responded by deliberately shutting down the nation's productive facilities so as to foster the scarcity on which their profits depend. "Warehouses bulge," Chase charged, "and children cry for food." Soule was equally troubled by the paradox of plenty. "We have made so many goods that many of us are in danger of starving and freezing to death."[14]

Although Chase, Soule, and Lynd were as convinced as Johnson that abundance was "a savage threat to . . . price levels," they parted company with him over the solution. If the price system could not function in an economy of abundance, the solution, they maintained, was certainly not to get rid of abundance and "retreat to the economy of scarcity," with its "strangled, standard of living." Indeed, Chase doubted that it would be possible to eliminate abundance even by practicing the most aggressive forms of sabotage. "If we do not accept [leisure and abundance] intelligently and gracefully," he warned, "we get them anyway—leisure in the breadline, and abundance in a mile-long pile of rotting oranges." Only by replacing an economy "of production for individual profit" with "an economy controlled for consumption ends," the three concluded, would abundance cease to threaten the nation's very economic survival.[15]

That Chase, Soule, and Lynd rejected the profit motive was far less significant than the fact that they did so for Veblenian rather than Marxist reasons. In their view the real problem with the profit motive was not that it encouraged inequities or resulted in class conflict but that it was inefficient. "It is not the profit which the fortune hunter actually takes which makes the bulk of the trouble," Chase insisted. "It is the waste and maladjustment he creates in trying to take it." Indeed, Chase was confident that "the payment of profits at a reasonable rate on the going technological value of the enterprise would not break the back of a functional economy." What such an economy could not tolerate was the "the shower of monkey wrenches thrown into the mechanism" by capitalists as they pursued their profit. "No society, particularly a highly specialized one," he cautioned, "can stand the continuous impact of such blows. A luxury class it can support, if it must, but not a chaotic menagerie trying—and mainly failing—to crash the luxury gate."[16]

How, then, to stop the "shower of monkey wrenches"? According to Chase, the first step was to remember "what an economic system is for," namely "to provide food, shelter, clothing and comforts" to "the whole community" at a level that "natural resources and the state of the technical arts permit." The existing capitalist system had failed to do so because its function was "not to supply people with things which they want" but, instead, to provide capitalists with profits. "When used as a channel for personal aggrandizement," Chase warned, "a system's function and meaning collapse. It becomes an industrial whirlpool, throwing out a certain amount of goods and services as a by product, but susceptible to frightful stoppages [and] reverse twists."[17] The only way to prevent those "stoppages" and "twists" was to make general well-being, rather than profit, the economic goal. And that, Chase, Soule, and Lynd agreed, would require economic planning.

But the three Veblenian thinkers meant economic planning of a particular kind. Chase, Soule, and Lynd were quick to point out that economies could be planned with a variety of goals in mind. Indeed, they suggested, economic planning and capitalism had long coexisted as those engaged in business tried to substitute the visible hand of planning for the invisible hand of competition. What made this planning capitalist was that its purpose was "to make more profit." "Social planning," by contrast, would substitute "social direction of our economy for the power of private wealth." It would make the requirements of the "masses of the people" rather than profit the "major objectives of the system." It was this substitution of public welfare for private profit, rather than any increasing interference in the economy, the three insisted, which made a socially planned economy fundamentally different from a capitalist one.[18]

Although Chase, Soule, and Lynd were convinced that "every step in the direction of planning for social ends must be a step away from capitalism" and although they believed that "the more advanced stages of a planned society must be something closely akin to the broad ambitions of socialism," their version of a planned economy differed from that of the socialists. The most important difference involved the "matter of ownership." Soule granted that social planning might collectivize the "important power of the rulers of business," thereby demoting them to the position of a "salaried manager." But he insisted that "it is barely conceivable" that a socially planned economy might "be brought about . . . without any confiscation of property except by the customary and sanctioned means of regulation and taxation." Chase shared these sentiments. Like Soule, he agreed "with socialists in preferring to see the people own the chief means of production." But, like Soule, he was also convinced that "the title to a factory, important as it is, matters far less than the running of that factory." "Even if workers owned their factories," he pointed out, "they would be as helpless without a market as their sometime bosses. You cannot eat crankshafts, or clothe yourself in spark plugs." "Industry," he concluded, "can be managed in the public interest without necessarily revolutionizing the status of the legal title."[19]

That Chase, Soule, and Lynd were willing to allow capitalists to retain the "title to a factory" highlighted the distance between their version of a planned economy and a socialist version. But, even more significantly, it revealed how much their version of planning relied on what was a capitalist understanding of the economy. One of the ways in which capitalism differed from socialism was that it gave priority to efficiency rather than equity. So, too, did Chase, Soule, and Lynd. Even Soule, the consumerist left liberal most intent on claiming the socialist label, did not denounce capitalists or their system for being exploitative. For him the major flaw in the capitalist system was its "inefficiency," the most serious failing of the capitalists their "incompetence."[20] Like Chase and Lynd, Soule may have condemned capitalism and flirted with socialism. But he was as convinced as they and, more to the point, as convinced as any classical economist that the key to general well-being was a highly productive economy. And the best way to achieve such an economy was to maximize efficiency. Chase, Soule, and Lynd may have preferred socialist means. But they remained deeply committed to capitalist ends.

The extent to which their emphasis on efficiency gave Chase, Soule, and Lynd a perspective on the economy which was far more compatible with capitalism than socialism becomes evident when one compares the features of capitalism to which they objected with those to which socialists took exception. To socialists the private ownership of the means of production violated their most basic notions of equity and was therefore an issue on which they were unwilling to compromise. Chase, Soule, and Lynd, by contrast, had no problem with capitalists' retaining the title to a factory as long as it did not compromise the efficient running of that factory.

Similarly, both socialists and the Veblenian consumerists condemned the profit motive but for different reasons. Socialists objected to profits because they believed profits resulted from the capitalist expropriation of labor. Not surprisingly, they found it difficult to compromise on what they considered gross exploitation. Chase, Soule, and Lynd, on the other hand, were opposed to profit because they considered it an inefficient way to motivate the production and distribution of goods. But, if profits could be made to encourage rather than frustrate "production for abundance," if the "interests of money-makers" ever ceased to be "at right angles to the needs and desires of consumers," then whatever objections Chase, Soule, and Lynd had to profits would disappear.[21]

Chase's, Soule's, and Lynd's analyses revealed once again how much consumerist ideas pushed consumerist thinkers in political directions they did not want to go. Even in the depths of the Great Depression, a depression that the three blamed on capitalism, they nevertheless found it impossible to dismiss capitalist principles completely. And, ironically, the very collapse of the economy which had prompted them to condemn capitalism highlighted this system's consumerist potential and downplayed that of socialism. In the depressed economy of the 1930s expanded production, the hallmark of capitalism, seemed to offer consumers far more than the redistribution of income which the socialists advocated.

Equally significantly, the Depression all but nullified one of the most powerful consumerist objections to capitalism. Since Bellamy's time consumerist thinkers had emphasized the distinction between a consumption-oriented and a consumer-oriented system. Capitalism, they had long argued, might maximize consumption but often at the expense of real consumer well-being. Well into the 1920s the distinction between a consumption-oriented capitalism and a consumer-oriented alternative seemed a valid one. With the onset of the Depression in the early 1930s, however, this distinction became obscured. In the face of pervasive poverty no economy seemed more consumer oriented than a consumption-oriented one.

The blurring of the distinction between a consumer-oriented and a consumption-oriented system weakened what had been one of the few consumerist objections to capitalist ends. Consumerist critics of capitalism did not relinquish this distinction easily—indeed, it was what initially made them uncomfortable with a Keynesian solution to the economic crisis. But they were well aware that in the face of widespread poverty their critique of what were capitalist means was far more powerful than any objection to the capitalist emphasis on increasing consumption. They therefore shifted their arguments from those that distinguished between a consumer-oriented and a consumption-oriented system to those that stressed the inability of such capitalist means as profit, competition, and self-interest to achieve the sort of economy which Adam Smith had predicted they would. Eventually, however, even the Veblenian critics of capitalism would conclude that the solution was not to abandon capitalism in favor of some alternative economic system but, rather, to find new means of accomplishing Smithian ends.

Like Chase, Soule, and Lynd, AAA left liberals Tugwell and Means had reservations about capitalism. And, like them, Tugwell and Means owed many of their reservations to a Veblenian analysis of the economy. They, too, were skeptical about the business community's ability or willingness to function in a socially responsible manner. And they, too, were convinced that profit was an ineffective motivator. But they stopped short of rejecting capitalism in the 1930s in large part because they did not use their Veblenian analysis to arrive at Veblenian conclusions.[22]

Chase's, Soule's and Lynd's reading of Veblen convinced them that the interests of corporate capitalists were inevitably antithetical to those of consumers and that corporate capitalism was fundamentally incompatible with abundance. Tugwell and Means reached no such conclusions. They were as quick as Veblen and his disciples to insist that, "with an equipment adequate to this purpose," "the system of unregulated business enterprise has failed" to provide a "minimum of security." But they were confident that capitalism could "be modified and regulated to repair the failure."[23]

More significantly, Tugwell and Means were convinced that such repairs would prove as beneficial to the business community as to the consuming population. Chase, Soule, and Lynd had occasionally made concessions to the capitalists. But they had been willing to tolerate private control of the means of production and a continuation of profits only because they saw neither as a threat to their goal of a consumer-oriented economy of abundance. Business well-being never entered into their calculations. It did enter into the calculations of Tugwell and Means. While the two advocated abundant production because it was good for consumers, they were quick to point out that it was also good for capitalists. Indeed, it was the only way that corporate capitalism could survive.

Tugwell and Means may have endorsed what had been a central tenet of Adam Smith's theories, namely that a capitalist economy could function on behalf of both producers and consumers. But they were as quick as any left liberal to reject laissez-faire as a means to these Smithian ends. Smith and the classical economists, Tugwell maintained, mistakenly believed in "an invisible hand which beneficently guided warring business men to the promotion of the general welfare." In Tugwell's view, however, reliance on an invisible hand, far from promoting the general welfare, had plunged the nation into the worst depression in its history. "The jig is up," Tugwell declared. "The cat is out of the bag. There is no invisible hand. There never was. . . . We must now supply a real and visible guiding hand to do the task which that mythical, nonexistent, invisible agency was supposed to perform, but never did."[24]

Means was as convinced as Tugwell that there was currently "no invisible hand." But he disagreed that "there never was." For Means laissez-faire had once functioned reasonably effectively. And, more to the point, it had done so in a consumer-oriented fashion. "Indeed," he explained, "the primary justification for a system of laissez faire has been the assertion that if each individual were allowed to produce and sell freely in the market in the interests of his own profit, the net result would be a system which approached the ideal from the point of view of the consumer."[25] Much like Veblen late in his career, Means concluded that, under the sorts of competitive conditions which had prevailed in the late eighteenth and early nineteenth centuries, a laissez-faire economy had been a consumer-oriented one.

Just as significantly, this economy had been a consumer-directed one. "In the minds of classical theorists," Means explained, "the consumer has been regarded as someone who in large measure determined the course of economic activity through his purchasing here or there, through his buying or refraining from buying." Indeed, according to Means, it was precisely because a laissez-faire economy was a consumer-directed one that it had benefited producers as well as consumers. Moreover, it was because consumers had lost their influence over the economy that laissez-faire had ceased be an effective means of promoting the welfare of either consumers or producers.[26]

But why had consumers lost their influence over the economy? And, more important, why had this loss had such devastating consequences? According to Means, the answer to both questions was the rise of the corporation. As "countless numbers of small enterprises" gave way to large corporations, he explained, corporate managers, who were largely immune from competition, acquired control over price and production levels. Like their predecessors, these corporate managers surveyed the economy from a "producer point of view." This meant that, like their predecessors, their main concern was "producing values" rather than "producing goods." In the highly competitive economy of the nineteenth century the only way that business leaders could produce values was to produce goods. In the far less competitive corporate economy, however, corporate managers discovered that they could create values by limiting production while maintaining or even increasing prices. Without competitive market forces, Means concluded, the "producer point of view," with its emphasis on values, was transformed into "a Frankenstein, destroying even the values that producer-minded people would attempt to produce."[27]

If the rise of the corporate economy had transformed the producer point of view into a Frankenstein, then the solution, Means suggested, was to replace this producerist monster with a consumer point of view. Means was quick to emphasize, however, that this would not require a return to the competitive economy. Consumers might only be able to regulate business in a highly competitive market, but the government operated under no such constraints. It had the power to do directly what market forces had only done indirectly: force businesses to function in a consumer-oriented fashion. The result would be an economy that benefited not only consumers but also producers.[28]

What Means had done was to reconcile Smithian ideas with the economic conditions of the twentieth century. Like Smith, he assumed that the economy could serve the interests of both consumers and producers. And, like Smith, he believed that the best way to bring these competing interests into harmony was through abundant consumption.[29] He merely suggested that it was necessary to replace Smith's invisible hand with the visible hand of government. If government would do what competitive forces had once done—namely force businesses to operate in a consumer-oriented fashion—the result would be an economy that was simultaneously producer and consumer oriented. And such an economy would be far closer to what Smith had envisioned than were the producer-oriented laissez-faire policies that were defended in Smith's name.

Like Means, Tugwell looked to an economic system that would function on behalf of both producers and consumers. And, like Means, he did not advocate such an economy because of any concern for business well-being. Indeed, he was as convinced as Chase, Lynd, and Soule that, given half a chance, "our financial and industrial autocrats" would continue to "manipulate materials, natural forces and social institutions for their own good at the expense of all the rest." But he did part company with the Veblenian consumerist thinkers over whether the only solution was to overthrow the "autocrats." Having long maintained that the interests of consumers and those of industry "are ultimately identical," he suggested that the real question was: "what can the Government do to protect industry against itself?"[30]

According to Tugwell, there were at least two ways in which government could allow industry to remain under private control and still make sure that the consuming population was able to "take possession of the vast flow of goods" made possible by the productive "power of our industrial machine." One option was for government to adopt "a socially wise economic policy" and require manufacturers "to define the quality of the goods it offers and to sell them at prices which are suitably low." The alternative was for government to adopt a policy of "socialistic taxation." Businesses would be allowed "to proceed with the policy of establishing high prices and maintaining them by limitation, and of selling goods whose qualities are mysterious to most consumers." Government would then take "much of the resulting profits . . . in taxes" and return it "to consumers as free goods . . . in the form of facilities for health and recreation, insurance against old age, sickness and unemployment, or in other ways." Tugwell preferred the former, but, should the business interests refuse to cooperate, he had no objections to the latter.[31]

What was ultimately most significant about Means's and Tugwell's version of a consumer-oriented economy was that its potential appeal extended beyond the handful of political thinkers associated with the *New Republic* and the League for Independent Political Action. As long as a consumer-oriented system was associated with the abolition of private property and profit, it was a system that was unlikely to find much support outside a minority on the left. Means and Tugwell, however, managed to reconcile consumerist and capitalist ideas by suggesting that only by focusing on the needs of the consuming population could capitalism survive. And, in so doing, they helped to move consumerist ideas out of the margins of political discourse and into the mainstream.

Nor were they alone. At the same time that Tugwell and Means were removing some of the antibusiness bias of a consumerist worldview, consumerist corporate liberals such as retail magnate Edward Filene and economist William Trufant Foster were developing its pro-business potential. Unlike the consumerist left liberals, Foster and Filene were enthusiastic supporters of a system of "production for profit." Foster was adamant "that the greatest gains in per capita output have been achieved under the spur of the profit motive." He was willing to concede that, "if the profit incentive is not the most effective one, we should find a better one." But he insisted that, "until we do find a better one, we should use the old one for all it is worth. . . . it is stupid to hammer away at its foundations, weakening first one support and then another, until we find out how much weakening . . . [it] will stand without collapsing." Filene was equally committed to the profit system, although he was more interested in establishing the equity than the efficiency of such a system. "I cannot see, as hard as I have tried to follow the arguments of those who favor it," he admitted, "that we need any legislation looking toward the elimination of profits." More than willing to support measures to prevent "the accumulation of profits into useless and even dangerous reservoirs of disservice," he remained convinced that profits were "the legitimate wages of capital which is being used for human service."[32]

Foster and Filene were as committed to consumer well-being as they were to business prosperity. Indeed, for them the two were inextricably intertwined. They were as convinced as any corporate liberal that consumers were the source of business profits and that, the more abundantly consumers consumed, the better off business would be. But, if the goal was high levels of consumption, then, they reasoned, the more an economy functioned on behalf of consumers, the more consumers would be able to consume. "Modern machinery," Filene maintained, "made it not only possible but imperative from the true business standpoint that the masses should live lives of comfort and of leisure." "We must . . . recognize that there can be no prosperity for producers, excepting as they produce prosperity for the consuming public."[33] It was their conviction that it was as important to grant consumers rights as it was to assign them responsibilities that made Foster and Filene consumerist thinkers.

As one of the most successful retailers in the country, Filene might have been expected to be more sympathetic to consumerist ideas than many a corporate liberal. After all, he was in a business that depended more on the consumer's ability to buy. But it was not only his commitment to business prosperity which pushed him in a consumerist direction. As founder and president of the Twentieth Century Fund, he had long been a supporter of progressive causes. And he would later defend Roosevelt's tax policies by asking: "why shouldn't the American people take half my money from me? I took all of it from them."[34] What Filene found in a consumer-oriented corporate liberalism was a system of ideas which seemed consistent with both his commitment to capitalism and his strong sense of social responsibility.

An economist and one-time president of Reed College, Foster was even more convinced than Filene that the very survival of capitalism depended upon consumer-oriented policies. In the 1920s he had coauthored a series of popular economics books with industrialist Waddill Catchings in which the two had emphasized business's dependence on buyers. "In this money-and-profit world . . . which is the only economic order yet discovered which is at all workable on a large scale," the two declared, "consumption regulates production." The problem, in their view, was that in a capitalist economy the ability to consume inevitably lagged behind the ability to produce. Therefore, they concluded, "in the future we must provide as effectively for financing consumption, as in the past we have provided for financing production." By the early 1930s Foster had become convinced that the future had arrived. If the government did not take steps "directed toward sustaining the consuming power of the people," he warned, it would be "impossible to have sustained prosperity under capitalism" and, perhaps, even capitalism itself.[35]

Foster's and Filene's commitment to the profit system might have prompted them to adopt the sorts of attitudes toward the consumer and consumption which characterized the thinking of producer-oriented corporate liberals such as Hugh Johnson. And, indeed, the two shared Johnson's conviction that consumers were responsible for business prosperity. "This is a world of mass production," Filene declared, "and it must become a world of mass consumption. This means that everybody must do his part—as a consumer. That and only that will keep production running smoothly." Foster was equally quick to emphasize the role that consumption played in furthering business well-being. "Nothing but money spent by consumers," he emphasized, "can make the wheels of business go round."[36]

Ultimately, however, what was most striking about a comparison of Filene's and Foster's ideas with those of Johnson was not the similarities but the differences. Johnson seemed the personification of what Gardiner Means labeled "producer-minded." "To the producer-minded," Means explained, "the curtailment of production, limitation of hours, and lifting of prices can appear to be a satisfactory solution to a specific problem." This was because their primary concern was how "the existing producing instruments [can] be made to return values." Foster and Filene, by contrast, were what Means called "consumer-minded." Their primary concern was whether "the effect of the program [would] be to make people able to eat more or live better."[37] Their consumer-mindedness, however, did not compromise their capitalist allegiances. Indeed, what Foster and Filene demonstrated was that a commitment to capitalism could be completely compatible with a consumer-minded approach to the economy.

Precisely because Foster and Filene were consumer minded, they refused to go on what Means called the "sidetrack of creating value through scarcity." The producer-minded Johnson was quick to blame the depression on overproduction. The industrial sector, he insisted, was so phenomenally productive that consumers could not possibly use all that industry produced. It was, therefore, necessary to limit production. Foster disagreed. "First of all," he insisted, ". . . let us set down the unquestioned fact that the entire country now suffers from chronic underproduction. Even in years of greatest prosperity, industry falls far, far short of using its resources, human and material, to produce all that might readily be produced." If the "aim of the New Deal" really was "increased wealth for all the people," he maintained, then it was not going to achieve that aim "by reducing the output of wealth." Limiting production would raise prices. And it would increase the "dollar valuation of wealth." But it would do nothing to improve the standard of living, which was, Foster insisted, the real measure of a nation's wealth. "No way has yet been discovered of eating oranges which have not been grown, or wearing shoes which have not been made." Only by "increas[ing] per capita consumption of wealth" would the New Deal realize its goal of "increased wealth for all the people."[38]

Foster's and Filene's consumer-mindedness not only encouraged them to reject Johnson's producer-minded explanation of why the economy had collapsed. It also pushed them toward an explanation that was remarkably similar to that of the consumerist left liberals. According to Foster and Filene, "the crux of the economic problem" was neither excess production nor insufficient profit margins, as Johnson suggested. "The reason we cannot sell the goods . . . is because the people who would like to buy them do not have sufficient incomes." Economic recovery, they agreed, would depend on "an adequate, sustained, properly-distributed flow of consumer income."[39]

Johnson was not oblivious to the fact that producer well-being depended upon consumer purchasing power. He merely believed that the best way to increase that power was to make production profitable.[40] This was, he insisted, precisely why limitation of production was necessary. Without surpluses industrialists would find it once again profitable to produce and would hire more workers. It was the money in the pockets of those newly employed workers, Johnson maintained, which represented the best hope for renewed consumer spending and with it expanded production. To Johnson government could best increase consumer purchasing power by increasing profits.

Foster disagreed. Government, he insisted, could best increase consumer purchasing power by increasing consumer purchasing power. Conceding that "the flow of money to consumers depends mainly on productive activity," he was quick to point out that just the opposite was true: "Productive activity depends mainly on the flow of money to consumers." "Where are we to break into this circle?" he queried. His answer was at the point of consumption. The only way to have any permanent impact on the circle was to "increase the flow of money to consumers." "If we increase productive activity without proportionately increasing the flow of money to consumers," Foster warned, "prosperity is short-lived." Only consumer-oriented government policies would bring a sustained prosperity.[41]

Filene was equally convinced that consumer-oriented government policies would be good for business. "We Businessmen," he insisted, ". . . want like everything to sell a greater volume of goods; and we cannot, obviously, sell more than the buying public can buy." The only solution was a "program for the mass consumer." Such a program, Filene believed, could take many forms, but at its heart was an approach to the economy which would guarantee "that more productive methods will always bring greater benefits and greater leisure to the masses. To the masses this naturally seems attractive. To the business man it is imperative." "If the masses do not buy, and are not provided with both power to buy and leisure to consume, business can never again be profitable for any long period."[42]

At the same time that Foster's and Filene's consumerist leanings prevented them from embracing a producer-oriented version of corporate liberalism, their capitalist leanings made it impossible for them to adopt all the ideas of the consumerist left liberals. Most problematic among them was the left liberal assumption that business was part of the problem rather than part of the solution. Lynd, Soule, and Chase were convinced that business was fundamentally incapable of functioning in a consumer-oriented fashion. Even Tugwell and Means, who advocated a modified capitalist system, nevertheless assumed that extensive regulation would be necessary to force businesses to operate in a consumer-friendly manner. Foster and Filene, by contrast, were confident that businesses were both able and willing to function in a consumer-oriented fashion. The two may have joined consumerist left liberals in calling for modifications to the capitalist system, but the changes they demanded were not designed to constrain corporate greed so much as liberate a corporate sense of social responsibility.[43]

Like most corporate liberals, Foster and Filene were convinced that the key to prosperity was a partnership between business and government. But they parted company with the majority of corporate liberals in their conviction that this partnership should manage the economy in the public rather than the business interests. To Foster this could best be accomplished if government functioned as the senior partner. Although he was firmly convinced that, "if capitalism is to survive, there must be better management of private industry *by private industry*," he looked to government to make sure that "each major industry . . . plan[s] production, distribution, and conditions of labor in the public interest." Filene also believed it was important for industry to be directed in the public interest. But he believed that this goal could best be realized if the government-business partnership was one of equals. He called on the two to "plan together to eliminate waste, so that human labor may produce the greatest human results." And he suggested that they could cooperate to get more money into the hands of workers. "Many employers who believed in high wages," Filene maintained, ". . . have been afraid to pay them lest their competitors would not do the same." Government could prevent these competitors from frustrating social progress by forcing them to pay the same high wages that the more socially responsible businesses were paying.[44]

What was striking about Filene's and Foster's version of a business-government partnership was the extent to which it diverged from the standard corporate liberal version. Producer-oriented corporate liberals believed that government and business would work together to maximize business prosperity, which would, in turn, improve everyone's standard of living. Filene and Foster, however, rejected the trickle-down version of a government-business partnership. Both were adamant that "the first principle of . . . government must be to provide for adequate consumption." Indeed, Filene suggested that much of the economic problem came about because "we have had no understanding of what business is for." "Business," he insisted, "is not for finance," and it "is not for production. . . . Business is for the consumer—the mass consumer."[45] Convinced that consumer well-being would translate into producer well-being, Filene and Foster subscribed to what might be called "trickle-up economics."

The extent to which consumerist ideas prompted Filene and Foster to adopt a trickle-up approach was also evident in their conviction that far-reaching and relatively radical social policies were the best way to advance business interests. What Foster saw in "old-age pensions, unemployment insurance and a federal system of employment agencies" was not socialism but, rather, a way "to sustain the buying power of consumers." Similarly, Filene believed it was imperative that business and government cooperate "in eliminating unemployment and in arranging for an adequate income to those too young and those too old to work." The real danger, he warned, was doing nothing, because, if those groups "fail[ed] to consume, they [could] clog the wheels of industry."[46]

Perhaps nowhere was the impact of consumerist ideas on a corporate liberal worldview more striking than in Foster's and Filene's call for what Tugwell called "socialistic taxation." For Tugwell "rigorous regulation, . . . extreme taxation, and . . . [the] widespread provision of free social goods" were not particularly efficient ways to achieve a "more abundant life" for the American people. He advocated income redistribution only as a last resort, to be used as a disciplinary measure if businesses refused to produce an abundant supply of fairly priced goods. Chase and Soule were equally quick to dismiss income redistribution, convinced that "taking money from the rich to give to the poor" would do little to "raise the level of life of the majority of the people." Only "capacity operation of [the industrial] plant" and "an unhampered flow of goods to consumers," they insisted, could usher in the economy of abundance.[47]

Filene and Foster, by contrast, were confident that income redistribution could play an important role in maximizing prosperity. To Foster "higher income taxes on the upper groups, higher taxes on excess profits, much higher taxes on inheritances, and a gradual reduction of the volume of non-taxable securities" were not so much a matter of "social justice" as "arithmetic." "Consumers," he pointed out, "cannot long buy without money." Therefore, in "the interests of the well-to-do, . . . we should take from them a sufficient amount of their surplus to enable consumers to consume and business to operate at a profit." "The aim," he emphasized, "is not 'to soak the rich' but to save [them]."[48]

Unlike Foster, Filene advocated income redistribution as much for its social as its economic impact. But, then, he had always been far more convinced than Foster that social responsibility and economic prosperity were inextricably linked. Inheritance taxes, Filene maintained, could play an important role in encouraging a more socially responsible and productively efficient business community. By taking the fortunes of "irresponsible, inefficient, untrained persons" whose money gave them "power over millions of lives," income redistribution would cull from the ranks of business those individuals "whose sole claim to . . . power is based not upon anything which they contribute to society, but solely on what they have received from society."[49] The result would be an economy that would function more efficiently and more in the public interest.

Filene's and Foster's call for income redistribution highlighted, once again, the power of consumerist ideas to push political thinkers in directions they would not normally have traveled. In the case of left liberals these ideas prevented critics of profit-oriented capitalism from joining left-leaning contemporaries in completely rejecting that system. In the case of corporate liberals consumerist ideas prompted staunch supporters of profit-oriented capitalism to call for many of the same sorts of policies which social democrats were advocating.

What was striking about consumerist ideas, however, was not merely that they forced political thinkers in surprising political directions but that they pushed proponents of varied political views toward a common political ground—a "vital center." At the same time that consumerist ideas were having a moderating influence on left liberals, they were having a progressive influence on corporate liberals. The result was that left and corporate liberals who embraced consumerist ideas ultimately shared much more common ground than did their nonconsumerist counterparts.

But perhaps most striking was the extent to which the same economic conditions that polarized the left and the right only increased the common ground that left and corporate liberals shared. The Depression was a radicalizing experience for many Americans. The labor movement, moribund in the 1920s, emerged with renewed energy in the 1930s. In 1934 alone nearly 1.5 million workers went out on strike. Two years later the Congress of Industrial Organizations was born, ushering in, at least initially, a far more confrontational approach to labor/industrial relations. Nor was it only workers who were moving left in the 1930s. Liberal intellectuals became increasingly disillusioned by capitalism. A few joined the Communist Party, and many more cooperated with Communists in the creation of the Popular Front. Finally, even middle-class Americans were flirting with radical ideas in the Depression decade. Hundreds of thousands supported Upton Sinclair's EPIC plan to "End Poverty in California" and Floyd Olson's Farmer-Labor Party. Millions embraced Huey Long's "Share Our Wealth" program. By contrast, few conservatives actually moved farther to the right. A handful of intellectuals including Ezra Pound and Lawrence Dennis flirted with fascism. But most conservatives remained loyal to the Republican Party and continued to champion the same sorts of ideas they had espoused a decade earlier. Even the wealthy businessmen who founded the American Liberty League merely wanted a return to business as usual. Nevertheless, the very fact that most American conservatives did not modify their political ideas at a time when so many Americans were moving leftward meant that the gap separating left and right increased considerably.

It is, therefore, striking that, in the very years that the distance between left and right was growing, proponents of consumerist ideas found themselves converging on common political ground. Consumerist corporate liberals, who saw mass consumption as the foundation for business prosperity, came to believe that the best way to encourage mass consumption was to ensure the well-being of the consuming masses. In short, they concluded that few economies were more consumption oriented than a consumer-oriented one. Similarly, consumerist left liberals—who had long emphasized the differences between an economy dedicated to the consuming masses and one that was merely dedicated to mass consumption—became convinced that few economies were more consumer oriented than a consumption-oriented one.

Despite Filene's and Foster's endorsement of income redistribution and welfare policies, it was not the consumerist corporate liberals but their left liberal counterparts who ultimately had the longer distance to travel to the common ground that would eventually be called New Deal liberalism. This was, in part, because the New Deal would remain committed to the very profit system that the left liberals had so long denounced. Corporate and left liberals alike agreed that the New Deal "was not a revolution." Foster thought that "the chief economic consequence of the New Deal will be the discovery that a profit economy, when we maintain conditions under which it can work, makes possible higher standards of living than any other, but that a profit economy cannot work without profits." And Filene emphasized that the consumer- and consumption-oriented policies of the New Deal were ultimately good for business. He chastised those "business men who believe most profoundly in the profit system" for not recognizing that "the President's recovery program is their program—*their* way out of chaos." As for the left liberals, most agreed with Soule that, instead of "excercis[ing] real power over industry," the administration had "handed the system back to the old rulers, with enough help so that they were able to carry on."[50]

It was not only the New Deal's commitment to the "old rulers" which meant consumerist left liberals would have to travel farther than their corporate liberal counterparts. It was also the New Deal's eventual reliance on a consumption-oriented approach to the economy, namely countercyclical government spending. According to the proponents of this approach, government could offset any economic decline in the private sector by pumping money into the economy. Because such spending would get money into the hands of consumers, it would maintain the purchasing power on which businesses depended.

Although countercyclical spending would come to be associated with John Maynard Keynes, consumerist left liberals first encountered these ideas in the writings of none other than William Trufant Foster. Foster identified the same potentially fatal flaw in a capitalist economy which Karl Marx had identified several decades earlier. When capitalists used part of their profits to expand production, he warned, they reduced the amount of money paid out in wages. But money not paid out in wages was money that could not be spent by consumers. Marx had predicted that this leak would bring about capitalism's downfall. Foster, however,was convinced that it was possible to plug the leak or, at least, compensate for it. The problem, he insisted, was not that "the profit economy does not work," only that it "does not work automatically." If the "Lazy Fairies," as Foster disparagingly referred to laissez-faire, could not ensure "the proper flow of money to consumers," then government would have to do so. Either through the dole or public works projects—Foster preferred the latter—it could get "additional purchasing power into the hands of consumers" and, in so doing, could go a long way toward "establishing the only conditions under which business as a whole can operate at a profit."[51]

It was not particularly surprising that consumerist left liberals would have little interest in Foster's version of countercyclical government spending, designed, as Foster put it, "to prime the pump of private business." For them pump priming was only "a means to restore the old formula," when what was needed was "a new formula."[52] But consumerist left liberals initially had almost as little interest in these ideas when presented by an "intelligent and distinguished" economist such as John Maynard Keynes.[53] Lynd was frustrated by much of the "current economic research" because it "tacitly assumes that private, competitive business enterprise, motivated by the desire for profit, is the way for a culture to utilize its technical skill to supply its people with needed goods." The challenge, as he saw it, was not to fix capitalism but to replace it. Chase agreed. "Most of the programs for reform which have been pouring in upon us ever since the depression started—including those of Keynes . . . have, to my mind, one fatal defect. They do not ask what an economic system is for." Keynesian spending sought to repair the "prevailing system," putting "only patches on a boiler which is destined ultimately to explode." In his view "the fires must be drawn and the boiler redesigned. Unlimited purchasing power for unlimited junk, and a managed currency to underwrite the claims of creditors to perpetuity," he insisted, "will only make the final explosion worse." Not until 1940 would Chase fully embrace Keynesian economics.[54]

Soule was even slower to do so. Until the end of the decade he remained convinced that, for at least two reasons, government spending was inferior to economic planning. First, it used government money to give people "beautiful buildings, art museums, parks, and what not," when what they really needed was "enough nourishing food." The more serious defect, however, was that it was not effective. "Pump-priming works," he insisted, "as long as we keep priming the pump, but fails as soon as we stop pouring water in." If the goal was "to increase the flow of money and to make proper adjustments in the valves of the system through which the flow occurs," then government could best accomplish this goal not by spending on public works but by entering "those types of enterprise where the circumstances of private business have obstructed the necessary expansion of our economy." Soule denied that his recommendation was "based on any doctrinaire belief in socialism." Instead, it was "based on the fact that government can do a specific job in our national economy that private enterprise has failed to do in important sectors." By running certain industries, government "can reduce prices, improve quality, and so increase consumption." And, just as important, "it can greatly enlarge and continue the investment of new capital." Finally, "by virtue of both these activities it can aid employment and enhance the national income."[55] In short, he concluded, government operation of what had once been private industries could accomplish the goals of Keynesianism far better than Kenynesian spending could.

If, in the 1930s Chase and Soule considered countercyclical government spending only to dismiss it, Tugwell and Means largely ignored it. Both were convinced that the economic crisis could be solved without scrapping the existing system. But they insisted that the solution was economic planning on behalf of the consumer, rather than manipulation of the money supply. Although Tugwell occasionally suggested that it was necessary to "put into circulation . . . a new flow of buying power [through the public works program]," he placed far more emphasis on "increasing production and raising wages to the industrial worker faster than industrial prices are raised." According to Tugwell, what had destroyed purchasing power was not so much an insufficient money supply as excessive profits. In the 1920s, he suggested, huge gains in efficiency "steadily, almost spectacularly, reduced" costs. "Prices were reduced somewhat but by no means in proportion to the reduction in costs. The result of this disparity between costs and prices was that profits rose enormously." For Tugwell it was these high profits that had caused the collapse of the economy. When businesses decided to keep all "the gains from the efficiency movement" for themselves and refused to allow consumers "to share in [those] gains . . . the demand for the goods produced began to fail."[56] Businesses responded to the fall in demand by limiting production, and the result was economic depression.

According to Tugwell, the only way to end the Depression was to reverse this process. Businesses, he insisted, would have to increase production, maintain or even lower prices, and raise wages. "At first thought you will ask how the wage bill can be increased by an industry without increasing the prices charged. This," Tugwell suggested, "is the very crux of the recovery program. It was by reducing production and wages in some industries, without a corresponding drop in prices, that we destroyed exchangeability. To restore it the process must be reversed." "Profits will have to follow from new efficiencies." Nor would such a process necessarily be bad for business. "In fact," he suggested, "the best guarantee of profits is capacity operation at low cost and prices; this involves the preservation of purchasing power, the conservation of markets. It may mean smaller earnings at once, but it ought to insure their steady continuance."[57]

Ultimately, it was not surprising that consumerist left liberals initially showed so little interest in countercyclical government spending, even as propounded by Keynes, because such spending would do nothing to fix what they considered the primary flaws in the capitalist system. It would not transform what Chase called an "acquisitive economy . . . concerned with price in terms of money" into "a functional economy . . . concerned with supplying human wants."[58] It would not reduce the waste within the capitalist system. It would not even encourage the abundant production of high-quality, fairly priced goods. All it would do was put more money into the hands of consumers so that they could continue to support business as usual. Consumerist left liberals may have come to believe that some versions of a consumption-oriented economy functioned in a consumer-oriented way. But into the late 1930s they doubted that the Keynesian version was one of them.

Instead, consumerist left liberals continued to call for a planned economy as the most effective way to usher in an economy of abundance. Whether they looked to a system in which government would actually direct economic activity in a consumer-oriented direction—as did Chase, Soule, and Lynd—or whether they favored one in which extensive government regulations would force businesses themselves to operate in a consumer-oriented way, as did Tugwell and Means, all placed their faith in economic planning. That faith was seriously shaken in the mid-1930s, when the NRA provided consumerist left liberals with one example of a planned economy in action.

The impact of the NRA experiment on consumerist ideas extended far beyond its effect on the left liberal faith in economic planning. First, by its failure it went a long way toward discrediting economic planning among most political thinkers. Second, by creating a Consumers' Advisory Board alongside the Labor Advisory Board (LAB) and the Industrial Advisory Board (IAB), it recognized the right of the consuming public to influence economic policy. Third, by bringing together consumerist thinkers as diverse in their ideas as James Peter Warbasse, Paul Douglas, Lynd, Means, and Foster, the Consumers' Advisory Board (CAB) exposed its members to alternative ways of understanding the consumer. And, finally, the NRA would play a critical role in determining exactly how the consumer would be defined.

From the outset it was clear that those involved with the NRA did not all define the consumer in the same way. And, though it was perhaps to be expected that producerist thinkers relied on definitions that were at odds with those of consumerist thinkers, it was surprising that consumerist thinkers failed to achieve a consensus even among themselves. Was the consumer an interest that all people shared? Was it the primary economic identity of all humans? Was it the primary economic identity of some individuals but not others? How such questions would be answered would not only go a long way toward determining what rights and responsibilities the consumer would have. Even more important, the answers would play an important role in shaping the economic assumptions that would be at the heart of New Deal liberalism.

Not surprisingly, given his conviction that any gains for consumers came at the expense of producers, Johnson's definition of the consumer was one that would limit whatever influence consumers might seek to exert on NRA policy. To Johnson government could develop policies that were in the public interest by balancing the interests of distinct groups. Consumers, he insisted, should not be included in the balancing process, because, according to Johnson, their interest was the public interest. They would therefore be the primary beneficiaries of the balancing process. Indeed, he suggested, precisely because the consumer and the public interest were one and the same, not some board of consumer representatives but "the President himself is the real representative of Consumers, i.e., of the whole people of the United States."[59]

Johnson was not only convinced that recognizing the consumer interest was unnecessary. Even more to the point, he argued, it was absurd. Treating consumers as a specific interest only pit the interests of consumers against the interests of producers and, in so doing, divided "a man against himself." If the consumer interest was to be involved in economic recovery at all, he decided, it should be understood as "a composite of labor, economic, industrial and popular representation." As such, it could balance "diverse policies for the best interest of the people as a whole." Johnson's consumer interest, it would seem, was an even more public interest than the "popular" interest.[60]

Johnson's determination to make the consumer interest synonymous with the public interest was evident in his initial appointments to the CAB. The people he chose to represent the consumer were all individuals with little connection to the consumer interest. Sociologist William F. Ogburn, president of University of North Carolina–Chapel Hill, Frank Graham, League of Women Voters officers Belle Sherwin and Mrs. Joseph J. Daniels, and Junior League founder and Washington socialite Mary Rumsey were all committed to reform. But it was reform on behalf of the public rather than the consumer interest. They had little background in consumption economics, consumer activism, or even consumerist thought.[61]

Consumerist thinkers were well aware that Johnson's definition of the consumer would limit the influence of the CAB. Means was profoundly troubled by Johnson's equation of the consumer with the public interest. "Probably no single element in the thinking of the past year," he asserted, "has done more damage to the consumer that this confusion." "The public interest and the consumer interest," he emphasized, "are not identical." The former was a broad interest covering "all spheres of human activity—religious, political, economic, social." The latter was a purely economic interest and only one interest among many. "To confuse the public interest with the much more specific consumer interest is to lose sight of the even-handed balance which is implicit in the term 'the public interest.'"[62]

Lynd also had concerns about Johnson's definitions, but, unlike Means, he was far more troubled by Johnson's definition of the business interest than by any definition of the consumer interest. According to Lynd, Johnson assumed that business prosperity was the key to everybody's welfare. This assumption meant that Johnson allowed "a special group, business men, to preempt the right to speak for 'everybody.'"[63] Most of the problems with the NRA, Lynd concluded, could be traced to Johnson's assumption that *business interest* and *public interest* were synonymous.

As for Johnson's definition of *consumer*, Lynd agreed with Means that Johnson was confused about who consumers were. Indeed, Lynd suggested, Johnson was so confused that he relied on at least two definitions. At times Johnson treated consumers as members of a distinct interest, often blocking "action by a Consumers' Board on the ground that [it] represents a special group." At other times he defined the consumer interest as a public interest. It was this definition, Lynd argued, which accounted for the CAB's "heterogeneous membership," which was "recruited from a variety of sources—club women, college professors, etc."[64]

Lynd was far less troubled by Johnson's definition of the consumer interest as the public interest, in large part because it was a definition that he shared. He granted that it may have prevented the CAB from functioning as "a pressure group to get what it can for the consumer." But it was precisely because CAB members tended to identify their mission in terms of "general public policy rather than class interest," Lynd maintained, that the CAB was the one board not intent on "getting the old bus back on the road and humming along profitably as in the past" or "seeking to fatten the winnings of any group at the expense of any or all others." It alone went beyond the "immediacies of recovery." It alone was committed to a "fundamental reconstruction of the traditional vested interest and procedures of business." This broader view may have meant that the CAB was less effective at influencing NRA policy than were the other boards, but, according to Lynd, it also meant that the CAB was the one board with radical potential.[65]

As Johnson and the left liberals debated how much influence the consumer should have over recovery policy, they employed whatever rhetorical weapons they could find. One of the most powerful turned out to be gender. Convinced that the political arena was a male domain, both sides took for granted that the gender of the consumer would go a long way toward determining whether or not consumers would gain access to it. A male consumer would be entitled to take his place beside labor, industry, and agriculture as one of the major players in interest group politics. A female consumer, by contrast, would not be allowed to participate in the creation of public policy but would have to rely on public policy makers to represent her interests.

What is striking about the debates over the gender of the consumer was that they highlighted a fundamental difference between advocates of a consumer-orientated economy and proponents of a consumption-oriented system. Those who sought to gender the consumer were all thinkers who approached the economy as an arena of conflict rather than consensus. Chase, Soule, F. J. Schlink, and, for that matter, Johnson all assumed that consumers and producers had antithetical interests. And all were far more interested in victory for their side than in peaceful coexistence. They all hoped that gender connotations might help them vanquish opposing ideas.

By contrast, consumerist thinkers such as Tugwell, Means, Foster, and Filene, who looked to a consumption-oriented economy, tended to ignore gender. And they did so because they were not intent on achieving victory in the conflict between consumers or producers so much as ending that conflict. Indeed, it had been their desire to find a common ground for the various economic interests that had drawn them to a consumption-oriented system in the first place. Because establishing the gender of consumers and producers would emphasize differences rather than similarities between these two identities, consumerist proponents of a consumption-oriented economy tended to avoid the category altogether.

Few thinkers relied as heavily on gender as did Johnson. And, not surprisingly, given his determination to limit the influence of the consumer on NRA policy, he defined the consumer as female. It was a definition that was evident as he staffed the three advisory boards of the National Recovery Administration. No women sat on the Industrial Advisory Board, and only one woman, Rose Schneiderman of the National Women's Trade Union League, sat on the Labor Advisory Board. As a longtime labor activist, Schneiderman had valid producer credentials. She was appointed to the LAB in spite of her gender, not because of it. By contrast, during his tenure as NRA administrator, Johnson appointed numerous women to the CAB. These women were prominent but, in most cases, their prominence had nothing to do with consumption. Neither vice chairwoman of the Democratic National Committee Emily Newell Blair nor president of the National League of Women Voters Belle Sherwin nor president of the Indiana League of Women Voters Mrs. Joseph J. Daniels were consumer economists or consumer activists, but they were women and, as such, qualified for board membership.

The same, however, could not be said of Johnson's male appointees, all of whom were considered specialists in consumer issues. In addition to Means, Lynd, Foster, and Warbasse, Johnson eventually appointed Frederic Howe, who was an authority on consumer cooperation; Walton Hamilton, who had written on consumer issues from a legal perspective; and Paul Douglas, who had become increasingly interested in a consumerist approach to the economy.[66] In short, men were appointed to the CAB only after establishing their consumer credentials. Women could establish these credentials merely by being female.

Feminizing the consumer went a long way toward marginalizing CAB members within the NRA. But Johnson made that marginalization even more complete by masculinizing both producers and the recovery effort. As he saw it, the purpose of the NRA codes of fair competition was to "eliminate eye-gouging and knee-groining and ear-chewing in business." "Above the belt any man can be just as rugged and just as individual as he pleases."[67] Recovery, it would seem, was no place for ladies.

The extent to which Johnson relied on gender to establish his producer-oriented version of recovery was also evident in the language he used to describe his lieutenants as he "prepar[ed] for attack on the NRA front." It was not particularly surprising that Johnson drew his lieutenants from the producer-oriented advisory boards nor that they were all men. What is striking is how determined Johnson was to show that they were *manly* men. What Johnson liked about John Lewis, the rugged United Mine Workers president, was that he was "a man from the sole of his foot to the mane on his shaggy head." There were no parlor manners about Lewis. Indeed, Johnson noted, "he may not be as gentle as a perfumed zephyr in the heat of an argument," but he got the job done. As for George Berry, leader of the pressmen's union, Johnson acknowledged that he might be "gentle and polished and suave." But he was quick to point out that "it is the velvet glove on the iron hand." Berry was no more of a pushover in an argument than was Lewis. "When he is thoroughly aroused," Johnson was pleased to note, ". . . you know that you are up against a man."[68]

As it turned out, Johnson did envision a role for women in the recovery process. Political command might be a male prerogative, but he looked to women to function as his shock troops. Thus was hatched the Blue Eagle campaign, designed to harness consumer purchasing power on behalf of industrial recovery. Only businesses that cooperated with the NRA would be permitted to display the Blue Eagle. If consumers limited their purchasing to Blue Eagle enterprises, then, Johnson reasoned, businesses would voluntarily cooperate with NRA policies.

By *consumers* Johnson meant women. While he was quick to point out that in previous wars it had been "our men" who "made," "united," and "glorified" the nation, "this time, it is the women who must carry the whole fight of President Roosevelt's war against depression, perhaps the most dangerous war of all. It is women in homes—and not soldiers in uniform—who will this time save our country from misery and discord and unhappiness." Johnson was confident that women were up to the challenge. "They will go over the top," he predicted, "to as great a victory as the Argonne. It is zero hour for housewives." Nor was Johnson relying only on the pluck of his feminized troops. He was also counting on their domestic instincts. "A woman in support of her home," he warned male producers, "is about as safe for triflers as a Royal Bengal Tigress at the door of a dam full of cubs."[69]

Johnson did have one concern. Although he was sure that his troops had the instincts and the emotions necessary to achieve victory, he was far less confident about their intellectual abilities. Convinced that women were not particularly adept at abstract reasoning, he worried that his womanly warriors might fail to grasp "that the Blue Eagle on everything that she permits to come into her home is a symbol of its restoration to security." But, if he could make them understand the larger significance of their individual purchases, then there would be no holding them back, and "may God have mercy on the man or group of men who attempt to trifle with this bird."[70]

The consummate trickle-down economist, Johnson placed business at the center of his political economy and never had any intention of allowing consumers, whether male or female, to influence NRA policy. But defining consumers as female made it much easier for Johnson to marginalize them and with them the Consumers' Advisory Board. His feminized consumer was a consumer-shopper not a consumer-citizen, her job to support business through her purchases. There was no question of her helping to direct public policy. Nor was there any question of the economy revolving around her needs.

Consumerist thinkers were as quick as Johnson to employ gender connotations to strengthen their arguments. And, precisely because they understood that any overtones of femininity would undercut the political potential of their consumer, most sought to establish that identity as male. Few, however, did so with the zeal of F. J. Schlink. By the early 1930s Schlink had come to view the consumer through the lens of radical politics. As he saw it, the conflict between consumers and producers was "as real and inescapable as the class struggle—however thick you slice it." It was pointless, he insisted, for the consumer to look to government for help because "service to the general population is not and has not been the function of government in America, or any other plutocratic country of the world." Instead, consumers had to take matters into their own hands. In a mass production economy "utterly dependent for its functioning on continuous large volume consumption . . . the consumer, if and when he is conscious of his power, has one invincible weapon at his command. He can refuse to buy beyond his bare necessities." Doing so, Schlink predicted, would topple the business system. "The consumer" he warned, "had better be served."[71]

Not surprisingly, Schlink's barricade-storming consumer bore little resemblance to Johnson's domestic tigress. For Schlink "nice respectable middle-class enterprisers' wives" should not be considered a part of the "class-category of consumers." "You don't develop a consumer interest among people whose woman's club, or Sunday school, or study circle or some other interest is dominant." On the contrary, he continued, "the real consumer is sometimes hardly distinguishable from a truck driver."[72] Like Johnson's "knee-groining" producer, Schlink's truck-driving consumer was an individual who was not only male but also manly.

Precisely because he was so sensitive to the political implications of gender, Schlink found Johnson's definition of the consumer alarming. This definition guaranteed that the CAB as a "formal protection to consumers' interests is at best a defense so weak as hardly to warrant serious consideration at this time." Rather than consisting of virile, hard-hitting males, the board was made up partly of "college professors of economics with . . . no guts and no capacity to see that the NRA was an economic conflict of the powerful against the weak, and not a Sunday School or a Chautauqua." The rest of the members, he insisted, were even worse, "a sort of highly respectable and dull person of the social worker type," who lacked both the class affiliation and the technical expertise necessary to represent the consumer. Mary Rumsey, Johnson's choice to head the CAB, was, in Schlink's view, typical of this group. She not only belonged to the wrong class to represent the consumer—"an astonishing sort of Lady Bountiful (the railroad Harrimans, you know) right out of Shaw and the 1890s"—but also lacked the necessary technical expertise. Schlink was, therefore, dismayed that "to her unskilled and economically unschooled mind, unaware by either training or experience of either the consumption or income problems of consumers, were turned over the destinies of 120,000,000 consumers in these United States in that year of Chaos, 1933." Schlink and Johnson agreed that within the rugged environment of the NRA a board consisting of effeminate professors and society matrons would be incapable of "forcefully or militantly pressing the rights of consumers as against those of big and little business."[73] They merely parted company over whether that was a good thing.

Like Schlink, Lynd wanted to see the consumer play a far more dominant role in the political arena. Therefore, it was not surprising that his consumer was not only male—the "forgotten man," Lynd dubbed him—but manly. According to Lynd, this forgotten man was an individual who "stands there alone—a man barehanded, against the accumulated momentum of 43,000,000 horse power and their army of salesmen, advertising men and other jockeys," a veritable David against the Goliath of corporate America.[74]

Lynd's David-like consumer personified his understanding of conflict as effectively as Schlink's truck driver reflected his. To Schlink the task was to develop the consumer consciousness of potentially powerful consumers. Lynd, by contrast, envisioned a struggle between powerful capitalists and weak consumers. The task, as he saw it, was to empower both consumers and their representatives. Indeed, when Schlink criticized the CAB, suggesting that "the existence of an agency that does not function and is not allowed to function may be worse for the consumer than its complete abolition," Lynd disagreed. Conceding to Schlink that the CAB might not be doing as much as it should, he nevertheless was adamant that "it's important to keep a consumer body going within the government until we can strengthen it." Lynd was willing to wait until his David acquired the wherewithal to slay Goliath.[75]

Unlike Lynd and Schlink, Chase had no interest in establishing the consumer as a political player. Having little patience with what he dismissed as "democratic nonsense," Chase wanted to see the economy directed on behalf of the consuming population by a National Planning Board staffed by experts. He, therefore, insisted that "the consumer is not a man but a woman." A female consumer, he realized, would be in a far better position than a male consumer to lay claim to such traditionally female prerogatives as being provided for and being protected.

Chase's female consumer had several faults. She had not been the most discriminating shopper, having "time and again paid scandalously high prices for sleazy goods and services." She had allowed herself to be "shamelessly exploited" by "shrewd advertisers" who promised "her beauty by the jar, health by the bottle, sex appeal by the vial, superiority to her neighbors by the yard, well-being for her children by the pound." But her biggest failing had been her inability to keep the economy operating. As Chase explained it, all the productive energies of the economy went "into a gigantic hopper with a little valve in the bottom. The consumer has her finger on the valve. If she pulls it open the hopper discharges, to fill again. If she failed to pull it, or pulls it only half way, the hopper chokes." According to Chase, the little lady was more than willing to pull it open but had proved incapable of doing so. "The hopper choked and will remain choked until she is able to buy again."[76]

Chase replaced Lynd's forgotten man and Schlink's truck driver with a consumer who was gullible, naive, and mechanically inept. This was not a consumer who was able to take care of herself. But then Chase did not expect her to. Instead, he wanted to see her "provided for." That meant giving her the necessary funds so that she could consume at the requisite levels. And it meant protecting her.[77] As for the political implications of a female consumer, Chase considered them irrelevant. Convinced that the political arena should be reserved for experts, he never found it necessary to establish the political credentials of the consumer by masculinizing *her*. Indeed, defining the consumer as female only reinforced his version of a political order in which consumers did not represent themselves but relied on others to represent their interests.

While consumerist critics of capitalism such as Chase and Lynd appreciated the power of gender connotations, they were reluctant to rely on the connotations associated with class. At one level this reluctance was surprising. Their consumer was a member of the middle class. The connotations associated with this class were not particularly useful for discrediting the capitalist system. But the same could not be said for those surrounding *working class*. Evoking images of brutal capitalists in conflict with the exploited masses, these connotations had long been useful to critics of capitalism. Why, then, did consumerist left liberals not take advantage of them and abandon their middle-class consumer in favor of one who belonged to the working class?

It was certainly not because it was impossible to construct a working-class version of the consumer. Workers on both sides of the Atlantic had been doing so for years. Indeed, if membership in consumer cooperatives was any indication, European workers were even more comfortable with their identity as consumers than producers. When World War I began, more of them belonged to a consumer cooperative than to either a labor union or a political party, prompting two historians of consumer cooperation to suggest that "by 1914 consumer cooperation was the largest and strongest working-class movement in Europe." Even in the United States, where workers did not launch a broad-based cooperative movement, they were nevertheless more than willing to organize around their consumer identity, agitating for "a living wage" and using "purchasing power" as a weapon in their struggles against capitalists. And, in the 1930s, the increasing awareness among workers that they shared a common identity as consumers played a critical role in revitalizing the labor movement.[78]

Nor were labor activists the only Americans to suggest that workers were consumers as well as producers. The middle-class intellectuals who wanted to see the United States follow a social democratic rather than a Marxist road to a new order expressed similar views. Convinced that workers were as exploited in the marketplace as in the workplace, they insisted that any attempt to construct an equitable system would have to address the consuming as well as the producing interests of the working class.

In the 1930s American social democrats found their most prominent spokesman in John Dewey. Dewey, however, was only a recent convert to socialism. Indeed, as late as 1931, he explicitly rejected socialism. And he did so, in large part, because he placed his hopes in the middle rather than the working class. The good society that he envisioned was one that would establish a middle-class standard of living for all, "extend[ing] the advantages of this standard, in both its cultural and economic aspects, to those who do not enjoy it" while simultaneously leveling down the "idle, luxurious and predatory group." Dewey granted that it would be necessary "to adopt many measures which are now labeled socialistic." And he was confident that "such measures in the concrete . . . will win support from American people." Nevertheless, he cautioned American proponents of a new order not to look to European socialism for a model. "In spite of the disparaging tone in which 'bourgeois' is spoken," he emphasized, "this is a bourgeois country." Any attempt to organize a new party would have to be "couched in the language which the American people understand." Into the early 1930s he remained convinced that this language was middle-class.[79]

Even more to the point, he remained convinced that this language was consumerist. As late as 1931, Dewey identified "the clash between property interests and human interests" as the fundamental conflict in society. By property interests he meant those "of production, of industry, transportation and finance." Human interests he defined as those concerned with "consumption and the standard of living." Tracing the cause of "much of our present distress" to the "neglect of the consumer and his standard of living at the expense of fostering production," Dewey concluded that the only way to resolve the conflict between the human and the property interests was to "regulate production in the interest of consumption."[80]

Dewey was quick to insist that any program designed to regulate production in the interest of consumption would benefit members of not only the middle but also the working class. It would do so, in part, because wage workers were also consumers. But, even more significant, it would do so by moving workers into the middle class. In the consumerist lexicon *class* was associated with the standard of living rather than the means of production.[81] Therefore, any worker who enjoyed a middle-class standard of living was, by definition, a member of the middle class. Socialists might have proposed to eliminate class by bringing all members of society into the working class. As late as 1931, Dewey implied that it was possible to do so by making everyone a member of the middle class.[82]

After 1931 Dewey began moving rapidly in a socialist direction.[83] And, as he did so, he found it necessary to rethink many of his consumerist ideas. That Dewey abandoned much of his consumerist perspective in the very years in which he was embracing democratic socialism was not particularly surprising. Socialism was a producerist system of thought, one that defined such basic concepts as "class," "conflict," and "exploitation" in terms of the producer and production. In the socialist lexicon *class* was determined by the relationship of the individual to the means of production, *conflict* referred to the struggle between the working and the capitalist class, and *exploitation* meant the expropriation of the fruits of another's labor. Even the exploitation of the consumer was, for socialists, exploitation of the producer. In their view high prices were merely an attempt by capitalists to recoup in the marketplace wages they had had to pay in the workplace.

The extent to which socialism pushed Dewey in a producerist direction was evident in his new thinking about class. Whereas once he had relied on a consumerist definition of that term, equating class with standard of living, he now adopted a producerist definition, namely one that associated class with the means of production. Whereas once he had looked to a time when workers would move into the consuming "middle classes," he now emphasized the producer interests of the middle class as salary workers. And, finally, whereas once he had assumed that the consumer was primarily a middle-class identity, he now concluded that "Peter consumer" was merely the alter ego of "Paul producer."[84]

Not surprisingly, once Dewey replaced his consumerist definition of *class* with a producerist one, he found it necessary to rethink his ideas about conflict. By 1933 he no longer assumed that the fundamental struggle in society divided the producing, property interests and the consuming, human ones. Instead, he adopted a producerist understanding, one that located the divide in society between "property and producers." Similarly, when it came to figuring out the causes of the "present so-called 'depression,'" he no longer blamed the producer-oriented approach to the economy. Instead, in good socialist fashion he attributed the crisis to the "exploitation through the profit system."[85]

Dewey's intellectual journey went a long way toward suggesting why consumerist critics of capitalism refused to replace their middle-class version of the consumer with a working-class version. Dewey had done so because his primary concern was with what he saw as the inequity of the existing economic system. A working-class version of the consumer might have compromised his consumerist analysis of the economy, but it gave him yet another example of capitalist perfidy, namely, exploitation of workers in the marketplace. To Dewey it was a worthwhile trade-off. Consumerist left liberals, by contrast, were primarily concerned with the inefficiency of the system. Replacing their middle-class consumer with a working-class version would do little to highlight this flaw. And, even worse, it would undercut their argument that the real conflict in society was the one that divided those who were primarily interested in consumption and those who focused on production, since working-class consumers were obviously interested in both. Not surprisingly, consumerist left liberals were unwilling to risk their consumerist worldview merely to gain access to connotations that were of dubious value for their purposes.

Perhaps no one more effectively highlighted the tensions between a socialist and a consumerist worldview than F. J. Schlink. Like Dewey, Schlink was more concerned with issues of exploitation than with those of inefficiency. And, like Dewey, his concern with exploitation pushed him toward socialism. But, because Schlink was first and foremost a consumerist thinker, he was unwilling to shift his focus from the consumer to the producer. Instead, he was determined to do what neither the consumerist left liberals nor Dewey had even attempted, namely, reconcile a consumerist and a socialist worldview.

At some level Schlink realized that the tension between the two worldviews had its roots in the producerist definitions of socialist categories such as *class, exploitation,* and *conflict.* If he hoped to reconcile these worldviews, he would need definitions that were rooted in the consumer and consumption. Such definitions were available. Indeed, Schlink's political mentor, the radical eccentric J. B. Matthews, had developed them.

Matthews constructed his consumerist version of class conflict by shifting the focus from the means to the products of production. The real division in society, he decided, was between "those whose relationship to goods is primarily a function of use" and "those whose relationship to goods is primarily a function of exploitation." By *exploitation* Matthews did not mean the capitalist expropriation of labor. His victims were consumer-workers. And they were exploited when business "lower[ed] their living standards, both in terms of quantity and quality." As for those who suggested that shifting the focus to a universal activity such as consumption could reduce conflict, Matthews was adamant that "the principle of the 'primacy of consumption' makes the struggle of classes" not less but "more evident."[86]

Matthews was ultimately unable to resolve the tensions between a consumerist and a socialist worldview. Indeed, his consumer-worker turned out to be a highly unstable combination. When employees at Consumers' Research (CR) went out on strike in 1935, both he and Schlink quickly decided that workers were not consumers after all. On the contrary, they were producers and, as such, had interests that were antithetical to those of consumers. The two rejected socialism in favor of capitalism and the working class in favor of the middle class, insisting that there was "more chance of bringing about decent conditions for consumers—viz., the population—by leadership of some residually honest middle-class groups than by any plan that is likely to be laid down in Moscow and forwarded here by Browder, Hathaway, Broun, or Thomas."[87]

Once Schlink decided that capitalism rather than socialism was the economic system with the greater consumerist potential, he found it necessary to rethink the mission of the product testing agency. In the early 1930s, when he had been moving in a socialist direction, he had assumed that government was the only institution with the power necessary to force capitalists into line.

The role he envisioned for CR was to politicize consumers, who would then demand that government use its power on their behalf. But, once Schlink rejected socialism, he concluded that no government would ever function in a consumer-oriented way. Instead, it was up to consumers to discipline capitalists, rewarding businesses that provided high-quality, low-cost goods and punishing those that did not. As for CR, Schlink still believed that its job was to empower consumers. But it would do so economically rather than politically. By providing consumers with the information they needed to make informed purchases, CR could play a critical role in preserving the consumer orientation of capitalism which Adam Smith had identified almost two centuries earlier. Schlink's twenty-year political odyssey had landed him at free market conservatism. And there he would remain. The author of *Your Money's Worth* had found his home.[88]

Although Schlink, Johnson, Dewey, Chase, and Lynd traveled different political paths, they nevertheless shared certain basic assumptions. All were convinced that the political economic arena was a site of conflict. And all treated the consumer as the primary identity of some members of society rather than an interest that everyone shared. It was because of these assumptions that they all sought to establish the gender or class of the consumer. Doing so gave them a way to emphasize the differences between those whom they championed and those whom they hoped to see defeated.

While the consumerist thinkers who devoted most of their attention to industrial recovery were quick to harness the connotations associated with gender or class, those whose primary affiliation was with the AAA ignored both categories. And they did so precisely because they were affiliated with the AAA. On the staff of a department dedicated to promoting the well-being of agricultural producers, they knew that any conflict between consumers and producers would be resolved in the producer's favor. Therefore, unlike the consumerist thinkers who focused primarily on industrial recovery, those involved in agricultural recovery had a real stake in finding whatever common ground consumers and producers shared. The key to establishing this common ground, they decided, was "not to organize *individuals as consumers* but to organize the *consumer interest.*"

For AAA left liberals what made the consumer interest such a powerful vehicle for ushering in a consumer-oriented system was that it was a universal interest. As Gardiner Means explained, this interest was, of course, evident in consumer organizations such as consumer cooperatives. But it also existed in groups that did not focus specifically on either the consumer or the producer, such as "teachers' societies, organizations of Government employees, churches, women's organizations, [and] engineering societies." And, perhaps most significant, it could be found in "organizations which primarily approach economic problems from the producer point of view." Members of both farm and labor organizations, Means insisted, had interests "on specific issues" which were "frequently as strong on the side of the consumer as on the side of the producer." It was precisely these common interests shared by all members of society, Means concluded, rather than the "conflict between the interests of either farmers or workers as producers and their interest as consumers," which were the key to a healthy and balanced economy in which all members of society would prosper.[89]

While the organizational structure of the AAA encouraged efforts to build consensus, that of the NRA promoted conflict. Within the industrial recovery agency consumer, worker, and business were considered distinct identities rather than a universal interest that all members of society shared. These identities—or interest groups, as they were often called—were each represented by a board whose job it was to secure as much as possible for its own constituency, often at the expense of the constituencies of other boards. This interest group approach went a long way toward making NRA public policy making a highly contentious process.

It was soon clear that the interest group approach placed representatives of the consumer at a distinct disadvantage. Because the boards were merely advisory and had no legislative power, all three depended upon an organized backing to give their suggestions weight. The LAB could mobilize organized labor; the IAB could count on the chambers of commerce and other business organizations. The CAB, however, could rely on only a limited organized backing. It could appeal to consumer organizations such as CR or the consumer cooperatives. But these organizations represented only a small fraction of the nation's consumers. The vast majority of consumers had no institutional affiliation. This meant, as Tugwell later complained, that in the recovery effort "the consumer organizations have been spear heads without shafts."[90]

If the CAB's problem was that it lacked a broad, organized backing, then the solution was obvious. All it had to do was to create such a backing. This proved far from easy. In the fall of 1933 the CAB announced that it would establish 3,000 consumers' councils across the country. To direct the project, it appointed Paul Douglas. Initially, the CAB envisioned an ambitious role for the councils. But that vision was seriously curtailed when Johnson approved only two of the more limited functions. The councils, he decided, would serve as clearinghouses for complaints and sources of information on NRA policy but nothing more. As it turned out, the consumers' councils never were able to provide the CAB with the backing it wanted. Indeed, when Douglas resigned in April 1934, only 150 were in existence.[91]

Theoretically, at least, the CAB had an additional option. If it could not count on organized consumer support, perhaps it could rely on a more informal backing. Representing as it did the entire consuming public, the CAB could conceivably harness mass support on behalf of the consumer interest. All it had to do was appeal directly to the public. This, too, proved far from easy. Concerned about the constitutionality of the NIRA, Johnson was determined to maintain as low a profile for the recovery agency as possible. He, therefore, enforced a rigorous press censorship within the organization and refused to approve any press releases that he deemed controversial.

Despite Johnson's censorship, the CAB managed on occasion to bring the anticonsumer bias at the NRA to national attention. It got some press coverage, for example, when its executive director, William Ogburn, resigned in protest of Johnson's press censorship. The *New Republic* haled Ogburn's resignation a "patriotic act" and praised him for using the only "weapon" available to him. And Schlink suggested that the best service the CAB could render for consumers was for all the members to resign because, in so doing, they would "at least focus light on the conflict."[92]

The members of the CAB did not follow Schlink's suggestion. But, shortly after Ogburn's resignation, Schlink himself managed to get a little light focused on the conflict. In January 1934 CBS canceled its broadcast of Schlink's speech on national recovery because, according to the head of the New York CBS office, it was "slanderous," "suspicious," and "a direct attack on the N.R.A." The cancellation led to precisely the press coverage that Johnson so wanted to avoid. "Is Free Speech a Joke to the Radio Trust?" "'News' or Propaganda?" "Is This Freedom of Speech?" queried headlines in several of the nation's newspapers. Worried that the radio broadcaster's decision might be traced back to the NRA, Johnson quickly issued a statement to the press. "I did not know of Dr. Schlink's address," he told reporters, "and I did not know it had been banned. We never have made any attempt to interfere with any criticism." "The Roosevelt Administration and myself," he added, "always have invited and always will invite constructive criticism." CBS broke under the pressure and asked Schlink to give the address at a later date.[93]

Ironically, it was not the CAB, Schlink, or Douglas but, rather, Johnson who proved most successful at creating an organized consumer pressure group. Because of his concerns about a constitutional test of the NIRA, Johnson looked to consumers to be the enforcement arm of the recovery administration. He created the Blue Eagle so that consumers would keep industry in line, thereby making it unnecessary for government to do so. Consumers quickly rallied behind Johnson, signing pledges by the hundreds of thousands. And in September 1933 almost two million Americans attended the Blue Eagle parade in New York City. The potential power of Johnson's pressure group was not lost on business. In an attempt to reassure consumers that "we do our part," over two million employers displayed an NRA sticker in their storefront window.[94]

The various attempts to mobilize the consumer may not have resulted in a stronger CAB. But they did play a role in bringing the consumer to public attention. The consumers' councils, William Ogburn's resignation, the cancellation of Schlink's speech by CBS, the Blue Eagle Campaign, all forced not only New Deal officials but the American public to think about the place of the consumer within the recovery program in particular and the political economy in general. Throughout the Roosevelt Administration individuals who had never paid much attention to consumer issues suddenly found it necessary to defend their policies in terms of the consumer interest. They may not have embraced an exclusively consumerist worldview. But most of them became increasingly aware of the vulnerability of the consuming population. And most were willing to recognize certain rights associated with the consumer identity.

The NRA not only brought the consumer into the spotlight. It also had a profound impact on consumerist ideas. For one, it called into question the consumerist potential of an interest group approach to politics. At first glance such an approach seemed one that would give consumers all the advantage. After all, everyone was a consumer. Therefore, those representing the consumer should have been able to dominate the public policy–making process.

The inability of the CAB to mobilize consumers, however, suggested that Americans were far more willing to organize around their producer than their consumer identity. By the time the NRA experiment ended, most consumerist thinkers had concluded that an interest group approach to politics was much more likely to result in policies that were producer rather than consumer oriented.

The NRA experience also discredited planning. Neither Johnson's business-oriented approach to the consumer—which treated the consumer as little more than a source of profits—nor the anticapitalist, antidemocratic approach, which Chase, Lynd, and Soule advocated, emerged victorious. Ironically, however, it was the defeat of both versions which proved significant in the evolution of a consumer-oriented approach to the political economy. By the time the Supreme Court declared the NIRA unconstitutional, planning had lost much of its appeal. Veblenian left liberals such as Chase, Lynd, and Soule may have continued to advocate a planned economy until the end of the decade. But by the mid-1930s most New Dealers had begun casting about for alternative ways to regulate the economy.[95]

Finally, the NRA experiment gave consumerist left liberals a new appreciation of democracy. Having seen how easily powerful business interests had hijacked the planning process, Chase, Lynd, and Soule all began to rethink their earlier reservations concerning democracy and to emphasize the democratic potential of a consumer-oriented system. In 1936 Lynd identified consumers as "democracy's third estate." Three years later Soule—who in 1932 had insisted that "consumer democracy does not work any better than political democracy"—was arguing that economic planning would enable democracy to outlast its enemies. And even Chase, always the least democratic of the three, no longer dismissed democracy as just so much "nonsense." The NRA experiment was certainly not the only force in the 1930s pushing Chase, Soule, Lynd, and, indeed, most American intellectuals in a more democratic direction. The rise of totalitarian regimes in Europe played a critical role in this process. But to consumerist left liberals the NRA and totalitarianism were not unrelated. Indeed, Soule suggested that the NRA had been America's experiment with the "economics of fascism."[96]

When the smoke had cleared from the NRA battlefield, the ground was littered with casualties. Economic planning had been discredited. So, too, had the idea that an interest group approach could result in a consumer-oriented system. So, too, had the belief that organized consumers could play a pivotal role in transforming the economy. Even the very notion of a consumer-oriented system had been called into question if, by such a system, one meant the antithesis of a producer-oriented economy.

There was, however, one definition of a consumer-oriented system which did survive the NRA recovery effort largely unscathed. This was the version that treated *consumption oriented* and *consumer oriented* as synonyms. Rooted in consensus rather than conflict, it was a version that envisioned consumers and producers not as opposing combatants but as allies with a mutual interest in abundant consumption. "Enough buyers to take away the current output of finished goods is a project upon which everybody can unite with enthusiasm," Foster had declared in the 1920s, "for it looks not only to the welfare of the people generally, but to the welfare of each and every class."[97] This consumption-oriented economy would only become more compelling as the AAA approach to recovery unfolded. And, eventually, it would provide the foundation for what would come to be called "New Deal liberalism."

CHAPTER SEVEN

The Common Ground of Abundance, 1933–1940

In June 1933 Secretary of Agriculture Henry Wallace sent a memorandum to the head of the Agricultural Adjustment Administration (AAA), George Peek. "You have already provided . . . for adequate representation of the producer and the distributor and processor," he told Peek. "If we are to justify our decisions before Congress and other political groups, however, the record must show that we have given equal consideration to the consumers' interests."[1]

Wallace's emphasis on "consumers' interests" was neither particularly consumerist nor particularly surprising. Instead, it was an attempt to forestall the criticism that he knew would inevitably be directed at one of the most producer-oriented programs of the New Deal. The AAA intended to bring about agricultural recovery by paying farmers to limit production. The funds for these payments would come from a processing tax, which would ultimately be passed on to consumers. As Walter Lippmann explained it, "if the plan worked, the consumer would find himself paying the farmer to raise the price by limiting the supply."[2] The task confronting the AAA was to convince consumers that it was in their best interest to foot the bill.

One way to do so was to assure consumers that the AAA would give serious attention to the consumer's stake in agricultural recovery. To that end the AAA established the Office of the Consumers' Counsel. From the outset this office enjoyed a legitimacy that had all but eluded its counterpart within the

National Recovery Administration (NRA). Consumers' Counsel recommendations might be rejected in favor of more producer-oriented policies, but, unlike the Consumers' Advisory Board, those in the Office of the Consumers' Counsel could always count on their proposals receiving a serious hearing.

The differences in the AAA's treatment of the Office of the Consumers' Counsel and the NRA's treatment of the Consumers' Advisory Board stemmed in part from the fundamentally different notions of "consumer" to which each of the recovery administrations subscribed. Within Hugh Johnson's NRA the consumer interest was equated with a social reform movement. It evoked connotations of public-minded citizens demanding fair play in the marketplace. It was seen as voluntaristic, idealistic, and ultimately feminine. The choice of socialite and Junior League founder Mary Rumsey as its chair, the volunteer status of those who served on the board, even the broad range of academic fields and social reform organizations from which members were drawn reflected and reinforced the sense of dilettantism associated with the consumer interest within the NRA.

By contrast, within the AAA the connotations that came to be associated with the consumer in the agricultural recovery effort were more scientific, professional, and male. Thus, the individual chosen as Consumers' Counsel was not a society matron but, instead, an individual with a distinguished record in progressive politics, Frederic Howe. And the office itself was staffed with paid government officials, economists almost to a man. And, indeed, they were men. Hugh Johnson might attempt to marginalize the CAB by feminizing it; the Office of the Consumers' Counsel was never considered the ladies' auxiliary of the AAA.

AAA regard for the consumer interest was not limited to the creation of a "unit specially charged with examining each proposed action from the consumer's point of view." Throughout the Department of Agriculture individuals with consumerist leanings held influential positions. Rexford Tugwell served as assistant secretary and later undersecretary of agriculture and was a constant confidant of Henry Wallace. Gardiner Means was appointed economic advisor to the secretary. And, although Department of Agriculture economist Mordecai Ezekiel—who also served as an economic advisor to Wallace—did not place consumers at the center of his worldview, he did advocate economic planning as the best method of achieving abundance.[3] Johnson might have little patience with the "Apostles of Plenty"; Wallace surrounded himself with them.

Why was Wallace so much more willing than Johnson to incorporate the consumer point of view into the recovery effort? The ideological differences between the two men were certainly a factor, but, at least initially, their economic ideas were not that different. During the early days of the New Deal, Wallace was no more of a consumerist than Johnson. Only later did he begin to incorporate into his worldview the very ideas he had initially espoused for tactical reasons.

Ironically, the Agricultural Adjustment Administration granted the consumer a legitimacy that the National Recovery Administration never did because the AAA program was more exclusively producer oriented than the NRA program. Both agencies sought to effect recovery by furthering the interests of producers, but in the public's view there was a fundamental difference between the two. To most Americans the NRA looked out for the interests of workers and consumers by forcing businesses "to do their part," while the AAA plowed under cotton and slaughtered pigs at a time when much of the population lacked adequate food and clothing. Because of such popular perceptions, AAA officials were under far more pressure to justify policy decisions in terms of the consumer than were those on the NRA staff.

The producer orientation of the agricultural recovery effort also had an impact on the drafting of the legislation that created the AAA. Because the AAA was designed to raise prices, Congress believed it was necessary to include certain safeguards for the consumer within the Agricultural Adjustment Act. These included a limit for price increases as well as authorization to the secretary of agriculture to make public any information he deemed necessary whenever a processing tax was applied. The publication of such information, it was hoped, would not only deter processors and distributors from raising prices unfairly but would also give consumers the knowledge necessary to resist unfair price hikes.[4] Thus, for legal as well as public relations reasons, the AAA was forced to address the consumer interest in a way that the NRA never was.

Finally, the organizational structure of the New Deal recovery effort inadvertently strengthened the consumerist perspective within the AAA while weakening it within the NRA. Because the NRA was an independent administration, Johnson reported directly to the president. Although the first administrator of the AAA, George Peek, insisted that he have the same access to the president as his counterpart in the NRA, he never enjoyed the same free hand in determining policy. The AAA was organized not as an independent administration but, rather, as part of the Department of Agriculture. This meant that Wallace as secretary of agriculture and, more significantly, Tugwell as second in charge were both in a position to exert considerable influence over the AAA. Thus, when Johnson adopted policies that sacrificed consumers on behalf of producers' interests, he encountered at most an objection from the Consumers' Advisory Board; Peek's attempt to follow a similar course within the AAA resulted in his removal as administrator.

Ultimately, the NRA—Johnson's intentions to the contrary—did help to establish the consumer interest as distinct from the public interest. But the AAA played a far more significant role in influencing the direction of New Deal liberalism. Because the AAA's primary goal was the well-being of producer-farmers, the left liberals who served within that agency found it necessary to emphasize the ways in which consumer and producer interests coincided. By the mid-1930s their efforts had resulted in a widespread belief among most AAA officials that the recovery effort could and should further the interests of both consumers and producers. And they agreed that the best way to do so was to develop policies that would foster a "balanced abundance."[5]

By the end of World War II, New Deal liberals finally reached a consensus concerning the proper role of government in the economy. As they saw it, government should further the interests of all members of society by creating an economy of balanced abundance. The best way to create such an economy, they agreed, was through Keynesian countercyclical spending.[6] The liberal reliance on Keynesianism was recent, a response to the impact of World War II on the economy. The liberal commitment to balanced abundance was far older, in certain respects going back as far as Adam Smith. But the specific version that New Deal liberals embraced took shape in the 1930s. And it originated within the halls of the AAA.

The roots of the agricultural problem went back to World War I. At that time American farmers had expanded production to meet the increased demand for agricultural products brought on by the war. With the end of hostilities, however, European acreage was brought back into cultivation. The expanded American production, the resumption of European production, and the generally high level of production worldwide which existed during the

1920s flooded the market with agricultural goods, which in turn pushed down prices. American farmers, however, did not respond by limiting production. In fact, many responded to the price decline by increasing production.[7]

Farmers did not respond to declining prices in the same way as industrialists because fundamentally different conditions prevailed in the industrial sectors of the economy than in agriculture. Many sectors of the industrial economy were controlled by one or two corporations. Corporate leaders were therefore frequently in a position to respond to falling prices by cutting production. The agricultural sector of the economy, on the other hand, consisted of roughly six million individual producers. Simultaneously limiting their production seemed all but impossible. The only way an individual farmer could hope to maintain a constant level of income when prices began to fall was to sell more.

The economic difficulties that beset farmers during the 1920s seemed doubly unfair because they occurred at a time when the rest of the nation seemed to be enjoying unprecedented prosperity. With farm incomes declining at the very time that urban incomes were on the rise, a number of farm leaders began to advocate measures to reestablish parity, namely the price relationship that had existed between farm commodities and industrial goods in the period from 1910 to 1914.

But how to achieve parity? Farmers had a number of ideas. But few were as popular as the "two-price system" outlined by Peek and Johnson in a pamphlet entitled *Equality for Agriculture*. Under this system farmers would sell all they could at an "American" price, which would be based on parity. The government would then pay farmers the American price for whatever surplus farmers had not been able to sell and would dump the surplus overseas at the prevailing foreign price. A high tariff would keep foreign competitors out of what would become an attractive American market. By dumping the surplus, the government would give farmers the economic control they needed to employ the sorts of price-fixing strategies upon which many of the corporations relied.[8]

Introduced into Congress by Senator Charles L. McNary and Congressman Gilbert N. Haugen, the Peek-Johnson proposal—or McNary-Haugenism, as it came to be called—was repeatedly defeated and never managed to become law. With good reason. The approach had two major flaws. First, it would not curtail overproduction. Indeed, it would encourage it. Because the American price was ultimately guaranteed by the federal government, farmers who produced more would make more. Second, it would have had a negative impact on U.S. foreign relations.

Late in the 1920s, farm economists offered an alternative solution to the "farm problem"—one that would make it in the farmers' interest to limit production. Under the domestic allotment plan the government would pay farmers to take acreage out of production. Ezekiel, Tugwell, and Wallace were early proponents of the domestic allotment approach to the farm problem. By the 1932 Democratic convention, Roosevelt, who, like Wallace, had initially favored McNary-Haugenism, had also become a convert.[9]

Despite Roosevelt's support for domestic allotment, the Agricultural Adjustment Act did not endorse one approach at the expense of the other. Instead, it provided legislative authority for both the two-price system and domestic allotment.[10] It established parity price levels as the goal. But it also stipulated that corrections would be made "in view of the current consumption demand in domestic and foreign markets." By mentioning both domestic and foreign markets, it provided authority for Tugwell's domestic allotment as well as Peek's foreign dumping.[11]

Because the implementation of agricultural recovery would depend so heavily on the administrator of the AAA, Tugwell and Wallace thought long and hard about who that person should be. Convinced that "the administration of this farm bill . . . can make or break this whole Democratic venture," Tugwell admitted that "it would be foolish to take any avoidable risk with it." At the very least, he decided, the position should go to someone who was a skilled administrator. And it would probably be a good idea to choose someone who would not alienate the business interests, because "this is a new thing and much depends upon cooperation among the processors who are affected."[12] Peek satisfied both counts.

Tugwell and Wallace agreed that there were certain drawbacks with Peek. He was "conservative in philosophy and . . . rather opposed to crop control." He was also a Baruch man. "We do not like this crowd particularly," Tugwell confessed, "and would rather have a hard-boiled progressive." But, as Wallace pointed out, "Peek's business experience, his aggressiveness, and his unvarying sympathy for farmers, among other qualities, seemed to recommend him for the job of making the new machinery work." Tugwell agreed, reassuring himself that, in appointing Peek, "we shall advance in our chosen direction more slowly, no doubt, but perhaps more surely."[13] Tugwell was wrong.

Peek did not approach agricultural recovery from the same perspective as

Tugwell. The undersecretary and, indeed, most left liberals involved in agricultural recovery saw the Agricultural Adjustment Act as an endorsement of the allotment plan. Peek, however, insisted that it provided "the needed machinery to run the two-price system—an American price for American consumption and competitive foreign prices for export." Not domestic allotment but McNary-Haugenism, he insisted, was the approach to recovery implicit in the AAA legislation.[14]

It was not merely pride of authorship which made Peek prefer McNary-Haugenism to domestic allotment. As director of the Moline Plow Company in the 1920s, he had experienced firsthand how much the crisis in agriculture affected businesses that depended upon farmers. The experience convinced him that any recovery program would have to benefit "middlemen" as well as farmers. The two-price system promised to do just that. Because it would eliminate the surplus only after it had been harvested and processed, McNary-Haugenism would help farmers while still maintaining the high levels of production which processors and farm machinery manufacturers wanted.

What bothered Peek about the allotment plan was that it rested on what he called "planned scarcity." Domestic allotment, he maintained, sought to reduce the acreage under cultivation and, in so doing, would lower profits for farmers and middlemen. The abundance that Peek advocated, however, was a far cry from that which the AAA left liberals envisioned. McNary-Haugenism would not have made goods any more available to consumers than would the allotment plan. What it would have done, or so Peek believed, was to provide producers, be they farmers, processors, or agricultural machinery manufacturers, with abundant profits.[15]

It was no surprise that consumerist left liberals rejected McNary-Haugenism. Veblen himself could not have come up with a more perfect illustration of the price system's obsession with curtailing production. But the domestic allotment plan was no more immune to charges of "sabotage" than was the two-price system, as the pronouncements of some of its harshest critics indicated. "No wonder people are asking what sort of a crazy economic system we have," John Dewey declared, "when at a time when millions are short of adequate food, when babies are going without the milk necessary for their growth, the best remedy that experts can think of and that the Federal Government can recommend, is to pay a premium to farmers to grow less grain with which to make flour to feed the hungry and pay a premium to dairymen to send less milk to market." F. J. Schlink was equally critical. "The destruction of useful and needed goods," he concluded, "is apparently the last and most convincing evidence of the failure of capitalistic enterprise to perform the function of supplying human beings with useful goods at prices they can afford to pay."[16]

Consumerist left liberals who supported the AAA struggled long and hard with the seeming contradictions between their endorsement of domestic allotment and their commitment to a consumer-oriented system. On the one hand, they were as convinced as Dewey and Schlink that crop destruction and crop limitation were dubious remedies for an economic crisis that was already denying many Americans the most basic of necessities. To Robert Lynd, crop limitation was a perfect example of the "effort of production to force consumption to production's own private ends." To Chase, crop destruction was Veblenian sabotage at its best, an "attempt to maintain price levels by waste." "Plow under your wheat and cotton, slaughter your brood sows, that the curse of abundance may no longer fall upon you." Even Tugwell, one of the architects of the legislation and a proponent of domestic allotment, admitted that crop destruction in the midst of a depression highlighted the "paradox of want in the midst of plenty, and it goes to the very heart of our economic system."[17]

Despite such concerns, consumerist left liberals ultimately concluded that the AAA was the New Deal agency with the greatest consumerist potential. They reached this conclusion, in part, because of the political sympathies of those who served within the agency. While consumerist left liberals agreed that there were "of course, lapses in the A.A.A.'s behavior," they insisted that these lapses "were by no means so serious as in the N.R.A." That was because those on the AAA staff "such as Peek who have the same attitude in this matter as Johnson . . . are usually checkmated by the more progressive members of the staff when the matter goes up to Wallace." Wallace's progressivism as well as that of other AAA officials, the fact that "recommendations of the consumers' group will get real attention," and the extent to which these recommendations "are reinforced by the economists and the lawyers," convinced consumerist left liberals that the New Deal agency most committed to increasing profits by reducing supply was also the one most likely to usher in a consumer-oriented system.[18]

It was not only the political sympathies of much of the staff which prompted consumerist left liberals to hold up the AAA as the most consumerist of the New Deal agencies. They also supported the AAA because they believed its policies were the best example of economic planning within the New Deal. Lynd praised the agency for "taking literally the conception of the partnership of industrial ownership—labor and the consumer in industry—and the fiduciary role of the businessman." Chase was equally enthusiastic about the larger implications of agricultural recovery. As he saw it, the AAA had responded to the inability of agriculture to function "as a self-sustaining sector of private business" by establishing farming as "a quasi-public business." It was this "process of collectivizing the largest private business in the nation," Chase insisted, that made the AAA the most "immediately significant" of the New Deal programs.[19]

While it was the progressivism of the AAA staff and the scope of its economic planning that convinced most consumerist left liberals of the consumerist potential of agricultural recovery, Chase identified an additional feature that contributed to this potential. Like Edward Bellamy before him, Chase believed that only by separating consumption from production would it be possible to establish a "right to consume." Relief agencies were helping to sever these connections by supporting "the unemployed and their families." But the AAA was also involved in the process. By paying farmers not to produce, Chase suggested, it was helping to break down the connection between consumption and production and in so doing was taking "another step . . . to the establishment of guaranteed subsistence to every citizen from birth to death."[20]

Although consumerist left liberals were quick to identify the AAA as the New Deal agency with the most consumerist potential, few of those who served in the agency came to their jobs with a well-developed consumerist worldview. Even those on the staff of the Office of the Consumers' Counsel arrived with a far stronger commitment to political than consumer activism. Gardner (Pat) Jackson, who served as assistant to the consumers' counsel, was typical. He had no real background in consumer issues. But he had been deeply involved in the campaign to prevent the executions of Nicola Sacco and Bartolomeo Vanzetti. In the late 1930s he would devote his energies to helping the Southern Tenant Farmers Union. Even consumers' counsel Frederic Howe had more impressive credentials as a political than a consumer activist, having been involved in progressive politics since the 1910s. But he did have some experience with consumer issues, having written on the agricultural cooperative movement. Despite that experience—or, indeed, because of it—he came to his office as committed to producers as consumers, confident that the economy could be made to function on behalf of both groups and convinced that the best way to guarantee that it would do so was to "exile . . . the middlemen."[21]

Howe may have begun his tenure at the AAA as committed to producers as consumers, but it was not long before he began to develop a more exclusively consumerist outlook. Indeed, he quickly decided that he had only "a minor interest in the attempts to police prices," which were ostensibly the main responsibility of his office. But he had a "major interest . . . in any movements which look to the creation of consumer self-consciousness and consumer philosophy." The greatest contribution he could make as consumers' counsel, he concluded, was to build up "consumer thinking and consumer organization in the belief that something far more important than the saving of pennies here and pennies there will eventually come from [such efforts]." That "something more important" was what Howe called "a Consumers' Society," one in which the interests of consumers would be "a definite objective of organized society" and "wealth will be viewed as something to be consumed."[22]

Howe's attitude toward middlemen and his insistence that the consumers' interests be the ultimate objective of all public policy did little to endear him to Peek. Indeed, Peek would later point to Howe's appointment as one of his greatest errors (the other being his acceptance of Jerome Frank as general counsel). "Dr. Howe," Peek insisted, "had been seriously bitten by some kind of pink bug and had accumulated a hazy, half radical, half uplifter set of views and attitudes." Howe's determination to make sure that agricultural recovery came at the expense of the middlemen, rather than the consumer, convinced Peek that Howe "was against the profit system and was all for abolishing it—without, however, exactly knowing what he wanted to put in its place."[23]

Nor was Howe the only AAA staff member whose attitude toward middlemen, the profit system, and consumers alarmed Peek. The administrator was equally concerned about the political attitudes of the "intense young men" in the Office of the General Counsel whom he believed were "out gunning for the profit system as though it were some kind of rapacious wolf."[24] Most of the AAA lawyers were actually far more in favor of reforming the existing system than abolishing it. But the reforms that they wanted were designed to limit corporate profits and discipline business interests. Their left-liberal—and in some cases radical—convictions were precisely the sort to bring them into conflict with Peek.

Jerome Frank, who served as general counsel (and shared a house with

Tugwell), was typical of this group. Frank considered himself a "reformer." He had spent the 1920s as a corporate lawyer in Chicago—representing among others the very banks that had liquidated Peek's Moline Plow Company. But he had also been involved in progressive politics. He had been active in literary circles, counting among his acquaintances such left-leaning literary luminaries as Sherwood Anderson, Carl Sandburg, Floyd Dell, and Max Eastman. And, with the publication of *Law and the Modern Mind* (1930), Frank placed himself at the forefront of what was a radical challenge to legal orthodoxy, the legal realist movement.[25]

Frank brought to the AAA a number of "brilliant young men with keen legal minds and imagination" who shared, or so he thought, many of his political convictions. He recruited heavily from the Ivy League law schools. And he chose individuals who possessed not only considerable legal talent—Alger Hiss, for example, had clerked for Supreme Court Justice Oliver Wendell Holmes and was, according to Felix Frankfurter, "first rate in every way"—but also a passion for using that talent on behalf of reform. Frank's initial appointments included not only Hiss but also two members of the Yale Law School faculty, Abe Fortas and Thurman Arnold, as well as three attorneys, Lee Pressman, John Abt, and Nathan Witt, whose political sympathies, it turned out, were far more left leaning than Frank had realized. All three belonged to a Communist discussion group that would be at the center of the celebrated Alger Hiss trial in the 1940s. Eventually, the Office of the General Counsel had over sixty lawyers on its staff, almost all of whom possessed both the legal skills and the political convictions that Frank desired.[26]

The political sympathies of those serving within the AAA went a long way toward explaining why it became the consumerist stronghold within the New Deal. But equally significant were their urban roots and their lack of any agricultural background. (According to one story, Lee Pressman demanded to know what the macaroni code would do for macaroni growers.) These roots made the AAA left liberals far more sympathetic to the needs of urban consumers than were Peek and the farm leaders. And it also gave them a broader view of agricultural recovery. To the Peek faction agricultural recovery was an agricultural issue, its only purpose to improve profits for farmers and processors. The AAA left liberals disagreed. As they saw it, the collapse of agriculture was intimately connected to the collapse of industry. Only by bringing these two sectors back into balance would it be possible to solve the nation's economic problems. Their larger reform goals were not lost on Peek, who once declared in frustration that the Department of Agriculture was just that, the Department of Agriculture, and not the "Department of Everything."[27]

The AAA turned out to be one of the most important crucibles for what would come to be called New Deal liberalism. Charged with improving well-being of agricultural producers, the left liberals who served in the AAA were under considerable pressure to identify ways in which the interests of consumers and producers coincided. On occasion they adopted an approach similar to that of Chase and Soule, suggesting that the most significant interest wage earners and farmers had was as consumers. "Never forget," Frank told a radio audience in 1933, "that the farmer is a consumer—that largely, he is a farmer in order that he can be a consumer."[28] But far more often Frank and the other AAA left liberals made room for wage-earning and farming producers by shifting the focus from the consumer to consumption.

While the AAA left liberals were under pressure to find the common ground between producers and consumers, those involved within the NRA were pushed in a different direction. The organizational framework of the NRA highlighted, even exacerbated, the conflict among consumer, labor, and industrial interests. As each of the NRA advisory boards struggled to get code provisions that would benefit its own particular constituency, they found that, more often than not, their victories came at the expense of the other advisory boards. The battles within the NRA made it easy for consumerist thinkers to assume that a consumer-oriented system was the antithesis of a producer-oriented one.

The NRA approach to recovery also made it easy for consumerist thinkers to assume that a profit-oriented capitalist system was incapable of functioning in a consumer-oriented fashion. Johnson's determination to protect profits by reducing production seemed only to confirm what consumerist left liberals such as Chase and Soule had long suspected, that capitalism depended upon scarcity. If abundance threatened profits, then, they concluded, the solution was to get rid of not abundance but the profit system.

AAA left liberals may have shared many of Chase's and Soule's anticapitalist sentiments. But they were government officials on the staff of an agency whose goal was to improve the well-being of agricultural producers. This meant, for one, that they had to develop an analysis of the Depression which did not require the elimination of capitalism. And it meant, for another, that the only way they would be able to push policies that furthered the interests of consumers was if those policies did not come at the expense of the producing farmers.

While the primary goal of the agricultural recovery effort may have been producer well-being, the effort itself rested on certain premises that had consumerist potential. Parity was one example. When Peek originated the term, he had meant the price relationship between agricultural and industrial commodities. But in general usage—and even in the Agricultural Adjustment Act—*parity* came to refer to the relationship between urban and rural incomes as well as urban and rural purchasing power. Prices, income, and purchasing power were, of course, related. But what was significant about the shift from prices to purchasing power was that the former was rooted in production concerns—how much could agricultural goods command—while the latter was concerned with consumption.

Parity was not the only element of agricultural recovery that had a consumerist potential. So, too, did the concept of balance. Although the Agricultural Adjustment Act had sought "to establish and maintain [the] balance between the production and consumption of agricultural commodities," the term soon acquired a number of meanings. To Peek balance meant parity.[29] An economy that consistently produced too much was in balance as long as it dumped that excess overseas, thereby keeping domestic prices high.

Hugh Johnson had a different definition, one that focused on the relationship between the various sectors of the economy rather than the supply of and demand for agricultural products. "If only we could give the agricultural half of our population a fair price for its products," he maintained, "we could create—in our own backyard—one of the richest markets for industry in the whole world." And, by the same token, "if only we could see to it that the working segments of our population . . . get a fair wage for their labor, we could create in our country the best market for our farm products that we could expect if we combed the whole round earth."[30]

Tugwell and the AAA left liberals also used *balance* to refer to the relationship among the various sectors of the economy. But they parted company with Johnson over how to restore balance. The producer-minded Johnson insisted that the only way to reverse the downward spiral was to provide farmers with higher prices, workers with higher wages, and businesses with higher profits. Blaming the Depression on an "unmanageable surplus," he believed that the best way to increase the income of all producers was to eliminate that surplus, in industry as well as in agriculture. Indeed, he asked, "if the presence of it hanging over a market will destroy agriculture, why will it not destroy industry?"[31]

Johnson may have posed his question rhetorically, but left liberals were more than willing to give him an answer. Granting that an unmanageable surplus may have existed in agriculture, they were adamant that it did not exist in industry. And it did not exist, they maintained, because manufacturers had responded to the collapse of purchasing power in a different way than farmers had. Between 1929 and 1933 farmers had reduced their prices by more than 60 percent while holding their production steady. In the same years, however, most industries had cut their production, in some cases by as much as 80 percent, dropping their prices only slightly. The different responses, left liberals concluded, meant that the "restoration of balance would require a lowering of production and a lifting of prices in agriculture, but a lifting of production and in some cases even a lowering of prices in industry."[32]

The AAA left liberals not only dismissed the notion that balance could be achieved by applying the same policies to the agricultural as the industrial sector. They also pointed out that getting more money into the pockets of Americans would not necessarily increase purchasing power. If industry merely passed its higher costs on to the consumer, then, Frank argued, "purchasing power will not have been augmented." The solution, he insisted, was not merely "to pay the farmers more," as Peek and Johnson wanted to do, but to do so "without making the consumers invariably pay all the increase."[33]

What the AAA left liberals found in the concept of balance was a way to reconcile their antibusiness sentiments and their consumerist sympathies with their responsibilities to agricultural producers. Their focus on balance allowed them to place the blame for not merely the economic crisis but even the cotton plow-up and the hog slaughter on industrial capitalists. When capitalists had decided to cut production rather than prices, the left liberals argued, they had made a bad situation far worse. And when they had refused to reverse their policies, they had left AAA officials with only one option. If industry would not produce more, then farmers would have to produce less. But, as far as left liberals were concerned, this did not change the fact that at the AAA, unlike the NRA, "the attempt . . . is for balance, not for scarcity."[34]

Equally significantly, although the focus on balance called into question the actions of industrial capitalists, it did not necessarily discredit capitalism itself. To Chase and Soule the limitation of production to protect prices was merely the most egregious example of capitalism's dependence on scarcity. Only by abandoning capitalism in favor of some sort of economic planning, they argued, would it be possible to establish an economy of abundance. The AAA left liberal focus on balance, however, implied that the problem was not a fundamental flaw within capitalism but merely the aberrant behavior of capitalists. And aberrant behavior could be modified. By focusing on balance, the AAA left liberals were able to do what Chase and Soule throughout the 1930s could not. They were able to envision a capitalist system that was compatible with plenty.

The focus on balance not only allowed left liberals to criticize capitalists while remaining "inside the profit system." It also highlighted the common ground that consumers and producers shared. The only way to improve the well-being of farmers, the AAA left liberals argued, was to improve the purchasing power of consumers. Indeed, Tugwell insisted, protecting consumers was "not simply . . . a matter of justice to the general public." It was "an aid to farm relief itself." Frank echoed such sentiments. "If this depression ought to teach us anything," he declared, "it is precisely this: that no one group of people in the society can, for long, prosper, if the general run of men as consumers are in bad shape. Exploitation of the consumer means exploitation of and disaster for everybody."[35]

Finally, the focus on balance helped to shift the emphasis in left liberalism from the consumer to consumption and, in so doing, began to replace the Veblenian analysis that had dominated left liberal thought since the 1920s with an analysis far closer to that of Simon Patten. To Veblenians such as Chase and Soule the interests of consumers and profit-oriented producers were so fundamentally at odds that it was impossible to construct an economy that would function on behalf of both. Even as the Depression encouraged them to rethink their earlier conviction that a consumption-oriented system was far more producer than consumer oriented, the consumption-oriented system that they envisioned bore no relationship to that of Patten. In the Veblenian version of a consumption-oriented economy, capitalists, far from enjoying higher profits because of expanded demand, were merely managers, their job to churn out high-quality, low-cost goods for consumers.

By contrast, their focus on balance convinced many AAA left liberals that an economy could function on behalf of both consumers and producers. Such an economy might not be exclusively consumer oriented, but its emphasis on increased purchasing power would nevertheless benefit consumers even as it served producers. Consumers would have increased access to goods, and producers would see an expanded demand for them. Thus, like Patten, the AAA left liberals came to see an economy dedicated to abundance as one that could simultaneously further the interests of consumers and producers.

The left liberals within in the AAA never acknowledged their intellectual debt to Patten. Indeed, they were far more likely to sing the praises of Veblen. Thurman Arnold listed the works of Veblen—as well as those of one of Veblen's most devoted disciples, Stuart Chase—as among the most influential books of recent times. Frank framed the economic struggle in terms of those who committed "industrial sabotage" and those who were the "victims of sabotage." Even Tugwell—who, by all accounts, continued to see Patten as a "great man"—wrote the section on Veblen in *Books That Changed Our Minds*.[36]

Despite their determination to modify rather than replace capitalism, AAA left liberals quickly ran afoul of Peek. Indeed, as Peek saw it, he was locked in a struggle with "the socialists or, more strictly, the collectivists . . . headed by Felix Frankfurter, Rexford G. Tugwell, and Jerome Frank." At issue, Peek believed, was whether the AAA would be a "device to aid the farmers" or one "to introduce the collectivist system of agriculture into this country." By *collectivist system* he meant domestic allotment, which, he charged, threatened "the whole individualistic system of the country" because it took control of the land away from farmers and "put [it] at the disposal of a Washington bureaucracy." It sought to control profits when "legitimate profits" were "a proper reward for individual initiative, industry, and thrift." And it would eliminate competition by "subsidizing . . . farmers for not producing," even though competition had played a critical role in raising "our country and its people . . . to a high level of wealth and prosperity." Without competition, he warned, "the fit and . . . the unfit. . . . regardless of ability, would be on the same level of mediocrity." For Peek domestic allotment threatened profits, competition, and private property and, in so doing, threatened the very survival of the American political and economic system.[37]

Much of the struggle between the left liberals and Peek came down to how each viewed the place of the consumer within the agricultural recovery process. To the AAA left liberals it was imperative that recovery not come at the expense of consumers. They tried, therefore, to negotiate marketing agreements that would prevent processors and distributors from passing the increased costs of farm products on to consumers. And they looked to business interests to absorb the costs of agricultural recovery, through lower profits and greater efficiency.

Peek, by contrast, believed that consumers should foot the bill for agricultural recovery. As he saw it, the consumer had been the primary beneficiary of a system that, in essence, "took the farmer's crop away from him without paying for it." Throughout the 1920s agricultural prices had been "ruinously below their fair relation to other prices." The task of the AAA, Peek maintained, was "to bring about economic justice—to right a social wrong," and that would require raising prices. The increase, Peek believed, should be paid by consumers, who had long enjoyed inexpensive agricultural commodities at the farmers' expense, and not by the middlemen, who had been performing "a necessary service between the farmer and the consumer."[38]

The struggle between Peek and the AAA left liberals came to a head late in 1933 over the flue-cured tobacco marketing agreement. Tugwell, Frank, and the Office of the Consumers' Counsel all sought to include in it a provision that would grant the secretary of agriculture access to all company records, thereby making it possible for the government to monitor profits and to prevent unreasonable price hikes. They defended such a clause by arguing that the government had granted the processors immunity from antitrust and was therefore responsible for making sure that the processors did not use this immunity to rake in excessive profits. Peek believed, however, that their demand was nothing short of "a drive to take over control of the industry." He appealed to Roosevelt to intervene "for unless the drive to control business were halted in the Department, we were going to get just nowhere in helping the farmer through marketing agreements."[39]

Roosevelt responded with what George Soule described as "a characteristic compromise which failed to face the issue." The president transferred Peek out of the AAA. But he also urged the AAA to accept the tobacco agreement with only a limited books and records clause. Finally, he transferred authority over most of the food industries from the AAA to the NRA, where these industries were sure to receive more lenient treatment.[40] Roosevelt's response meant that Peek's pro-industry sentiments would no longer frustrate left-liberal attempts to regulate industry, but it also meant that there were almost no industries under AAA jurisdiction for the left liberals to regulate.

Two years later it was not Peek but several of the AAA left liberals who were the victims of a purge. The immediate issue was an opinion, signed by Francis Shea and initialed by Hiss and Frank, which interpreted Section 7 of the master cotton contract to mean that plantation owners did not have the right to remove their tenants. Peek's replacement, Chester Davis, was outraged by the opinion, which, he believed, could threaten the Senate appropriations for the AAA by alienating Southern senators such as "Cotton Ed" Smith of South Carolina, Majority Leader Joe Robinson of Arkansas, and chairman of the Senate Agricultural Committee John Bankhead of Alabama, all of whom were far more sympathetic to the planter interests than to those of the tenants. Davis went to Wallace and demanded that Frank be fired.[41]

If Section 7 was the immediate issue, the underlying cause of the purge was more far-reaching. Davis was not merely upset about the tenant farmer issue. He was frustrated by the repeated refusals of the legal and consumer divisions to certify marketing agreements on the grounds that these agreements failed to provide what they considered adequate protection for consumers. Pressured by the processors and convinced that the primary goal of the AAA should be to help farmers, Davis denounced the legal and consumer divisions for their "doctrinaire insistence that certain ideal requirements be met." By February 1935 he had become convinced the left liberals had to go. Within the Office of the General Counsel he asked not only Frank and Shea, who had been directly involved in the Section 7 opinion, but also Lee Pressman and Victor Rotnem to leave. And within the Office of the Consumers' Counsel he fired Gardner Jackson and demoted Frederic Howe. Alger Hiss, who had been involved in the drafting of the Section 7 opinion, was not asked to leave.

Tugwell had been out of town when the purge occurred. But, as soon as he heard about it, he was "mad all through." Convinced that the Section 7 opinion "had little significance," he saw the purge as "part of Davis' studied plan to rid the Department of all liberals and to give the reactionary farm leaders full control of policy," most of whom, he insisted, "are owned body and soul by the processors." Rushing back to Washington, Tugwell tried to reverse what had happened but to no avail. He then tried to offer his resignation to Roosevelt, but the president requested that Tugwell stay. So, too, did Wallace, stipulating, however, that Tugwell was not to have anything to do with the AAA. Tugwell found such a situation intolerable and a few months later left the Department of Agriculture to head the new Resettlement Administration. In 1936 he departed the New Deal.[42]

Shortly after the purge, Raymond Graham Swing of the *Nation* suggested that the departure of the left liberals was the "defeat of the social out look in agriculture." Tugwell went even farther. "Tugwell," Harold Ickes noted in his diary, "is of the opinion that this Administration has done all that it can be expected to do in the way of social advance. He thinks too that the president is slipping and that the big business interests have him stopped."[43] As it turned out, Tugwell and Swing were too quick to see the purge as an end rather than a beginning. For one, by pushing AAA left liberals into other departments, the purge helped to disseminate the AAA brand of consumerist ideas throughout the New Deal administration. Frank was sent over to the Reconstruction Finance Corporation and was later appointed commissioner of the Securities Exchange Commission. Gardner Jackson went on to chair the National Committee on Rural Social Planning. And Lee Pressman joined Tugwell at the Resettlement Administration.

Nor was it only those whom Davis fired who were responsible for disseminating the AAA version of a consumerist left liberalism throughout the New Deal administration. Many who were not part of the purge eventually moved on to other jobs, taking the AAA brand of left liberalism with them. Alger Hiss, for example, had not been one of the victims of the purge. But, even before it occurred, he had already begun to focus his energies elsewhere, serving as counsel for the Nye Committee, a Senate investigating committee that was trying to determine whether weapons manufacturers had influenced the Wilson Administration's decision to enter World War I. Gardiner Means left the Department of Agriculture in 1935 to become director of the National Resources Committee, where he quickly decided that he would expand the committee's duties from a study of employment and industrial plant capacity to a consideration of the "problem of over-all balance" and "what would constitute a balance of production and consumption at high level."[44] But perhaps the best illustration of the impact of the AAA experience on New Deal left liberalism can be found in Thurman Arnold's tenure at the Justice Department.

In 1938 Arnold was appointed head of the Antitrust Division. While more than willing to use his newly acquired legal powers—he set a record for the number of cases filed and won—Arnold did not use these powers to eliminate economic concentration. Indeed, as he saw it, "Big Business is not an economic danger so long as it devotes itself to efficiency in production and distribution." The best antitrust policy, in his view, sought to eliminate not corporations but those corporate practices that "hamper the production and distribution of a product from raw material to consumer." As long as businesses used their bigness to produce abundant high-quality, fairly priced goods, they had nothing to fear from Arnold and the Antitrust Division.[45]

For a number of reasons Arnold's approach to antitrust enforcement was significant. For one, it was an approach that made consumer well-being the test of whether corporations had violated antitrust regulations. Only trusts that operated in a consumer-oriented manner would be immune from prosecution. Second, Arnold's approach was based on the assumption that a consumer-oriented and a consumption-oriented economy were one and the same. The best way that a corporation could avoid prosecution was to produce an abundant supply of fairly priced goods. Third, Arnold believed that capitalism could function in a consumer-oriented way. All that was necessary was the sort of regulation which the Antitrust Division was providing. And, finally, Arnold's version of a consumer-oriented economy, committed as it was to high levels of production under capitalism, was as good for businesses as it was for consumers. Arnold may have listed Veblen and Chase as two of the most influential thinkers of the era. But his approach to antitrust seemed to rely on a view of the economy that had far more in common with that of Patten.

It was not only the AAA left liberals who took their consumerist sympathies with them into other New Deal agencies who pushed New Deal liberalism in a consumerist direction. So, too, did those who remained within the agricultural recovery administration. Indeed, for a number of reasons AAA policies were more explicitly consumerist after the purge than before. For one, Peek's departure in 1934 and that of Frank, Pressman, and Howe in 1935 reduced the level of tension within the AAA. While those who remained might continue to disagree on issues involving the consumer, they managed to do so in a less confrontational manner. Furthermore, by 1935 the AAA was coming increasingly under attack not only by the legal system but also by consumers themselves. AAA officials, Wallace included, felt compelled to highlight both the stake that consumers had in the AAA recovery program and the extent to which consumer welfare was a central goal of the program.[46] Finally, the purge did not remove all consumerist thinkers from the AAA staff. Into the 1940s it included individuals who had consumerist sympathies.

That Howe's eventual replacement as consumer counsel, Donald Montgomery, should adopt a consumerist perspective was to be expected. What was surprising was that Montgomery managed far more than Howe to identify producer and consumer interests with each other, so much so that, when he left the AAA in the early 1940s, he began working for the United Automobile Workers as their lobbyist in Washington, D.C., on consumer issues.

Montgomery came to the AAA shortly after the Supreme Court declared the Agricultural Adjustment Act unconstitutional. As AAA staff members worked feverishly on new legislation to replace the old act, Montgomery urged the inclusion of provisions within the new legislation which would provide "adequate recognition and safeguard of the consumer interest." What was striking about his arguments on behalf of such provisions was how heavily they emphasized the common ground that consumers and producers shared.[47]

Montgomery was as determined as any other AAA advocate of the consumer to show that the consumer's interest was not "antagonistic to the farmer's." Like his predecessors, he insisted that farmers had a stake in consumer well-being; after all, they were themselves consumers. But, Montgomery was quick to point out, they also had a stake as producers. "The farm program itself cannot succeed," Montgomery warned, "unless it is built upon the principle that adequate and sufficient consumption of farm products is the necessary foundation of farm prosperity."[48]

Montgomery was able to identify a common ground between producers and consumers in large part because he concentrated on supply rather than price. As he saw it, when it came to prices, consumers and producers were "trying to ride the same horse at the same time in diametrically opposite directions." Consumers wanted lower prices, producers higher ones. But, unlike the Veblenians, whose emphasis on the price system had convinced them that a producer-oriented and a consumer-oriented system were antithetical, Montgomery was confident that consumers and producers could "come to some understanding with each other." The key was to shift the focus on both sides from price to volume. "Increased production. . . . is one national goal which no group and no school of thought repudiates."[49]

Probably no issue highlighted the intellectual differences between the consumerist thinkers who were involved in agricultural recovery and those who were primarily interested in industrial recovery as much as the issue of production levels. Veblenians such as Chase and Soule had long maintained that, because business profits depended upon scarcity and consumers were best served by abundance, it was impossible to satisfy the interests of consumers and producers in the same economic system. Montgomery disagreed. "All economic interests," he insisted, "have a stake in finding the balanced relationships that will bring abundance."[50]

It was not merely that the AAA experience encouraged consumerist left liberals to shift their focus from price to supply. It also forced them to think about these two categories in fundamentally different ways than did those who were primarily involved in industrial recovery. The latter found it easy to conclude that the collapse of purchasing power had been caused by layoffs that had accompanied production cuts. Within the AAA, however, consumerist left liberals were forced to confront the possibility that too much production was as bad for the consumer as too little. "When too much cotton and wheat and pork are forced into trade channels," Tugwell maintained, "prices received by farmers dwindle to levels so low that they themselves cannot buy the goods which city workers manufacture. The result is that factories close down and employees are thrown out of work." "Let us not be confused in our thinking," he counseled. "We can arrange to have abundance where abundance is needed and can be consumed. We need not waste our energies producing that which is not needed and which must inevitably pile up in warehouses, as nearly 400,000,000 bushels of American wheat piled up in 1932 and 1933."[51]

Conditions within agriculture also forced left liberals to devote far more attention to the issue of a fair price. To Chase and Soule prices were something that were used to exploit the consumer. Within the AAA, however, they were seen as something that exploited the farmer. Far from making goods scarce and dear, the price system operated in the agricultural sector to make farm commodities abundant and cheap. Even consumerist left liberals found it hard to escape the conclusion that conditions in agriculture made it necessary to raise prices. Although they found it "inexcusable" that some Americans did not have enough to eat, they agreed with Tugwell that "it certainly was *not* the responsibility of the farmers, who themselves were in sore straits, to feed the destitute."[52]

In the early years of the AAA Tugwell, and indeed many AAA left liberals, never completely managed to reconcile their conviction that it was necessary to eliminate "wasteful overabundance" with their commitment to a consumer-oriented economy of abundance. While focusing on balance allowed them to emphasize the connection between farmer and consumer well-being and while it enabled them to blame crop destruction on the limited production policies of industrial capitalists, it nevertheless implied a reduction in supply. Tugwell tried to justify reduction by insisting that "one of the important causes of the lack of consumer purchasing power" was "the glut of farm products." This glut, he maintained, had forced down agricultural prices, which had reduced the incomes of farmers, who in turn had been unable to buy manufactured products, thereby throwing urban workers out of their jobs. "The Nation's economic machine, gorged with an excess of farm and other products, [broke] down." Gardiner Means agreed, suggesting that AAA production control was justified, "so long as it is an effort to eliminate a surplus or take care of a reduced export."[53]

By the mid-1930s, however, AAA liberals began to develop a different understanding of balance. And they did so, in large part, because of changing conditions in agriculture. By early 1934 the country was within the grip of a severe drought, which affected not only the Far West but also much of the East. One AAA official from Montana remarked that the parched fields of western Maryland reminded him of home. Exacerbating the crisis were dust storms that had begun occurring as early as 1931 and by 1934 had taken on alarming proportions. Western soil flew eastward as far as the nation's capital and even beyond.[54]

The drought and dust storms eliminated the agricultural surpluses far more rapidly than the AAA had ever hoped to do. "What the A.A.A. had planned to do in three years," Wallace noted, "the drought did—except for cotton and tobacco—in one." By 1935 the United States actually found it necessary to import wheat, its surpluses having been so completely eliminated. And agricultural prices were rising. In some cases, as in cotton, that rise was due to AAA policies. In others, such as wheat, it was the weather. In still others, such as corn, it was a combination of the two. But the results were the same. Between 1932 and 1936 farmers saw a 50 percent increase in their income. And they saw the ratio between the price of agricultural goods and the price of industrial products improve significantly.[55]

The rapid improvement in agricultural prices meant that by mid-1934 the AAA found it necessary to begin to "overhaul its programs with the drought in mind," shifting the focus from cutting production to increasing it. What was significant about this shift was that it allowed AAA liberals to portray agricultural programs as seeking not merely balance but abundance. Indeed, in the mid- and late 1930s AAA officials increasingly linked the two concepts. The challenge confronting the AAA, they suggested, was to find a balance that would bring abundance.[56]

The shift to increasing production gave the AAA some immunity to the charges that it was committed to a policy of scarcity. And it allowed those at the AAA to distinguish between their approach to recovery and the approach that industrial leaders favored. Indeed, Montgomery chastised industry for continuing to rely on scarcity, thereby preventing the mass purchasing power on which an economy of abundance rested. "Agriculture alone cannot build up consumers' income," he insisted. "Industry has a grave obligation to increase its production which is still far below normal."[57]

Finally, while Montgomery was adamant that producers had as great a stake in abundance as did consumers, he nevertheless maintained that consumers would ultimately have to take most of the responsibility for ushering in such an economy. As business and labor addressed questions concerning profits and wages, he warned, they were as likely as not to do so from a producerist perspective. Only consumers were capable of taking the "broader view." Therefore, Montgomery concluded, it was consumers who would have "to insist that these questions be answered on the side of MORE not LESS, that restriction of output be not invariably the solution dictated by business expediency."[58]

Even more than his predecessors, Montgomery was determined to show that his consumer-oriented economy of abundance could benefit producers. Ultimately, however, for him an economy of abundance had to be a consumer-oriented one. "Larger consumption is the goal we should set for ourselves. The road to that goal is getting enough income to consumers, to farm families as well as to city families."[59] It was consumers who would and should be the primary beneficiaries of an economy of abundance. And, just as important, it was the consumer's perspective that would be instrumental in maintaining this economy.

Montgomery's version of a consumer-oriented economy of abundance was not the only version to come out of the AAA in the late 1930s. Wallace's financial advisor Mordecai Ezekiel, who had been in the Department of Agriculture since the early 1920s, was also calling for a planned economy of abundance. What was striking about Ezekiel's version was that it was not particularly consumer oriented. Indeed, Ezekiel did not spend much time discussing the consumer at all. His focus was on the ways in which an economy of abundance would advance the interests of producers, be they workers, farmers, or capitalists.[60]

Although Ezekiel's version of an economy of abundance was far closer to that of Patten than Veblen, Ezekiel did agree with the Veblenians on one point. Like them, he believed that capitalism was flawed because it forced producers "to think primarily in terms of making more money, not of making more goods," which meant that "profits must come first." And, even more disturbing, it meant that the "volume of production is only incidental." Indeed, because "scarcity creates values," many economic players devoted far more effort to creating scarcity than creating goods. "Unless ways are found to create abundance through modifying the profit system," he warned, "the issue may finally be drawn as between the present economy of profits and poverty on one side, and a promised economy of socialism and abundance on the other."[61]

Ezekiel parted company with the Veblenian left liberals over whether the defects in the capitalist system meant that the only choice was between capitalist scarcity and socialist abundance. Throughout the 1930s Chase and Soule insisted that the answer was yes, whereas Tugwell and the AAA left liberals settled for a definite maybe. Ezekiel, however, believed that capitalism could, and, even more to the point, should, be saved. The task was not to find an alternative to capitalism but "to correct its faults." Only by doing "so can the best features of the old system long be retained."[62]

Ezekiel was far more determined to save capitalism than were either the Veblenian or the AAA left liberals because he saw far more productive potential in "private enterprise." Indeed, as far as he was concerned, private enterprise had "worked miracles in achieving efficient production and closely-knit, smooth-running organization within individual plants or within the successively integrated plants owned by a single concern." Where it was far less efficient, Ezekiel conceded, was at "dovetail[ing] operations between the various competitive units of an industry and between related industries." But government could do this. The task, Ezekiel concluded, was to find an approach to the economy which could "combine the best points of private enterprise and government coordination."[63]

Ezekiel was also determined to save capitalism because he believed its flaws were easily remedied. To the Veblenians capitalism could not ever produce enough to go around because it was committed to waste and sabotage, what Chase had called "the shower of monkey wrenches thrown into the mechanism" by those bent on "getting rich." To Tugwell and the AAA left liberals the problem was not so much sabotage as insufficient purchasing power, which they blamed on excessive profits and production inefficiencies. Ezekiel, however, was convinced that the reason "we don't produce more" was only "because it is nobody's business to see that we produce more. It is everybody's business to make a profit, to make wages, to make money. But profits and wages and money are not goods and services." "No person or agency in this country is directly concerned with trying to expand production for a balanced abundance. And what is nobody's business—doesn't get done." What was needed, therefore, was a program that could "organize and utilize fully our resources of materials and men," without abandoning "capitalism or private enterprise."[64]

Ezekiel believed that Industrial Adjustment was just such a program. Based on agricultural adjustment, his plan would organize industry around voluntary contracts. The difference was that, whereas the AAA had used these contracts to make it in farmers' interest to produce less, Ezekiel's Industrial Adjustment would use them to make it in each business' interest to produce more. Industrial Adjustment, he concluded, would provide "democratic mechanisms through which private enterprises could coordinate in full activity, and thus renew their ability to produce abundantly."[65]

What was significant about Ezekiel's economy of abundance was that it was consumption oriented. Since the early twentieth century political thinkers had increasingly defined an economy of abundance as a consumer-oriented one. It was a definition that was rooted in conflict and had anticapitalist overtones. Most of those who embraced such a definition assumed that, either through ineptitude or design, capitalist producers would thwart the emergence of an economy of abundance. Because Ezekiel focused on maximizing "production and consumption, employment and buying power," rather than consumer well-being, he was able to argue that an economy of abundance would benefit everyone. Aimed "squarely at the prime economic necessity—fuller employment and greater output and consumption," his economy of abundance "would assure producers of markets, workers of jobs, and consumers of improved standards of living." And it would owe its existence and survival to capitalists, who would willingly increase production because they were well aware that "the pie must be made bigger before everyone can have a generous slice."[66]

Despite the differences between Montgomery's and Ezekiel's versions of an economy of abundance, what was ultimately most significant were the similarities. Building on the ideas of the AAA left liberals, both had constructed versions of the economy which would benefit producers as well as consumers. Both had done so by shifting the focus from price, an arena of conflict, to production, an arena of consensus. And both identified balance as the key.

Their approach was significant for two reasons. First, it helped to reunite liberal and consumerist ideas. Although Adam Smith had identified consumption as the "sole end and purpose of all production" and had denounced a system that "seems to consider production, and not consumption, as the ultimate end and object of all industry and commerce," nineteenth-century classical liberals had quickly placed the producer at the center of their political economy.[67] The efforts of a handful of thinkers in the early twentieth century to construct a consumer-oriented alternative to classical liberalism might have been expected to bring about some sort of reconciliation. But they had developed their ideas as a critique of producer-oriented liberalism. Into the early 1930s consumer-oriented and producer-oriented liberals had little interest in rapprochement.

Montgomery's and Ezekiel's versions of an economy of abundance, however, could appeal to those who championed the consumer as well as those who focused on the producer. Their emphasis was on "a balanced expansion in both buying power and production." Both Ezekiel's "balanced abundance" and Montgomery's "coordinated program of increasing production" helped to reestablish the consumerist assumptions that had been at the heart of the Smithian system, namely a balanced and productive economy that simultaneously advanced the interests of producers and consumers.[68]

The focus on balanced abundance was not only important because it reestablished the consumerist perspective within liberalism. It was also significant because it provided the intellectual foundation for the Keynesian policies that would be central to post–World War II liberalism. Ezekiel may have been an enthusiastic proponent of planning, and Montgomery may have ultimately favored a consumer-oriented economy. But, in identifying abundance as the one interest that consumers and producers shared and suggesting that balance was the most effective means of achieving abundance, they embraced a view of the economy which was ultimately far closer to that of postwar Keynesian liberals than the consumer-oriented planned economy of the prewar left liberals.

The extent to which AAA consumerist ideas left their mark on New Deal liberalism was nowhere more evident than in the evolution of Henry Wallace's political ideas during his tenure as secretary of agriculture. When Wallace came to the Department of Agriculture, he was no consumerist thinker. Born and raised in Iowa, his background and, to a certain extent, his outlook resembled that of farm leaders such as Peek and Davis. Indeed, in the 1920s he, too, had been a proponent of McNary-Haugenism. "I was for agriculture first, last, and all the time," he would later remember. "I wasn't battling for either labor or business, except insofar as labor and business helped the farmer."[69] Wallace's deep commitment to the farmer and his producerist perspective were firmly in place when he took up his duties as secretary of agriculture.

Wallace's producerist and agrarian sympathies were evident in his initial understanding of the agricultural crisis. Like most of those involved with the AAA, he believed that the goal was balance. But in his early years as secretary he understood balance much as Peek and Davis did, as something that involved income and prices rather than purchasing power. The goal of agricultural recovery, he insisted, was "to encourage price and production policies that will maintain a continually balanced relationship between the income of agriculture, labor, and industry." And, if that meant that the consumer would have to pay higher prices, then so be it. "Consumers," he insisted, "cannot expect to be fed indefinitely at prices which represent a return to the farmer so low as to make it impossible for him to buy his customary quantity of city products."[70]

Wallace, however, was not only an agrarian. He also had roots in the progressive tradition that went back to his grandfather. The elder Wallace had been a major force on Theodore Roosevelt's Country Life Commission and had supported the Bull Moose Party in 1912. Young Henry had not only read Herbert Croly, John Dewey, Richard Ely, and Thorstein Veblen about the same time that Stuart Chase, Rexford Tugwell, and George Soule were reading them, but he had also voted the Progressive Party ticket in 1924 (he later insisted that he had done so as a protest). Finally, Wallace had spent much of his adult life on the staff of the family newspaper the *Wallace Farmer,* a job that kept him immersed in agrarian progressivism.[71]

In his early years as secretary Wallace's progressive and agrarian sympathies were often at odds, and more often than not the latter prevailed. While he was sympathetic to the idea of economic abundance, suggesting that "perhaps in time we shall be able safely to unleash the productive capacities of all our industries, including agriculture," he nevertheless insisted that the AAA's first responsibility had to be to farmers. The AAA had to "play with the cards that are dealt." It would be nice if farmers could continue producing at high levels, but, he insisted, agriculture "cannot survive in a capitalistic society as a philanthropic enterprise." If industry "controlled production," so too must farmers. "The condition of greater balance and justice we now seek, in a capitalistic structure hastily mended, can certainly not be obtained by arranging that everybody work under the profit system except the farmer."[72]

While Wallace's producerist perspective and his deep commitment to the farmer went a long way toward explaining his initial approach to agricultural recovery, so too did the personnel conflicts within the AAA. As Peek and the farm leaders faced off against what Wallace referred to as the "extreme liberal group," Wallace believed that it was his job to mediate between the factions. But the same commitment to a "middle course" also pushed him in a consumerist direction after the purge. When a reporter suggested that, in firing Frank and the other left liberals, the AAA had "thrown out all the left-hand ballast" and might "shift too much to one side," Wallace conceded that "we might have to take on some more left-side ballast so we can go straight ahead." Ironically, it would turn out to be Wallace himself who would provide much of that "left-side ballast."[73]

It was not only the shift in personnel which encouraged Wallace to move in a consumerist direction in 1935. Equally influential was the increasing criticism leveled at the AAA for its anticonsumer policies. One year earlier Wallace had defended these policies by suggesting that agriculture had to play with the cards it was dealt. By 1935, however, he was denying that the AAA had ever tried to create scarcity. Such a policy, he insisted, had been "the farthest thing from our thoughts." Instead, the AAA had implemented what Wallace called "an adjustment policy providing for increases when such increases make for the welfare of the consumer, and for decreases when such decreases make for the welfare of the producer."[74]

Like the AAA left liberals before him, Wallace found that the easiest way to incorporate the consumer into a recovery effort on behalf of the producer was to find the common ground that the two shared. "There can be no manner of doubt," he insisted, "that farmers and consumers have interests in common that are far deeper and more important than their differences." At the most basic level this was because "most consumers are also producers." But, he insisted, it was also because consumer well-being depended upon producer well-being and vice versa. If producers tried to push prices "too high," consumers would not be able to buy farm products. Similarly, if consumers tried to push prices too low, it would be impossible for farmers "to buy what they need from cities." The goal was "a point of balance, then, between too high and too low prices, a point where the welfare of both the farmer and the consumer is best served."[75]

Although Wallace initially tried to find this common ground by suggesting that balanced prices would be good for all concerned, he soon found it far easier to find it by redefining balance in terms of production. It was, he suggested, at the point of "increased balanced production. . . . that producer goals and consumer goals become identical." "The American home needs abundance of food and clothing. The American farmer needs buyers for the abundance he produces so that he may enjoy some of the abundance that industry can produce." For Wallace the "formula for the general welfare" had become "increased balanced abundance." And this formula, he insisted, would provide "an adequate basis around which to build an economic democracy to sustain and perpetuate our political democracy."[76]

Wallace had initially incorporated the consumer into his political economic view in an effort to counter the anticonsumer charges being leveled at the AAA. His attempt to establish the agency's consumerist credentials, however, had a profound impact on his own thinking, transforming him from an agrarian progressive into a New Deal liberal. And it was this liberalism, which relied on abundant production to further the interests of all members of society, that Wallace would take with him as he left the Department of Agriculture to serve as Roosevelt's vice president.[77]

In 1933 consumerist left liberals focused most of their attention on the National Recovery Administration, all but ignoring the Agricultural Adjustment Administration—and with good reason. Convinced that the key to consumer well-being lay in increased industrial productivity and confident that the best way to reach this goal was through economic planning, they saw the NRA as the New Deal agency most likely to usher in a consumer-oriented economy. By contrast, few agencies seemed less likely to do so than the AAA. For one, this agency focused on agriculture, a sector of the economy that consumerist left liberals had largely ignored. For another, the AAA was committed to limiting agricultural production in order to raise prices. A less consumer-oriented approach was hard to imagine. Yet it soon became clear that the AAA and not the NRA was the recovery agency more sympathetic to consumerist ideas.

The different degrees to which Johnson and Wallace were willing to incorporate consumerist ideas into their recovery policy had an impact not only on NRA and AAA recovery efforts but also on consumerist thought. Johnson's hostility toward the consumer quickly polarized the debate within the NRA, intensifying the anticapitalist, antiproducer convictions that many of the consumerist left liberals had brought with them. This hostility made it easy for both Johnson and the consumerist left liberals to conclude that one side's gain came at the expense of the other side. And it forced the consumerist left liberals to spend most of their time trying to establish the legitimacy of the consumer interest rather than developing consumerist approaches to industrial recovery.

Within the AAA, by contrast, the legitimacy of the consumer interest was a given. But, because the agency was created to advance the interests of agricultural producers, it was also a given that in any conflict the producer interest would take precedence. The result was that those who were most committed to the consumer had the biggest incentive to find the common ground that consumers and producers shared. Not conflict but cooperation was the dominant mood at the AAA.

While Johnson's militaristic style and the cooperative, Christian approach of Wallace went a long way toward setting the tone at each recovery administration, the consumerist left liberals who were drawn to each agency also left their mark. Those who served within the NRA or spent much of their time writing about it were the most left of the consumerist left liberals. In the early 1930s Stuart Chase, George Soule, Paul Douglas, and Robert Lynd were all convinced that the very logic of capitalism, with its reliance on profit, prevented it from functioning in a consumer-oriented fashion. Little wonder that they and the business-oriented Johnson clashed so violently.

Those who served in the AAA, by contrast, were the least left of the consumerist left liberals. Tugwell and Means had both come to the New Deal committed to planning and convinced that capitalists often made decisions at the expense of the consuming population. But, unlike many consumerist left liberals, they did not assume that a consumer orientation and a business orientation were, inevitably, mutually exclusive approaches to the economy. Frank and many of the AAA left liberals were equally willing to work within the profit system. Indeed, as Frank once complained to Chase, "We socialists are trying to save capitalism and the damned capitalists won't let us."[78] To most of the AAA critics of capitalism the system needed to be reformed but not necessarily replaced.

Ultimately, what was most significant about the AAA version of a consumer-oriented system was that it played a role in preparing the ground for a Keynesian approach to the economy. In the American version of a Keynesian economy, which emerged by the end of World War II, a consumer-oriented and a consumption-oriented economy were all but synonymous. And, just as significantly, a consumption-oriented economy was assumed to be in the best interests of all members of society, not just consumers. Both assumptions, while antithetical to the most fundamental beliefs of most Veblenian consumerist left liberals, had been well established within the AAA by the late 1930s.

What was significant about these AAA assumptions—and Keynesian assumptions, for that matter—was that they went a long way toward establishing within modern American liberalism the logic that had been behind the classical liberalism of Adam Smith. By the 1940s liberalism was rooted once again in the idea that the primary purpose of the capitalist economy was to serve consumers and that, in doing so, such an economy would further the interests of producers. The ultimate irony was that it was not the recovery administration charged with jump-starting industry but the one designed to limit production which developed the consumerist potential of a consumption-oriented economy.

Conclusion

By the 1940s American liberals found it easy to identify freedom from want as one of the "four essential human freedoms." They found it easy to do so because late-nineteenth- and early-twentieth-century American intellectuals had transformed the economic, social, and political meanings associated with consumer and consumption. Those new meanings were the basis for not one but two versions of a political economy in which the focus was on the consumer and consumption rather than the producer and production. One version emphasized abundant consumption as the key to general well-being. The other, far more critical of capitalism, called for extensive government regulation to force business leaders to operate industry on behalf of consumers.

The two versions began coalescing into a single consumerist system of thought in the 1930s as individuals across the liberal spectrum responded to the economic crisis. Those corporate liberals, who saw abundant consumption as the key to business prosperity, began to advocate consumer-oriented policies, convinced that the best way to maximize consumption was to maximize consumer well-being. Left liberals, who were appalled by the widespread misery caused by the Depression, came to believe that few systems were more consumer oriented than a consumption-oriented one. It took some left liberals more time than others to identify capitalism as the system most compatible with an economy of abundance. But even the most skeptical had lost whatever doubts remained after witnessing the phenomenal productivity of American industry during World War II. By 1945 liberals had found the common ground that in the post–World War II period would be called "New Deal liberalism."

The consumerist ideas that had been so instrumental in transforming classical liberalism into its modern American counterpart did not displace producerist ideas. Instead, the two coexisted. How much so was evident in many of the New Deal programs that became the foundation for modern American liberalism. New Deal liberals may have advocated unemployment insurance and social security benefits because they recognized a governmental responsibility to prevent citizens from starving, but in doing so they created programs that favored "producing" over "nonproducing" citizens.[1] Similarly, New Deal support for farm subsidies and minimum wage legislation may have severed the direct connection between labor and income, but in both cases it was producers who ultimately benefited. And, while Roosevelt's Economic Bill of Rights of 1944 may have insisted that all citizens had a right to a minimum standard of living, it did so at the same time that he and other liberals were coming to believe that full employment was the best way to guarantee that right.[2] In short, the New Deal did not see the ascendancy of consumerist ideas so much as a blending of both producerist and consumerist ideas into a new understanding of the relationship between government and citizens.

The new liberal system was not without its detractors. Critics became increasingly concerned that freedom from want was being equated with a right to plenty. And they worried that material plenty was being treated as a precondition for democracy. Their concerns were not unfounded. By the early 1950s historian David Potter was suggesting that only because Americans were a "people of plenty" had they been able to make democracy work. And at the end of the decade Richard Nixon told Nikita Khrushchev in the Kitchen Debates that the United States was superior to the Soviet Union not because American citizens had a right to freedom from want—Soviet citizens had that—but because Americans had access to abundant consumer goods.

The most vehement critique of the new consumption-oriented liberalism, that of economist John Kenneth Galbraith, highlighted the extent to which the tensions between a consumer-oriented and a consumption-oriented political economy survived within liberal discourse. In 1958 Galbraith published *The Affluent Society,* his stinging indictment of a consumption-oriented liberalism. According to Galbraith, the biggest problem with American liberalism was that its "economic creed . . . is more production." Liberals, he insisted, gave no thought to "the kinds of private goods and services that are produced." "The question of the distribution of the product so produced—who gets it—is decidedly secondary."[3] They were merely interested in the total output. A consumption-oriented system, Galbraith concluded, was not consumer but producer oriented

Galbraith's consumerist indictment of the new liberalism was not totally unexpected. He admired Thorstein Veblen, whom he lauded as "the greatest voice from the frontier." (He was less enthusiastic about Simon Patten, describing him as "a singularly interesting and original figure" who had received "the neglect reserved for American heretics.") In addition, Galbraith had also served in two of the strongholds of left liberal consumerist thought within the Roosevelt Administration, the Agricultural Adjustment Administration and the Office of Price Administration.[4] And in 1952 he had published *American Capitalism and the Concept of Countervailing Power,* in which he identified consumers as one of the groups that could use "countervailing power" to keep corporations in line.

In denouncing an economic system that was dedicated to increasing consumption, Galbraith joined a long-standing intellectual tradition, one that extended back through Stuart Chase and Robert Lynd to Edward Bellamy. Like those thinkers, Galbraith wanted Americans to spend less time working and consuming (he joined the Lynds in assuming that the two were inextricably intertwined) and more time enjoying leisure. He also called on Americans to spend less money on private goods like "mauve and cerise, air-conditioned, power-steered, and power-braked automobile[s]" and more on public goods like education, paved roads, clean parks, and unpolluted water. And, to those who insisted that in a democratic society consumers themselves decided what the balance between private and public goods should be, he responded that consumers were not free to choose. The consumer, he insisted, "is subject to the forces of advertising and emulation by which production creates its own demand." Only government could alter the balance between public and private goods.[5]

What was ultimately striking about Galbraith's critique of a consumption-oriented system, however, was not so much the similarities with earlier critiques but the difference. Whereas consumerist thinkers from Bellamy and Veblen to Chase and Lynd had all blamed capitalism for emphasizing consumption at the expense of genuine consumer well-being, Galbraith blamed modern liberalism. It was, he insisted, liberals, with their Keynesian policies, who were primarily responsible for an economy that did far more to improve the bottom line of the business interests than the living standard of the consuming masses.[6] The real irony was that Bellamy and Veblen, Chase and Lynd, had all participated in the creation of such a liberalism. Their denunciations of a system that focused on the interests of producers and their calls for one that would further the interests of consumers, had helped to push liberalism in a consumption-oriented direction.

Galbraith's book may have been the opening salvo in a renewed conflict between those who equated well-being with prosperity and those who insisted that increasing consumption actually threatened genuine well-being. But ultimately the participants in that renewed conflict, be it Galbraith, the liberals he targeted, or the New Left critics of a consumption-oriented system, did agree on one thing. All believed that citizens should have the right to freedom from want. They merely parted company over how best to guarantee such a right.

In the early 1980s that right itself came under siege. When Ronald Reagan came into office, conservatives in his administration, led by budget director David Stockman, saw an opportunity to cut government spending by eliminating many of the liberal entitlement programs. Their targets were not only welfare programs such as food stamps and Aid to Families with Dependent Children (AFDC) but also social security, veterans' benefits, and farm subsidies. Their successes and failures revealed much about both the limits of an American commitment to freedom from want and the enduring power of producerist ideas.

Stockman soon discovered that, although Congress was willing to go along with the cuts to welfare programs, it—and, even more surprisingly to Stockman—Ronald Reagan drew the line at curtailing or abolishing such benefits as social security, veterans' payments, and farm subsidies. Reagan's refusal to go after such programs was certainly politically motivated. Social security, veterans' benefits, and farm subsidies had powerful lobbies behind them. What was striking about these programs, however, was that, unlike food stamps and AFDC, they guaranteed a freedom from want for producers. Whether recipients had worked in the armed forces, produced the nation's food, or diverted some of their wages into the social security fund, they had all "earned" their payments. Those who received food stamps and AFDC, by contrast, were guaranteed a freedom from want which was completely severed from any role in production.[7]

Ten years after a Republican president had blocked a challenge to programs guaranteeing entitlements to producers, Democratic president Bill Clinton signed into law legislation that further limited entitlements to nonproducers. The aim of the welfare reform bill of 1996 was to move welfare mothers from the consuming into the producing ranks. And it sought to do so at the same time that the federal government remained committed to farm subsidies and corporate tax deductions, both of which benefited producers. Critics of these programs were quick to recognize that producerist ideas had played a role in determining the amount of support the government and, indeed, Americans gave to the various programs. And they used these ideas on behalf of their own cause, quickly dubbing the assistance to farmers and corporations "corporate welfare." Like the opponents of AFDC, they knew that the most powerful indictment of a government entitlement program was one that charged recipients with not "working" for their payment.

While the debates over welfare in the 1980s and 1990s highlighted the enduring potency of producerist ideas, they also revealed the extent to which producerist ideas coexisted with consumerist ones. The welfare reform bill may have relied far more on producerist principles than its critics would have liked. But, even as Congress limited how long a recipient could remain on the welfare rolls, it endorsed the concept of welfare payments. And it did not put similar limits on other programs for the poor such as Medicaid. Most of those who supported welfare reform endorsed some version of a freedom from want. They merely wanted to limit that freedom. That they wanted to limit it suggests the extent to which consumerist ideas had not completely displaced producerist ones. That they recognized a governmental responsibility to the poor highlights the extent to which consumerist ideas had fundamentally altered the parameters of the political-economic discourse. The welfare reform bill that Congress passed may have seemed far too limited to its opponents. To William Graham Sumner it would have seemed positively libertine.

In the late twentieth century the idea of a freedom from want confronted a far more profound challenge than the one implicit in Newt Gingrich's "Contract with America." In the United States that freedom had always rested on the notion of abundance. Not the redistribution of wealth but its continual increase would allow all Americans to enjoy a comfortable standard of living.

By the 1980s, however, activists throughout the world had begun to call such assumptions into question. The earth's resources, they repeatedly insisted, were finite. Denouncing what had once been termed "abundant production" and "abundant consumption" as "unsustainable production" and "unsustainable consumption," they pointed out that 80 percent of the planet's resources went to 20 percent of its population. "Each new child born in North America or Europe," one observer noted, "will consume 10 or 100 times as much of the world's resources and contribute as many times as much pollution. . . . A three-child American family is, in logic, many more times as dangerous to the planet than an eight- (or even an eighty-) child African family."[8] The American right to live free from want, these critics concluded, threatened the very survival of the planet and that of many, indeed most, of its inhabitants.

What was striking about this critique of an American freedom from want was that it turned the consumerist critique of capitalism on its head. Although proponents of this critique employed many of the same arguments that consumerist thinkers had, they used those arguments not to establish a right to consume but to deny it. Thus, for example, critics of American-style consumption were as quick as any early-twentieth-century consumerist thinker to insist that one's role in the production process should not determine how much one was entitled to consume. But they did so only because they wanted to argue that, regardless of how much Americans produced, they did not have the right to consume at the levels they did. Similarly, these critics were as committed as any consumerist thinker to establishing a freedom from want. But the very fact that they focused on such goods as food, water, and medicine rather than cars and televisions called into question the American assumption that freedom from want and abundant consumption were one and the same.

Perhaps it was inevitable that once critics of American-style consumption shifted the debate from consuming to nonconsuming, they would resurrect the category of "luxury." When the Washington-based World Resources Institute (WRI) proposed at the 1992 "Earth Summit" in Rio de Janeiro to slow the growth of greenhouse gases through a worldwide stabilization of carbon emissions, activists were outraged. How, they wanted to know, could the WRI possibly "equate the carbon dioxide contributions of gas guzzling automobiles in Europe and North America or, for that matter, anywhere in the Third World with the methane emissions of draught cattle and rice fields of subsistence farmers in West Bengal or Thailand?" A distinction had to be made, they insisted, between the "survival emissions" of the poor and the "luxury emissions" of the rich.[9] The luxury debate, it would seem, had come full circle.

By the early twenty-first century the consumerist ideas that had helped liberals reconcile the ideas of Adam Smith with the realities of a corporate world had come under siege. This time, however, the debate was not between those who wanted government to maximize the interests of producers and those who were committed to an economy that functioned on behalf of consumers. Indeed, to the critics of ever-increasing material prosperity, abundant production was merely the alter ego of abundant consumption. But, if, as the critics charged, it was impossible to sustain ever-increasing prosperity indefinitely, then the very foundation on which the liberal economic order rested was made of sand. Perhaps it was not as easy as some modern American liberals had assumed to reconcile liberal principles forged in an industrializing economy with the realities of a postindustrial world.

Notes

Introduction

1. William Graham Sumner, "The Forgotten Man" (1883), in *On Liberty, Society, and Politics: The Essential Essays of William Graham Sumner,* ed. Robert C. Bannister (Indianapolis: Liberty Fund, 1992), 209–10.

2. Christopher Lasch and Nancy Cohen have also emphasized the connections between liberalism and ideas about consumption. My interpretation differs from theirs both in timing and in the political implications of those ideas. Lasch suggests that liberalism became consumer oriented with the publication of Adam Smith's *Wealth of Nations* and never deviated from that orientation. Cohen sees that orientation occurring in the late nineteenth century as a way to contain working-class discontent. Both see the focus on consumption as something that undercuts radical social change. Christopher Lasch, *The True and Only Heaven: Progress and Its Critics* (New York: Norton, 1991); and Nancy Cohen, *The Reconstruction of American Liberalism: 1865–1914* (Chapel Hill: University of North Carolina Press, 2002).

3. Sumner, "Forgotten Man," 209–10; Daniel T. Rodgers, *The Work Ethic in Industrial America, 1850–1920* (Chicago: University of Chicago Press, 1978), 1–15; Daniel Horowitz, *The Morality of Spending: Attitudes toward the Consumer Society in America, 1875–1940* (Baltimore: Johns Hopkins University Press, 1985), 1–12; Dorothy Ross, *The Origins of American Social Science* (Cambridge: Cambridge University Press, 1991), 43–44.

4. Quoted in Robert L. Heilbroner, *The Worldly Philosophers: The Lives, Times, and Ideas of the Great Economic Thinkers* (New York: Simon and Schuster, 1953), 81.

5. Several historians have discussed the deep-seated American reservations concerning consumption. See, for example, J. E. Crowley, *This Sheba, Self: The Conceptualization of Economic Life in Eighteenth-Century America* (Baltimore: Johns Hopkins University Press, 1974); Horowitz, *Morality of Spending;* David E. Shi, *The Simple Life: Plain Living and High Thinking in American Culture* (New York: Oxford University Press, 1985). The negative ideas concerning consumption, while an important strain in the colonial intellectual tradition, did not go uncontested. Theorists outside of the Puritan and republican traditions were far more tolerant of consumption. See, for example, Joyce Appleby, *Capitalism and the New Social Order: The Republican Vision of the 1790s* (New York: New York University Press, 1984); Richard L. Bushman, *The Refinement of America: Persons, Houses, Cities* (New York: Knopf, 1992); Cary Carson, Ronald Hoffman, and Peter J. Albert, eds., *Of Consuming Interests: The Style of Life in Eighteenth Century America* (Charlottesville: Published for the United States Capitol Historical Society by the University Press of Virginia, 1994); John E. Crowley, *The Invention of Comfort: Sensi-*

bilities and Design in Early Modern Britain and Early America (Baltimore: Johns Hopkins University Press, 2001).

6. Rodgers, *Work Ethic in Industrial America.*

7. Neil McKendrick, John Brewer, and J. H. Plumb, *The Birth of a Consumer Society: The Commercialization of Eighteenth-Century England* (Bloomington: Indiana University Press, 1982); Carole Shammas, "How Self-Sufficient Was Early America?" *Journal of Interdisciplinary History* 13 (fall 1982): 247–72; Lorena S. Walsh, "Urban Amenities and Rural Sufficiency: Living Standards and Consumer Behavior in the Colonial Chesapeake, 1643–1777," *Journal of Economic History* 43 (March 1983): 109–17; Jack P. Greene, *Pursuits of Happiness: The Social Development of Early Modern British Colonies and the Formation of American Culture* (Chapel Hill: University of North Carolina Press, 1988); Laura Thatcher Ulrich, *The Age of Homespun: Objects and Stories in the Creation of an American Myth,* 1st ed. (New York: Knopf, 2001); Stuart M. Blumin, *The Emergence of the Middle Class: Social Experience in the American City, 1760–1900* (Cambridge: Cambridge University Press, 1989); Mary Ryan, *Cradle of the Middle Class: The Family in Oneida County, New York, 1790–1865* (Cambridge: Cambridge University Press, 1981); Bushman, *Refinement of America;* Carson, Hoffman, and Albert, *Of Consuming Interests;* Crowley, *Invention of Comfort.*

8. Alan Brinkley, *The End of Reform: New Deal Liberalism in Recession and War* (New York: Vintage Press, 1995).

9. Adam Smith, *An Inquiry into the Nature and Causes of the Wealth of Nations* (Chicago: University of Chicago Press, 1976), 2:179.

CHAPTER 1: The Producerist Worldview, 1870–1900

1. Adam Smith, *An Inquiry into the Nature and Causes of the Wealth of Nations* (Chicago: University of Chicago Press, 1976), 2:179.

2. Joyce Oldham Appleby, *Economic Thought and Ideology in Seventeenth Century England* (Princeton: Princeton University Press, 1978); "Ideology and Theory: The Tension between Political and Economic Liberalism in Seventeenth-Century England," *American Historical Review* 81, no. 3 (June 1976): 499–515.

3. A survey of the tables of contents and the indexes of Adam Smith's *Wealth of Nations,* David Ricardo's *Principles of Political Economy and Taxation,* and John Stuart Mill's *Principles of Political Economy* suggests the extent to which consumption was, at most, only a peripheral interest.

4. Smith, *Wealth of Nations, 179.*

5. Jean-Baptiste Say, *A Treatise on Political Economy, or the Production, Distribution, and Consumption of Wealth* (Philadelphia: Claxton, Remsen and Haffelfinger, 1880), 387, 391, 394, 402–3.

6. Ibid., 399, 407.

7. Smith, *Wealth of Nations, 179.*

8. Joyce Oldham Appleby, *Capitalism and a New Social Order: The Republican Vision of the 1790s* (New York: New York University Press, 1984), 27–28.

9. James Livingston, *Pragmatism and the Political Economy of Cultural Revolution, 1850–1940* (Chapel Hill: University of North Carolina Press, 1994), 16, 18, 31–40.

10. Livingston, *Pragmatism and the Political Economy of Cultural Revolution,* 18–56; William Leach, *Land of Desire: Merchants, Power, and the Rise of a New American Culture*

(New York: Pantheon Books, 1993), 15–38; Richard S. Tedlow, *New and Improved: The Story of Mass Marketing in America* (New York: Basic Books, 1990), esp. 3–32; Susan Porter Benson, *Counter Cultures: Saleswomen, Managers and Customers in American Department Stores, 1890–1940* (Urbana: University of Illinois Press, 1986), 12–30; Susan Strasser, *Satisfaction Guaranteed: The Making of the American Mass Market* (New York: Pantheon Books, 1989).

11. Bonamy Price, "One Per Cent," *Contemporary Review* 29 (1877); David A. Wells, "How Shall the Nation Regain Prosperity?" *North American Review* 125 (1877); U.S. Commissioner of Labor, *First Annual Report: Industrial Depression* (Washington, D.C., 1886), both quoted in Daniel T. Rodgers, *The Work Ethic in Industrial America, 1850–1920* (Chicago: University of Chicago Press, 1974), 116, 118–19.

12. William Graham Sumner, "The Forgotten Man" (1883), in *On Liberty, Society, and Politics: The Essential Essays of William Graham Sumner*, ed. Robert C. Bannister (Indianapolis: Liberty Fund, 1992), 208–11. See also William Graham Sumner, "The Power of Capital" (1899), in *Earth Hunger and Other Essays*, ed. Albert Galloway Keller (New Haven: Yale University Press, 1913), 345; "The Challenge of Facts" (1880s), in *The Challenge of Facts and Other Essays*, ed. Albert Galloway Keller (New Haven: Yale University Press, 1914), 34; "Examination of a Noble Sentiment" (1887–89), in *Earth Hunger*, 213–16.

13. Sumner, "Forgotten Man," 217–19.

14. William Graham Sumner, *What Social Classes Owe to Each Other* (1883; rpt., Caldwell, Idaho: Caxton Printers, 1982), 19.

15. Henry George, *Progress and Poverty* (New York: D. Appleton, 1879), 75.

16. Ibid., 270–71.

17. Ibid., 341–42.

18. Ibid., 453.

19. Ibid., 168.

20. Sumner, *What Social Classes Owe to Each Other*, 43–44.

21. George, *Progress and Poverty*, 308.

22. Like most thinkers in the late nineteenth century, Sumner assumed that the producer was a male.

23. Sumner, "Liberty and Responsibility" (1887–89), in *Earth Hunger*, 182; "Challenge of Facts," 25–27.

24. George, *Progress and Poverty*, 285.

25. Ibid., 272, 274.

26. Sumner, "Challenge of Facts," 33–34; "Forgotten Man," 217–19; Henry George, *Social Problems* (1884; rpt., London: Henry George Foundation of Great Britain, 1931), 185–86; *Progress and Poverty* 274, 246.

27. William Graham Sumner, "The Abolition of Poverty" (1887–89), in *Earth Hunger*, 236–37; "Power of Capital," 244–45.

28. Sumner, "Abolition of Poverty," 236; "Power of Capital," 244–45; "Challenge of Facts," 35–36.

29. John L. Thomas, *Alternative America: Henry George, Edward Bellamy, Henry Demarest Lloyd, and the Adversary Tradition* (Cambridge, Mass.: Belknap Press, 1983), 110–11; George, *Social Problems*, 185–86.

30. George, *Social Problems*, 185–86.

31. Ibid., 28, 44; George, *Progress and Poverty*, 548.

32. George, *Social Problems,* 110, 545.

33. Ibid., 112.

34. Ibid., 64.

35. Ibid., 100, 112.

36. Ibid., 63–64, 68.

37. Ibid., 66, 102–4.

38. Introduction by David Wells to Jerome Adolphe Blanqui's *History of Political Economy in Europe* (1880). Quote from Joseph Dorfman, *The Economic Mind in American Civilization,* vol. 3: *1865–1918* (New York: Viking Press, 1949), 80–84; see also Daniel Rodgers, *The Work Ethic in Industrial America* (Chicago: University of Chicago Press, 1974), 114–17.

39. Sumner, "Power of Capital," 347–48; "Challenge of Facts," 52; "Sociological Fallacies" (1884), in *Earth Hunger,* 357.

40. George, *Progress and Poverty,* 75; William Graham Sumner, "Another Chapter on Monopoly" (1887–89), in *Earth Hunger,* 293–94.

41. Sumner, "Challenge of Facts," 33–34; "Some Points in the New Social Creed" (1887–89), in *Earth Hunger,* 211; "Power of Capital," 339–40; "Some Natural Rights" (1887–89), in *Earth Hunger,* 223; "Another Chapter on Monopoly," 293–94.

42. Sumner, "Challenge of Facts," 26–27; George, *Social Problems,* 82; Sumner, "Liberty and Responsibility," 182.

43. Richard T. Ely, *The Labor Movement in America* (New York: Thomas Y. Crowell, 1886), 113–14.

44. Ibid., 3–4, 313.

45. Ibid., 136–38, 201.

46. Ellen Furlough and Carl Strikwerda, eds., *Consumers against Capitalism? Consumer Cooperation in Europe, North America, and Japan, 1840–1990* (Lanham, Md.: Rowman and Littlefield, 1999).

47. Carl J. Guarneri, *Brotherly Tomorrows* (Ithaca: Cornell University Press, 1991), 292–320; Rodgers, *Work Ethic in Industrial America,* 44–45; Ellis Cowling, *Co-operatives in America: Their Past, Present, and Future* (New York: Coward-McCann, 1938), 81; Edwin Charles Rozwenc, *Cooperatives Come to America: The History of the Protective Union Store Movement, 1845–1867* (Mount Vernon, Iowa: Hawkeye-Record Press, 1941), 117–18.

48. Rodgers, *Work Ethic in Industrial America,* 42–44; Guarneri, *Utopian Alternative,* 296, 315–18.

49. Ely, *Labor Movement in America,* 169–73, 180–81, 205–7; Richard T. Ely, intro., *History of Coöperation in the United States* (Baltimore: Johns Hopkins University, 1888), 6.

50. Ely, *Labor Movement in America,* 149–52, 166, 300–302.

51. Ibid., 317–18. Richard T. Ely, *Social Aspects of Christianity* (New York: Thomas Y. Crowell, 1889), 37.

52. Bernard Mandeville, *The Fable of the Bees* (1714), quoted in Neil McKendrick, John Brewer, and J. H. Plumb, *The Birth of a Consumer Society: The Commercialization of Eighteenth-Century England* (Bloomington: Indiana University Press, 1982), 17–18; Christopher Berry, *The Idea of Luxury: A Conceptual and Historical Investigation* (Cambridge: Cambridge University Press, 1994), 126–34; Appleby, "Ideology and Theory," 499–515; *Economic Thought and Ideology in Seventeenth-Century England,* 257.

53. Ely, *Social Aspects of Christianity,* 28, 34–37.

54. Furlough and Strikwerda, *Consumers against Capitalism.*

55. The Knights of Labor, for example, frequently sought advice from British cooperators. John Samuel Papers (microfilm ed., 1976), State Historical Society of Wisconsin.

56. E. R. Bowen, foreword, in Beatrice Webb, *The Discovery of the Consumer* (New York: Cooperative League, 1930); John Graham Brooks, intro. to Albert Sonnichsen, *Consumer's Cooperation* (New York: Macmillan, 1919), vi; Sonnichsen, *Consumers' Cooperation*, 44–45, 77–78, 175, 196; Horace M. Kallen, *The Decline and Rise of the Consumer: A Philosophy of Consumer Coöperation* (New York: D. Appleton–Century, 1936), 182.

57. Beatrice Potter, *The Co-operative Movement in Great Britain* (London: Swan Sonnenschein, 1891), 156, 167–68.

58. Ibid., 194.

59. Ibid., 193–203.

60. Ibid., 204–6, 221.

61. Daniel Horowitz, *The Morality of Spending: Attitudes toward the Consumer Society in America, 1875–1940* (Baltimore: Johns Hopkins University Press, 1985).

62. Charlotte Perkins Gilman, *Women and Economics* (Boston: Small, Maynard, 1898), 9, 116–18, 157–58.

63. Ibid., 6–7, 10–11.

64. Ibid., 9–10, 15.

65. Ibid., 117–21, 139–40.

66. Ibid., 118–19.

67. Thorstein Veblen, *The Theory of the Leisure Class* (1899; rpt., New York: Random House, 1934), 154–55.

68. Ibid., 34, 96–99, 154–55.

69. George, *Progress and Poverty*, 75, 270, 288; *Social Problems*, 68.

70. Veblen, *Theory of the Leisure Class*, 208–9, 235.

71. Ibid., 229, 243.

72. George, *Social Problems*, 75.

73. Veblen, *Theory of the Leisure Class*, 210–11, 243–44.

74. Linda K. Kerber, *Women of the Republic: Intellect and Ideology in Revolutionary America* (Chapel Hill: Institute of Early American History and Culture / University of North Carolina, 1980), 8, 36–41, 44–45; Stuart M. Blumin, *The Emergence of the Middle Class: Social Experience in the American City, 1760–1900* (Cambridge: Cambridge University Press, 1989), 185–86; Mary P. Ryan, *Cradle of the Middle Class: The Family in Oneide County, New York, 1790–1865* (Cambridge: Cambridge University Press, 1981), 198–201; Roland Marchand, *Advertising the American Dream: Making Way for Modernity, 1920–1940* (Berkeley: University of California Press, 1985), 66–72. On Veblen and the "Barbarian Status of Women," see John P. Diggins, *The Bard of Savagery: Thorstein Veblen and Modern Social Theory* (New York: Seabury Press, 1978), chap. 8.

75. Veblen, *Theory of the Leisure Class*, 43, 52.

76. Ibid., 63.

77. Ibid., 170–72.

78. Ibid., 1–2, 181–82.

79. Ibid., 83.

80. Ibid., 208–9, 30.

81. Ibid., 8–33, 39–43.

82. Kathleen G. Donohue, "What Gender Is the Consumer? The Role of Gender

Connotations in Defining the Political," *Journal of American Studies* 33, no. 1 (April 1999): 19–44.

CHAPTER 2: Legitimizing the Consumer, 1880–1900

1. On Patten, see Daniel Fox, *The Discovery of Abundance: Simon Patten and the Transformation of Social Theory* (Ithaca: Cornell University Press, 1967).

2. Simon Nelson Patten, *The Premises of Political Economy* (Philadelphia: J. B. Lippincott, 1885), 17–18.

3. Ibid., 14–18, 71.

4. Ibid., 113–14.

5. Ibid., 14–17, 47–48, 93–94.

6. Ibid., 113.

7. Ibid., 132–35.

8. Ibid., 11–12, 63–64.

9. Ibid., 11–12.

10. William Graham Sumner, *What Social Classes Owe to Each Other* (1883; rpt., Caldwell, Idaho: Caxton Printers, 1982), 113–15.

11. Patten, *Premises of Political Economy*, 113–14.

12. Ibid., 59.

13. Lawrence B. Glickman, *A Living Wage: American Workers and the Making of Consumer Society* (Ithaca: Cornell University Press, 1997).

14. Patten, *Premises of Political Economy*, 118–19.

15. Ibid.

16. Ibid., 17–18.

17. Horace M. Kallen, *The Decline and Rise of the Consumer: A Philosophy of Consumer Coöperation* (New York: D. Appleton–Century, 1936), x; Charlotte Perkins Gilman, *Women and Economics* (Boston: Small, Maynard, 1898), 157–58.

18. Edward Bellamy, *Looking Backward* (1888; rpt., New York: Random House, 1982), 142–43.

19. Ibid.

20. William Graham Sumner, "The Challenge of Facts," (1880s), in *The Challenge of Facts and Other Essays*, ed. Albert Galloway Keller (New Haven: Yale University Press, 1914), 26–27, 52; "The Power of Capital" (1899), in *Earth Hunger and Other Essays*, ed. Albert Galloway Keller (New Haven: Yale University Press, 1913), 244–45; "Another Chapter on Monopoly" (1887–89), in *Earth Hunger*, 293–94.

21. Bellamy, *Looking Backward*, 63.

22. Ibid., 78, 84.

23. Ibid., 230–31.

24. Ibid., 61–62, 68.

25. Michael Katz, *In the Shadow of the Poorhouse: A Social History of Welfare in America* (New York: Basic Books, 1986), 18–57; Robert H. Bremner, *The Discovery of Poverty in the United States* (New Brunswick, N.J.: Transaction Publishers, 1992), 48–49.

26. Bellamy, *Looking Backward*, 95–96.

27. Ibid., 94–95.

28. Ibid., 95–97.

29. Ibid., 96.

30. Ibid., 97. See also Edward Bellamy, *Equality* (New York: D. Appleton, 1897), 88–91.

31. Sumner, "Challenge of Facts," 33–34.

32. John Dewey, "A Great American Prophet" (first published in *Common Sense* [April 1934]), in *John Dewey, The Later Works, 1925–1953*, vol. 9, ed. Jo Ann Boydston (Carbondale: Southern Illinois University Press, 1986) 106.

33. Ibid., 8.

34. Ibid., 172–74.

35. Adam Smith, *An Inquiry into the Nature and Causes of the Wealth of Nations* (Chicago: University of Chicago Press, 1976), 2:179.

36. Bellamy, *Equality*, 159, 171–72.

37. Dorfman, *Economic Mind*, 82–84; Joseph A. Schumpeter, *History of Economic Analysis* (New York: Oxford University Press, 1954), 825–29, 909–20, 1054–73; Eric Roll, *A History of Economic Thought*, rev. 5th ed. (London: Faber and Faber, 1992), 336.

38. James Livingston, *Pragmatism and the Political Economy of Cultural Revolution, 1850–1940* (Chapel Hill: University of North Carolina Press, 1994), 50–52.

39. Livingston, *Pragmatism and the Political Economy of Cultural Revolution*, 49–56; Dorothy Ross, *The Origins of American Social Science* (Cambridge: Cambridge University Press, 1991), 118–20, 172–86; Nancy Cohen, *The Reconstruction of American Liberalism, 1865–1914* (Chapel Hill: University of North Carolina Press, 2002), 186–92.

40. Schumpeter, *History of Economic Analysis*, 952–63.

41. Richard T. Ely, *An Introduction to Political Economy* (New York: Chautauqua Press, 1889), 181; *Outlines of Economics* (New York: Macmillan, 1893), 121–23, 127.

42. Ely, *Outlines of Economics*, 126.

43. Smith, *Wealth of Nations*, 1:359; Jean-Baptiste Say, *A Treatise on Political Economy* (Philadelphia: Claxton, Remsen and Haffelfinger, 1880), 391, 394; John Stuart Mill, *Principles of Political Economy*, abridged ed. (1848; rpt., New York: D. Appleton, 1884), 61–62.

44. Ely, *Introduction to Political Economy*, 269.

45. Ely, *Outlines of Economics*, 221.

46. Ely, *Introduction to Political Economy*, 153–54, 159.

47. Ely, *Outlines of Economics*, 230, 236.

48. Ibid., 232–33; Richard T. Ely, *Social Aspects of Christianity* (New York: Thomas Y. Crowell, 1889), 37.

49. Richard T. Ely, *The Strength and Weakness of Socialism* (New York: Chautauqua Press, 1894), 14, 128, 178–79.

CHAPTER 3: At the Crossroads, 1899–1912

1. Simon Nelson Patten, *The New Basis of Civilization* (New York: Macmillan, 1907), 186–87; Simon Nelson Patten, *The Theory of Prosperity* (New York: Macmillan, 1902), 2–3, 167.

2. Patten, *Theory of Prosperity*, 168.

3. Thorstein Veblen, *The Theory of Business Enterprise* (New York: Charles Scribner's Sons, 1904), 37, 51–54, 177; Patten, *New Basis of Civilization*, 9, 66–67.

4. Veblen, *Theory of Business Enterprise*, 29.

5. Ibid., 29–34, 213–14.

6. Ibid., 214–17.

7. Ibid., 213–17.

8. Ibid., 229–30.

9. Ibid.

10. Ibid., 242–43, 255–58.

11. Veblen, *Theory of Business Enterprise*, 242–43, 257–58.

12. Ibid., 51, 59–60.

13. Ibid., 21, 177.

14. Ibid., 29, 157–58.

15. Ibid., 64–65, 157–58, 242–43, 256–57.

16. Veblen's wife, Ellen, would later suggest that reading *Looking Backward* was "the turning point of our lives" (qtd. in John Diggins, *The Bard of Savagery* [New York: Seabury Press, 1978], 36).

17. Simon Nelson Patten, *The Premises of Political Economy* (Philadelphia: J. B. Lippincott, 1885), 135.

18. Daniel T. Rodgers, *The Work Ethic in Industrial America, 1850–1920* (Chicago: University of Chicago Press, 1978), 120–22.

19. Patten, *Theory of Prosperity*, 60–61.

20. Ibid., 76.

21. Ibid., 74.

22. Ibid., 60–61.

23. Simon Nelson Patten, "The Political Significance of Recent Economic Theories" (1908), in *Essays in Economic Theory*, ed. Rexford Guy Tugwell (New York: Alfred A Knopf, 1924), 255; *Theory of Prosperity*, 74, 80.

24. Patten, *Theory of Prosperity*, 71–72, 74.

25. Patten, "Political Significance of Recent Economic Theories," 255.

26. Ibid., 256.

27. Patten, *Theory of Prosperity*, 62.

28. Simon N. Patten, *The Theory of Social Forces* (Philadelphia: American Academy of Political and Social Science, 1896), 75–85; *New Basis of Civilization*, 141–42, 161, 213, 215, 337–39; "Reconstruction of Economic Theory," 319, 337–39. The best treatment of the ambivalence toward consumption which characterized the thought of numerous individuals in the late nineteenth and early twentieth centuries is Daniel Horowitz, *The Morality of Spending: Attitudes toward the Consumer Society in America, 1875–1940* (Baltimore: Johns Hopkins University Press, 1985).

29. Edward Bellamy, *Looking Backward* (1888; rpt., New York: Random House, 1982), 97.

30. Edward Bellamy, *Equality* (New York: D. Appleton, 1897), 88–90.

31. Ibid., 88.

32. Bellamy, *Looking Backward*, 43, 96.

33. Patten, *Theory of Prosperity*, 19.

34. Ibid., 40.

35. Ibid., 19.

36. Ibid., 40.

37. Bellamy, *Looking Backward*, 97; *Equality*, 88.

38. Patten, *Theory of Prosperity*, 13–14, 19, 35–38.

39. Patten, *New Basis of Civilization*, 11; *Theory of Prosperity*, 36.

40. Patten, *Theory of Prosperity,* 13–14, 35–36, 38.

41. Patten, *New Basis of Civilization,* 9, 11, 47, 66–69; "Reconstruction of Economic Theory," 335.

42. Mary O. Furner, *Advocacy and Objectivity: A Crisis in the Professionalization of American Social Science, 1865–1905* (Lexington: University of Kentucky Press, 1975), chap. 7.

43. Patten, *Theory of Social Forces,* 99; "Reconstruction of Economic Theory," 280; *Theory of Prosperity,* 39–40; *New Basis of Civilization,* 9, 66–67, 115–16; "Conflict Theory of Distribution," in Tugwell, *Essays,* 238–39.

44. Patten, "Reconstruction of Economic Theory," 291–92, 322; William Graham Sumner, "The Forgotten Man" (1883), in *On Liberty, Society, and Politics: The Essential Essays of William Graham Sumner,* ed. Robert C. Bannister (Indianapolis: Liberty Fund, 1992), 208–9; Patten, *Theory of Prosperity,* 224, 233; *New Basis of Civilization,* 9.

45. Patten, "Reconstruction of Economic Theory," 322–28; "Conflict Theory of Distribution," 219–20, 238–39; *New Basis of Civilization,* 57–61, 115–16, 193; "Political Significance of Recent Economic Theories," 257; *Theory of Prosperity,* 215–33.

46. In *Theory of Prosperity* Patten listed a number of economic rights, ten of which could best be classified as consummatory rights, three as producer rights (the right to an open market, to publicity, and to cooperate), and three (the right to decision by public opinion, to homogeneity of population, and to wholesome social standards) as neither (*Theory of Prosperity,* 217–29; *Theory of Social Forces,* 99).

47. Patten, *New Basis of Civilization,* 57–58, 97, 125.

48. Patten, "Reconstruction of Economic Theory," 291–92, 324–25; *Theory of Prosperity,* 174, 233.

49. Patten, "Conflict Theory of Distribution," 219–20; *New Basis of Civilization,* 193; "Political Significance of Recent Economic Theories," 257–58.

50. Mary O. Furner, "Social Scientists and the State: Constructing the Knowledge Base for Public Policy, 1880–1920," in *Intellectuals and Public Life: Between Radicalism and Reform,* ed. Leon Fink, Stephen T. Leonard, and Donald M. Reid (Ithaca: Cornell University Press, 1996); "The Republican Tradition and the New Liberalism: Social Investigation, State Building, and Social Learning in the Gilded Age," in *The State and Social Investigation in Britain and the United States,* ed. Michael J. Lacey and Mary O. Furner (Washington, D.C.: Woodrow Wilson Center Press, 1993); "Knowing Capitalism: Public Investigation and the Labor Question in the Long Progressive Era," in *The State and Economic Knowledge: The American and British Experiences,* ed. Mary O. Furner and Barry Supple (Washington, D.C.: Woodrow Wilson International Center for Scholars, 1990); Dorothy Ross, "Socialism and American Liberalism: Academic Social Thought in the 1880s," *Perspectives in American History* 11 (1977–78): 5–79; James Kloppenberg, *Uncertain Victory: Social Democracy and Progressivism in European and American Thought, 1870–1920* (New York: Oxford University Press, 1986); Martin J. Sklar, *Corporate Reconstruction of American Capitalism, 1890–1916: The Market, the Law, and Politics* (Cambridge: Cambridge University Press, 1988); James Weinstein, *The Corporate Ideal in the Liberal State, 1900–1918* (Boston: Beacon Press, 1968).

51. Patten, *Theory of Prosperity,* 168; *New Basis of Civilization,* 61, 86–87.

52. Adam Smith, *An Inquiry into the Nature and Causes of the Wealth of Nations* (Chicago: University of Chicago Press, 1976), 2:179.

53. Patten, *New Basis of Civilization,* 86–87.

54. Alan Brinkley, *The End of Reform: New Deal Liberalism in Recession and War* (New York: Vintage Press, 1995); Alan Brinkley, "The New Deal and the Idea of the State," in *The Rise and Fall of the New Deal Order,* ed. Steve Fraser and Gary Gerstle (Princeton: Princeton University Press, 1989), 85–121.

55. Adding insult to injury, the *New Republic* had a Patten student and devoted admirer, Rexford Tugwell, write the section on Veblen. Malcolm Cowley and Bernard Smith, eds., *Books That Changed Our Minds* (New York: Doubleday, Doran, 1939), 98–99.

56. One of the few economists in the 1950s who did remember Patten was John Kenneth Galbraith (*The Affluent Society* [Boston: Houghton Mifflin, 1958], 52 n).

57. Patten, "Conflict Theory of Distribution," 220–21.

58. Michael Kazin, *The Populist Persuasion: An American History* (New York: Basic Books, 1995), 27–77.

59. Weinstein, *Corporate Ideal in the Liberal State,* 7.

60. Ibid., 252.

61. See David P. Thelen, *The New Citizenship: Origins of Progressivism in Wisconsin, 1885–1900* (Columbia: University of Missouri Press, 1972), 248–49, 270, 288, 290, 308, 311–12. See also "Patterns of Consumer Consciousness in the Progressive Movement: Robert M. La Follette, the Antitrust Persuasion, and Labor Legislation," in *The Quest for Social Justice: The Morris Fromkin Memorial Lectures, 1970–1980,* ed. Ralph M. Aderman (Madison: University of Wisconsin Press, 1983).

62. E. P. Thompson, "The Moral Economy of the English Crowd in the Eighteenth Century," *Past and Present* 50 (1971): 94–126; T. H. Breen, "'Baubles of Britain': The American and Consumer Revolutions of the Eighteenth Century," in *Of Consuming Interests: The Style of Life in the Eighteenth Century,* ed. Cary Carson, Ronald Hoffman, and Peter J. Albert (Charlottesville: University Press of Virginia, 1994).

63. Breen, "'Baubles of Britain,'" 462–82; Thompson, "Moral Economy of the English Crowd," 94–126; Florence Kelley, *Some Ethical Gains through Legislation* (New York: Macmillan, 1905), 229. Quotes from *A Report of the Record Commissioners of the City of Boston Containing the Boston Town Records, 1758 to 1769* (Boston, 1886), 227–28; Ellen D. Larned, *History of Windham County, Connecticut,* 2 vols. (1874–80; rpt., Chester, Conn.: Pequot Press, 1976), 2:116–19. Both cited in Breen, "'Baubles of Britain,'" 467–68.

64. Kelley, *Some Ethical Gains through Legislation,* 230; Florence Kelley, "Aims and Principles of the Consumers' League," *American Journal of Sociology* (November 1899): 290, 301.

65. William Graham Sumner, "The Forgotten Man" (1883), in *On Liberty, Society, and Politics: The Essential Essays of William Graham Sumner,* ed. Robert C. Bannister (Indianapolis: Liberty Fund, 1992), 208–11, 217–19; "The Power of Capital" (1899), in *Earth Hunger and Other Essays,* ed. Albert Galloway Keller (New Haven: Yale University Press, 1913), 345; "The Challenge of Facts," in *The Challenge of Facts and Other Essays,* ed. Albert Galloway Keller (New Haven: Yale University Press, 1914), 34; "Examination of a Noble Sentiment" (1887–89), in *Earth Hunger,* 213–16; Charlotte Perkins Gilman, *Women and Economics* (Boston: Small, Maynard, 1898), 118–19.

66. On Kelley, see Kathryn Kish Sklar, *Florence Kelley and the Nation's Work: The Rise of Women's Political Culture, 1830–1900* (New Haven: Yale University Press, 1995).

67. Kelley, "Aims and Principles of the Consumers' League," 289–90, 303; *Some Ethical Gains through Legislation,* 210, 227–29.

68. Kelley, "Aims and Principles of the Consumers' League," 293, 95, 300; *Some Ethical Gains through Legislation,* 212–13, 216, 230.

69. Kelley, "Aims and Principles of the Consumers' League," 290, 303.

70. Sumner, "Challenge of Facts," 34; Gilman, *Women and Economics,* 110–21.

71. For examples of Kelley's use of the term *producer,* see Kelley, "Aims and Principles of the Consumers' League," 293; and *Some Ethical Gains through Legislation,* 209–10, 212, 227–28. For examples of her use of the terms *worker, wage-earner,* or *employé,* see Kelley, *Some Ethical Gains through Legislation,* 230; and Kelley, "Aims and Principles of the Consumers' League," 295, 300, 301.

72. Sumner, "Forgotten Man," 209–10.

73. Veblen, *Theory of Business Enterprise,* 52. For examples of Veblen's use of the term *businessmen,* see Veblen, *Theory of Business Enterprise,* 29, 31–37, 51, 61–64. For examples of his use of the term *workmen,* see Veblen, *Theory of Business Enterprise,* 62–64, 211–12, 215–16, 241–42.

74. Thorstein Veblen, *The Instinct of Workmanship* (New York: Macmillan, 1914), 352.

75. On the rare occasion that Bellamy did use the term *producer,* he distinguished between capitalists and wage-working producers by referring to the latter as "original producers." For examples of Bellamy's use of the term *original producer,* see Bellamy, *Equality,* 167, 173. For examples of his use of the term *producer,* see Bellamy, *Equality,* 355; and *Looking Backward,* 171. For examples of his use of the term *worker,* see Bellamy, *Looking Backward,* 65, 95–98, 167–68; and *Equality* 56, 88, 90–91, 132–33, 162, 163, 183–84, 238–39, 359, 371. For examples of his use of the term *capitalist,* see Bellamy, *Looking Backward,* 38–39, 43; *Equality,* 7, 8, 9, 90, 98, 132–33, 159, 162–63, 165, 167, 172–74, 180–84, 238, 239, 241, 355, 359, 371.

76. Richard T. Ely, *The Labor Movement in America* (New York: Thomas Y. Crowell, 1886), 94, 180; *The Strength and Weakness of Socialism* (New York: Chautauqua Press, 1894), 126–27, 133, 135.

77. Lawrence B. Glickman, *A Living Wage: American Workers and the Making of Consumer Society* (Ithaca: Cornell University Press, 1997), 57–91.

CHAPTER 4: Politicizing the Consumer, 1909–1923

1. David Levy, *Herbert Croley and "The New Republic"* (Princeton: Princeton University Press, 1985); Charles Forcey, *The Crossroads of Liberalism: Croly, Weyl, Lippmann, and the Progressive Era, 1900–1925* (New York: Oxford University Press, 1961); Walter Steel, *Walter Lippmann and the American Century* (New York: Vintage, 1980).

2. Walter Lippmann, *Drift and Mastery* (New York: Mitchell Kennerley, 1914), 186–87; Walter Weyl, *The New Democracy* (New York: Macmillan, 1912), 75–76.

3. Lippmann, *Drift and Mastery,* 70.

4. Herbert Croly, *The Promise of American Life* (New York: Macmillan, 1909), 369–70; Weyl, *New Democracy,* 297; Lippmann, *Drift and Mastery,* 168.

5. Croly, *Promise of American Life,* 369–70.

6. Ibid., 362.

7. Weyl, *New Democracy,* 260, 279, 297; Lippmann, *Drift and Mastery,* 168.

8. Adam Smith, *An Inquiry into the Nature and Causes of the Wealth of Nations* (Chicago: University of Chicago Press, 1976), 2:179.

9. Lippmann, *Drift and Mastery,* 66–67.

10. Ibid., 68–70.

11. Ibid., 67–69.

12. Ibid., 71–73.

13. Ibid., 73, 75–76, 143–44.

14. Ibid., 78–81, 95, 143–44.

15. Ibid., 30–33, 86.

16. James Weinstein, *The Corporate Ideal in the Liberal State* (Boston: Beacon Press, 1968), 40–91.

17. Lippmann, *Drift and Mastery,* 73–75.

18. Daniel Joseph Singal, *The War Within: From Victorian to Modernist Thought in the South, 1919–1945* (Chapel Hill: University of Chapel Hill, 1982), esp. 26–33; T. J. Jackson Lears, *No Place of Grace: Antimodernism and the Transformation of American Culture: 1880–1920* (New York: Pantheon, 1981), esp. chap. 1.

19. Lippmann, *Drift and Mastery,* 115–18.

20. Ibid., 31–33.

21. Charles Forcey, *The Crossroads of Liberalism* (New York: Oxford University Press, 1961), 55, 165.

22. Ibid., 58–78; Daniel Fox, *The Discovery of Abundance: Simon N. Patten and the Transformation of Social Theory* (Ithaca: Cornell University Press, 1967), 155.

23. Weyl, *New Democracy,* 144, 146–47.

24. Thorstein Veblen, *The Theory of Business Enterprise* (New York: Charles Scribner's Sons, 1904), 229; Simon Nelson Patten, *The New Basis of Civilization* (New York: Macmillan, 1907), 11.

25. Stuart Chase considered Veblen "the greatest economist America has produced" and spent the 1920s popularizing Veblen's ideas. Robert Lynd listed several of Veblen's works as among the most influential in his intellectual development. Rexford Tugwell wrote the essay on Veblen in *Books That Changed Our Minds.* And one of the few books that F. J. Schlink ever recommended (other than his own) was *The Engineers and the Price System* by Veblen (1921; rpt., New Brunswick, N.J.: Transaction Publishers, 1983) (Stuart Chase, *Out of the Depression—And After: A Prophecy by Stuart Chase* [New York: John Day, 1931], 27; Malcolm Cowley and Bernard Smith, eds., *Books That Changed Our Minds* [New York: Doubleday, Doran, 1939], 18–19, 93; letter from F. J. Schlink to J. V. Hightower, November 22, 1933, box 738, Consumers' Research [CR] Collection, Rutgers University).

26. Daniel Bell, intro. to Veblen, *Engineers and the Price System,* 2, 13.

27. Rexford Guy Tugwell, intro. to Simon Patten, *Essays in Economic Theory,* ed. Tugwell (New York: Knopf, 1924), v; letter from Stuart Chase to Daniel Fox, March 25, 1963, quoted in Fox, *Discovery of Abundance,* 225 n. 5.

28. Forcey, *Crossroads of Liberalism,* 52–53, 70–76.

29. Lippmann's definition of *social surplus,* for example, bore little resemblance to Patten's definition but a considerable resemblance to Weyl's. Weyl had modified Patten's definition to include not merely wealth that had no cost but also that which George had called the "unearned increment." Lippmann's definition made social surplus synonymous with *unearned increment.* See Lippmann, *Drift and Mastery,* 102; Weyl, *New Democracy,* 200, 249, 297.

30. Weyl, *New Democracy,* 145–47.

31. Ibid., 192–94.

32. Ibid., 7–25, 206–7.

33. Ibid., 31–40, 43–45.

34. Richard T. Ely, *An Introduction to Political Economy* (New York: Chautauqua Press, 1889), 180–81.

35. Forcey, *Crossroads of Liberalism,* 64–70.

36. Simon Nelson Patten, "The Reconstruction of Economic Theory" (1912), in *Essays in Economic Theory,* 291–92, 324–25; *The New Basis of Civilization* (New York: Macmillan, 1907), 86; *The Theory of Prosperity* (New York: Macmillan, 1902), 168.

37. Weyl, *New Democracy,* 250.

38. Ibid., 251.

39. Ibid., 251, 292.

40. Edward Bellamy, *Equality* (New York: D. Appleton, 1897), 167, 173, 239.

41. Florence Kelley, "Aims and Principles of the Consumers' League," in *American Journal of Sociology* (November 1899): 301; *Some Ethical Gains through Legislation* (New York: Macmillan, 1905), 212, 216, 230.

42. Kelley, "Aims and Principles of the Consumers' League," 289; *Some Ethical Gains through Legislation,* 210.

43. Weyl, *New Democracy,* 200, 249, 251.

44. Ibid., 260.

45. Ibid., 73–74, 141–42, 149.

46. See also Walter Weyl, *Tired Radicals and Other Papers* (New York: B. W. Huebsch, 1921).

47. Patten, *Theory of Prosperity,* 168, 174; *New Basis of Civilization,* 86–87; "Reconstruction of Economic Theory," 291–92, 324–25.

48. Weyl, *New Democracy,* 78, 142, 146–47, 154, 161.

49. Ibid., 76, 146–47.

50. Ibid., 144–45.

51. Ibid., 145, 151–52.

52. Ibid., 76, 94, 140, 148–49, 191 n. 1.

53. Ibid., 76, 84, 140, 148–49.

54. Patten, *Theory of Prosperity,* 168; "Reconstruction of Economic Theory," 291–92, 324–25; *New Basis of Civilization,* 57–61, 86–87; "The Political Significance of Recent Economic Theories" (1908), in *Essays in Economic Theory,* 257–58.

55. Weyl, *New Democracy,* 249, 150.

56. Ibid., 189, 245.

57. Ibid., 189, 279, 297.

58. Ibid., 250–53, 320.

59. For Patten's use of *the public,* see, Patten, *Theory of Prosperity,* 217, 226; *New Basis of Civilization,* 86, 193; "Political Significance of Recent Economic Theories," 254–55; "Reconstruction of Economic Theory," 291–92, 324–25; For Weyl's use of *the people,* see Weyl, *New Democracy,* 145, 150–52, 200, 208, 249, 253, 320, 330. See also, Michael Kazin, *The Populist Persuasion* (New York: Basic Books, 1995), 27–77.

60. See, for example, William Jennings Bryan, "Cross of Gold Speech" (1896), in *A Treasury of Great American Speeches,* ed. Andrew Bauer (New York: Hawthorn Books, 1970), 149.

61. Adam Smith, *An Inquiry into the Nature and Causes of the Wealth of Nations*

(Chicago: University of Chicago Press, 1976), 2:179; Christopher Lasch, *The True and Only Heaven: Progress and Its Critics* (New York: Norton, 1991), 317–40.

62. Weyl, *New Democracy*, 251.

63. Dana Frank, *Purchasing Power: Consumer Organizing, Gender, and the Seattle Labor Movement, 1919–1929* (New York: Cambridge University Press, 1994), 49.

64. Ibid., 43.

65. Albert Sonnichsen, *Consumers' Cöoperation* (New York: Macmillan, 1919), xi, 185; James Peter Warbasse, *Co-operative Democracy* (New York: Macmillan, 1923), 30–34, 90.

66. Sonnichsen, *Consumer's Cöoperation*, 208, 210; Warbasse, *Co-operative Democracy*, 293.

67. Lawrence B. Glickman, *A Living Wage: American Workers and the Making of Consumer Society* (Ithaca: Cornell University Press, 1997), 1–6, 57–91; Lasch, *True and Only Heaven*, 329–44; "A Sketch of Political Economy, Chapter VIII. Consumption," *Journal of Union Labor*, December 25, 1884, 865, quoted in Glickman, *Living Wage*, 6.

68. Warbasse, *Co-operative Democracy*, 8, 270, 272, 362; Sonnichsen, *Consumer's Cöoperation*, 214.

69. Warbasse, *Co-operative Democracy*, 9, 11, 26–27, 271–72; Sonnichsen, *Consumer's Cöoperation*, 212, 214–15.

70. Sonnichsen, *Consumer's Cöoperation*, 214; Warbasse, *Co-operative Democracy*, 11, 315.

71. Horace M. Kallen, *The Decline and Rise of the Consumer: A Philosophy of Consumer Cöoperation* (New York: D. Appleton–Century, 1936), x, xiii, 108, 197.

72. Ibid., x, 12–14, 52–54, 105, 108, 422, 443; Kathleen Donohue, "From Cooperative Commonwealth to Cooperative Democracy: The American Cooperative Ideal, 1880–1940," in *Consumers against Capitalism: Consumer Cooperation in Europe, North America, and Japan, 1840–1990*, ed. Ellen Furlough and Carl Strikwerda (Lanham, Md.: Rowman and Littlefield, 1999), 128–30.

73. James T. Kloppenberg, *Uncertain Victory: Social Democracy and Progressivism in European and American Thought, 1870–1920* (New York: Oxford University Press, 1986), 247–98; Dorothy Ross, "Socialism and American Liberalism: Academic Social Thought in the 1880s," *Perspectives in American History* 11 (1977–78): 5–79.

74. Beatrice Potter, *The Co-operative Movement in Great Britain* (London: Swan Sonnenschein, 1891), 194; Mrs. Sidney Webb, *The Discovery of the Consumer* (New York: Co-operative League, 1930), 32.

75. Quoted from Ronald Steel, *Walter Lippmann and the American Century* (New York: Vintage, 1981), 227.

CHAPTER 5: "What's an Economic System For?" 1917–1933

1. John D. Hicks, *Republican Ascendancy: 1921–1933* (New York: Harper and Row, 1960); William J. Barber, *From New Era to New Deal: Herbert Hoover, the Economists, and American Economic Policy, 1921–1933* (Cambridge: Cambridge University Press, 1985); Eugene M. Tobin, *Organize or Perish: America's Independent Progressives, 1913–1933* (New York: Greenwood Press, 1986).

2. Casey Nelson Blake, *Beloved Community: The Cultural Criticism of Randolph Bourne, Van Wyck Brooks, Waldo Frank, and Lewis Mumford* (Chapel Hill: University of

North Carolina Press, 1990), esp. chap. 8; Daniel Horowitz, *Morality of Spending: Attitudes toward the Consumer Society in America, 1875–1940* (Baltimore: Johns Hopkins University Press, 1985), 134–35.

3. Gary Gerstle, "The Protean Character of American Liberalism," *American Historical Review* 99, no. 4 (October 1994): 1043–73.

4. Roderick Nash, *The Nervous Generation: American Thought, 1917–1930* (Chicago: Rand McNally, 1970), 55–67; Ronald Steel, *Walter Lippmann and the American Century* (Boston: Little, Brown, 1980), 181–83.

5. Guy Alchon, *The Invisible Hand of Planning: Capitalism, Social Science, and the State in the 1920s* (Princeton: Princeton University Press, 1985), 21–32; Ronald Schaffer, *America in the Great War: The Rise of the War Welfare Class* (New York: Oxford University Press, 1991), 31–46.

6. Hugh S. Johnson, *The Blue Eagle, from Egg to Earth* (Garden City, N.Y.: Doubleday, Doran, 1935), 172–73.

7. Stuart Chase, *The Tragedy of Waste* (New York: Macmillan, 1925), 10; George Soule, *A Planned Society* (New York: Macmillan, 1932), 186–87; Robert S. Lynd, "The Consumer Becomes a Problem," *Annals of the American Academy of Political and Social Sciences* (May 1934): 4.

8. Thorstein Veblen, *The Engineers and the Price System* (1921; rpt., New Brunswick, N.J.: Transaction Publishers, 1990), 38–42.

9. Ibid., 83.

10. Ibid., 119–20.

11. Ibid., 83.

12. Thorstein Veblen, *The Theory of Business Enterprise* (New York: Charles Scribner's Sons, 1904), 213–16, 255.

13. Ibid., 65.

14. Veblen, *Engineers and the Price System*, 78, 112.

15. Veblen, *Absentee Ownership*, 40–49, 69–100.

16. Ibid., 99.

17. Veblen, *Engineers and the Price System*, 72–74, 89, 98–99; *Absentee Ownership*, 106, 292–93.

18. Edward Bellamy, *Looking Backward* (1888; rpt., New York: Random House, 1982), 167–68; Walter Lippmann, *Drift and Mastery* (New York: Mitchell Kennerley, 1914), 70, 124–25; Walter E. Weyl, *The New Democracy* (New York: Macmillan, 1914), 76, 94.

19. Veblen, *Absentee Ownership*, 99.

20. Ibid., 78, 99.

21. Veblen, *Absentee Ownership*, 57; Lippmann, *Drift and Mastery*, 70.

22. Veblen, *Absentee Ownership*, 78.

23. Alan Brinkley, "The New Deal and the Idea of the State," in *The Rise and Fall of the New Deal Order* (Princeton: Princeton University Press, 1989), 112.

24. Veblen, *Absentee Ownership*, 306.

25. Bellamy, *Looking Backward*, 230–31.

26. Veblen, *Engineers and the Price System*, 114; *Absentee Ownership*, 306.

27. Walter E. Weyl, *The New Democracy* (New York: Macmillan, 1914), 330–31.

28. Lippmann, *Drift and Mastery*, 68–69; Bellamy, *Looking Backward*, 230–31; *Equality* (New York: D. Appleton, 1897), 59–61; Weyl, *New Democracy*, 330–31.

29. Weyl, *New Democracy,* 330.

30. Chase, *Tragedy of Waste,* 16; Stuart Chase, *Prosperity: Fact or Myth* (New York: Charles Boni Paper Books, 1929), 186–87. See also Robert Westbrook, "Tribune of the Technostructure: The Popular Economics of Stuart Chase," *American Quarterly* 32 (fall 1980): 387–408.

31. Rexford Guy Tugwell, *Industry's Coming of Age* (New York: Harcourt, Brace, 1927), 184–85.

32. Daniel Horowitz, *The Morality of Spending: Attitudes toward the Consumer Society in America, 1875–1940* (Baltimore: Johns Hopkins University Press, 1985), 111–14.

33. Westbrook, "Tribune of the Technostructure," 391.

34. Richard Wightman Fox, "Epitaph for Middletown: Robert S. Lynd and the Analysis of Consumer Culture," in *The Culture of Consumption: Critical Essays in American History, 1880–1980,* ed. Richard Wightman Fox and T. J. Jackson Lears (New York: Pantheon Books, 1983), 109.

35. Letter from Stuart Chase to Daniel Fox, March 25, 1963; and letter from Henry Wallace to Daniel Fox, March 6, 1963, both cited in Daniel Fox, *The Discovery of Abundance: Simon Patten and the Transformation of Social Theory* (Ithaca: Cornell University Press, 1967), 225 n. 5.

36. Simon Nelson Patten, *The Theory of Prosperity* (New York: Macmillan, 1902), 60–87; "The Reconstruction of Economic Theory" (1912), in *Essays in Economic Theory,* ed. Rexford Guy Tugwell (New York: Knopf, 1924), 291–92; *The New Basis of Civilization* (New York: Macmillan, 1907), 86–87.

37. Rexford Guy Tugwell, *The Economic Basis of Public Interest* (Menasha, Wis: George Banta, 1922), 16–19, 23–24; Patten, *Theory of Prosperity,* 71–72.

38. Tugwell, *Economic Basis of Public Interest,* 3, 29, 36–37.

39. Ibid., 18–19, 23.

40. Ibid., 20–21.

41. Ibid., 17, 21, 36–37, 80, 96.

42. Ibid., 16–17, 23–24.

43. Robert and Helen Merrell Lynd, *Middletown: A Study in Modern American Culture* (New York: Harcourt, Brace and World, 1929), 73, 81.

44. Blake, *Beloved Community,* 50–51, 210, 272–73; Lynd, Middletown, 82 n. 18, 87.

45. Stuart Chase, *The Tragedy of Waste,* 126–46, 149, 175–78, 205–7, 265–68.

46. Ibid., 30.

47. Lynd, *Middletown,* 28–29, 255–56.

48. Chase, *Tragedy of Waste,* 44–45.

49. Ibid., 44, 120–21.

50. Stuart Chase, *A New Deal* (New York: Macmillan, 1933), 188–89; Stuart Chase, *Prosperity: Fact or Myth* (New York: Macmillan, 1931), 17, 25–26.

51. Chase, *Nemesis of American Business,* 184–88.

52. Veblen, *Absentee Ownership,* 98.

53. For examples of Chase's attempt to modify capitalism through economic planning, see Stuart Chase and F. J. Schlink, *Your Money's Worth: A Study in the Waste of the Consumer's Dollar* (New York: Macmillan, 1927), 43; Stuart Chase, *Out of the Depression— And After: A Prophecy by Stuart Chase* (New York: John Day, 1931), 9, 23–24; *Nemesis of American Business,* 97; *New Deal,* 154–55, 241–48. For examples of Chase's conviction

that capitalism would have to be replaced, see Chase, *Prosperity: Fact or Myth*, 187; "Mr. Chase Replies," *New Republic*, February 10, 1932, 349; "The Consumer's Tomorrow," *Scribner's Magazine* (December 1933): 333–38; "The Age of Distribution," *Nation*, July 25, 1934, esp. 94–95; Stuart Chase, *The Economy of Abundance* (1934; rpt., Port Washington, N.Y.: Kennikat Press, 1971), 138–39, 223, 313.

54. Tugwell, *Economic Basis of Public Interest*, 36–37.

55. The terms *acquisitive society* and *functional society* were not original with Chase. He took them from R. H. Tawney (Chase, *Tragedy of Waste*, 23).

56. See, for example, Stuart Chase, "The Age of Distribution," 94; *Economy of Abundance*, 313.

57. Robert S. Lynd, "Democracy's Third Estate: The Consumer," *Political Science Quarterly* 51 (December 1936): 497–98.

58. Letter from F. J. Schlink to Neil Carothers, June 14, 1933, box 690; letter from Samuel H. Rosen to *Consumers Digest*, August 24, 1938, box 734, Consumers Research Collection, Rutgers University.

59. *Consumers' Research General Bulletin* (September 1932): 2.

60. Chase, *Tragedy of Waste*, 271; Frederick J. Schlink, "Safeguarding the Consumer's Interest—An Essential Element in National Recovery," *Annals of the American Academy of Political and Social Sciences* (March 1934): 117.

61. Chase, *Nemesis of American Business*, 161; F. J. Schlink, "Bear Oil," *New Republic*, July 31, 1929, 279.

62. Chase and Schlink, *Your Money's Worth*, 9–11, 26, 260.

63. Ibid., 66, 256.

64. Tugwell, *Economic Basis of Public Interest*, 36–37.

65. Chase and Schlink, *Your Money's Worth*, 43.

66. Ibid.

67. George Soule, "Hard-Boiled Radicalism," *New Republic*, January 21, 1931; Chase, "Mr. Chase Replies."

68. Soule, "Hard-Boiled Radicalism," 263; Chase, "Mr. Chase Replies," 349.

69. Edward A. Purcell Jr., *The Crisis of Democratic Theory: Scientific Naturalism and the Problem of Value* (Lexington: University of Kentucky Press, 1973), 95–114; Nash, *Nervous Generation*, 55–68.

70. Stuart Chase, "If I Were Dictator," *Nation*, November 18, 1931, 536; Sonnichsen, *Consumer's Coöperation*, 215.

71. Lynd and Lynd, *Middletown*, 502; Chase, "Mr. Chase Replies"; *New Deal*, 218–19.

72. Weyl, *New Democracy*, 251; Lippmann, *Drift and Mastery*, 73.

73. Roland Marchand, *Advertising the American Dream* (Berkeley: University of California Press, 1985).

74. See, for example, Neil Harris, "The Drama of Consumer Desire," in *Cultural Excursions: Marketing Appetites and Cultural Tastes in Modern America* (Chicago: University of Chicago Press, 1990); Martha L. Olney, *Buy Now, Pay Later: Advertising, Credit, and Consumer Durables in the 1920s* (Chapel Hill: University of North Carolina Press, 1991).

75. Schlink and Chase, *Your Money's Worth*, 264.

76. "Report of Consumers' Research: Fiscal Year Ending October 1, 1931"; "Report of Consumers' Research: Fiscal Year Ending October 1, 1932"; "Report of Consumers'

Research: Fiscal Year Ending October 1, 1934"; "List of Sponsors, 1932," all in box 743, CR Collection; Charles F. McGovern, "Sold American: Inventing the Consumer, 1890–1940" (Ph.D. diss., Harvard University, 1993).

77. Letter from Kitty Pollack to Mary Catherine Phillips, March 24, 1932, courtesy of F. J. Schlink; "The Buyers' Baedeker," *New Republic,* November 26, 1930.

78. Letter from George Soule to F. J. Schlink, September 21, 1933, box 743, CR Collection.

79. Letter from F. J. Schlink to George Soule, September 28, 1933, box 739, CR Collection; Schlink, "Safeguarding the Consumer's Interests"; "Producers Organize—Consumers Must," *Consumers' Research General Bulletin* (September 1932): 2.

80. Kathleen G. Donohue, "Conceptualizing the Good Society: The Idea of the Consumer in Modern American Political Thought" (Ph.D. diss., University of Virginia, 1995), chaps. 4–5.

81. J. B. Matthews, *Odyssey of a Fellow Traveler* (New York: Mount Vernon, 1938); Matthew Josephson and Russell Maloney, "Profiles: The Testimony of a Sinner," *New Yorker,* April 22, 1944.

82. J. B. Matthews and R. E. Shallcross, *Partners in Plunder: The Cost of Business Dictatorship* (New York: Covici, Friede, 1935), 4, 22, 30, 77, 145.

83. Ibid., 4–5, 22.

84. Schlink began denouncing liberals after he became involved with Matthews. See, for example, the note written by F. J. Schlink on the Discussion Group invitation October 12, 1933, box 736; letter from F. J. Schlink to Robert S. Lynd, July 18, 1934, box 729; letter from F. J. Schlink to Robert S. Lynd, October 17, 1934, box 743; F. J. Schlink, "How the Consumer Was Betrayed: The Acid Test of the New Deal Liberals," unabridged draft of article that appeared in *Common Sense* (September 1934), box 727, all in the CR Collection.

85. Report of the Investigating Committee on the Strike at the Plant of Consumers' Research, Washington, N.J. (the Niebuhr-Baldwin Report), issued November 16, 1935; telegram from the *New Republic* to F. J. Schlink, September 5, 1935, box 727; letter from George Soule to F. J. Schlink, January 22, 1936, box 727; letter from Robert A. Brady to Dewey Palmer, from CR photocopy dated December 5, 1935, box 739; letter from Mildred Edie to F. J. Schlink, August 31, 1935, box 739, all in CR Collection; *New Republic,* October 9, 1935, 230; James Rorty, "What's Wrong with Consumers' Research?" October 1935, box 739. On the strike, see Lawrence B. Glickman, "The Strike in the Temple of Consumption: Consumer Activism and Twentieth-Century American Political Culture," *Journal of American History* (June 2001): 99–128.

86. Donohue, "Conceptualizing the Good Society," chap. 5.

87. Lizabeth Cohen, *Making a New Deal: Industrial Workers in Chicago, 1919–1939* (Cambridge: Cambridge University Press, 1990); Dana Frank, *Purchasing Power: Consumer Organizing, Gender, and the Seattle Labor Movement, 1919–1929* (Cambridge: Cambridge University Press, 1994); Lawrence B. Glickman, *A Living Wage: American Workers and the Making of Consumer Society* (Ithaca: Cornell University Press, 1997).

88. Chase, "Age of Distribution," 94–95.

89. Lynd and Lynd, *Middletown,* 22.

90. Dana Frank, *Purchasing Power: Consumer Organizing, Gender, and the Seattle Labor Movement, 1919–1929* (Cambridge: Cambridge University Press, 1994).

91. George Soule, "What Planning Might Do," *New Republic,* March 11, 1931, 89.

92. George Soule, "The Challenge to the Engineers," *New Republic,* January 31, 1934, 327.

93. Rexford Guy Tugwell, *The Industrial Discipline and the Governmental Arts* (New York: Columbia University Press, 1933), 68; *Industry's Coming of Age,* 254.

94. Soule, "National Planning," 64; Chase, "Mr. Chase Replies," 349; *New Deal,* 178–79.

95. The account of the LIPA is based on R. Alan Lawson, *The Failure of Independent Liberalism: 1930–1941* (New York: G. P. Putnam's Sons, 1971), 39–43; Donald L. Miller, *The New American Radicalism: Alfred M. Bingham and Non-Marxian Insurgency in the New Deal Era* (Port Washington, N.Y.: Kennikat Press, 1979), 68–74; Eugene M. Tobin, *Organize or Perish: America's Independent Progressives, 1913–1933* (New York: Greenwood Press, 1986), 196–244.

96. John Dewey, "Who Might Make a New Party?" *New Republic,* April 1, 1931, 178.

97. Paul Howard Douglas, *The Coming of a New Party* (New York: McGraw-Hill, 1932), 15, 18–19.

98. Ibid., 115, 116, 121, 139, 172, 176–77, 192.

99. Ibid., 208.

100. Ibid., 139.

101. John Dewey, "The Need for a New Party II: The Breakdown of the Old Order," *New Republic,* March 25, 1931, 150–51; "The Need for a New Party I: The Present Crisis," *New Republic,* March 18, 1931, 116.

102. John Dewey, "Who Might Make a New Party?" 179; "Policies for a New Party?" *New Republic,* April 8, 1931, 205.

103. Dewey, "Who Might Make a New Party?" 179.

104. Ibid.

105. Ibid.

106. John Dewey, "What Do Liberals Want?" in *John Dewey: The Later Works, 1925–1953,* vol. 5: *1929–1930,* ed. Jo Ann Boydston (Carbondale: Southern Illinois University Press, 1984), 347–48.

107. Chase, *New Deal,* 252.

108. Robert Westbrook, *John Dewey and American Democracy* (Ithaca: Cornell University Press, 1991); John Dewey, "Policies for a New Party?" *New Republic,* April 8, 1931, 203.

CHAPTER 6: The Demise of Economic Planning, 1933–1940

1. "The Industrial Recovery Bill," *New Republic,* May 31, 1933, 58; Ellis Hawley, *The New Deal and the Problem of Monopoly: A Study in Economic Ambivalence* (Princeton: Princeton University Press, 1966), 35–46; Colin Gordon, *New Deals: Business, Labor, and Politics in America, 1920–1935* (Cambridge: Cambridge University Press, 1994), 35–40; Hugh Johnson, *The Blue Eagle, from Egg to Earth* (Garden City, N.Y.: Doubleday, Doran, 1935), 153, 162.

2. Adolf A. Berle Jr. and Gardiner C. Means, *The Modern Corporation and Private Property* (New York: Macmillan, 1933), 32.

3. John Kennedy Ohl, *Hugh Johnson and the New Deal* (Dekalb: Northern Illinois University Press, 1985), 36–84.

4. Johnson, *Blue Eagle,* 357.

5. Ibid., 168.

6. Ibid., 137, 188, 190–91.

7. Ibid., 161–62.

8. Ibid., 161–62, 178, 188.

9. Ibid., 137, 169, 190.

10. Stuart Chase, *The Economy of Abundance* (1934; rpt., Port Washington, N.Y.: Kennikat Press, 1971), 138; George Soule, *The Coming American Revolution* (New York: Macmillan, 1934), 253; "Roosevelt Confronts Capitalism," *New Republic,* October 18, 1933, 270.

11. Rexford Guy Tugwell, "Design for Government" (address delivered at the Eighth Annual Meeting of the Federation of Bar Associations for Western New York, June 24, 1933); "The Prospect for the Future" (address delivered at the Chicago Forum, October 29, 1933); "America Takes Hold of Its Destiny" (from an article, somewhat modified, in *Today,* April 28, 1934), all reprinted in Rexford Guy Tugwell, *The Battle for Democracy* (New York: Columbia University Press, 1935), 8, 58, 262; Gardiner C. Means, "The Consumer and the New Deal," *Annals of the American Academy of Political and Social Sciences* (May 1934): 13; Stuart Chase, "The Consumer's Tomorrow," *Scribner's Magazine* (December 1933): 333–34, 336.

12. Stuart Chase, *Prosperity: Fact or Myth* (New York: Charles Boni Paper Books, 1929), 78–79.

13. Thorstein Veblen, *The Engineers and the Price System* (1921; rpt., New Brunswick, N.J.: Transaction Publishers, 1990), 38–42; Stuart Chase, "On the Paradox of Plenty," *New Republic,* January 18, 1933, 258; George Soule, *The Future of Liberty* (New York: Macmillan, 1936), 149; Robert S. Lynd, "The Consumer Becomes a 'Problem,'" *Annals of the American Academy of Political and Social Sciences* (May 1934): 1; Robert S. Lynd, *Knowledge for What? The Place of Social Science in American Culture* (Princeton: Princeton University Press, 1939), 220.

14. Stuart Chase, "Our Capacity to Produce," *Harper's Monthly Magazine* (February 1935): 343; Stuart Chase, "The Economy of Abundance," in *Challenge to the New Deal,* ed. Alfred M. Bingham and Selden Rodman (New York: Falcon Press, 1934), 139; *A New Deal* (New York: Macmillan, 1933), 1–2; George Soule, *A Planned Society* (New York: Macmillan, 1932), 66, 208.

15. Stuart Chase, "This Age of Plenty," *Harper's Monthly Magazine* (March 1934): 379; "Consumer's Tomorrow," 335; *Economy of Abundance,* 275; "This Age of Plenty," 379; Robert S. Lynd, "Democracy's Third Estate: The Consumer," *Political Science Quarterly* 51 (December 1936): 504–13; Lynd, "Consumer Becomes a 'Problem'" 6; *Knowledge for What?* 220–23.

16. Chase, *New Deal,* 184–85; Soule, *Coming American Revolution,* 298; Lynd, "Democracy's Third Estate," 506–7.

17. Chase, *New Deal,* 22–23; "What Is Public Business?" *Current History* (April 1935): 10; *The Economy of Abundance* (1934; rpt., Port Washington, N.Y.: Kennikat Press, 1971), 138.

18. George Soule, "Planning—For Profit," in *Challenge to the New Deal,* 61, 64; *Planned Society,* 279–80; *Future of Liberty,* 149–50, 163, 165; *Coming American Revolution,* 261; Lynd, "Democracy's Third Estate," 508.

19. Soule, *Planned Society,* 254, 277–80; *Future of Liberty,* 163, 165; *Coming American*

Revolution, 280–81; Lynd, *Knowledge for What?* 220; Stuart Chase, "The Age of Distribution," *Nation,* July 25, 1934, 94–95; *New Deal,* 241.

20. Soule, *Coming American Revolution,* 283, 299, 302.

21. Soule, *Future of Liberty,* 149–50, 165; Chase, *Economy of Abundance,* 27.

22. Rexford Guy Tugwell, "Relief and Reconstruction" (address delivered at the National Conference of Social Work, Kansas City, May 21, 1934); "Freedom and Business" (written at some point between June and October 1933); "Prospect for the Future"; "The Economics of the Recovery Program" (address delivered at the Institute of Arts and Sciences, Columbia University, November 16, 1933); "The Return to Democracy" (address delivered before the American Society of Newspaper Editors, April 21, 1934); "America Takes Hold of Its Destiny," all reprinted in Tugwell, *Battle for Democracy,* 46, 58, 88–90, 197–98, 263–64, 314; Means, "Consumer and the New Deal," 10–14; Rexford Guy Tugwell, *The Industrial Discipline and the Governmental Arts* (New York: Columbia University Press, 1933), 20–21; "The Progressive Task Today and Tomorrow," *Vital Speeches of the Day* 2 (December 2, 1935): 131–34; Caroline F. Ware and Gardiner C. Means, *The Modern Economy in Action* (New York: Harcourt, Brace, 1936), 35–36, 53–55, 133.

23. Tugwell, *Industrial Discipline,* 198–99.

24. Tugwell, "Design for Government," 14.

25. Means, "Consumer and the New Deal," 7.

26. Ibid., 7, 10.

27. Means, "Consumer and the New Deal," 8, 10, 13–14; Ware and Means, *Modern Economy in Action,* 25–31, 133–41.

28. Means, "Consumer and the New Deal," 13–14; Ware and Means, *Modern Economy in Action,* 53.

29. Means, "Consumer and the New Deal," 13.

30. Tugwell, "Return to Democracy," 197–98; "Freedom and Business," 45–46; *Industrial Discipline,* 187–88.

31. Tugwell, "America Takes Hold of Its Destiny," 264–66; "Progressive Task Today and Tomorrow," 134.

32. William Trufant Foster, "Can Capitalism Be Trusted?" *Christian Century,* October 26, 1932, 1301–2; "Economic Consequences of the New Deal," *Atlantic Monthly* 152 (December 1933): 755; Edward A. Filene, "The New Relations between Business and Government," *Annals of the American Academy of Political and Social Science* 172 (March 1934): 42.

33. Filene, "New Relations between Business and Government," 37; "The Consumer in Modern Society," radio address, November 15, 1934, Harry Laidler Collection, box 14, Tamiment Library, New York University, New York.

34. Quoted in Arthur M. Schlesinger, *The Coming of the New Deal* (Boston: Houghton Mifflin, 1958), 494.

35. William Trufant Foster and Waddill Catchings, *Business without a Buyer,* 2d ed. (Boston: Houghton Mifflin, 1928), 20–21, 26–27, 86, 176–80; "Planning in a Free Country: Managed Money and Unmanaged Men," *Annals of the American Academy of Political and Social Science* 162 (July 1932): 51, 53; "Economic Consequences of the New Deal," 754–55.

36. Filene, "New Relations between Business and Government," 43; Foster and Catchings, *Business without a Buyer,* 27.

37. Means, "Consumer and the New Deal," 14.

38. Ibid.; Foster and Catchings, *Business without a Buyer*, 23; Foster, "Economic Consequences of the New Deal," 752.

39. Foster and Catchings, *Business without a Buyer*, 19; Filene, "Consumer in Modern Society"; Foster, "Can Capitalism Be Trusted?" 1302.

40. Johnson, *Blue Eagle*, 161.

41. Foster and Catchings, *Business without a Buyer*, 35; Foster, "Can Capitalism Be Trusted?" 1302–3.

42. Filene, "Consumer in Modern Society," 2; "New Relations between Business and Government," 43.

43. Foster and Catchings, *Business without a Buyer*, 26–27.

44. Foster, "Economic Consequences of the New Deal," 751; "Can Capitalism Be Trusted?" 1303; Filene, "New Relations between Business and Government," 43–44.

45. Filene, "New Relations between Business and Government," 42, 44; Foster, "Can Capitalism Be Trusted?" 1303.

46. Foster, "Can Capitalism Be Trusted?" 1303; Filene, "New Relations between Business and Government," 43.

47. Tugwell, "America Takes Hold of Its Destiny," 256, 264, 266; Soule, *Future of Liberty*, 152; Chase, *New Deal*, 21–22; *Economy of Abundance*, 308–10.

48. Foster, "Can Capitalism Be Trusted?" 1302; "Planning in a Free Country," 51–52; Filene, "New Relations between Business and Government," 42.

49. Filene, "New Relations between Business and Government," 42.

50. Foster, "Economic Consequences of the New Deal," 755; Filene, "New Relations between Business and Government," 42–43; George Soule, *The Coming American Revolution* (New York: Macmillan, 1934), 302.

51. Stuart Chase, *The Nemesis of American Business* (New York: Macmillan, 1931), 94; Soule, *Planned Society*, 56; Foster and Catchings, *Business without a Buyer*, 42–44, 48; Foster, "Planning in a Free Country," 51; "Economic Consequences of the New Deal," 748, 750.

52. Foster, "Economic Consequences of the New Deal," 750; Chase, "Consumer's Tomorrow," 338.

53. Chase referred to Keynes several times in *A New Deal*. Indeed, according to the index, Keynes was mentioned on seventeen pages, Veblen only on one. But for the rest of the decade Chase largely ignored Keynesian ideas. So, too, did Soule, Lynd, Tugwell, and Means. Indexes in their major works include almost no references to Keynes.

54. Lynd, *Knowledge for What?* 144, 220; Chase, *New Deal*, 188–89; *Idle Money, Idle Men* (New York: Harcourt, Brace, 1940).

55. Soule, *Coming American Revolution*, 276; *An Economic Constitution for Democracy* (New Haven: Yale University Press, 1939), 79, 90, 94. In neither work did Soule mention Keynes. George Soule, "After the New Deal: (II) The Legacy of the New Deal," *New Republic*, May 24, 1939, 70; "After the New Deal: (III) Suggestions for the Next Step," *New Republic*, June 7, 1939, 122–25.

56. Tugwell, "Economics of the Recovery Program," 89–92; "Freedom and Business," 44.

57. Tugwell, "Economics of the Recovery Program," 87; "Prospect for the Future," 58; "Consumers and the New Deal," 177–78.

58. Chase, "On the Paradox of Plenty," 258.

59. Johnson, *Blue Eagle,* 180.

60. Ibid., 180, 361.

61. Persia Campbell, *Consumer Representation in the New Deal* (New York: AMS Press, 1940), 40; Schlesinger, *Coming of the New Deal,* 128–30.

62. Means, "Consumer and the New Deal," 14.

63. Lynd, "Consumer Becomes a 'Problem,'" 3–4.

64. Ibid.; Lynd, "The Consumers' Advisory Board in the N.R.A.," *Publishers' Weekly,* April 28, 1934, 1607.

65. Robert S. Lynd, "The People as Consumers," in *Recent Social Trends in the United States: Report of the President's Research Committee on Social Trends* (New York: McGraw-Hill, 1934), 885; "Consumers' Advisory Board in the N.R.A.," 1607–8; "A New Deal for the Consumer," *New Republic,* January 3, 1934, 221; "Consumer Becomes a 'Problem,'" 5–6.

66. Walton H. Hamilton, "The Ancient Maxim Caveat Emptor" *Yale Law Journal* 40, no. 8 (June 1931); Paul H. Douglas, *Real Wages in the United States, 1890–1926* (1930; rpt., New York: A. M. Kelley, 1966).

67. Johnson, *Blue Eagle,* 282.

68. Ibid., 189, 217.

69. Ibid., 263–64.

70. Ibid.

71. Letter from F. J. Schlink to Charles Wyand, June 27, 1934, box 734, Consumers' Research (CR) Collection, Rutgers University; radio interview with F. J. Schlink, August 23, 1933, box 743, CR Collection; F. J. Schlink, "Safeguarding the Consumer's Interests: An Essential Element in National Recovery," *Annals of the American Academy of Political and Social Science, Philadelphia* (March 1934): 122.

72. Letter from Schlink to Wyand, September 12, 1934.

73. Schlink, "Safeguarding the Consumer's Interest," 115; "How the Consumer Was Betrayed: The Acid Test of the New Deal Liberals" (unedited version of an article that appeared in *Common Sense* [September 1934]); radio interview with F. J. Schlink, August 23, 1933, box 743, CR Collection.

74. Lynd, "Consumer Becomes a 'Problem,'" 3–4.

75. Letter from F. J. Schlink to Robert Lynd, January 16, 1934; letter from Robert Lynd to F. J. Schlink, April 9, 1934, both in box 738, CR Collection; "The New Deal and the Consumer" (radio debate between John T. Flynn and Robert S. Lynd, December 23, 1933, over NBC, box 743, CR Collection).

76. Chase, "Consumer's Tomorrow," 333–34, 336–37.

77. Ibid., 337–38.

78. Ellen Furlough and Carl Strikwerda, eds., *Consumers against Capitalism: Consumer Cooperation in Europe, North America, and Japan, 1840–1990* (Lanham, Md.: Rowman and Littlefield, 1999), 18; Lawrence B. Glickman, *A Living Wage: American Workers and the Making of Consumer Society* (Ithaca: Cornell University Press, 1997); Dana Frank, *Purchasing Power: Consumer Organizing, Gender, and the Seattle Labor Movement, 1919–1929* (New York: Cambridge University Press, 1994); Lizabeth Cohen, *Making a New Deal: Industrial Workers in Chicago, 1919–1939* (Cambridge: Cambridge University Press, 1990).

79. John Dewey, "Who Might Make a New Party?" *New Republic,* April 1, 1931, 178–79.

80. Ibid., 179; John Dewey, "The Need for a New Party I: The Present Crisis," *New Republic,* March 18, 1931, 116; "The Need for a New Party II: The Breakdown of the Old Order," *New Republic,* March 25, 1931, 150; "Policies for a New Party?" *New Republic,* April 8, 1931, 205.

81. The consumerist definition of *class* was a variation on Weber's idea of status. Max Weber, "Class, Status, Party," *From Max Weber: Essays in Sociology,* ed. H. H. Gertz and C. Wright Mills (New York: Oxford University Press, 1946), 180–95.

82. Dewey, "Who Might Make a New Party?" 179.

83. John Dewey, "No Half-Way House for America," in *John Dewey, Later Works, 1925–1953,* vol. 9, ed. Jo Ann Boydston (Carbondale: Southern Illinois University Press, 1986), 289–90 (first published in *People's Lobby Bulletin* [November 1934]: 1); Robert Westbrook, *John Dewey and American Democracy* (Ithaca: Cornell University Press, 1991), 429–43.

84. Dewey, "Need for a New Party I," 116; "Need for a New Party II," 150; "Who Might Make a New Party?" 179; "Wild Inflation Would Paralyze Nation," in *Later Works,* 9:267–68, 273–74 (first published in *People's Lobby Bulletin* [September 1933]: 1–2); "Inflationary Measures Injure the Masses," in *Later Works,* 9:265–66 (first published in *People's Lobby Bulletin* [July 1933]: 1–2); "President's Policies Help Property Owners Chiefly," in *Later Works,* 9:277–79 (first published in *People's Lobby Bulletin* [January 1934]: 1–2); "American Ideals (I) The Theory of Liberty vs. the Fact of Regimentation," in *Later Works,* 9:81 (first published in *Common Sense* [December 1934]: 10–11); "Unemployed and Underpaid Consumers Should Not Pay Billion Dollar Subsidy to Speculators," in *Later Works,* 9:251 (first published in *People's Lobby Bulletin* [January 1933]: 1–2).

85. Dewey, "Need for a New Party I," 116; "Need for a New Party II," 150; "Wild Inflation Would Paralyze Nation," 267–68, 273–74; "Inflationary Measures Injure the Masses," 265–66; "President's Policies Help Property Owners Chiefly," 277–79; "What Keeps Funds Away from Purchasers," *Later Works,* 9:83 (first published in *Congressional Record,* from a speech to the Joint Committee on Unemployment, April 21, 1934).

86. Letter from F. J. Schlink to Neil Carothers, June 14, 1933, box 690, CR Collection; J. B. Matthews and R. E. Shallcross, *Partners in Plunder: The Cost of Business Dictatorship* (New York: Covici, Friede, 1935), 4–6.

87. Letter from F. J. Schlink to E. G. Darbo. May 12, 1936, box 734, CR Collection. Schlink was referring to head of the Communist Party Earl Browder, editor of the *Daily Worker* Clarence Hathaway, left liberal newspaper columnist Heywood Broun, and Socialist Party leader Norman Thomas.

88. "Off the Editor's Chest," *Consumers' Research Bulletin* (June 1937): 1; (December 1937): 1; (December 1938): 1.

89. Means, "Consumer and the New Deal," 16.

90. Rexford G. Tugwell, "Consumers and the New Deal" (address delivered before the Consumers' League of Ohio, May 11, 1934), in *Battle for Democracy,* 268, 285.

91. Campbell, *Consumer Representation in the New Deal,* 64–65; National Recovery Administration Release No. 1759, November 1933, box 743, CR Collection; Paul H. Douglas, "The Role of the Consumer in the New Deal," *Annals of the American Academy of Political and Social Science* (March 1934): 105.

92. Campbell, *Consumer Representation in the New Deal,* 57–60: "The Consumer and

the N.R.A.," *New Republic,* August 30, 1933, 59; letter from F. J. Schlink to Robert Lynd, January 16, 1934; Johnson, *Blue Eagle,* 188.

93. *Philadelphia Record,* January 9, 1934, CR Collection.

94. Schlesinger, *Coming of the New Deal,* 115.

95. Hawley, *New Deal and the Problem of Monopoly,* 149–86.

96. Soule, *Coming American Revolution,* 261, 294; *Planned Society,* 68–69; *Economic Constitution for Democracy,* 101.

97. Foster and Catchings, *Business without a Buyer,* 6–7.

CHAPTER 7: The Common Ground of Abundance, 1933–1940

1. Memorandum from Henry Wallace to George Peek, June 10, 1933, Donald Montgomery Papers, Archives of Labor History and Urban Affairs, Wayne State University.

2. Walter Lippmann, "The Domestic Allotment Plan" (December 15, 1932), in Lippmann, *Interpretations, 1933–1935* (New York: Macmillan, 1936), 73.

3. Memorandum from Wallace to Peek, June 10, 1933; Ellis W. Hawley, *The New Deal and the Problem of Monopoly: A Study in Economic Ambivalence* (Princeton: Princeton University Press, 1966), 179.

4. Rexford Guy Tugwell, "Consumers and the New Deal" (address delivered before the Consumers' League of Ohio, Cleveland, May 11, 1934), reprinted in *The Battle for Democracy* (New York: Columbia University Press, 1935), 277; "Report on Consumers' Counsel Prepared for Mr. Harold L. Rowe, 1938 by Consumers' Counsel Division, AAA," 15–18, records of the Office of the Secretary of Agriculture, Consumer, 1939, National Archives; Persia Campbell, *Consumer Representation in the New Deal* (New York: Columbia University Press, 1940), 200.

5. As far as I can tell, it was Mordecai Ezekiel who first coined the term *balanced abundance.* Mordecai Ezekiel, *$2,500 a Year: From Scarcity to Abundance* (New York: Harcourt, Brace, 1936), 30.

6. Alan Brinkley, "The New Deal and the Idea of the State," in *The Rise and Fall of the New Deal Order, 1930–1980* (Princeton: Princeton University Press, 1989), 85, 111–12.

7. John D. Hicks, *Republican Ascendancy* (New York: Harper and Row, 1960), 193–96.

8. John Kennedy Ohl, *Hugh S. Johnson and the New Deal* (New York: Northern Illinois University Press, 1985), 59–64; David Hamilton, *From New Day to New Deal: American Farm Policy from Hoover to Roosevelt, 1928–1933* (Chapel Hill: University of North Carolina Press, 1991), 19–21.

9. Rexford Guy Tugwell, "New Strength from the Soil" (address delivered at Swarthmore College, November 26, 1933), reprinted in *Battle for Democracy,* 120.

10. Most historians include Jerome Frank as a participant at the drafting sessions, but Frank later denied involvement (Jerome Frank, *Save America First* [New York: Harper and Brothers, 1938], 271 n).

11. Agricultural Adjustment Act, 73d Cong., sess.1, May 12, 1933; Peter H. Irons, *The New Deal Lawyers* (Princeton: Princeton University Press, 1982), 111–18.

12. Rexford Guy Tugwell, *The Diary of Rexford G. Tugwell: The New Deal, 1932–1935,* ed. Michael Vincent Namorato (New York: Greenwood Press, 1992), 327–28.

13. Ibid.; Henry A. Wallace, *New Frontiers* (New York: Reynal and Hitchcock, 1934), 168–69.

14. George N. Peek, with Samuel Crowther, *Why Quit Our Own* (New York: D. Van Nostrand, 1936), 151; Irons, *New Deal Lawyers,* 118–28.

15. Peek, *Why Quit Our Own,* 14.

16. John Dewey, "Steps to Economic Recovery," in *John Dewey: Later Works, 1925–1953,* vol. 9, ed. Jo Ann Boydston (Carbondale: Southern Illinois University Press, 1986), 61 (first published from an April 28, 1933, radio address on the WEVD University of the Air); radio interview with F. J. Schlink, August 23, 1933, Consumers' Research (CR) Collection, Rutgers University, box 743.

17. Gardiner C. Means, "The Consumer and the New Deal," *Annals of the American Academy of Political and Social Sciences* (May 1934): 11–12; Stuart Chase, *The Economy of Abundance* (1934; rpt., Port Washington, N.Y.: Kennikat Press, 1971), 240; Robert S. Lynd, "Democracy's Third Estate: The Consumer," *Political Science Quarterly* 51 (December 1936): 494–95; Tugwell, "New Strength from the Soil," 119; see also George Soule, *The Coming American Revolution* (New York, Macmillan, 1934), 241.

18. Letter from George Soule to F. J. Schlink, October 5, 1933, CR Collection, box 739.

19. Robert S. Lynd, "A New Deal for the Consumer" *New Republic,* January 3, 1934, 221; Stuart Chase, "Government in Business," *Current History* (March 1935): 652; Rexford Guy Tugwell, "Relief and Reconstruction" (address delivered at the National Conference of Social Work, Kansas City, May 21, 1934), reprinted in Tugwell, *Battle for Democracy,* 319; "Consumers and the New Deal," 279.

20. Chase, *Economy of Abundance,* 284–85.

21. Arthur Schlesinger, *The Coming of the New Deal* (Boston: Houghton Mifflin, 1958), 51, 377; Frederic C. Howe, *Denmark: A Cooperative Commonwealth Ruled by Farmers* (New York: Harcourt, Brace, 1921); "The Most Complete Agricultural Recovery in History," *Annals* (March 1934): 126.

22. Howe, "Most Complete Agricultural Recovery in History," 126; "A Consumers' Society or Cooperation with Consumers" (address delivered August 1, 1934), 6, Consumers' Counsel Records, box 27, National Archives; letter from Frederic C. Howe to F. J. Schlink, January 10, 1934, Consumers' Counsel Records, box 4.

23. Peek, *Why Quit Our Own,* 107.

24. Ibid.

25. Irons, *New Deal Lawyers,* 118–26; Edward A. Purcell Jr., *The Crisis of Democratic Theory: Scientific Naturalism and the Problem of Value* (Lexington: University of Kentucky Press, 1973), 82–86.

26. Schlesinger, *Coming of the New Deal,* 50–54; Katie Louchheim, ed., *The Making of the New Deal: The Insiders Speak* (Cambridge: Harvard University Press, 1983), 25–32, 237; Leonard Baker, *Brandeis and Frankfurter: A Dual Biography* (New York: Harper and Row, 1984), 286; Irons, New Deal Lawyers, 118–26; Arthur M. Kennedy, *Freedom from Fear: The American People in Depression and War, 1929–1945* (New York: Oxford University Press, 1999), 211.

27. Schlesinger, *Coming of the New Deal,* 52.

28. Jerome Frank, *Save America First* (New York: Harper and Brothers,, 1938), 262.

29. Agricultural Adjustment Act; Peek, *Why Quit Our Own,* 7, 341, 351–53.

30. Hugh S. Johnson, *The Blue Eagle, from Egg to Earth* (Garden City, N.Y.: Doubleday, Doran, 1935), 161, 169.

31. Johnson, *Blue Eagle,* 137, 190.

32. Frank, *Save America First,* 259; Rexford Guy Tugwell, "The Economics of the Recovery Program" (address delivered at the Institute of Arts and Sciences, Columbia University, November 16, 1933), reprinted in Tugwell, *Battle for Democracy,* 83.

33. Jerome Frank, "Radio Talk," September 1933, in *Save America First,* 261–63.

34. Tugwell, "New Strength from the Soil," 119.

35. Rexford Guy Tugwell, *Agriculture and the Consumer* (Washington, D.C.: U.S. Government Printing Office, 1934); Frank, *Save America First,* 263.

36. Frank, *Save America First,* 255–63, 268–77; letter from Stuart Chase to Daniel Fox, March 25, 1963; and letter from Henry Wallace to Daniel Fox, March 6, 1963, both cited in Daniel Fox, *The Discovery of Abundance: Simon Patten and the Transformation of Social Theory* (Ithaca: Cornell University Press, 1967), 225 n. 5; Malcolm Cowley and Bernard Smith, eds., *Books That Changed Our Minds* (New York: Doubleday, Doran, 1939), 7–9, 91–107.

37. Peek, *Why Quit Our Own,* 13, 20–21, 24–25, 75, 82–83, 93, 97, 118, 121, 152, 342.

38. Ibid., 76, 102–4.

39. Irons, *New Deal Lawyers,* 128–32; Peek, *Why Quit Our Own,* 146–50; Ohl, *Hugh S. Johnson and the New Deal,* 165–66.

40. Soule, *Coming American Revolution,* 240.

41. Irons, *New Deal Lawyers,* 164–80.

42. Harold L. Ickes, *The Secret Diary of Harold L. Ickes: The First Thousand Days, 1933–1936* (New York: Simon and Schuster, 1953), 302–3; diary entry for February 10, 1935, in *Diary of Rexford G. Tugwell,* 217–18, 220.

43. Quoted in Campbell, *Consumer Representation,* 241; Ickes, *Secret Diary,* 303.

44. Hawley, *New Deal and the Problem of Monopoly,* 172–73.

45. Purcell, *Crisis of Democratic Theory,* 108–14; Alan Brinkley, *The End of Reform: New Deal Liberalism in Recession and War* (New York: Vintage Books, 1995), 112, 115–17; "New Deal and the Idea of the State," 89–91; Hawley, *New Deal and the Problem of Monopoly,* 420–28.

46. Memorandum from D. E. Montgomery to Chester Davis, January 21, 1936, Donald Montgomery Collection (1–2), Walter Reuther Library, Wayne State University; Irons, *New Deal Lawyers,* 175.

47. "The Need for Recognizing Consumer Interest," January 1936(?), Donald Montgomery Collection (1–3).

48. Ibid.

49. Donald E. Montgomery, "The Cost of Food" (address at the Conference on the High Cost of Living, December 14, 1935), 14, Consumers' Counsel Records, box 27, National Archives, Washington, D.C.

50. Ibid.

51. Tugwell, *Agriculture and the Consumer;* "Economic Freedom and the Farmers" (address delivered before the New York State Bankers Association, Buffalo, April 28, 1934), reprinted in *Battle for Democracy,* 231–32.

52. Ibid., 230; letter from D. E. Montgomery to Mrs. Emma Carlein, December 11, 1935, Consumers' Counsel Records, Office File of Dr. Donald E. Montgomery, 1935–38.

53. Tugwell, "New Strength from the Soil," 119; "Consumers and the New Deal," 277; *Agriculture and the Consumer;* Means, "Consumer and the New Deal," 11.

54. Henry Wallace, *Democracy Reborn,* ed. Russell Lord (New York: Reynal and Hitchcock, 1944), 81.

55. Ibid.; Schlesinger, *Coming of the New Deal,* 70–71.

56. Montgomery, "Cost of Food," 13–14.

57. Donald Montgomery, "Normal Food Supply of Past Years Is Not Sufficient as a National Goal," January 1936(?), Donald Montgomery Collection (1–3).

58. Ibid.; Montgomery, "Cost of Food," 14; D. E. Montgomery, "Consumers under Way," *Survey Graphic* (April 1938).

59. Montgomery, "Normal Food Supply of Past Years."

60. Ezekiel, *$2,500 a Year,* 246.

61. Ibid., 30, 66–67.

62. Ibid., 66–67.

63. Ibid., 197–98, 264.

64. Ibid., 18, 30, 66, 72; Stuart Chase, *A New Deal* (New York: Macmillan, 1933), 184–85.

65. Ezekiel, *$2,500 a Year,* 72.

66. Ibid., 72, 260, 294–95.

67. Adam Smith, *An Inquiry into the Nature and Causes of the Wealth of Nations* (Chicago: University of Chicago Press, 1976), 2:179.

68. Ezekiel, *$2,500 a Year,* 290; Montgomery, "Cost of Food," 11.

69. Quoted in Theodore A. Wilson, "Henry Agard Wallace and the Progressive Faith," in *Three Progressives from Iowa: Gilbert N. Haugen, Herbert C. Hoover, Henry A. Wallace,* ed. John N. Schlacht (Iowa City: Center for the Study of the Recent History of the United States, 1980), 37–44.

70. Wallace, *New Frontiers,* 22, 29; H. A. Wallace, "The Farmers' Problem—Everybody's Problem" (speech presented before the Civic Forum, November 24, 1933), 6, Consumers' Counsel Papers, box 26.

71. Wilson, "Henry Agard Wallace and the Progressive Faith," 37–44, 47 n.

72. Wallace, "Farmers' Problem," 16; *New Frontiers,* 139.

73. Irons, *New Deal Lawyers,* 175; press conference on February 6, 1935, quoted in Rexford Guy Tugwell, *The Diary of Rexford G. Tugwell: The New Deal, 1932–1935,* ed. Michael Vincent Namorato (New York: Greenwood Press, 1992), 208–9.

74. Henry A. Wallace, "A Joint Interest" (radio talk, April 18, 1935), 2, Consumers' Counsel Papers, box 27; "The Consumer and the Land" (address before the General Federation of Women's Clubs, June 7, 1935), 7, Consumers' Counsel Papers, box 26.

75. Wallace "Consumer and the Land," 2; "Joint Interest," 2.

76. Henry A. Wallace, "Producer Goals and Consumer Goals" (address before the Consumers Emergency Council, March 6, 1937), 5, 11, Consumers' Counsel Papers, box 26; letter from Henry Wallace to Rural and Urban Women in "Digest of the Rural-Urban Women's Conversations" (April 13–14, 1939), 1, Consumers' Counsel Papers, box 5, all in National Archives; *Whose Constitution: An Inquiry into the General Welfare* (New York: Reynal and Hitchcock, 1936), 294.

77. Henry A. Wallace, *The Century of the Common Man* (New York: Reynal and Hitchcock, 1943), 18–19.

78. Arthur M. Schlesinger Jr., *The Politics of Upheaval* (New York: Houghton Mifflin, 1960), 192.

Conclusion

1. See, for example, Gwendolyn Mink, "The Lady and the Tramp: Gender, Race, and the Origins of the American Welfare State" in *Women, the State, and Welfare,* ed. Linda Gordon (Madison: University of Wisconsin Press, 1990); and Alice Kessler-Harris, "Designing Women and Old Fools: The Construction of the Social Amendments of 1939," in *U.S. History as Women's History: New Feminist Essays,* ed. Linda K. Kerber, Alice Kessler-Harris, and Kathryn Kish Sklar (Chapel Hill: University of North Carolina Press, 1995).

2. Alan Brinkley, *The End of Reform: New Deal Liberalism in Recession and War* (New York: Knopf, 1995), 227–64.

3. John Kenneth Galbraith, *The Affluent Society* (Boston: Houghton Mifflin, 1958), 190.

4. Ibid., 52 n. On the OPA, see Meg Jacobs, "'How about Some Meat?': The Office of Price Administration, Consumption Politics, and State Building from the Bottom Up, 1941–1946," *Journal of American History* 84, no. 3 (December 1997): 910–41.

5. Galbraith, *Affluent Society,* 251–80, 334–48.

6. Ibid., 188–90, 192.

7. E. J. Dionne Jr., *Why Americans Hate Politics* (New York: Touchstone Press, 1991), 284–86.

8. Ramachandra Guha, *Environmentalism: A Global History* (New York: Longman Press, 2000), 142; "Failures of the Jo'burg Earth Summit," *Africa News Service,* September 16, 2002.

9. Guha, *Environmentalism,* 142.

Essay on Sources

Because I was primarily interested in the evolution of a public discourse, most of my primary sources were published. The most useful manuscript collections for this project were the records of the Agricultural Adjustment Administration (AAA) and the National Recovery Administration (NRA) at the National Archives, which contain extensive correspondence and speeches by numerous members of both administrations, and the Consumers Research (CR) Collection at Rutgers University. When I visited the CR Collection in the late 1980s, it was still in over a thousand file boxes, waiting to be catalogued. Nevertheless, it was still possible to find a considerable amount of useful material. F. J. Schlink corresponded with many of the most high-profile political thinkers of the day. And he clipped and filed all sorts of material covering a wide variety of topics, some of them only tangentially related to the consumer. The Consumers' Union Collection in Mount Vernon, New York, and the Donald Montgomery Papers at Wayne State University are both quite rich, but much of the material in those collections duplicated material found in the CR and AAA records.

A book that covers as much ground as this one obviously relied on the work of a great many historians. What follows, therefore, is anything but exhaustive. Instead, it is a brief discussion of those books that have had the greatest impact on my thinking.

A number of intellectual historians have looked at the producerist and the consumerist intellectual traditions. Daniel Rodgers, *The Work Ethic in Industrial America, 1850–1920* (Chicago: University of Chicago Press, 1974), is still the best book on producerist ideas. In *The Morality of Spending: Attitudes toward the Consumer Society in America, 1875–1940* (Baltimore: Johns Hopkins University Press, 1985) Daniel Horowitz convincingly argues that American thinkers retained their reservations concerning consumption even as they substituted a language of exploitation for an earlier language of morality. In *Pragmatism and the Political Economy of Cultural Revolution, 1850–1940* (Chapel Hill: University of North Carolina Press, 1994) James Livingston does an effective job of connecting the intellectual shifts with changing economic conditions.

Historians of liberalism have paid a great deal of attention to the transformation of classical liberalism into its modern American counterpart. Indispensable for an understanding of how American social thinkers ultimately came down on the side of liberalism rather than social democracy are James Kloppenberg's *Uncertain Victory: Social Democracy and Progressivism in European and American Thought, 1870–1920* (New York:

Oxford University Press, 1986); Dorothy Ross's article "Socialism and American Liberalism: Academic Social Thought in the 1880s," *Perspectives in American History* 11 (1977–78); as well as *The Origins of American Social Science* (New York: Cambridge University Press, 1991); Robert Westbrook's *John Dewey and American Democracy* (Ithaca: Cornell University Press, 1991); Mary O. Furner's articles "Social Scientists and the State: Constructing the Knowledge Base for Public Policy, 1880–1920," in *Intellectuals and Public Life: Between Radicalism and Reform,* ed. Leon Fink et al. (Ithaca: Cornell University Press, 1996); "The Republican Tradition and the New Liberalism: Social Investigation, State Building, and Social Learning in the Gilded Age," in *The State and Social Investigation in Britain and the United States,* ed. Michael J. Lacey and Mary O. Furner (New York: Cambridge University Press, 1993); and "Knowing Capitalism: Public Investigation and the Labor Question in the Long Progressive Era," in *The State and Economic Knowledge: The American and British Experiences,* ed. Mary O. Furner and Barry Supple (New York: Cambridge University Press, 1990).

The historical works that have examined the political implications of the consumer have fallen into two groups. On one side are those such as Christopher Lasch, *The True and Only Heaven: Progress and Its Critics* (New York: Norton, 1991), and Nancy Cohen, *The Reconstruction of American Liberalism: 1865–1914* (Chapel Hill: University of North Carolina Press, 2002), which see the incorporation of the consumer into political thought as something that undercuts radical social change. On the other side are works such as Lizabeth Cohen, *Making a New Deal: Industrial Workers in Chicago, 1919–1939* (New York: Cambridge University Press, 1990), Dana Frank, *Purchasing Power: Consumer Organizing, Gender, and the Seattle Labor Movement, 1919–1929* (New York: Cambridge University Press, 1994), and Lawrence B. Glickman, *A Living Wage: American Workers and the Making of Consumer Society* (Ithaca: Cornell University Press, 1997), which see far more political potential in the consumer identity. All three point out the ways in which workers were able to mount real challenges to the existing system by organizing around their identity as consumers.

The best work on the political economy of the New Deal is that of Alan Brinkley. In "The New Deal and the Idea of the State," in *The Rise and Fall of the New Deal Order, 1930–1980* (Princeton: Princeton University Press, 1989), and *The End of Reform: New Deal Liberalism in Recession and War* (New York: Vintage Press, 1995) Brinkley argues that the liberal conviction that the economy should function on behalf of the consumer became the foundational principle of New Deal liberalism. While Brinkley concentrates on the late 1930s and early 1940s, Ellis Hawley's classic, *The New Deal and the Problem of Monopoly: A Study in Economic Ambivalence* (Princeton: Princeton University Press, 1966), focuses on the intellectual crosscurrents within the New Deal during the 1930s. Gary Gerstle's article "The Protean Character of Liberalism," *American Historical Review* 99 (October 1994), suggests that between the two world wars liberalism shifted from a system of thought which focused on race and ethnicity to one that largely ignored these categories in favor of economics. Daniel T. Rodgers, in *Atlantic Crossings* (Cambridge, Mass: Belknap Press, 1998), traces the origins of many New Deal programs to European social democracy.

Index

AAA. *See* Agricultural Adjustment
Administration
*Absentee Ownership and Business Enterprise in
Recent Times* (Veblen), 157, 159
abundance, 5, 6, 24, 27, 212, 280–81; AAA
and, 259, 264, 266; AAA left liberals and,
247, 250, 258–59, 265–66; balanced, 247,
264–66, 270; Bellamy on, 54, 61; Chase
on, 205, 251; Ezekiel on, 267–70; Johnson
and, 201–2, 205; Kallen on, 147–48; left
liberals on, 224; Montgomery on, 264,
267, 270; Patten and, 46, 50, 74–75, 78,
84–86, 93–94, 97, 127, 132; Peek on, 250;
Potter on, 277; Soule on, 190, 205, 268;
Tugwell on, 251, 265; Veblenian left
liberals and, 202, 205–6, 208–10, 219, 255,
264, 276; Veblen on, 40, 127, 138; Wallace
on, 245, 271, 273; Weyl on, 132, 137–39,
148
Adams, Herbert Carter, 96–97
advertising, 14, 63, 81, 99, 181, 183, 199;
Bellamy on, 65; Galbraith on, 278; left
liberals on, 204–5; Lippmann on, 121;
New Republic liberals on, 116; Veblenian
left liberals on, 171–72, 176, 232; Veblen
on, 77–78, 80, 164. *See also* salesmanship
Agricultural Adjustment Administration
(AAA), 197–98; and abundance, 259, 264,
266; and consumer, 199, 228, 244–47,
254–55, 259, 264; consumerist orientation
of, 203, 251–59, 262–63; and
consumption, 255–56; and consumption-
oriented system, 258–59, 274–75; NRA,
compared with, 245–47, 264, 273; and
producer, 247, 255, 259, 263–64, 267;
producerist orientation of, 246–47; on

production, 244, 249–50, 256, 266, 273,
276; purge, 260–62, 272; sabotage, policies
as, 250–51, 259; Schlink and, 186–87
Arnold, Thurman, 259, 262–63

balance, 198–99, 247, 256–58, 264–66, 270,
271–73
Baruch, Bernard, 155, 200, 249
Bellamy, Edward, 5, 138; on abundance, 54,
61; on advertising, 65; on capitalism,
54–55, 61–65, 80, 87–88, 163, 278–79; on
class conflict, 50; on competition, 62–63,
160–62; on consumer, 51–52, 55, 57–58,
72, 80, 88, 90, 134, 160, 164, 180; on
consumer–oriented system, 51–64, 71,
112, 134, 162–64; on consumption, 52–57,
60, 71, 92; on consumption–oriented
system, 163; on creation of wealth, 60–61;
on democracy, 130, 180; on exploitation,
64–65, 87–88; on laissez-faire, 62; on
luxury, 53–56, 88; on producer, 52, 56–57,
58–59, 87–88, 90–91, 112–13, 133–34; on
producer-oriented system, 51–52, 56,
60–61, 64–65, 88–90, 92, 112, 134, 162;
on production, 53, 89; on profit, 62–65,
87; on profit motive, 55; on profit system,
61–63, 164–65; on self-interest, 62; on
socialism, 64, 112; on value, 54–55, 60,
87–91; on waste, 55, 160
Blair, Emily Newell, 228
Blue Eagle, 229–30, 241–42
Books That Change Our Minds (Cowley and
Smith), 99, 165–66, 259
Brandeis, Louis, 116

CAB. *See* Consumers Advisory Board

and the, 101, 141–42, 149, 152, 235–36;
Sonnichsen on, 145–47, 149; Soule on,
190, 228; Sumner on, 108, 110–11, 143;
Tugwell on, 91, 228; Veblenian left liberals
on, 258; Veblen on, 111–13, 143, 160,
162–63; Warbasse on, 145–47, 149,
153–54; Webb on, 148; Weyl on, 131,
133–35, 141–43, 149
producerist ideas. *See* producer-oriented
system
producer-oriented system, idea of, 2–4, 41,
73, 97, 101, 109, 113, 133, 151–53, 181,
188, 197, 270; AAA and, 246–47; Bellamy
on, 51–52, 56, 61, 64–65, 88–90, 92, 112,
134, 162; capitalism and, 37–38; Chase
on, 178, 188–89; in classical economic
theory, 6–15; cooperation and, 144–46;
Dewey on, 194, 235–36; Douglas and, 194;
Ely on, 25–32, 112; Filene on, 217; Foster
on, 217; George on, 16–25, 50; Johnson
on, 201, 215; Kelley on, 125, 134–35; and
liberalism, 2, 13, 101–2, 142, 270, 277;
and LIPA, 192; Lippmann on, 122, 124,
162; and marginalism, 65–68; Marx on,
64; Means on, 210–12; NCL and, 108;
NRA and, 199, 203–4; Patten on, 41–42,
46, 48, 50–51, 86–87, 89–92, 93, 95, 97,
99–100; Potter on, 30–32; in radical
theory, 142, 187; Schlink and, 178; Smith
on, 56, 62–64; Sumner on, 15–16, 18–20,
24–25, 50; and tripartite commissions,
123–24; Tugwell on, 210, 212; Veblen on,
34–39, 78–79, 129–30, 138, 157–60; Weyl
on, 129–31, 141, 162
production, 14, 41, 115, 197, 247–48; AAA
on, 244, 249–50, 256, 266, 273, 276; AAA
left liberals on, 257, 264–65; Arnold on,
262–63; Bellamy on, 89; Chase on, 171,
174, 189, 258; in classical economic
theory, 10–15; Dewey on, 194–95, 235; Ely
on, 68–69; Ezekiel, 268–70; Foster on,
214–15; left liberals on, 257; Lynd on,
251; meanings associated with, 11, 53,
105; Means on, 210, 262, 266;
Montgomery on, 264, 267, 269–70; NRA
and, 255; Patten on, 43, 90, 92, 96–97,
99–100, 137, 168; regulation of, 96–98;

Say on, 10–12; Soule on, 258; Tugwell on,
168–69, 210, 265–66; Veblenian left
liberals on, 264; Veblen on, 74–78, 137,
156–57, 159–62; Wallace on, 271–73; Weyl
on, 129, 133, 138–39; WIB and, 155
product testing, 175, 177, 182–84, 237–38
profit, 6, 152; AAA left liberals on, 205, 253,
259–60, 268; Bellamy on, 62–65, 87;
Chase on, 156, 165, 172, 174, 177, 204–8,
210, 274; and cooperation, 27, 30–32;
Croly on, 117; Douglas on, 274; Ezekiel
on, 267–69; Filene on, 216; Foster on, 216,
219; Johnson on, 202, 216, 242, 255–56;
left liberals on, 205; Lynd on, 204–8, 210,
274; Marx on, 64, 87, 221–22; Matthews
on, 185; Means on, 203, 210, 213, 251;
Montgomery on, 267; Patten on, 49–50,
82–83, 96, 100, 132; Peek on, 250, 254,
259; Potter, 30–32; Ricardo on, 13; Schlink
on, 177; Smith on, 80, 122, 168; socialism
on, 64, 208; Soule on, 204–8, 210, 274;
Sumner on, 18; Tugwell on, 165, 167–68,
203, 212–13, 223–24, 268; Veblenian left
liberals on, 170, 209, 258, 264; Veblen on,
78, 138, 156–57; Weyl on, 126, 130, 137,
140–41
profit motive, 27; Bellamy on, 55; Chase on,
174, 177, 206, 208; Filene on, 213; Foster
on, 213; Johnson on, 201; Kallen on, 148;
left liberals on, 170, 205–6, 209; Lynd on,
206, 208, 222; Means on, 209; *New
Republic* liberals on, 115–16; Smith on,
119; Soule on, 206, 208; Tugwell on,
169–70, 209; Veblen on, 168–69
profit system, 6, 75, 258; AAA left liberals
on, 274; Bellamy on, 61–63, 164–65;
Chase on, 166, 171; vs. cooperation, 153;
Dewey on, 236; Ezekiel on, 268; Filene
on, 213–15, 221; Foster on, 213–15,
221–22; Frank on, 274; George on, 24;
left liberals on, 202, 255; Lippmann on,
164–65; Lynd on, 171; marginalist
challenge of, 66; New Deal commitment
to, 221; Peek on, 253; Smith on, 61–63;
Soule on, 202–3; Veblen on, 80, 157–58;
Wallace on, 271–72; Weyl on, 135,
164–65. *See also* capitalism